THE ROYAL PALACE

GOONG

Park SoHee

W9-DAR-737

Yen Press

About the Creator

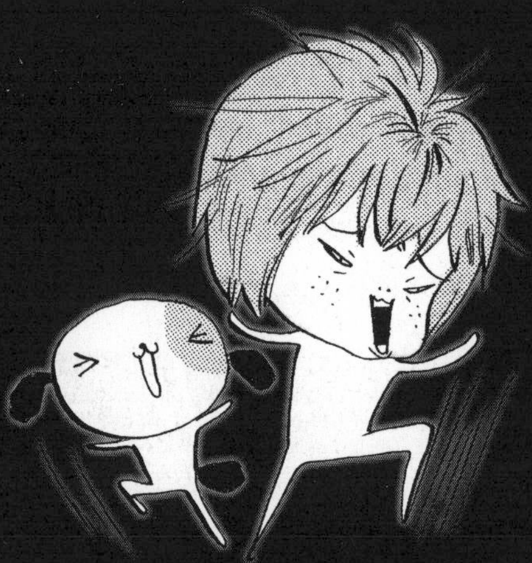

SoHee Park

Birthday: March 24, 1978

She graduated with a major in manhwa from Gongjoo Cultural University. She won Seoul Media's silver medal for Best New Manhwa Creator in 2000.

Major works: <Real Purple>, <Goong — The Royal Palace>

Words from the Creator

It's 2005, but I suddenly remembered myself ten years ago. There I was with a fluttering heart, drawing lines in a new sketchbook on my desk in class. I had gotten references from *Stories of Queens* and was working on **Goong** with all my might. When I think back to then, I was doing better than I am currently. Unlike in those days, all of my working tools are professional ones now, but I realize that my passion and dream for manhwa shouldn't change!
I have to do my best! Let's go!
Haiyah!

SoHee Park

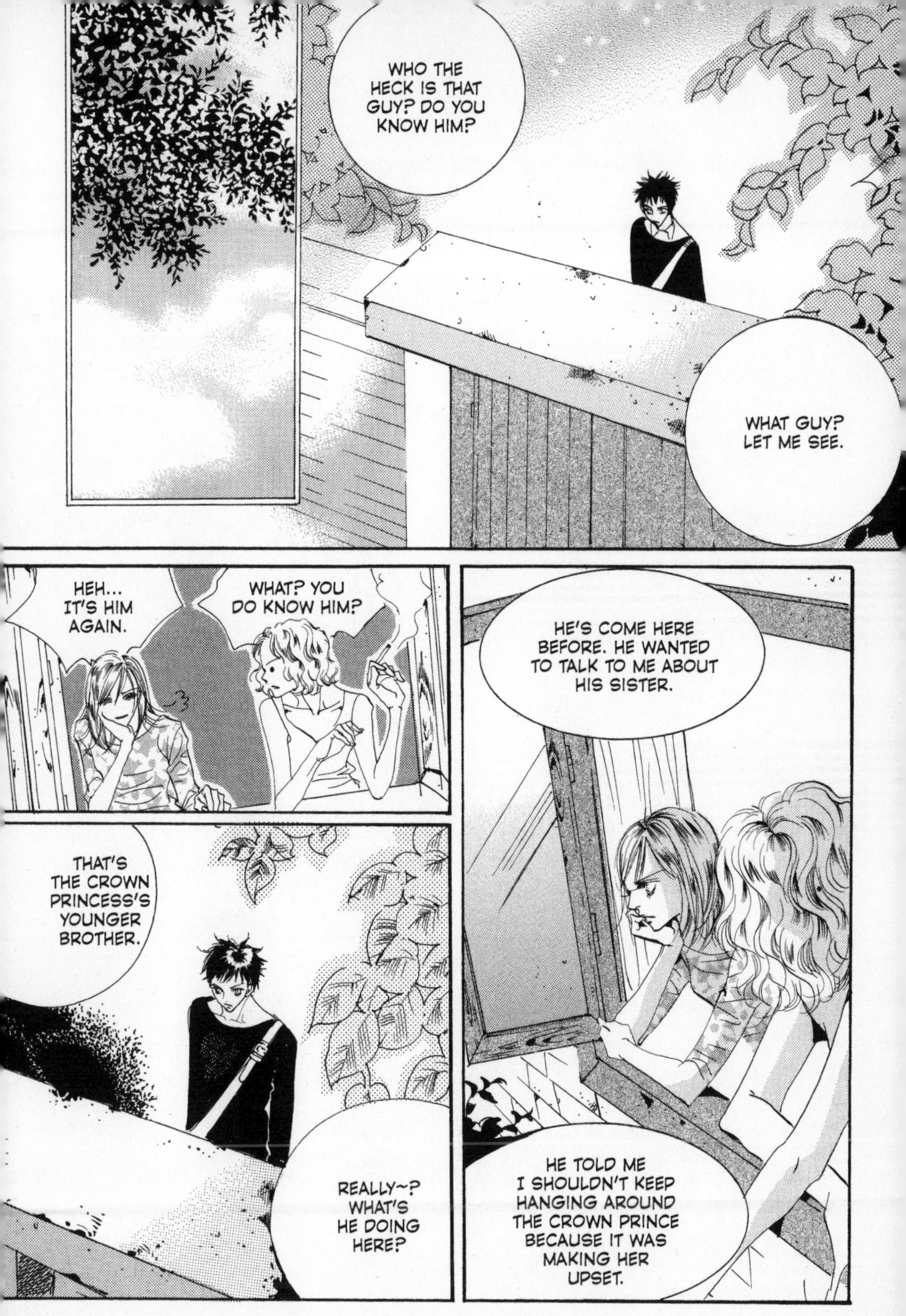
WHO THE HECK IS THAT GUY? DO YOU KNOW HIM?
WHAT GUY? LET ME SEE.
HEH... IT'S HIM AGAIN.
WHAT? YOU DO KNOW HIM?
THAT'S THE CROWN PRINCESS'S YOUNGER BROTHER.
REALLY~? WHAT'S HE DOING HERE?
HE'S COME HERE BEFORE. HE WANTED TO TALK TO ME ABOUT HIS SISTER.
HE TOLD ME I SHOULDN'T KEEP HANGING AROUND THE CROWN PRINCE BECAUSE IT WAS MAKING HER UPSET.

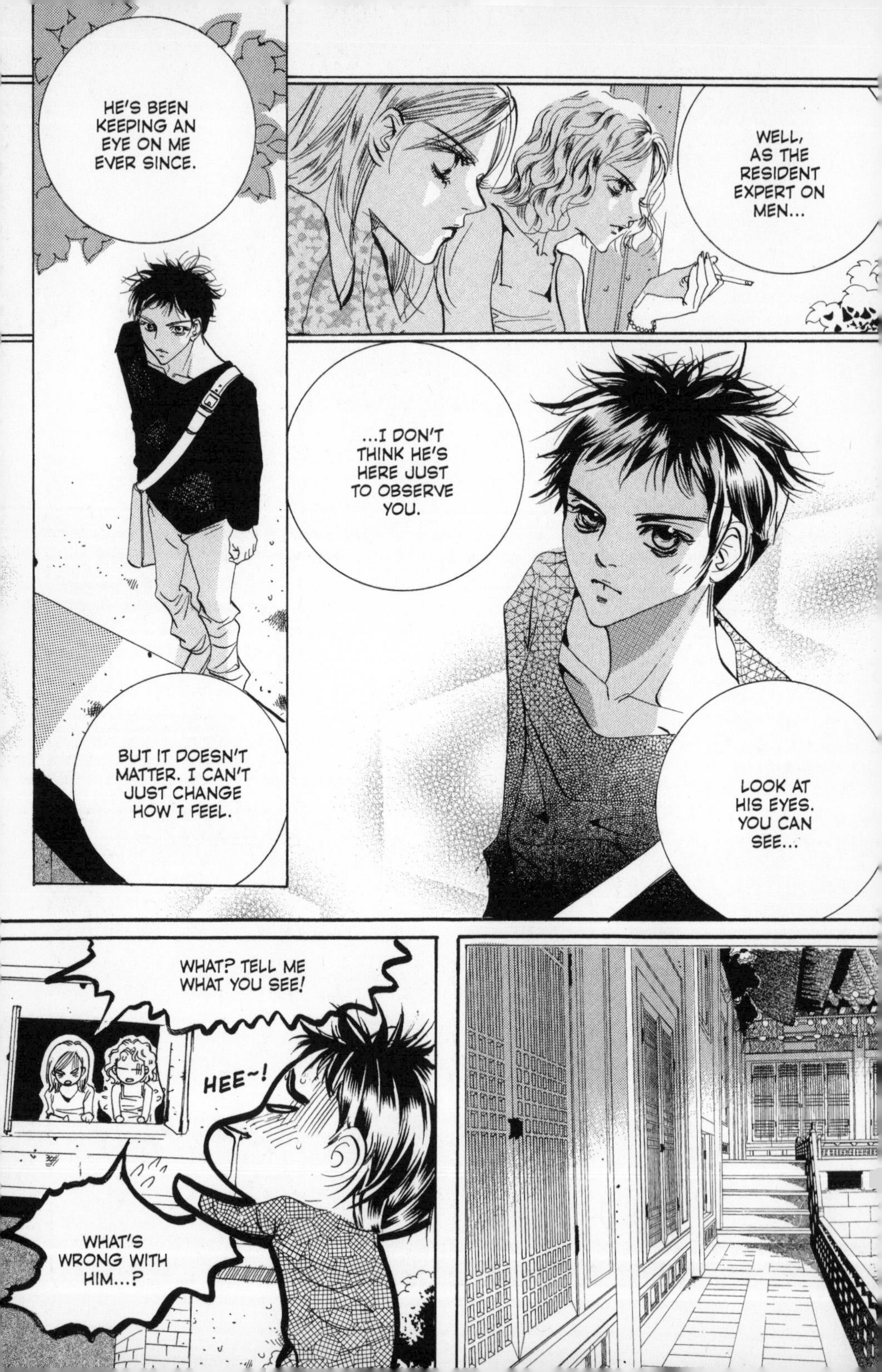
HE'S BEEN KEEPING AN EYE ON ME EVER SINCE.
BUT IT DOESN'T MATTER. I CAN'T JUST CHANGE HOW I FEEL.
WELL, AS THE RESIDENT EXPERT ON MEN...
...I DON'T THINK HE'S HERE JUST TO OBSERVE YOU.
LOOK AT HIS EYES. YOU CAN SEE...
WHAT? TELL ME WHAT YOU SEE!
HEE~!
WHAT'S WRONG WITH HIM...?

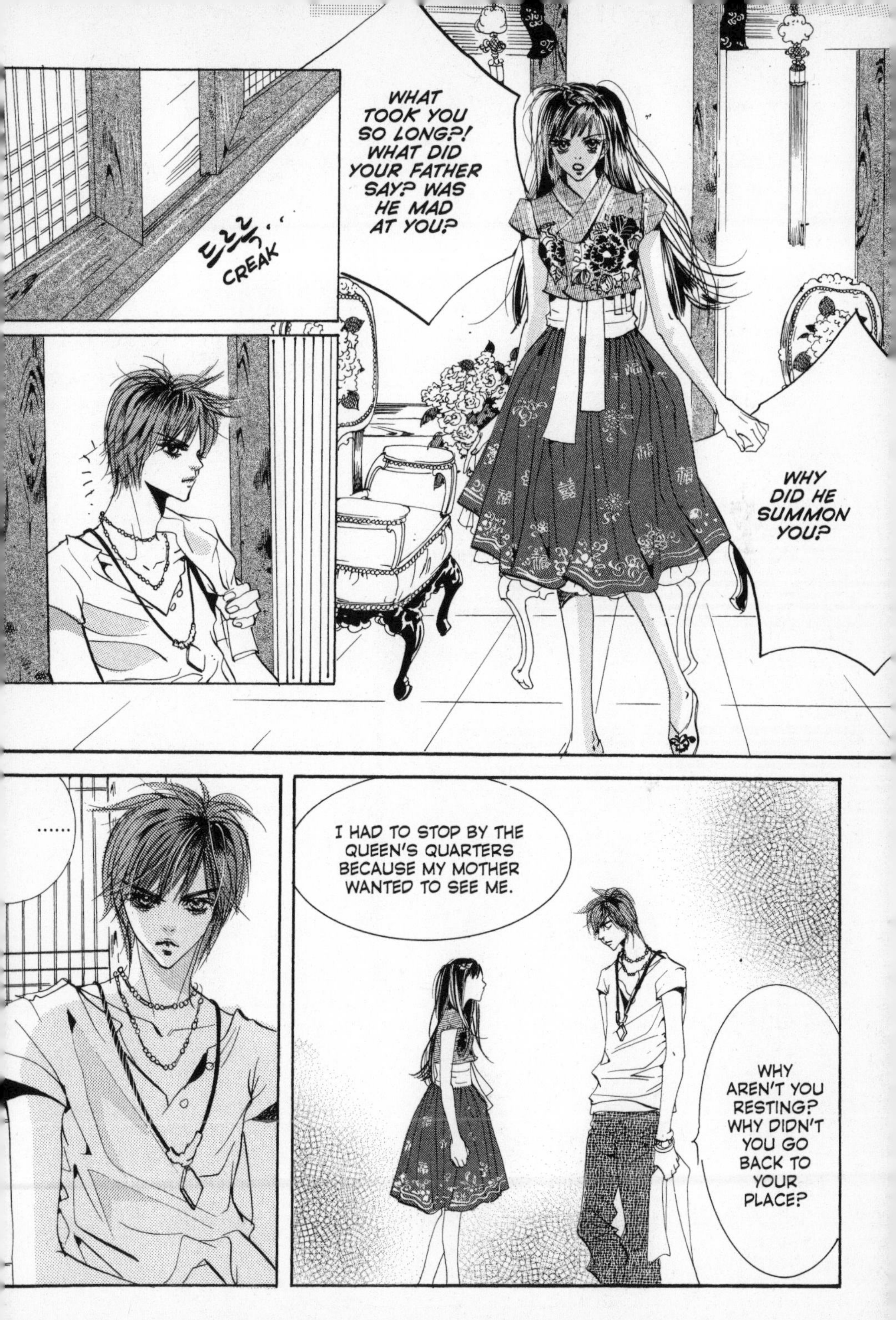
WHAT TOOK YOU SO LONG?! WHAT DID YOUR FATHER SAY? WAS HE MAD AT YOU?
CREAK
WHY DID HE SUMMON YOU?
......
I HAD TO STOP BY THE QUEEN'S QUARTERS BECAUSE MY MOTHER WANTED TO SEE ME.
WHY AREN'T YOU RESTING? WHY DIDN'T YOU GO BACK TO YOUR PLACE?

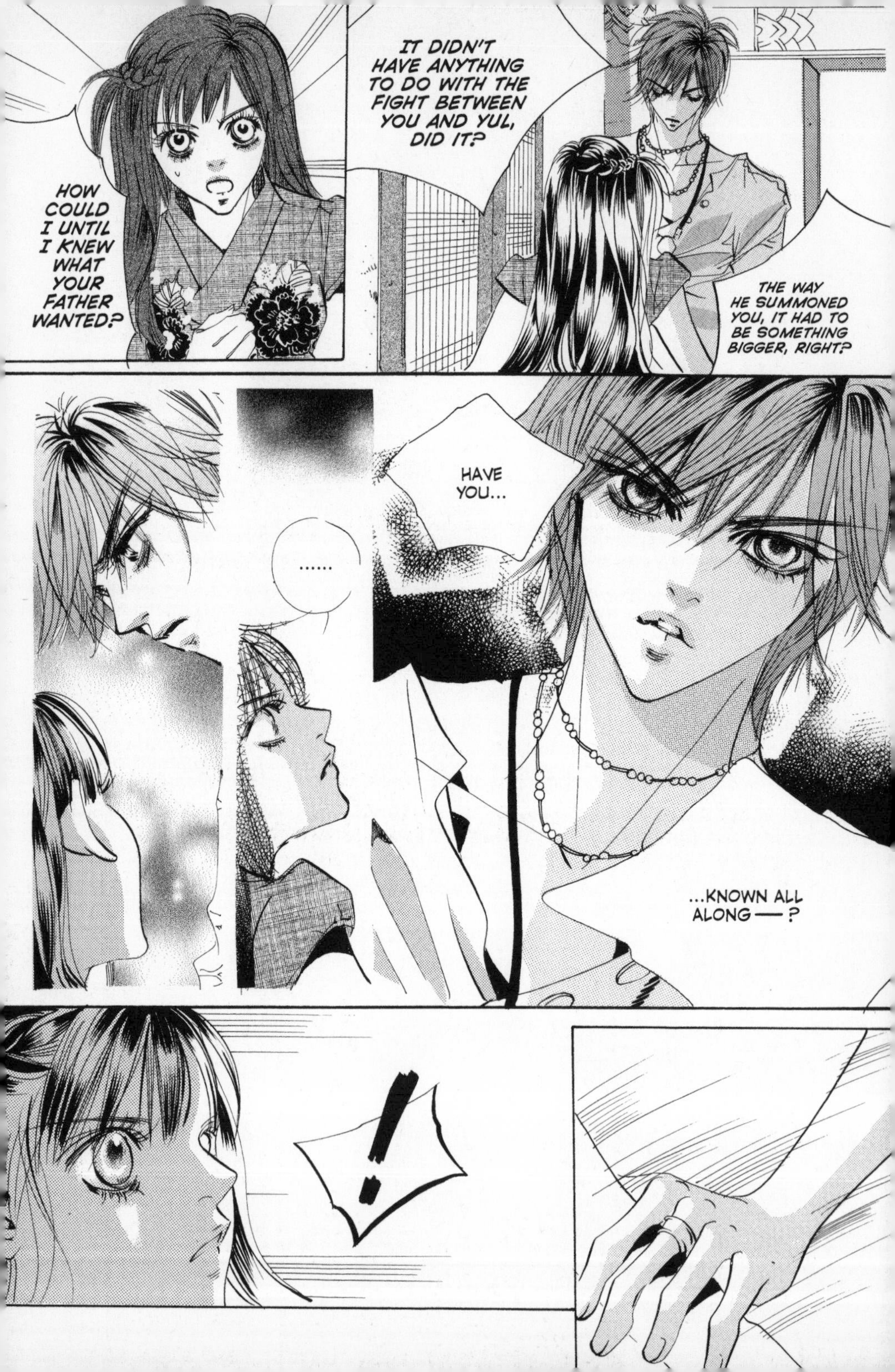
HOW COULD I UNTIL I KNEW WHAT YOUR FATHER WANTED?
IT DIDN'T HAVE ANYTHING TO DO WITH THE FIGHT BETWEEN YOU AND YUL, DID IT?
THE WAY HE SUMMONED YOU, IT HAD TO BE SOMETHING BIGGER, RIGHT?
......
HAVE YOU...
...KNOWN ALL ALONG—?
!

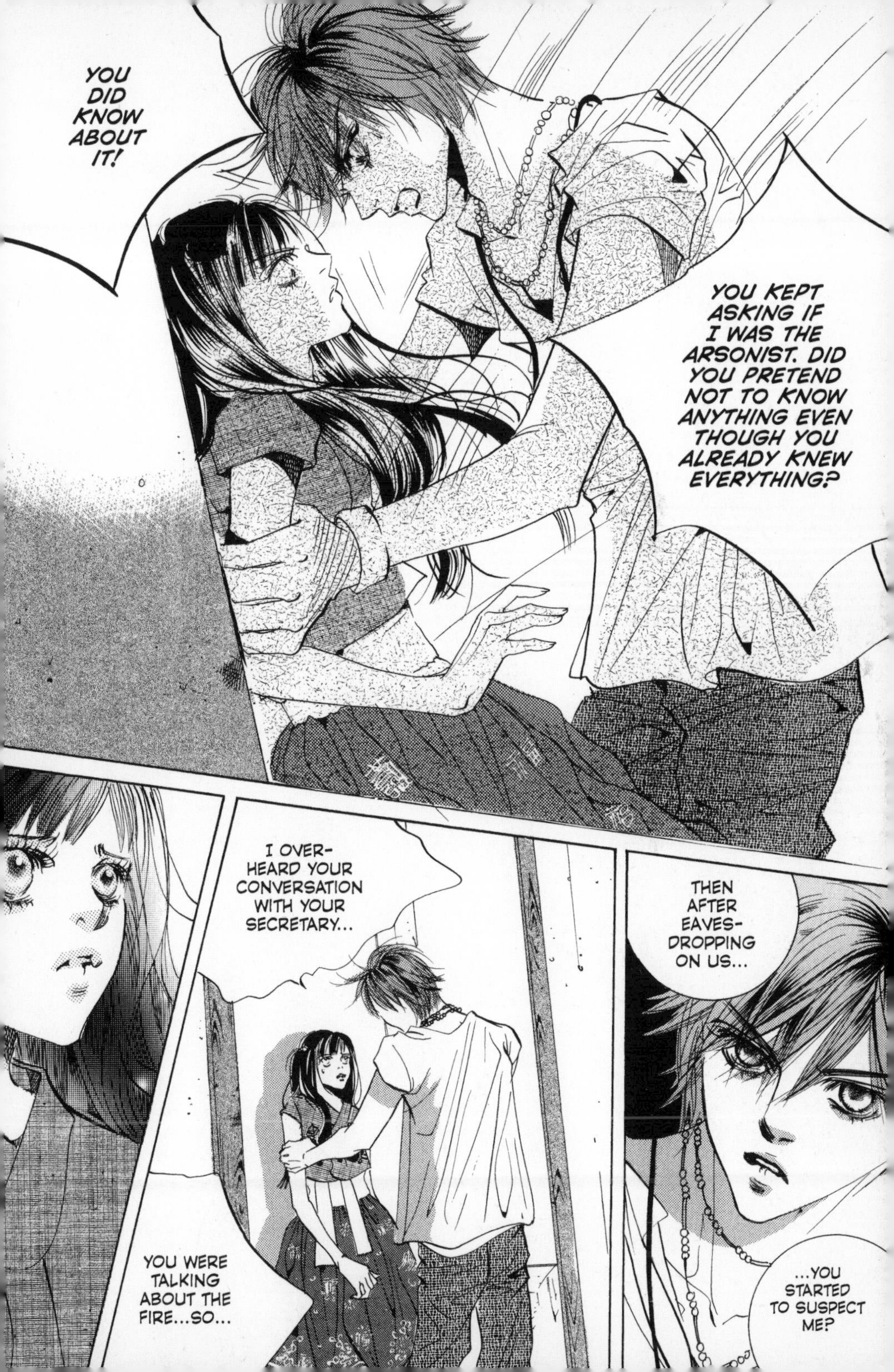
YOU DID KNOW ABOUT IT!
YOU KEPT ASKING IF I WAS THE ARSONIST. DID YOU PRETEND NOT TO KNOW ANYTHING EVEN THOUGH YOU ALREADY KNEW EVERYTHING?
I OVER-HEARD YOUR CONVERSATION WITH YOUR SECRETARY...
YOU WERE TALKING ABOUT THE FIRE...SO...
THEN AFTER EAVES-DROPPING ON US...
...YOU STARTED TO SUSPECT ME?

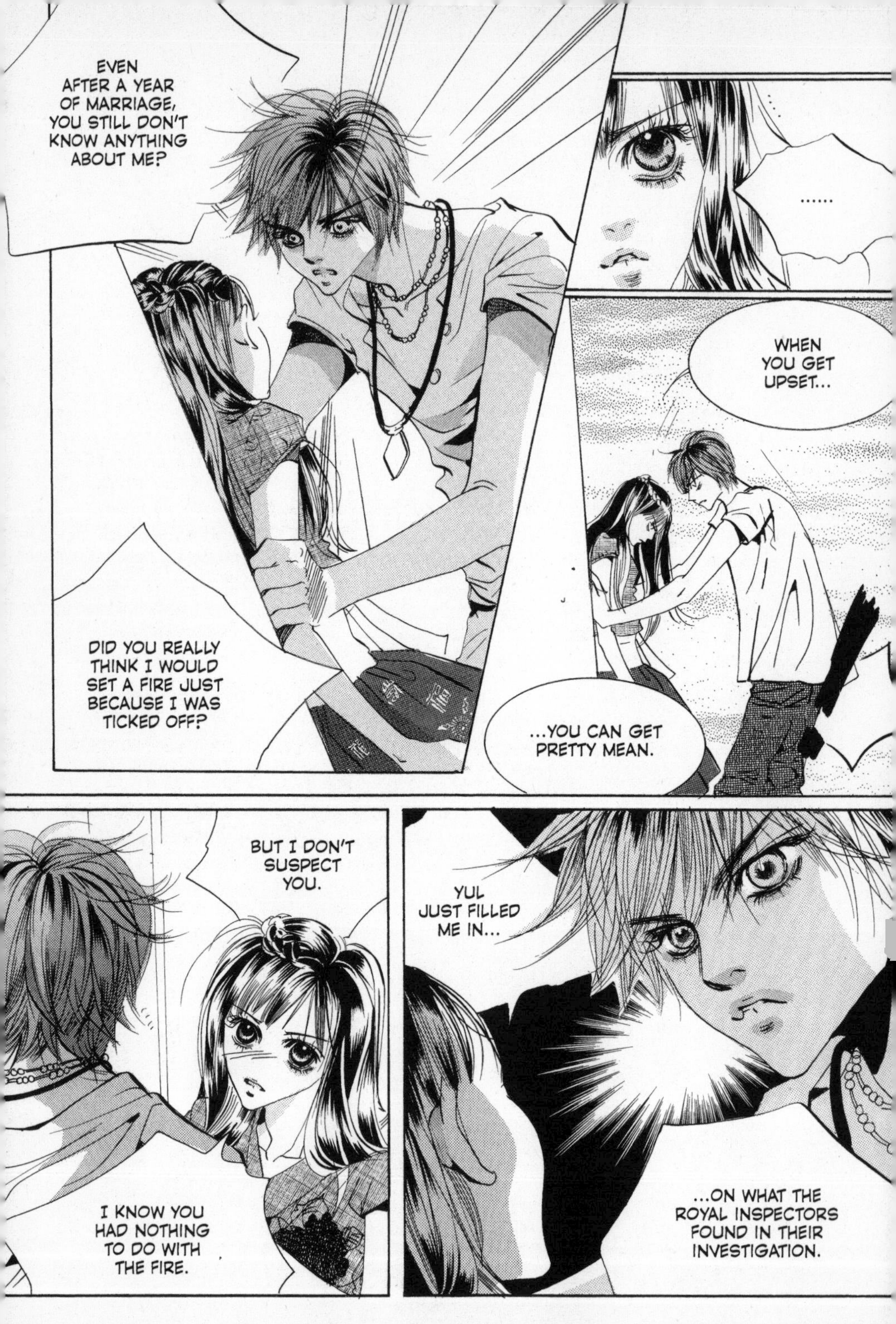
EVEN AFTER A YEAR OF MARRIAGE, YOU STILL DON'T KNOW ANYTHING ABOUT ME?
DID YOU REALLY THINK I WOULD SET A FIRE JUST BECAUSE I WAS TICKED OFF?
......
WHEN YOU GET UPSET...
...YOU CAN GET PRETTY MEAN.
BUT I DON'T SUSPECT YOU.
I KNOW YOU HAD NOTHING TO DO WITH THE FIRE.
YUL JUST FILLED ME IN...
...ON WHAT THE ROYAL INSPECTORS FOUND IN THEIR INVESTIGATION.

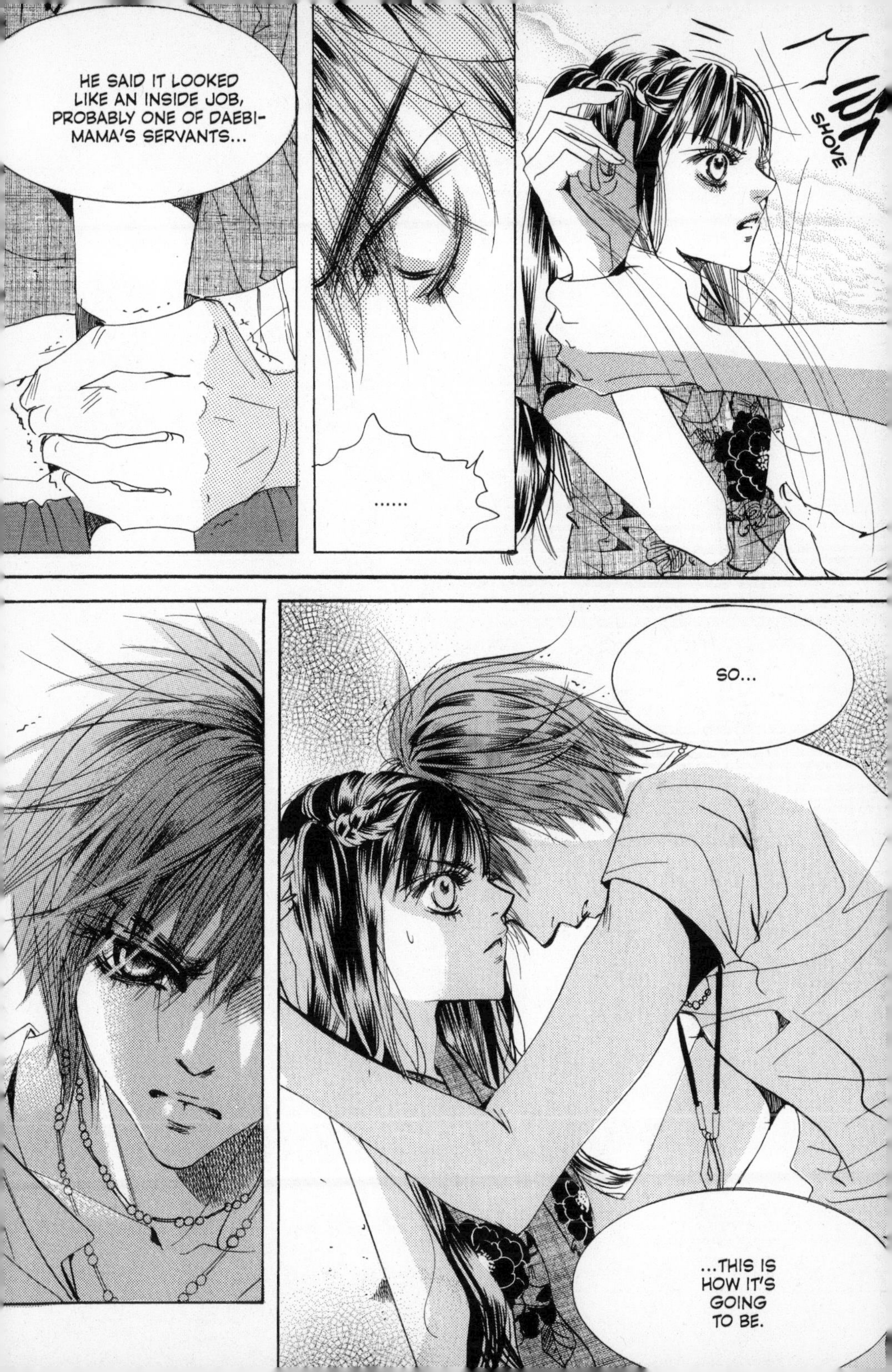
HE SAID IT LOOKED LIKE AN INSIDE JOB, PROBABLY ONE OF DAEBI-MAMA'S SERVANTS...
......
SHOVE
SO...
...THIS IS HOW IT'S GOING TO BE.

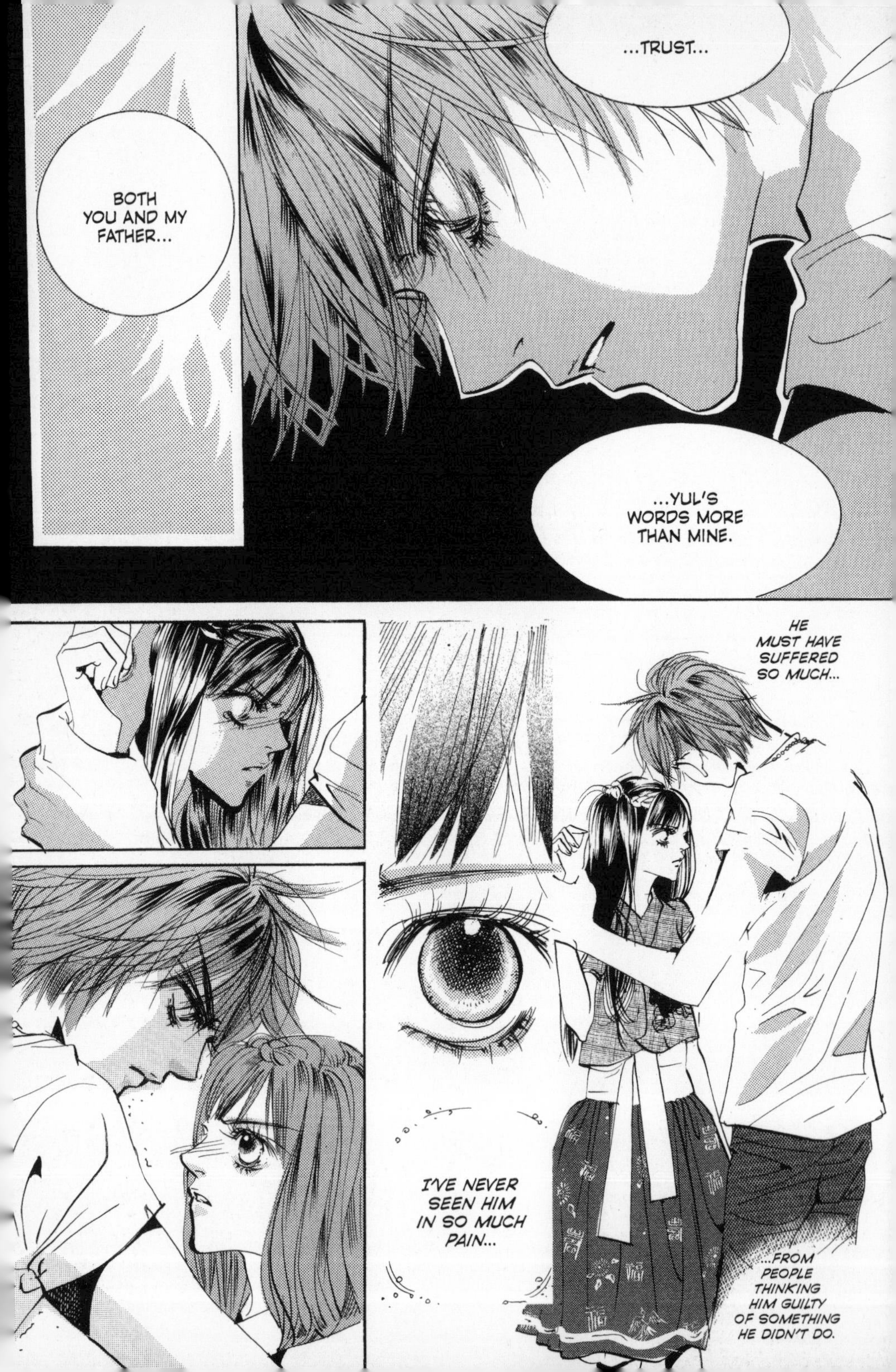
BOTH YOU AND MY FATHER...
...TRUST...
...YUL'S WORDS MORE THAN MINE.
HE MUST HAVE SUFFERED SO MUCH...
I'VE NEVER SEEN HIM IN SO MUCH PAIN...
...FROM PEOPLE THINKING HIM GUILTY OF SOMETHING HE DIDN'T DO.

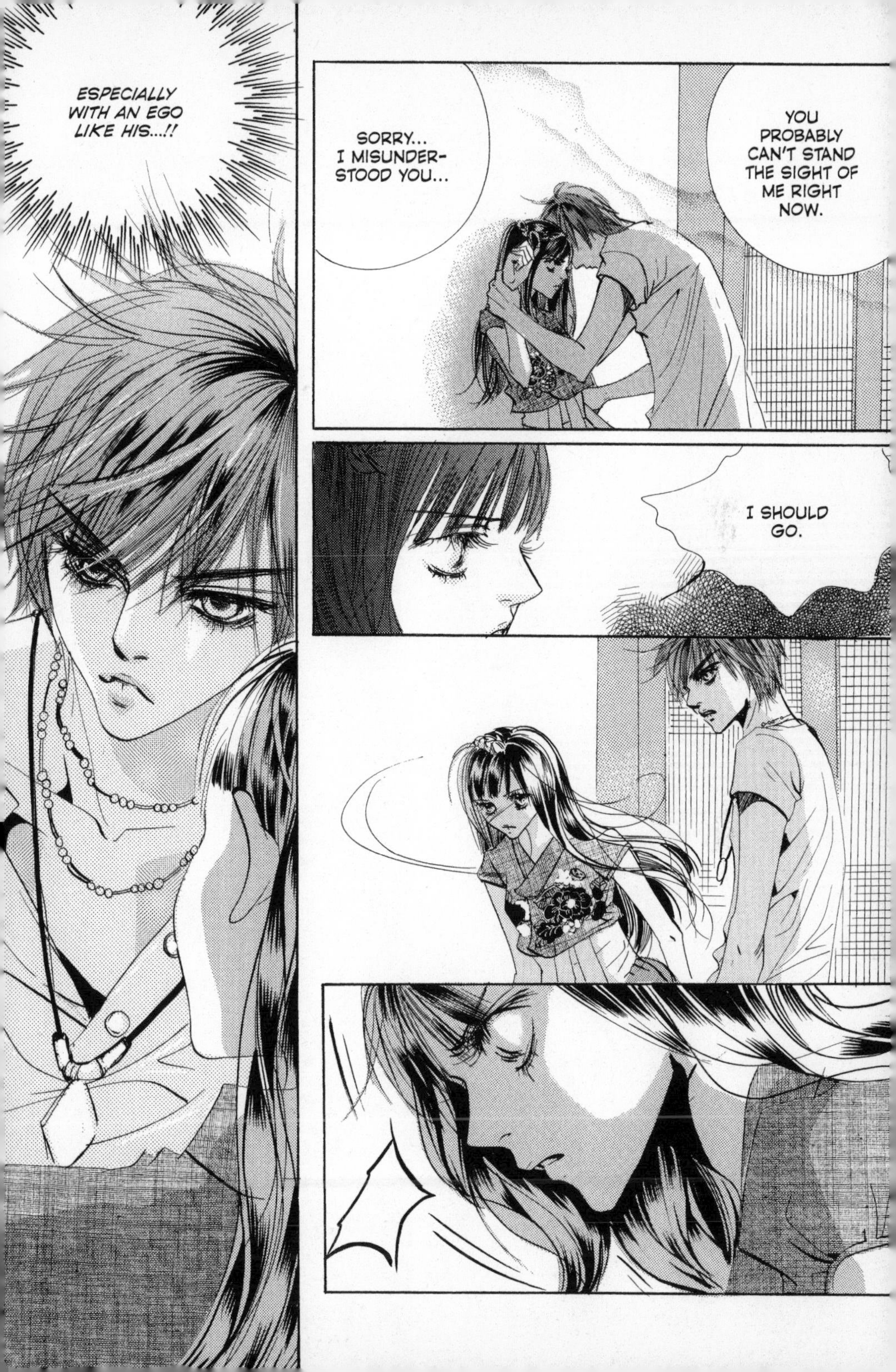
ESPECIALLY WITH AN EGO LIKE HIS...!!
SORRY... I MISUNDER-STOOD YOU...
YOU PROBABLY CAN'T STAND THE SIGHT OF ME RIGHT NOW.
I SHOULD GO.

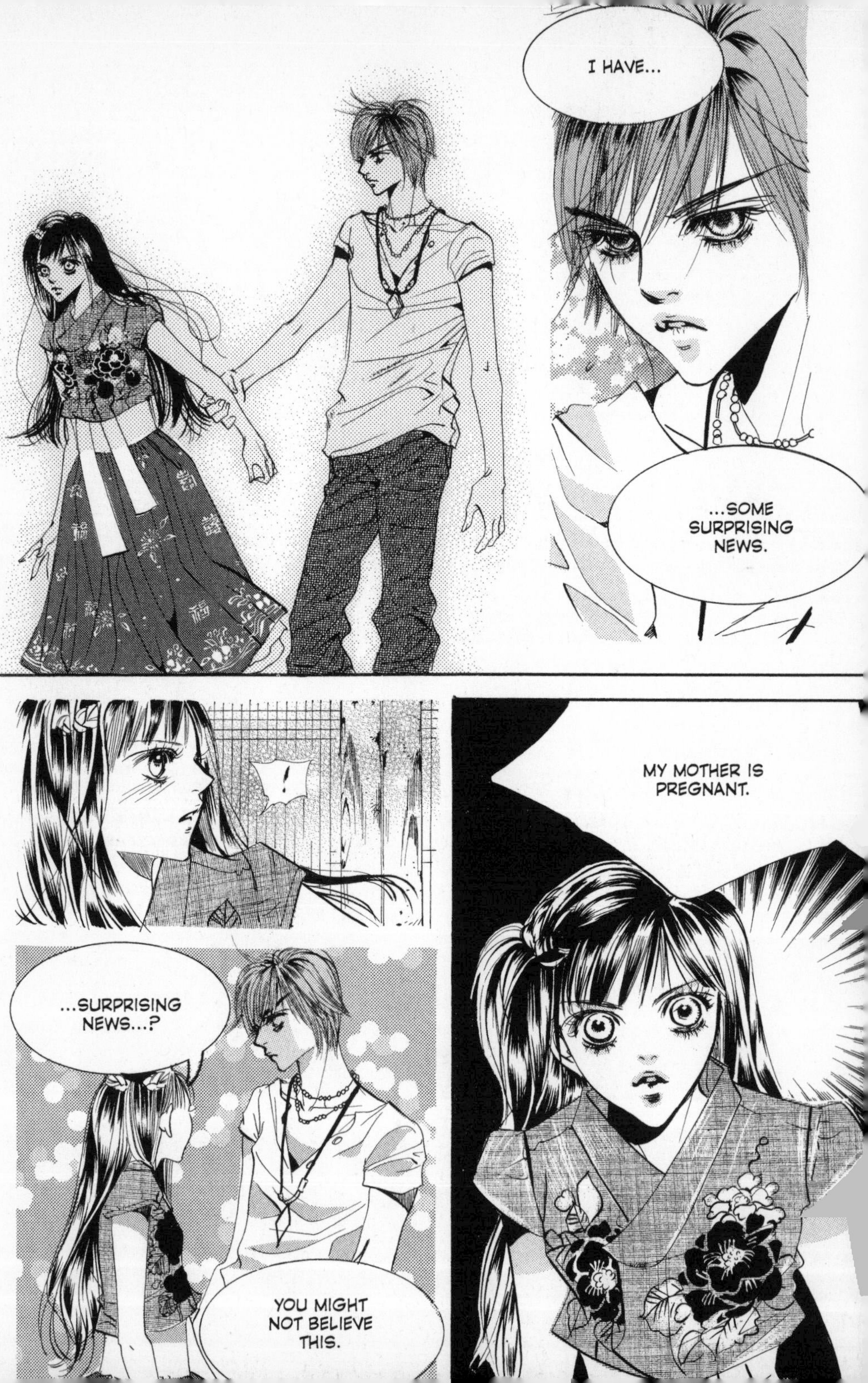
I HAVE...
...SOME SURPRISING NEWS.
!
...SURPRISING NEWS...?
YOU MIGHT NOT BELIEVE THIS.
MY MOTHER IS PREGNANT.

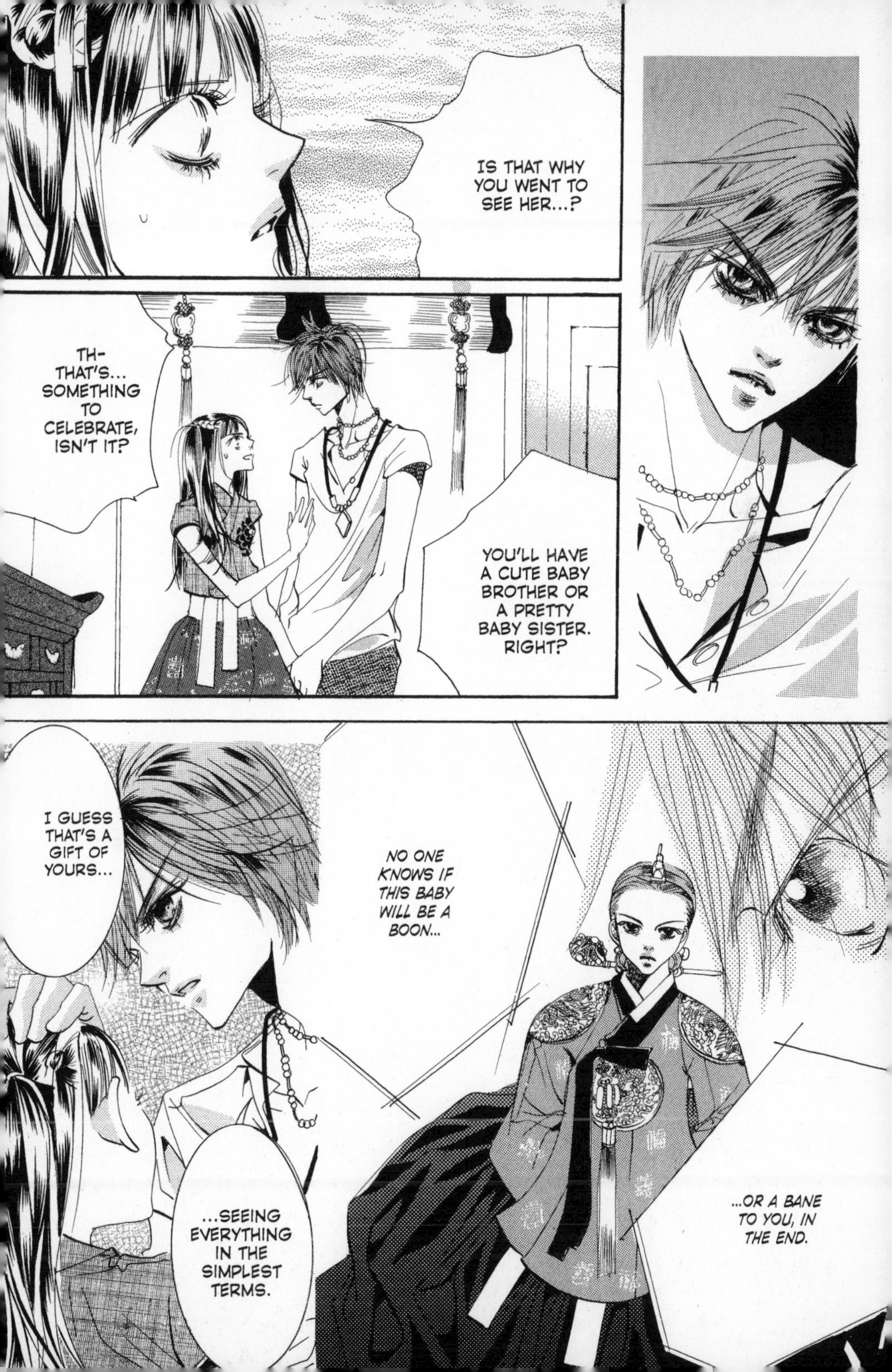
IS THAT WHY YOU WENT TO SEE HER...?
TH- THAT'S... SOMETHING TO CELEBRATE, ISN'T IT?
YOU'LL HAVE A CUTE BABY BROTHER OR A PRETTY BABY SISTER. RIGHT?
I GUESS THAT'S A GIFT OF YOURS...
...SEEING EVERYTHING IN THE SIMPLEST TERMS.
NO ONE KNOWS IF THIS BABY WILL BE A BOON...
...OR A BANE TO YOU, IN THE END.

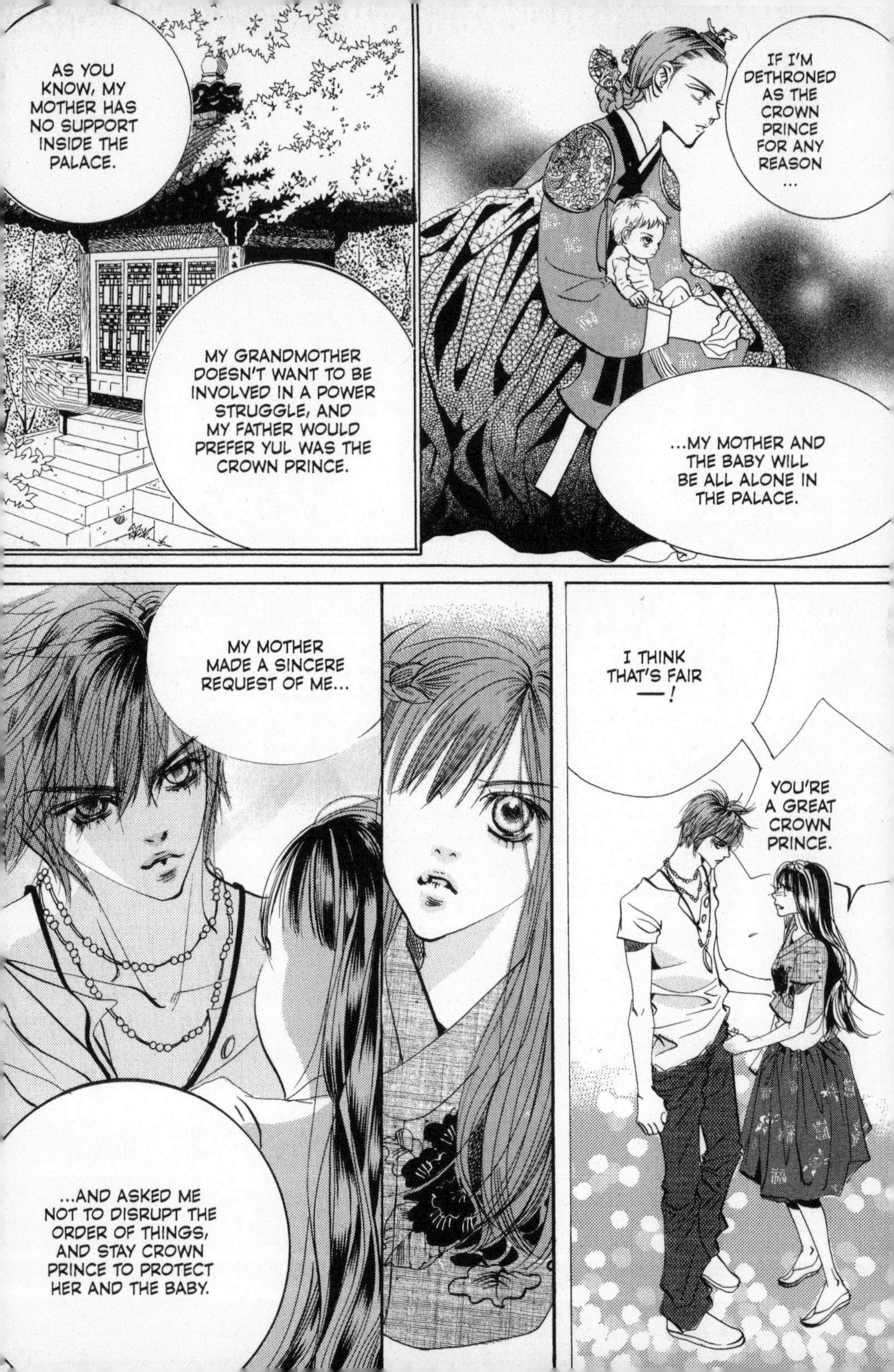
AS YOU KNOW, MY MOTHER HAS NO SUPPORT INSIDE THE PALACE.
MY GRANDMOTHER DOESN'T WANT TO BE INVOLVED IN A POWER STRUGGLE, AND MY FATHER WOULD PREFER YUL WAS THE CROWN PRINCE.
IF I'M DETHRONED AS THE CROWN PRINCE FOR ANY REASON ...
...MY MOTHER AND THE BABY WILL BE ALL ALONE IN THE PALACE.
MY MOTHER MADE A SINCERE REQUEST OF ME...
...AND ASKED ME NOT TO DISRUPT THE ORDER OF THINGS, AND STAY CROWN PRINCE TO PROTECT HER AND THE BABY.
I THINK THAT'S FAIR —!
YOU'RE A GREAT CROWN PRINCE.

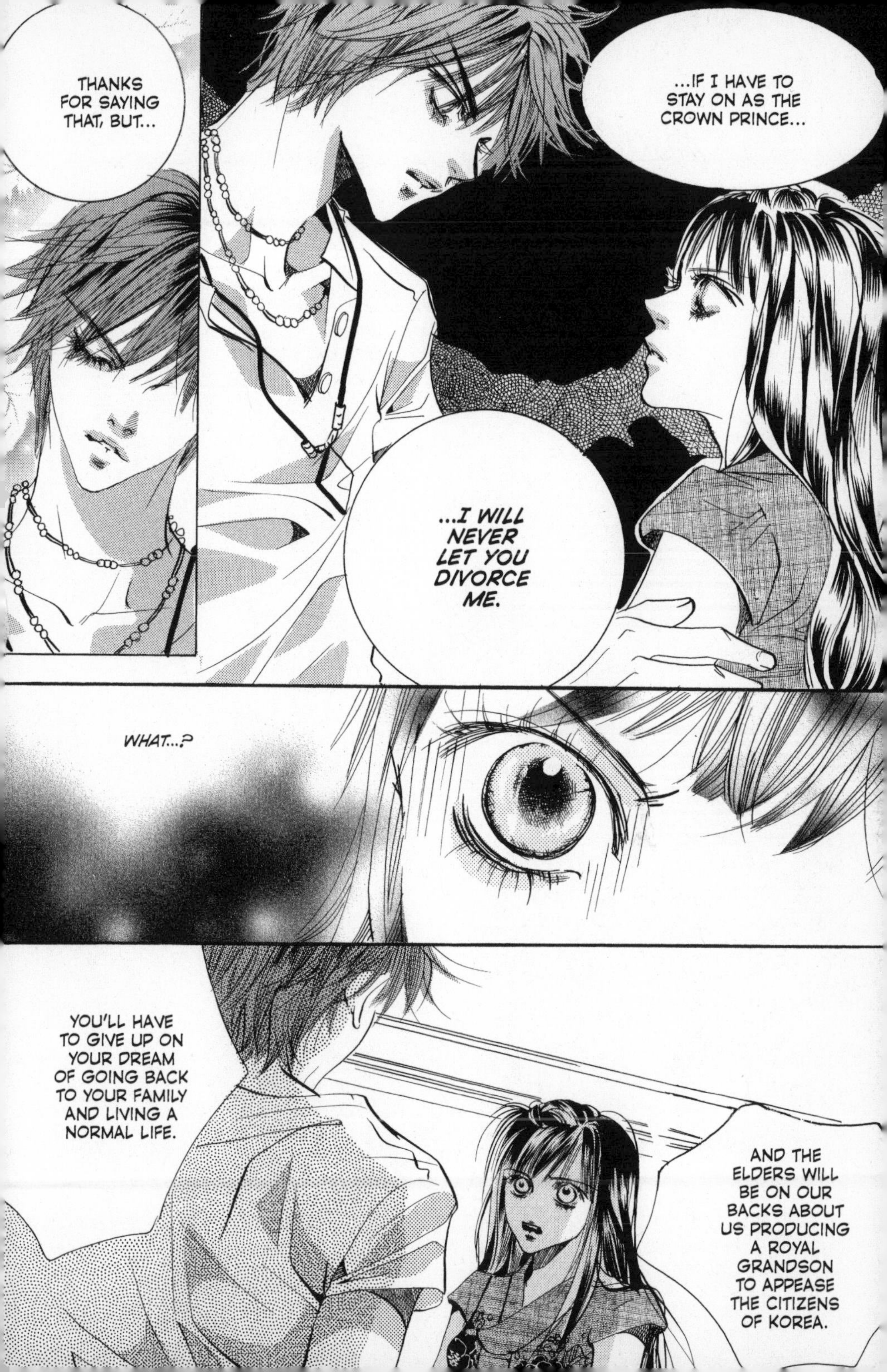
THANKS FOR SAYING THAT, BUT...
...IF I HAVE TO STAY ON AS THE CROWN PRINCE...
...I WILL NEVER LET YOU DIVORCE ME.
WHAT...?
YOU'LL HAVE TO GIVE UP ON YOUR DREAM OF GOING BACK TO YOUR FAMILY AND LIVING A NORMAL LIFE.
AND THE ELDERS WILL BE ON OUR BACKS ABOUT US PRODUCING A ROYAL GRANDSON TO APPEASE THE CITIZENS OF KOREA.

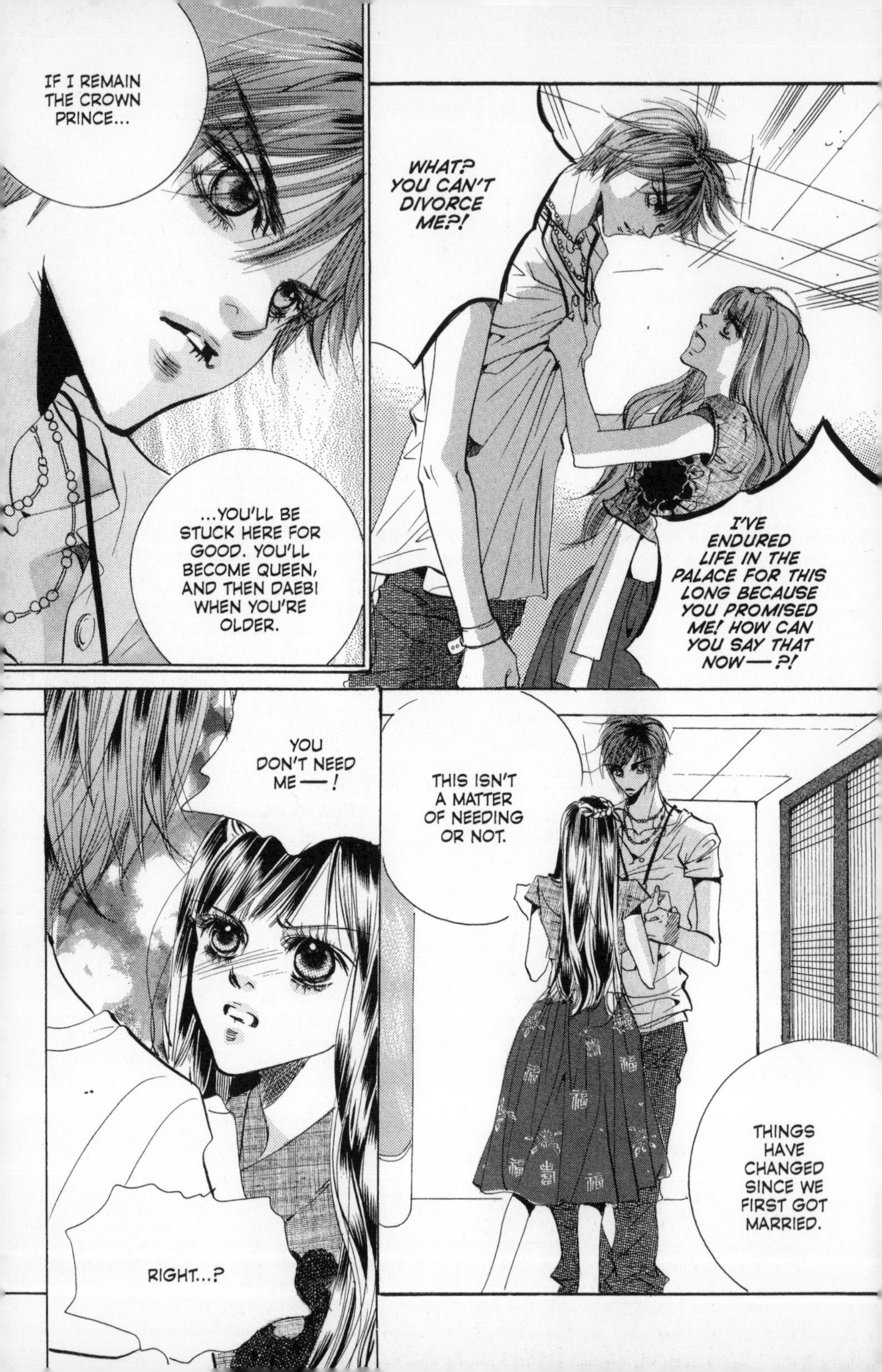
IF I REMAIN THE CROWN PRINCE...
...YOU'LL BE STUCK HERE FOR GOOD. YOU'LL BECOME QUEEN, AND THEN DAEBI WHEN YOU'RE OLDER.
WHAT? YOU CAN'T DIVORCE ME?!
I'VE ENDURED LIFE IN THE PALACE FOR THIS LONG BECAUSE YOU PROMISED ME! HOW CAN YOU SAY THAT NOW—?!
YOU DON'T NEED ME—!
RIGHT...?
THIS ISN'T A MATTER OF NEEDING OR NOT.
THINGS HAVE CHANGED SINCE WE FIRST GOT MARRIED.

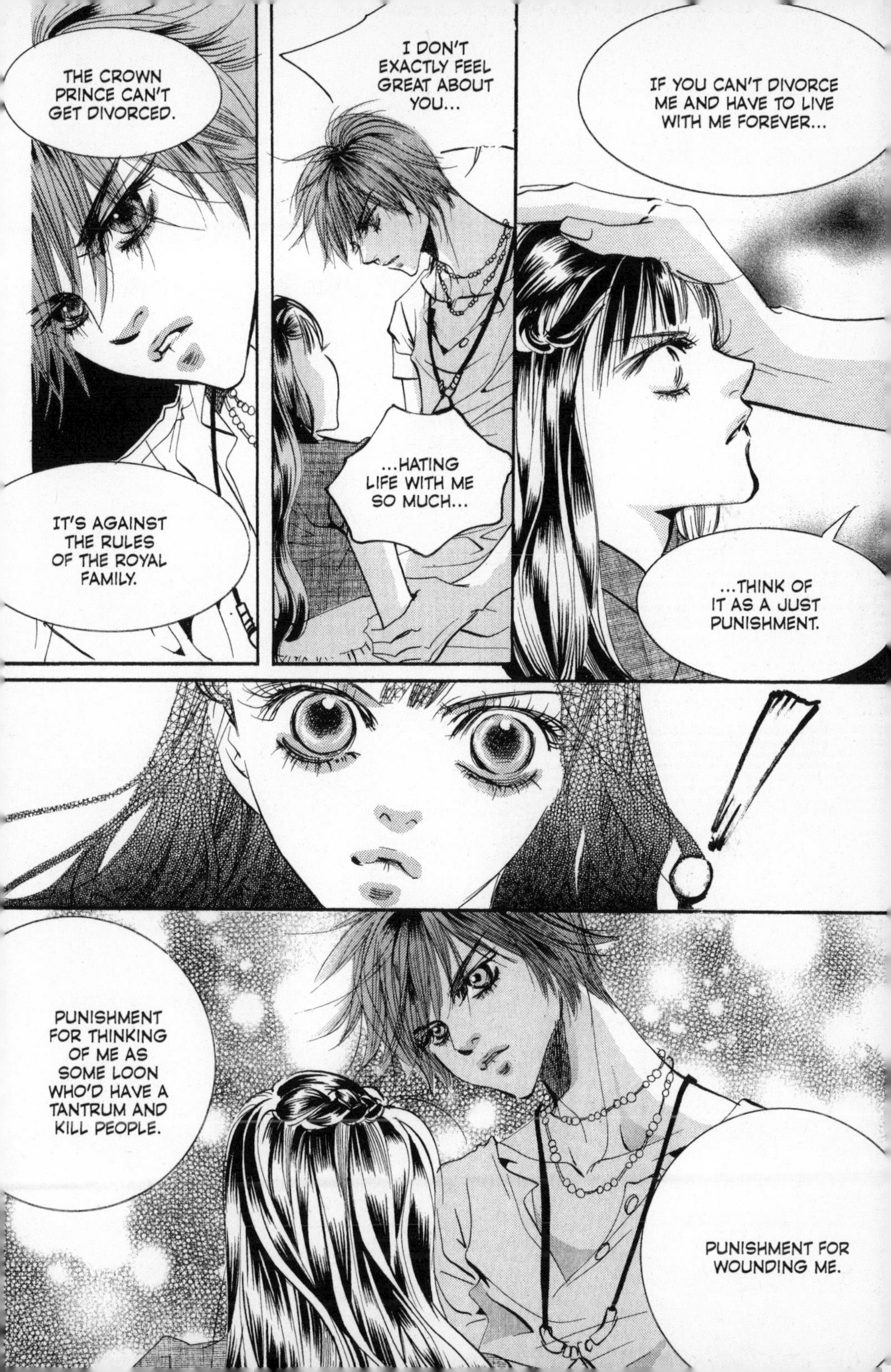
THE CROWN PRINCE CAN'T GET DIVORCED.
IT'S AGAINST THE RULES OF THE ROYAL FAMILY.
I DON'T EXACTLY FEEL GREAT ABOUT YOU...
...HATING LIFE WITH ME SO MUCH...
IF YOU CAN'T DIVORCE ME AND HAVE TO LIVE WITH ME FOREVER...
...THINK OF IT AS A JUST PUNISHMENT.
!
PUNISHMENT FOR THINKING OF ME AS SOME LOON WHO'D HAVE A TANTRUM AND KILL PEOPLE.
PUNISHMENT FOR WOUNDING ME.

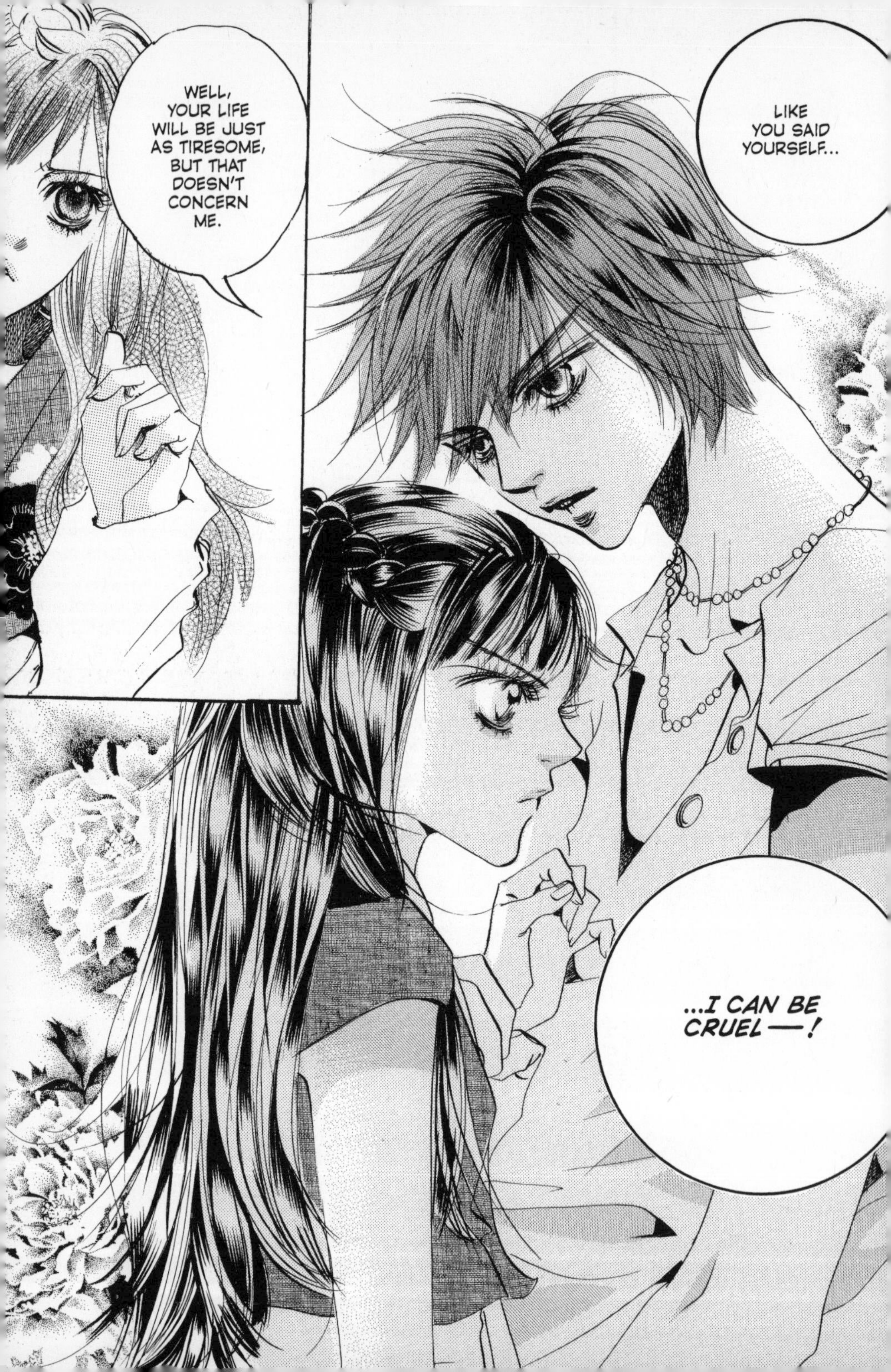
WELL, YOUR LIFE WILL BE JUST AS TIRESOME, BUT THAT DOESN'T CONCERN ME.
LIKE YOU SAID YOURSELF...
...I CAN BE CRUEL—!

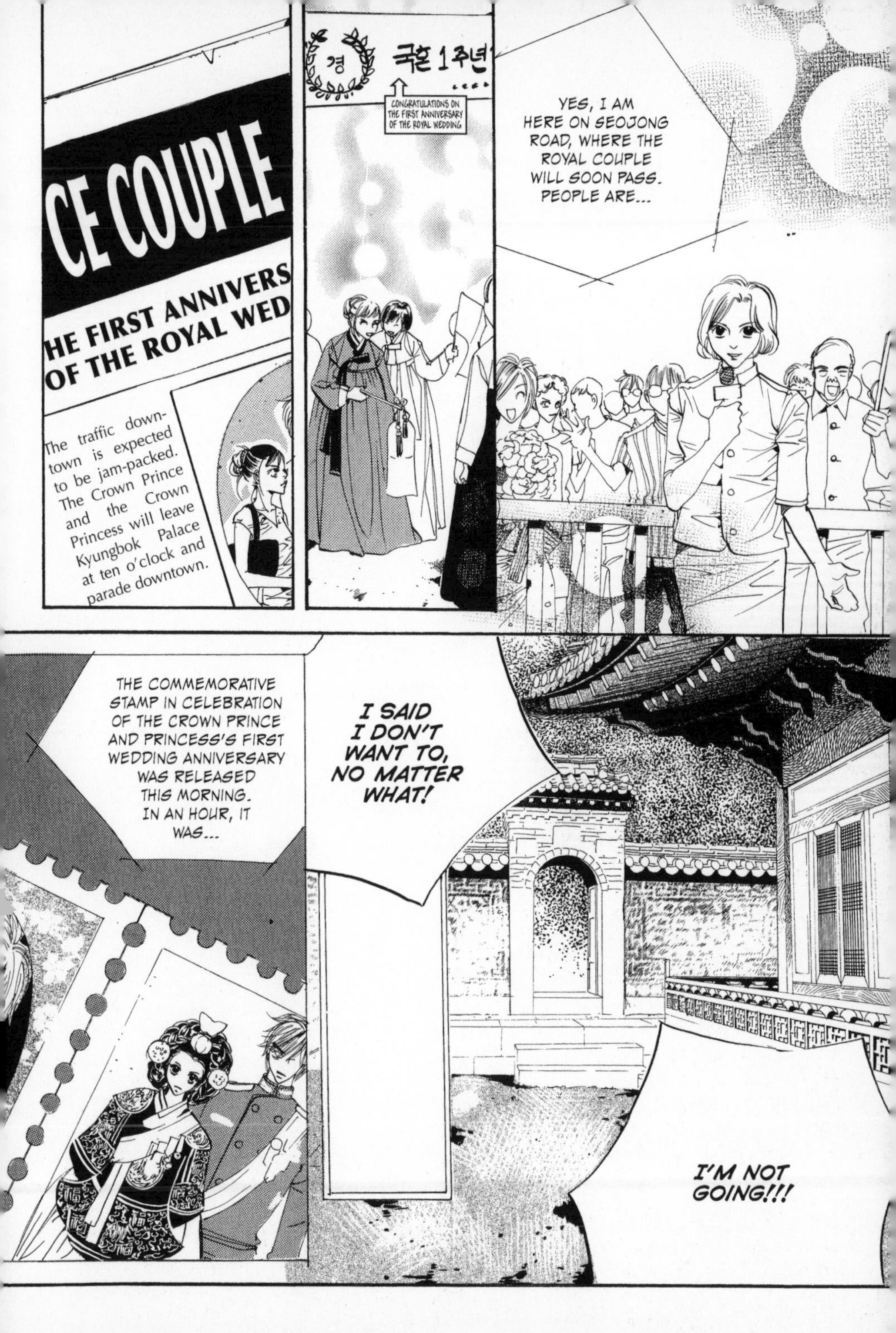
CE COUPLE
HE FIRST ANNIVERS
OF THE ROYAL WED
The traffic downtown is expected to be jam-packed. The Crown Prince and the Crown Princess will leave Kyungbok Palace at ten o'clock and parade downtown.
경 국혼 1주년
CONGRATULATIONS ON THE FIRST ANNIVERSARY OF THE ROYAL WEDDING
YES, I AM HERE ON SEOJONG ROAD, WHERE THE ROYAL COUPLE WILL SOON PASS. PEOPLE ARE...
THE COMMEMORATIVE STAMP IN CELEBRATION OF THE CROWN PRINCE AND PRINCESS'S FIRST WEDDING ANNIVERSARY WAS RELEASED THIS MORNING. IN AN HOUR, IT WAS...
I SAID I DON'T WANT TO, NO MATTER WHAT!
I'M NOT GOING!!!

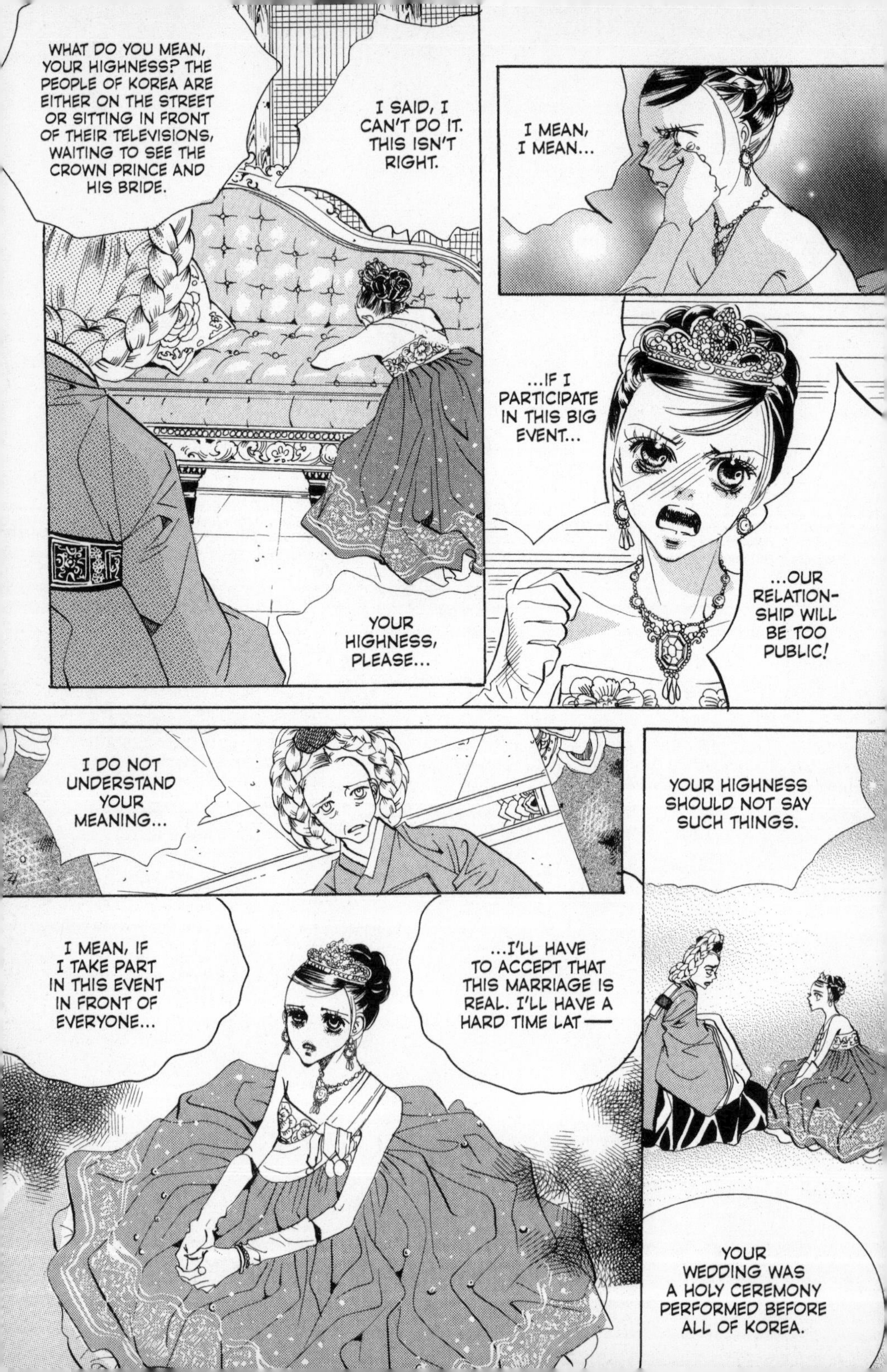
WHAT DO YOU MEAN, YOUR HIGHNESS? THE PEOPLE OF KOREA ARE EITHER ON THE STREET OR SITTING IN FRONT OF THEIR TELEVISIONS, WAITING TO SEE THE CROWN PRINCE AND HIS BRIDE.
I SAID, I CAN'T DO IT. THIS ISN'T RIGHT.
YOUR HIGHNESS, PLEASE...
I MEAN, I MEAN...
...IF I PARTICIPATE IN THIS BIG EVENT...
...OUR RELATION-SHIP WILL BE TOO PUBLIC!
I DO NOT UNDERSTAND YOUR MEANING...
I MEAN, IF I TAKE PART IN THIS EVENT IN FRONT OF EVERYONE...
...I'LL HAVE TO ACCEPT THAT THIS MARRIAGE IS REAL. I'LL HAVE A HARD TIME LAT—
YOUR HIGHNESS SHOULD NOT SAY SUCH THINGS.
YOUR WEDDING WAS A HOLY CEREMONY PERFORMED BEFORE ALL OF KOREA.

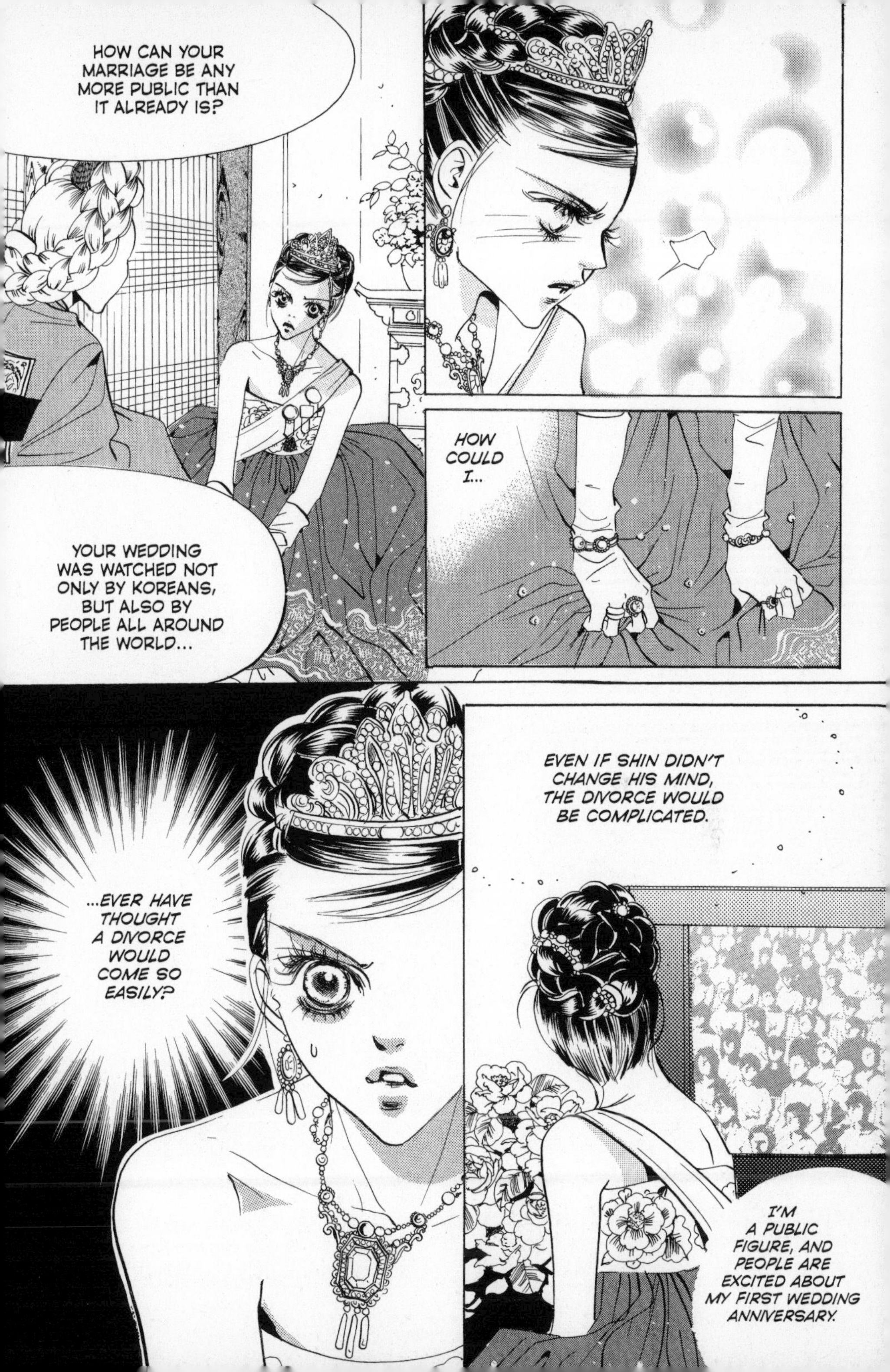
HOW CAN YOUR MARRIAGE BE ANY MORE PUBLIC THAN IT ALREADY IS?
YOUR WEDDING WAS WATCHED NOT ONLY BY KOREANS, BUT ALSO BY PEOPLE ALL AROUND THE WORLD...
HOW COULD I...
...EVER HAVE THOUGHT A DIVORCE WOULD COME SO EASILY?
EVEN IF SHIN DIDN'T CHANGE HIS MIND, THE DIVORCE WOULD BE COMPLICATED.
I'M A PUBLIC FIGURE, AND PEOPLE ARE EXCITED ABOUT MY FIRST WEDDING ANNIVERSARY.

PEOPLE ARE HAPPY TO SEE ME NOW, BUT THEY PROBABLY WON'T BE IF I DIVORCE SHIN.

THEY MIGHT DECIDE I'M SOME SHREW WHO DESTROYED THEIR BELOVED CROWN PRINCE.

THEY'D RUN ME RIGHT OUT OF THE COUNTRY.

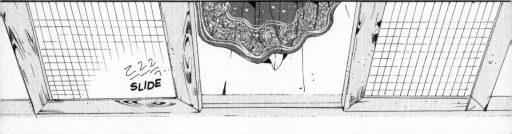

SLIDE

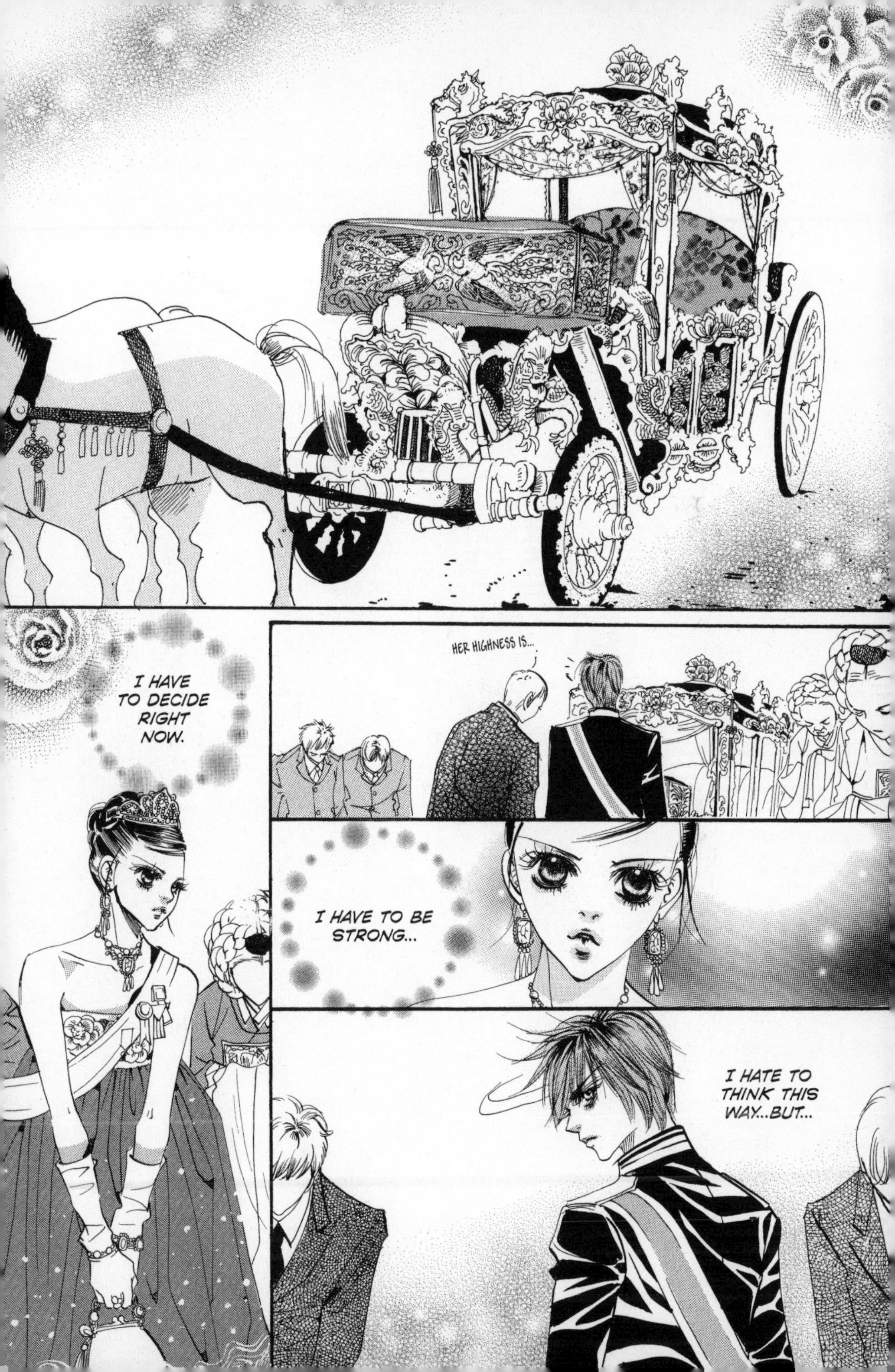
I HAVE TO DECIDE RIGHT NOW.
HER HIGHNESS IS...
I HAVE TO BE STRONG...
I HATE TO THINK THIS WAY...BUT...

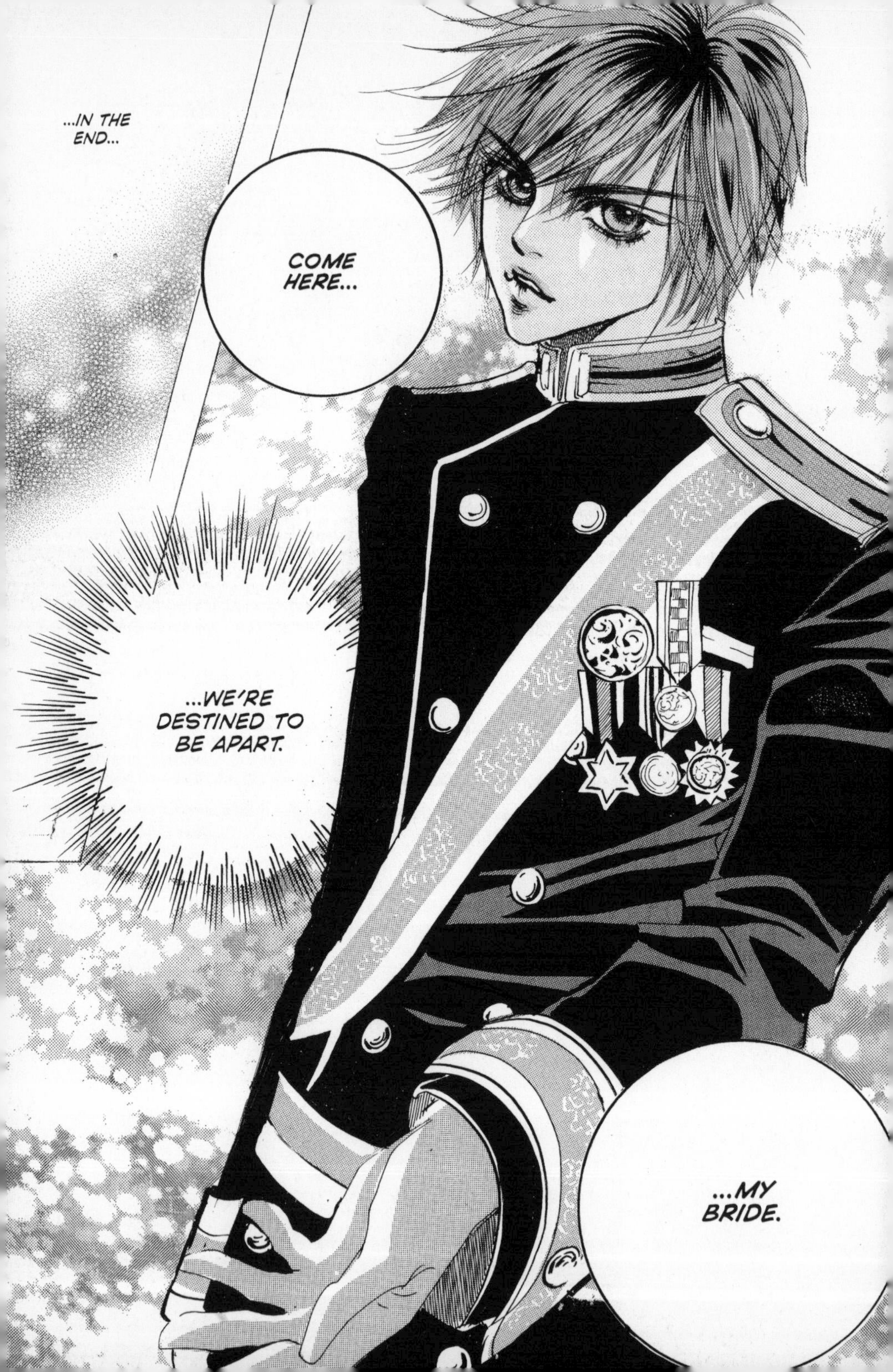
...IN THE END...
COME HERE...
...WE'RE DESTINED TO BE APART.
...MY BRIDE.

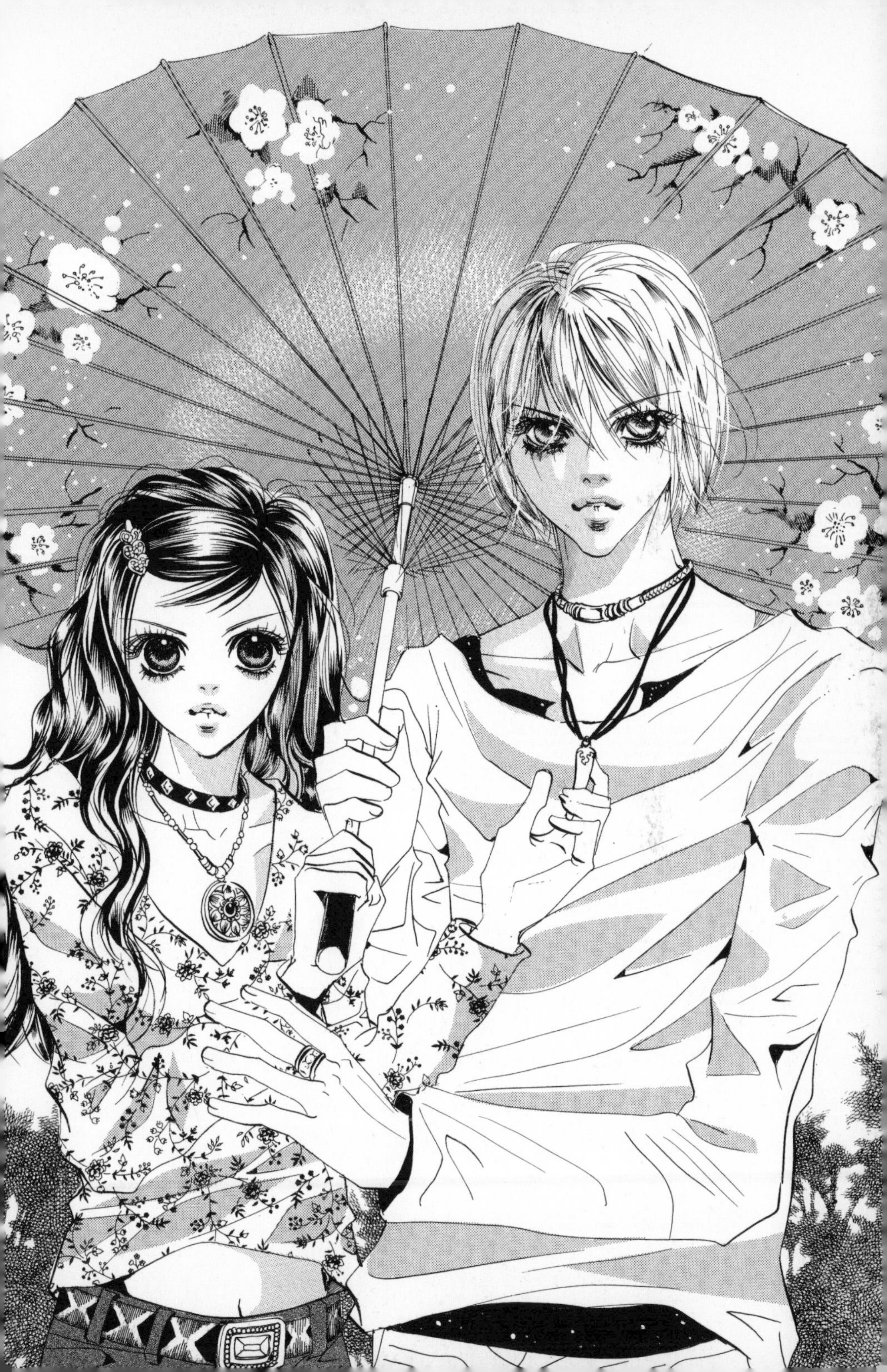

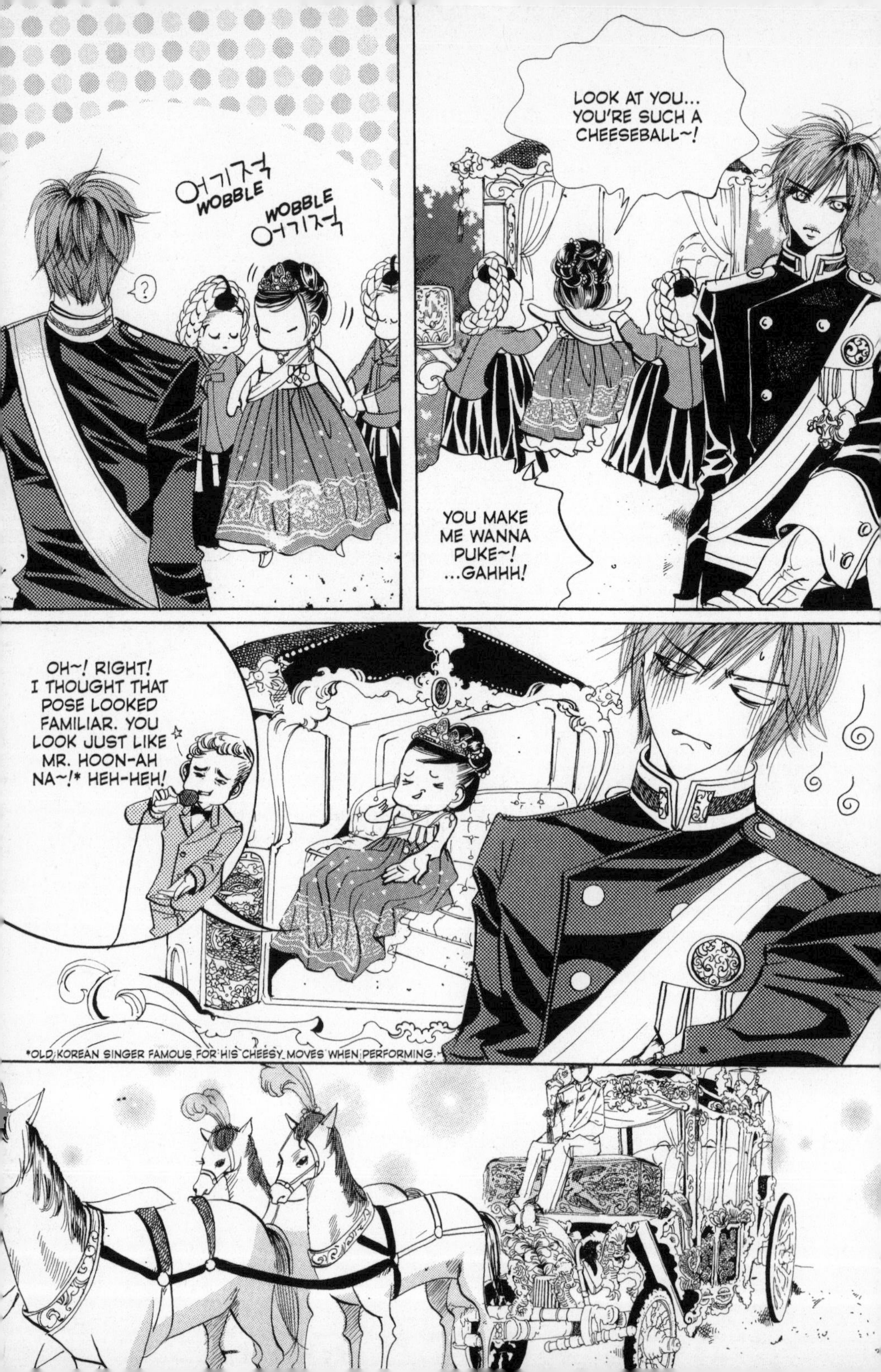
어기적
WOBBLE
WOBBLE
어기적
?
LOOK AT YOU... YOU'RE SUCH A CHEESEBALL~!
YOU MAKE ME WANNA PUKE~! ...GAHHH!
OH~! RIGHT! I THOUGHT THAT POSE LOOKED FAMILIAR. YOU LOOK JUST LIKE MR. HOON-AH NA~!* HEH-HEH!
*OLD KOREAN SINGER FAMOUS FOR HIS CHEESY MOVES WHEN PERFORMING.

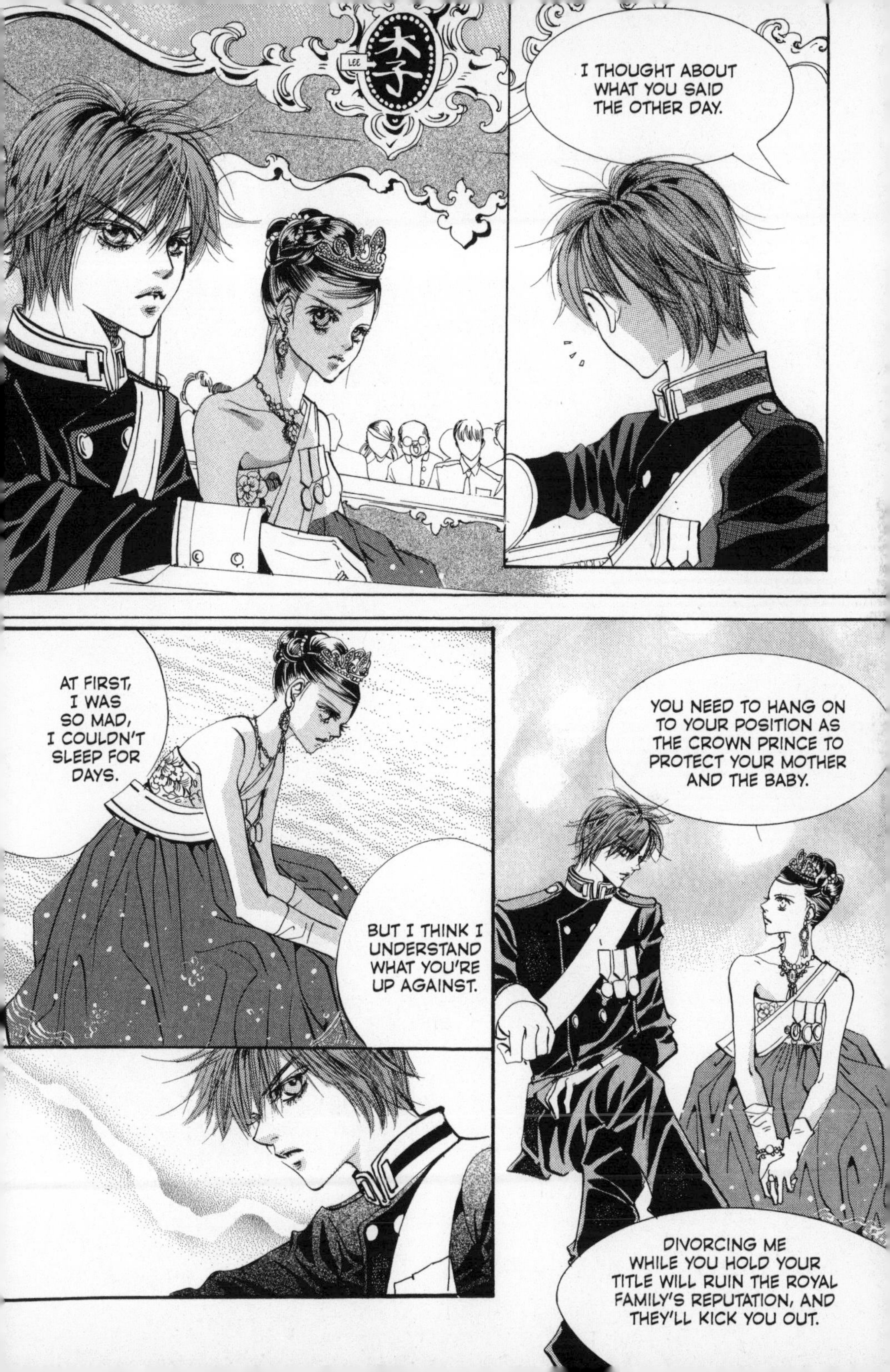
LEE
I THOUGHT ABOUT WHAT YOU SAID THE OTHER DAY.
AT FIRST, I WAS SO MAD, I COULDN'T SLEEP FOR DAYS.
BUT I THINK I UNDERSTAND WHAT YOU'RE UP AGAINST.
YOU NEED TO HANG ON TO YOUR POSITION AS THE CROWN PRINCE TO PROTECT YOUR MOTHER AND THE BABY.
DIVORCING ME WHILE YOU HOLD YOUR TITLE WILL RUIN THE ROYAL FAMILY'S REPUTATION, AND THEY'LL KICK YOU OUT.

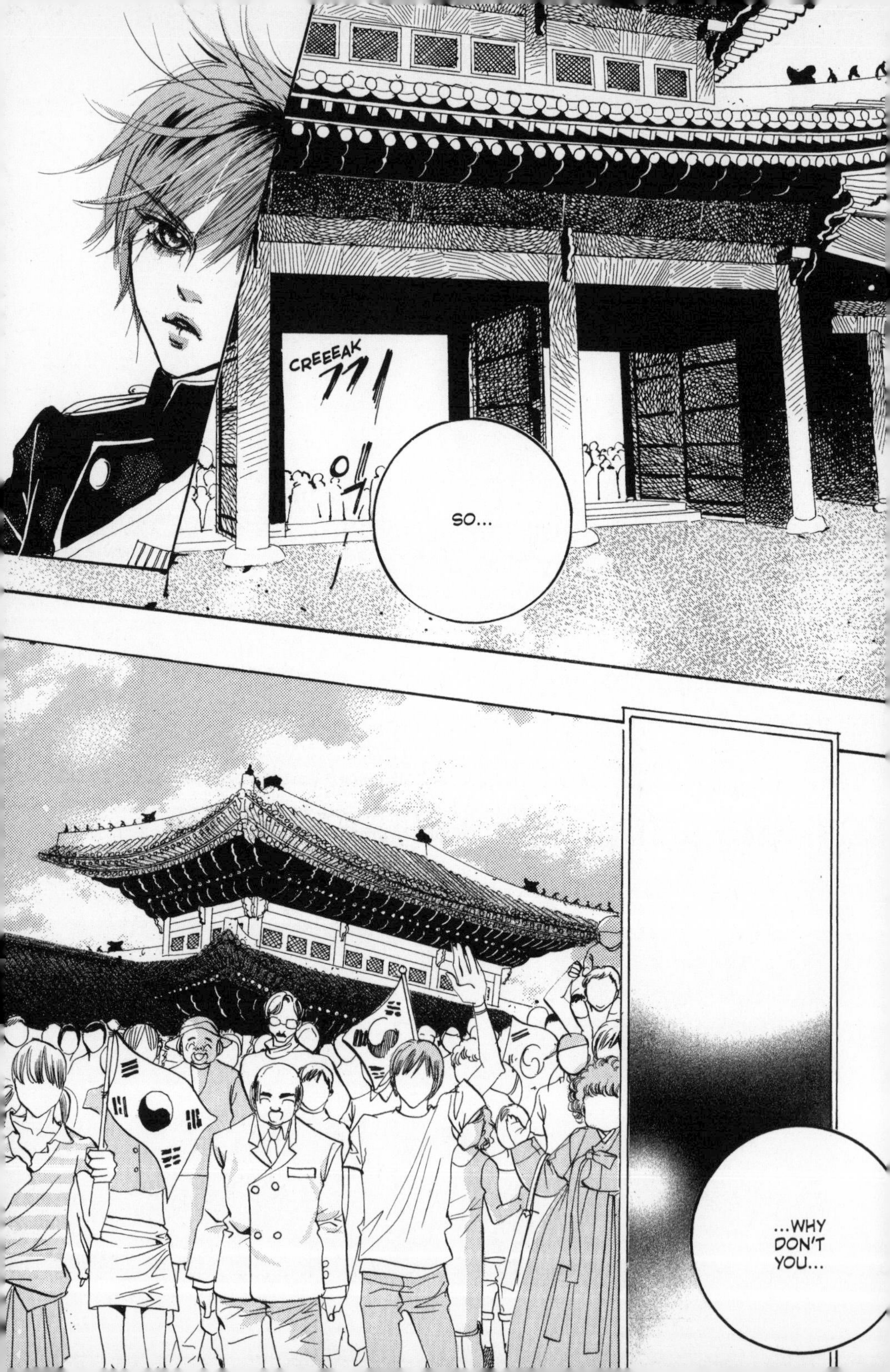
CREEEAK
SO...
...WHY DON'T YOU...

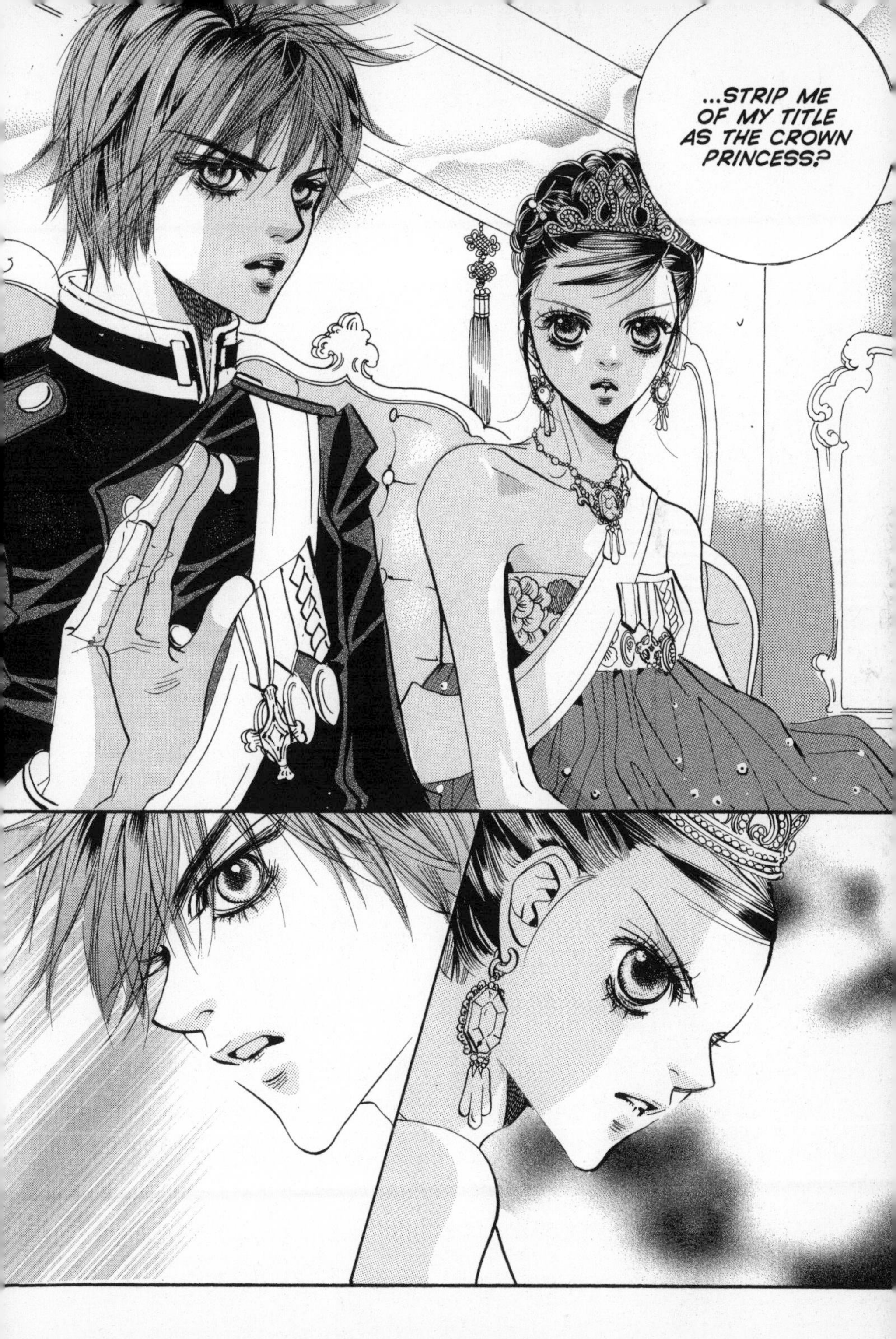
...STRIP ME OF MY TITLE AS THE CROWN PRINCESS?

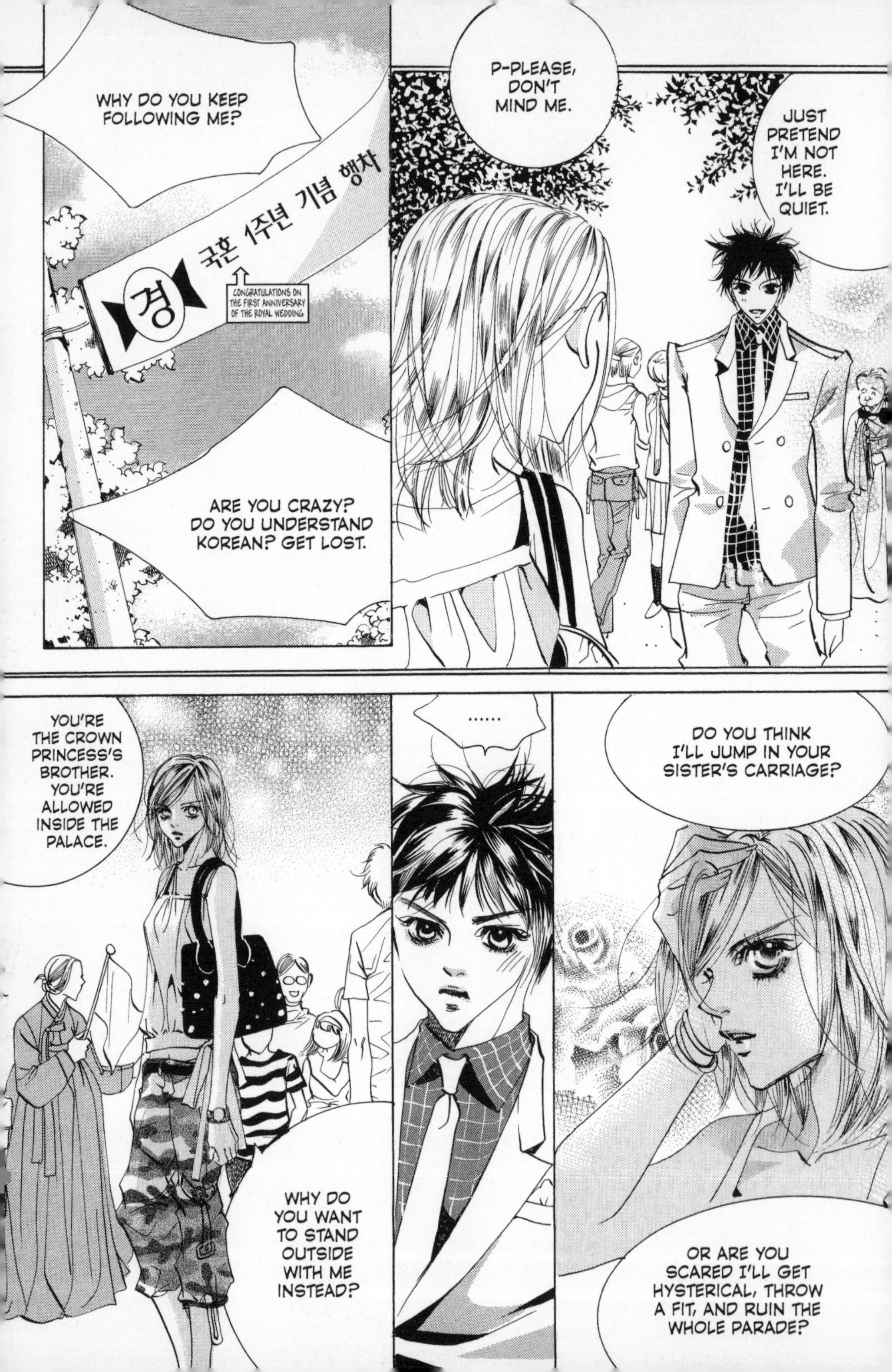

WHY DO YOU KEEP FOLLOWING ME?
경
국혼 1주년 기념 행차
CONGRATULATIONS ON THE FIRST ANNIVERSARY OF THE ROYAL WEDDING
ARE YOU CRAZY? DO YOU UNDERSTAND KOREAN? GET LOST.
P-PLEASE, DON'T MIND ME.
JUST PRETEND I'M NOT HERE. I'LL BE QUIET.
YOU'RE THE CROWN PRINCESS'S BROTHER. YOU'RE ALLOWED INSIDE THE PALACE.
WHY DO YOU WANT TO STAND OUTSIDE WITH ME INSTEAD?
......
DO YOU THINK I'LL JUMP IN YOUR SISTER'S CARRIAGE?
OR ARE YOU SCARED I'LL GET HYSTERICAL, THROW A FIT, AND RUIN THE WHOLE PARADE?

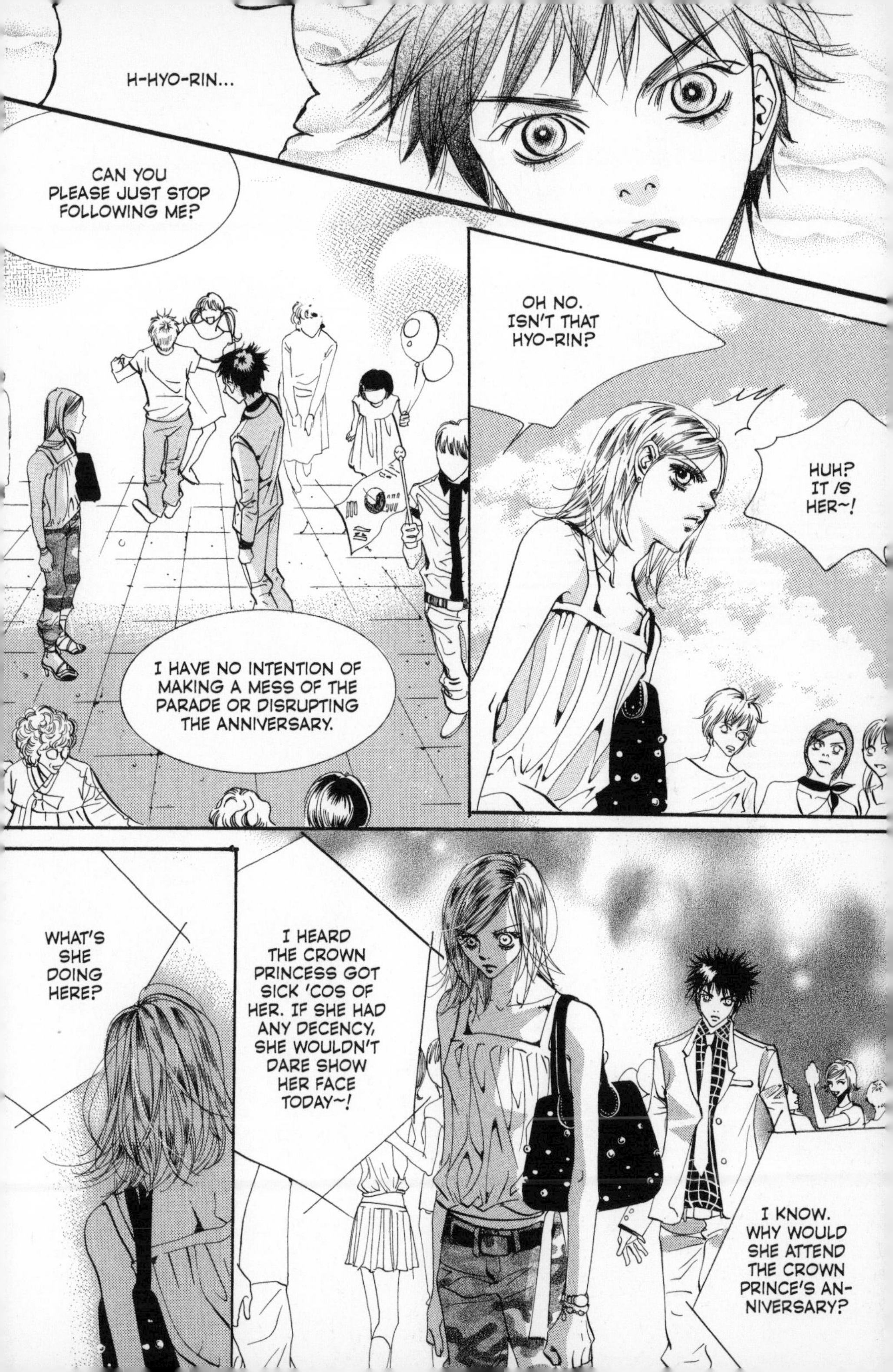
H-HYO-RIN...
CAN YOU PLEASE JUST STOP FOLLOWING ME?
I HAVE NO INTENTION OF MAKING A MESS OF THE PARADE OR DISRUPTING THE ANNIVERSARY.
OH NO. ISN'T THAT HYO-RIN?
HUH? IT IS HER~!
WHAT'S SHE DOING HERE?
I HEARD THE CROWN PRINCESS GOT SICK 'COS OF HER. IF SHE HAD ANY DECENCY, SHE WOULDN'T DARE SHOW HER FACE TODAY~!
I KNOW. WHY WOULD SHE ATTEND THE CROWN PRINCE'S AN-NIVERSARY?

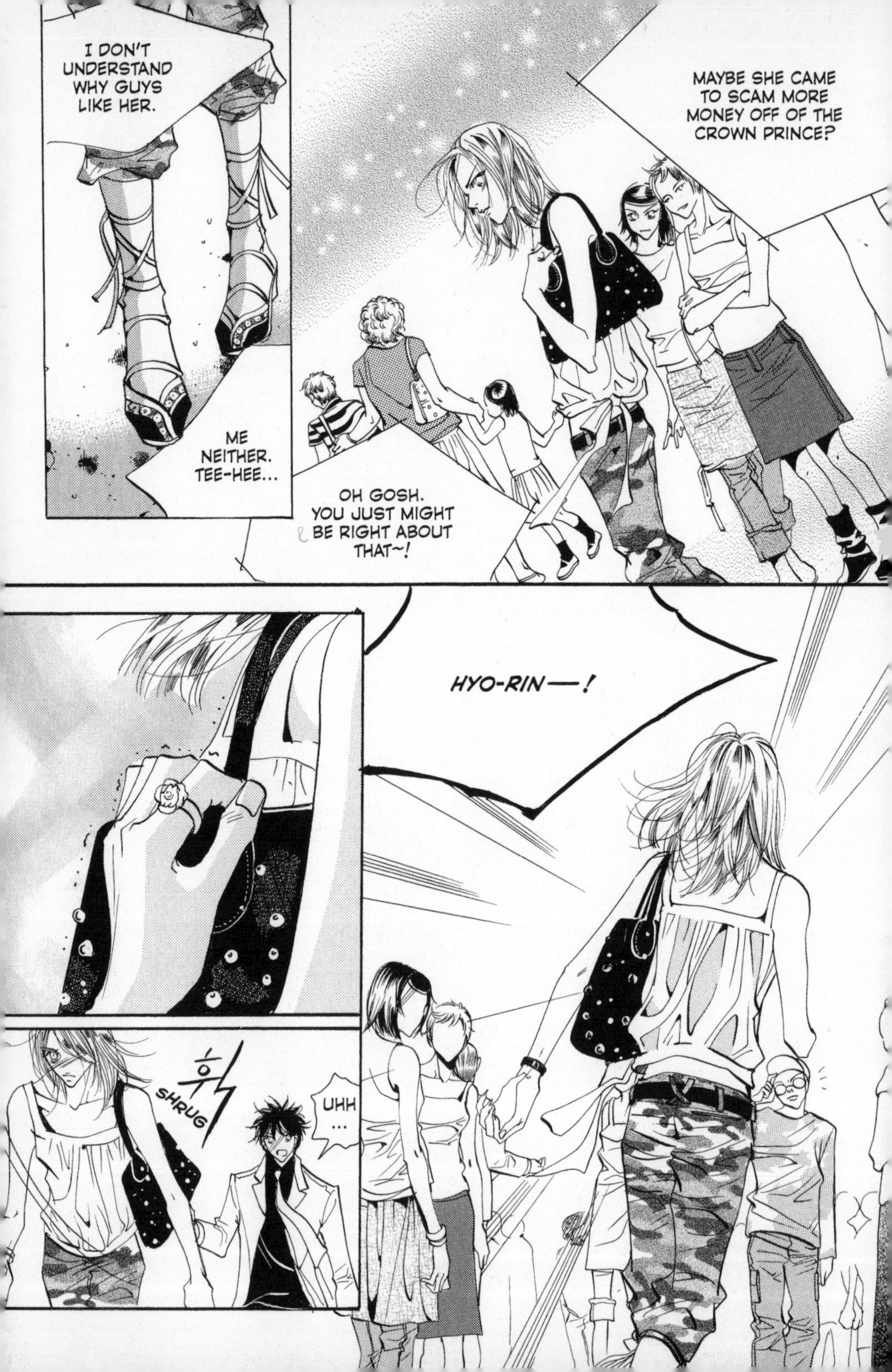

I DON'T UNDERSTAND WHY GUYS LIKE HER.
ME NEITHER. TEE-HEE...
MAYBE SHE CAME TO SCAM MORE MONEY OFF OF THE CROWN PRINCE?
OH GOSH. YOU JUST MIGHT BE RIGHT ABOUT THAT~!
SHRUG
UHH ...
HYO-RIN—!

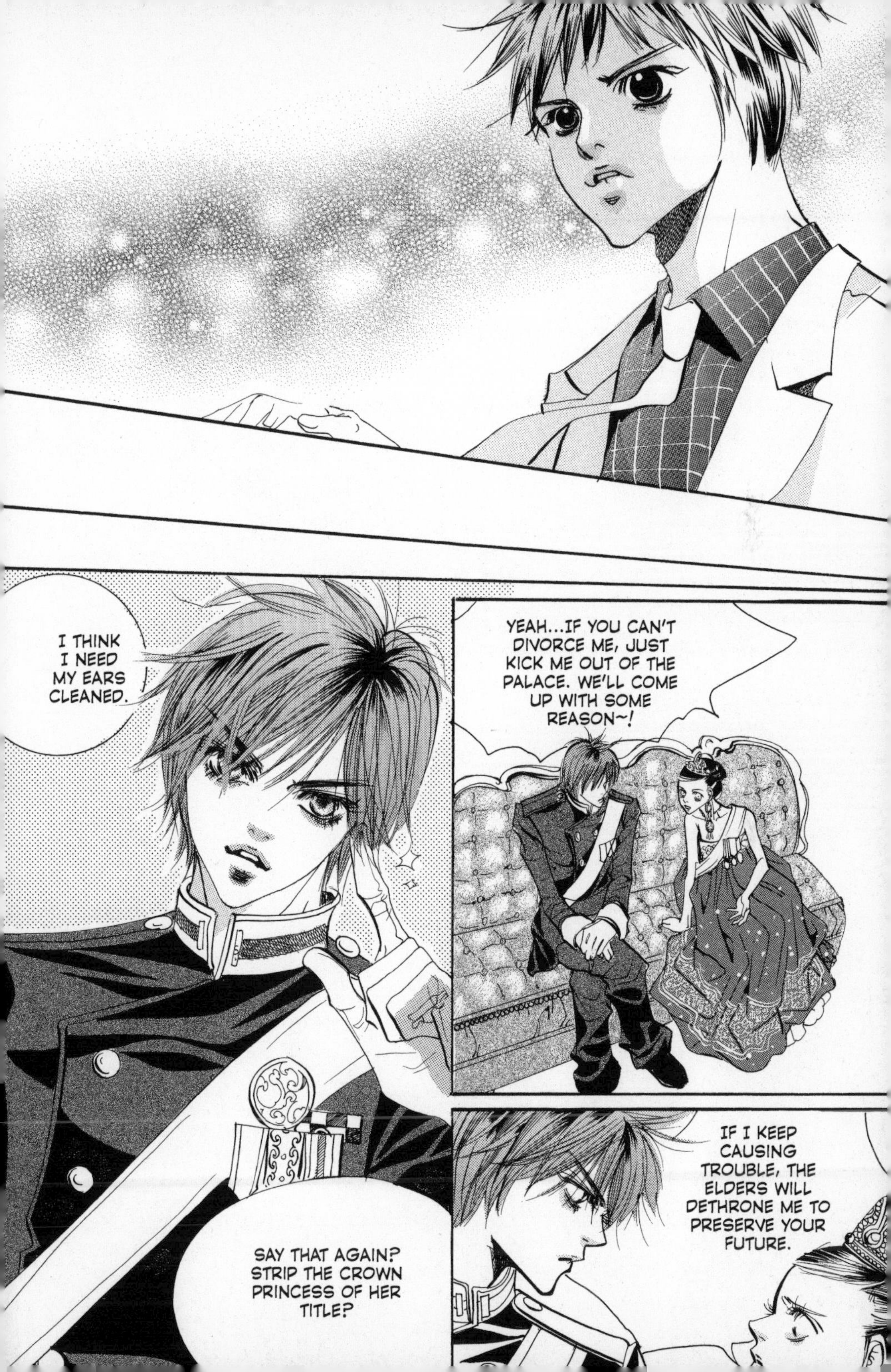
I THINK I NEED MY EARS CLEANED.
SAY THAT AGAIN? STRIP THE CROWN PRINCESS OF HER TITLE?
YEAH...IF YOU CAN'T DIVORCE ME, JUST KICK ME OUT OF THE PALACE. WE'LL COME UP WITH SOME REASON~!
IF I KEEP CAUSING TROUBLE, THE ELDERS WILL DETHRONE ME TO PRESERVE YOUR FUTURE.

MAKING THOSE OLD FARTS HATE ME WOULD BE LIKE TAKING CANDY FROM A BABY~!

CLENCH

I'M GOOD AT THAT~!!

IS THAT SOMETHING TO BRAG ABOUT...?

STOP TALKING NONSENSE AND WAVE TO YOUR SUBJECTS.

PEOPLE ARE WATCHING US.

I MEAN, COME ON~!

SHHH!

IS THAT HYO-RIN...?

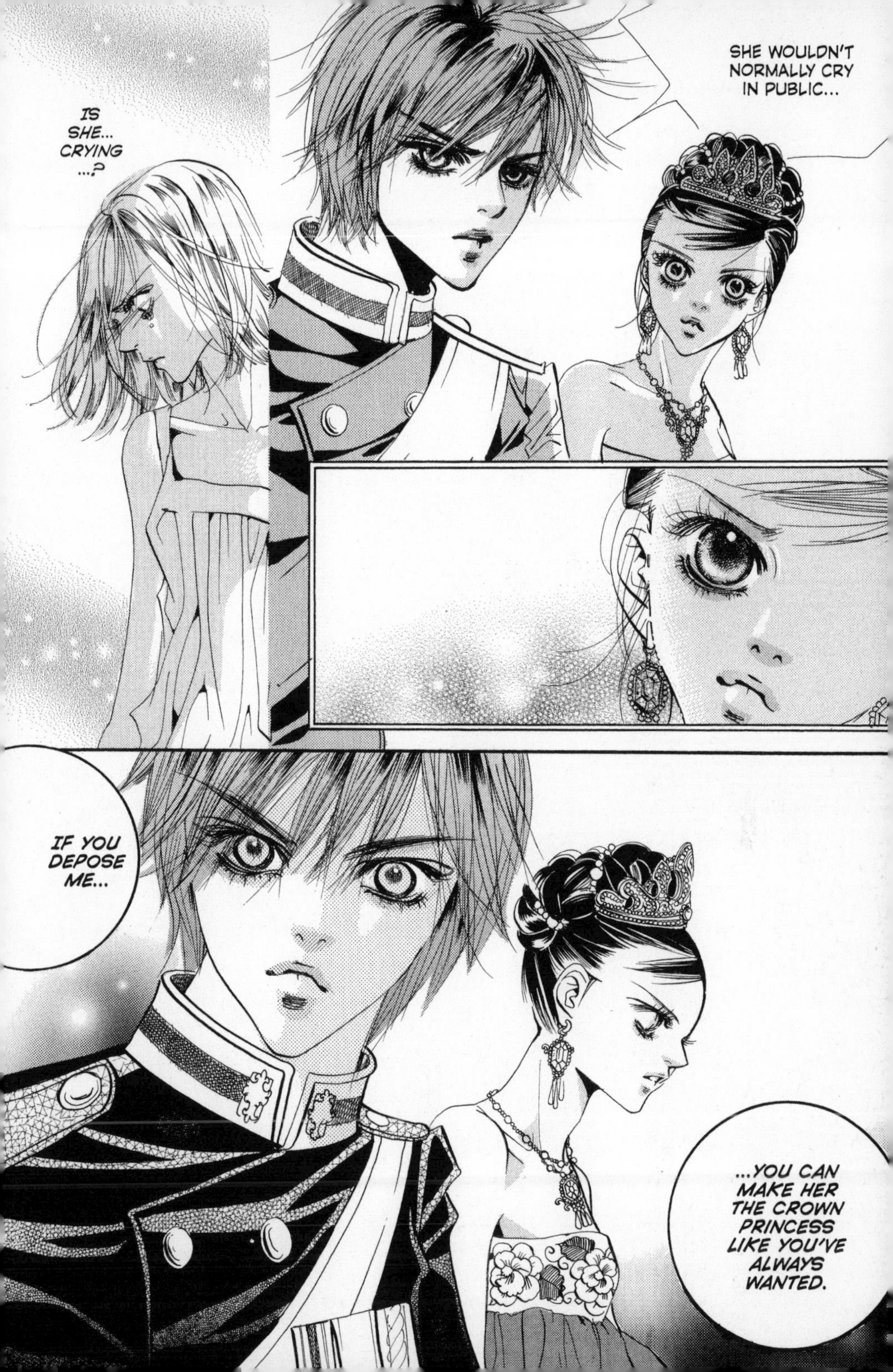
IS SHE... CRYING ...?
SHE WOULDN'T NORMALLY CRY IN PUBLIC...
IF YOU DEPOSE ME...
...YOU CAN MAKE HER THE CROWN PRINCESS LIKE YOU'VE ALWAYS WANTED.

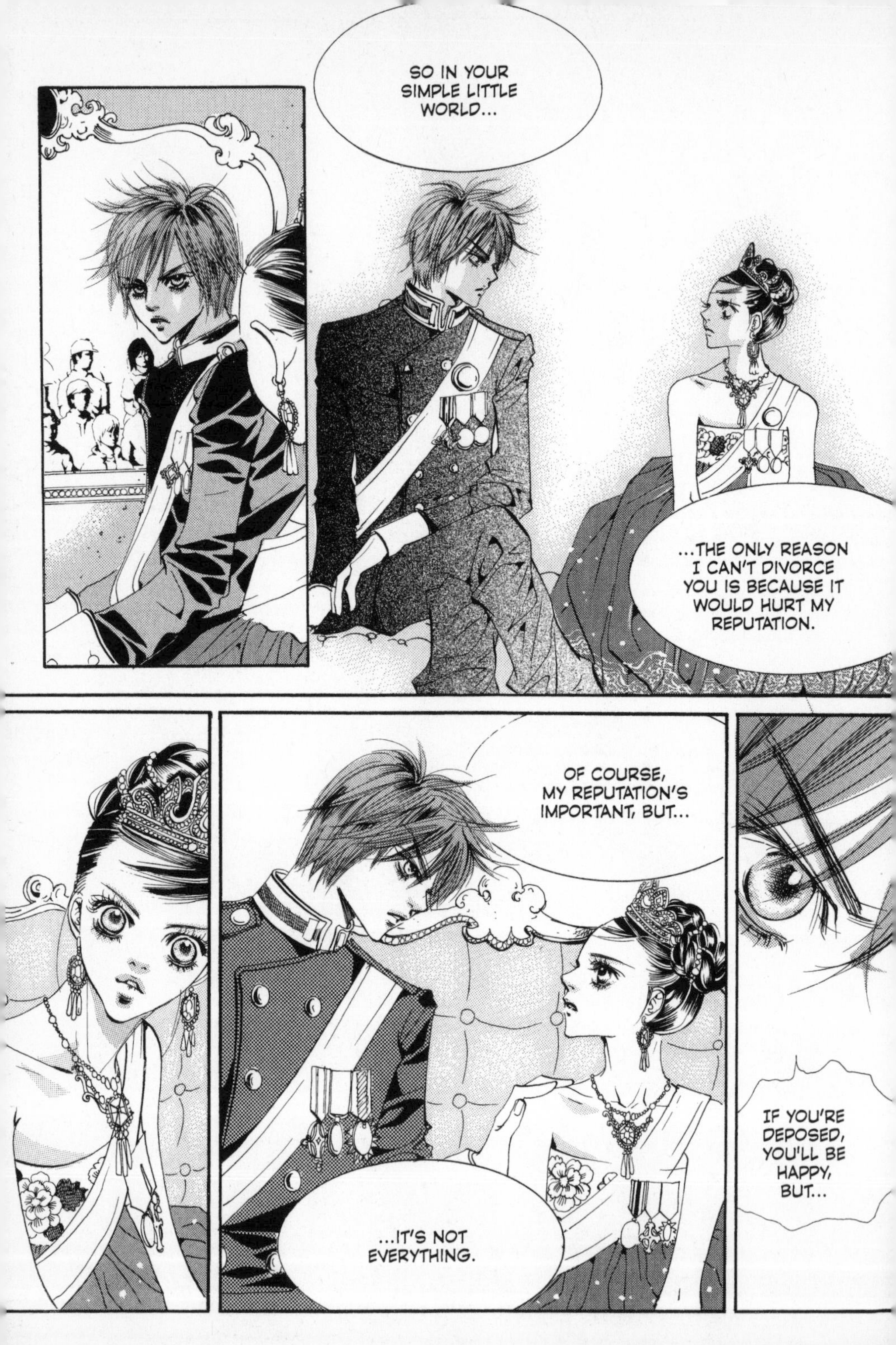
SO IN YOUR SIMPLE LITTLE WORLD...
...THE ONLY REASON I CAN'T DIVORCE YOU IS BECAUSE IT WOULD HURT MY REPUTATION.
OF COURSE, MY REPUTATION'S IMPORTANT, BUT...
...IT'S NOT EVERYTHING.
IF YOU'RE DEPOSED, YOU'LL BE HAPPY, BUT...

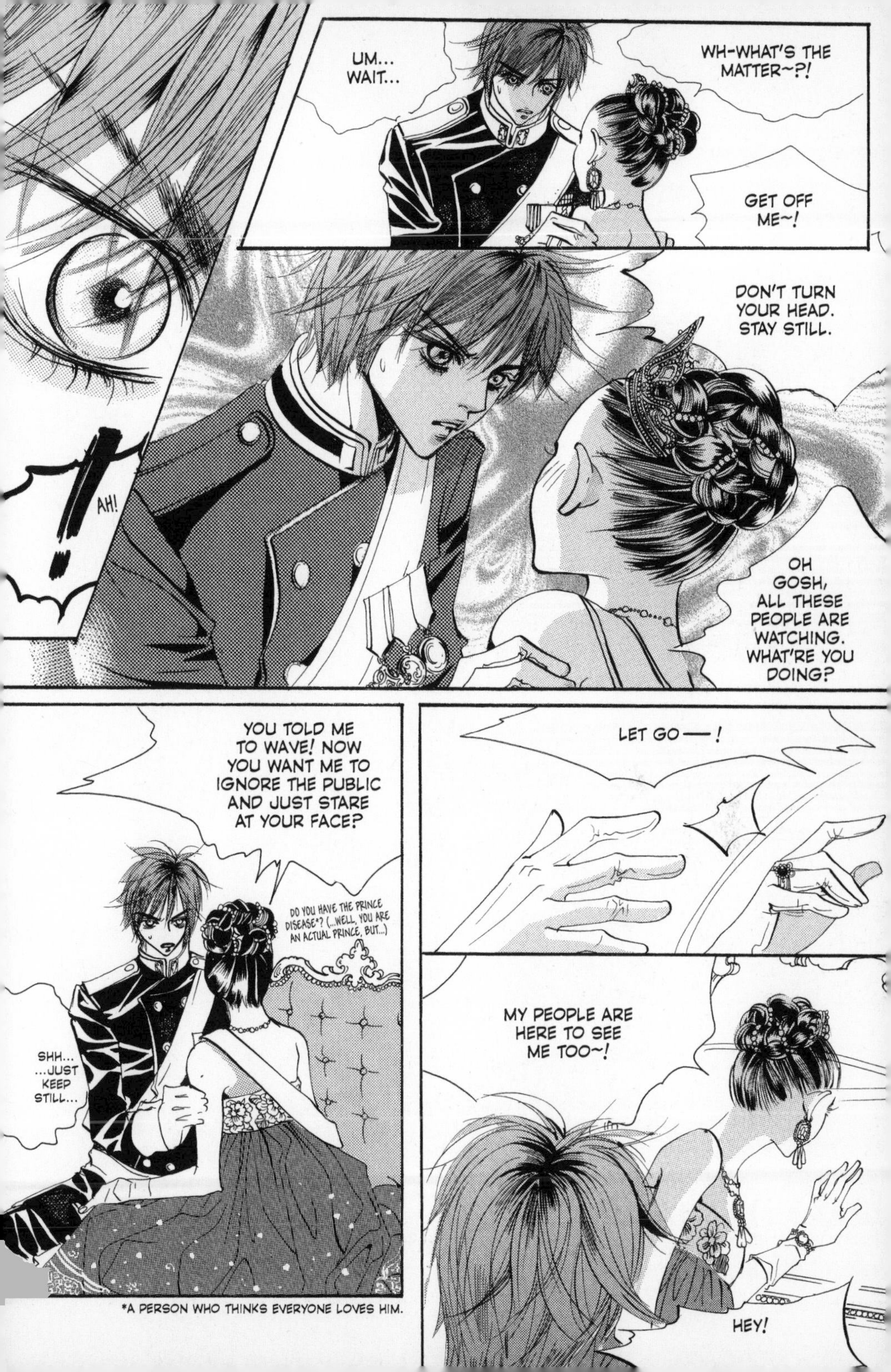
AH!
UM... WAIT...
WH-WHAT'S THE MATTER~?!
GET OFF ME~!
DON'T TURN YOUR HEAD. STAY STILL.
OH GOSH, ALL THESE PEOPLE ARE WATCHING. WHAT'RE YOU DOING?
YOU TOLD ME TO WAVE! NOW YOU WANT ME TO IGNORE THE PUBLIC AND JUST STARE AT YOUR FACE?
DO YOU HAVE THE PRINCE DISEASE*? (...WELL, YOU ARE AN ACTUAL PRINCE, BUT...)
SHH... ...JUST KEEP STILL...
LET GO—!
MY PEOPLE ARE HERE TO SEE ME TOO~!
HEY!

*A PERSON WHO THINKS EVERYONE LOVES HIM.

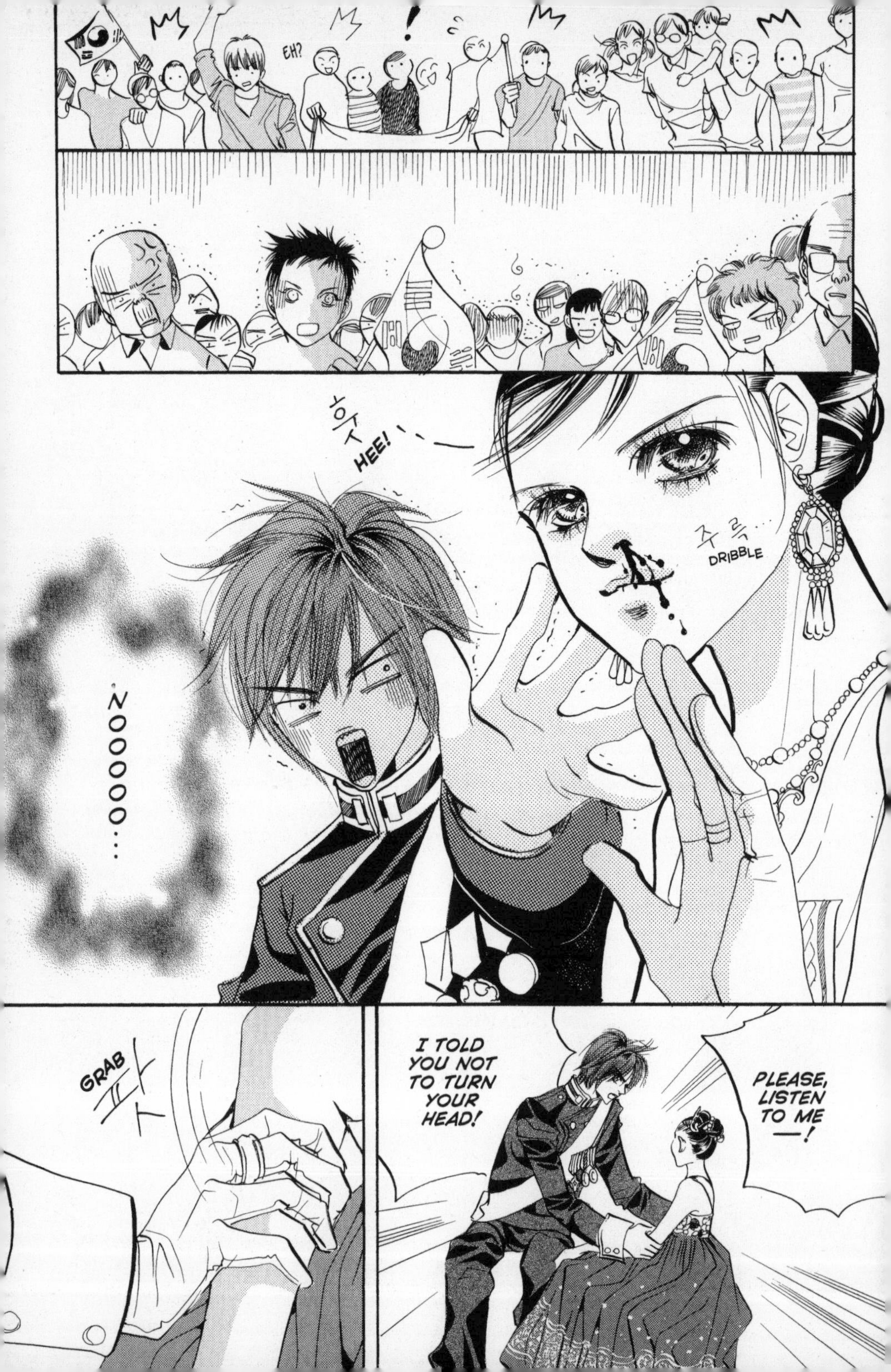
EH?
HEE!
주륵
DRIBBLE
NOOOOOO...
GRAB
I TOLD YOU NOT TO TURN YOUR HEAD!
PLEASE, LISTEN TO ME—!

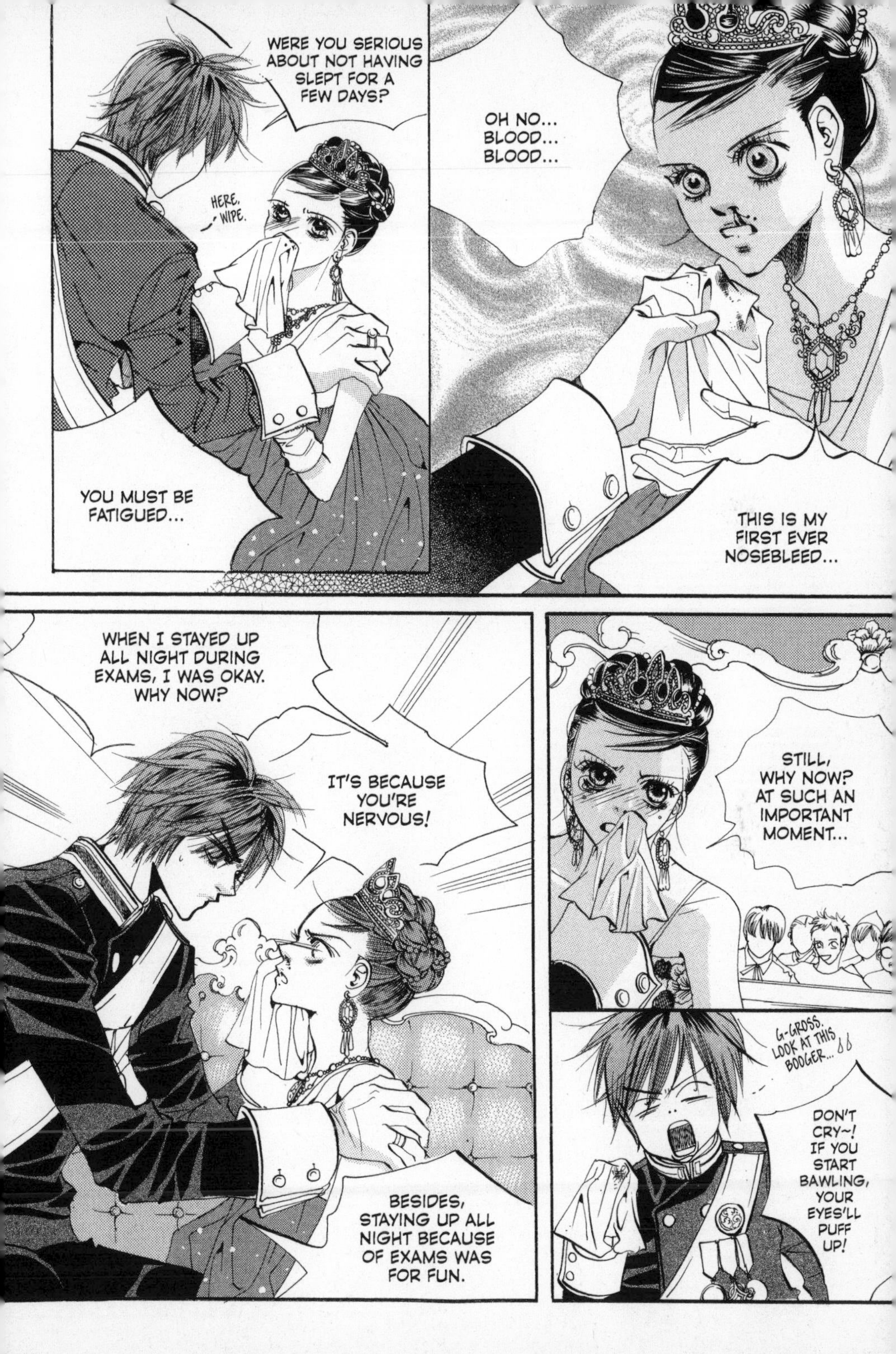
WERE YOU SERIOUS ABOUT NOT HAVING SLEPT FOR A FEW DAYS?
HERE, WIPE.
YOU MUST BE FATIGUED...
OH NO... BLOOD... BLOOD...
THIS IS MY FIRST EVER NOSEBLEED...
WHEN I STAYED UP ALL NIGHT DURING EXAMS, I WAS OKAY. WHY NOW?
IT'S BECAUSE YOU'RE NERVOUS!
BESIDES, STAYING UP ALL NIGHT BECAUSE OF EXAMS WAS FOR FUN.
STILL, WHY NOW? AT SUCH AN IMPORTANT MOMENT...
G-GROSS. LOOK AT THIS BOOGER...
DON'T CRY~! IF YOU START BAWLING, YOUR EYES'LL PUFF UP!

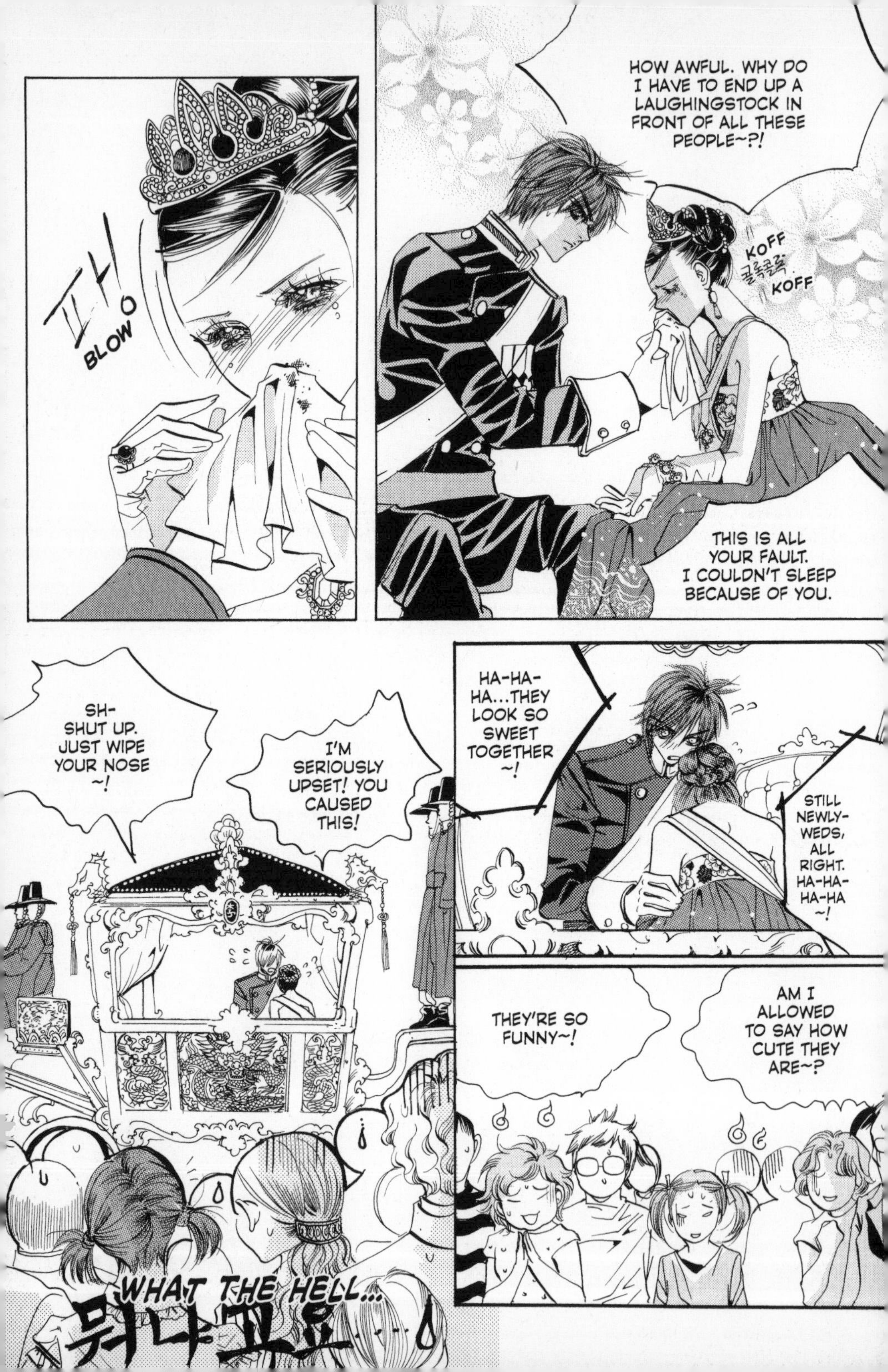
BLOW
HOW AWFUL. WHY DO I HAVE TO END UP A LAUGHINGSTOCK IN FRONT OF ALL THESE PEOPLE~?!
KOFF
KOFF
THIS IS ALL YOUR FAULT. I COULDN'T SLEEP BECAUSE OF YOU.
SH- SHUT UP. JUST WIPE YOUR NOSE ~!
I'M SERIOUSLY UPSET! YOU CAUSED THIS!
WHAT THE HELL...
HA-HA-HA...THEY LOOK SO SWEET TOGETHER ~!
STILL NEWLYWEDS, ALL RIGHT. HA-HA-HA-HA ~!
THEY'RE SO FUNNY~!
AM I ALLOWED TO SAY HOW CUTE THEY ARE~?

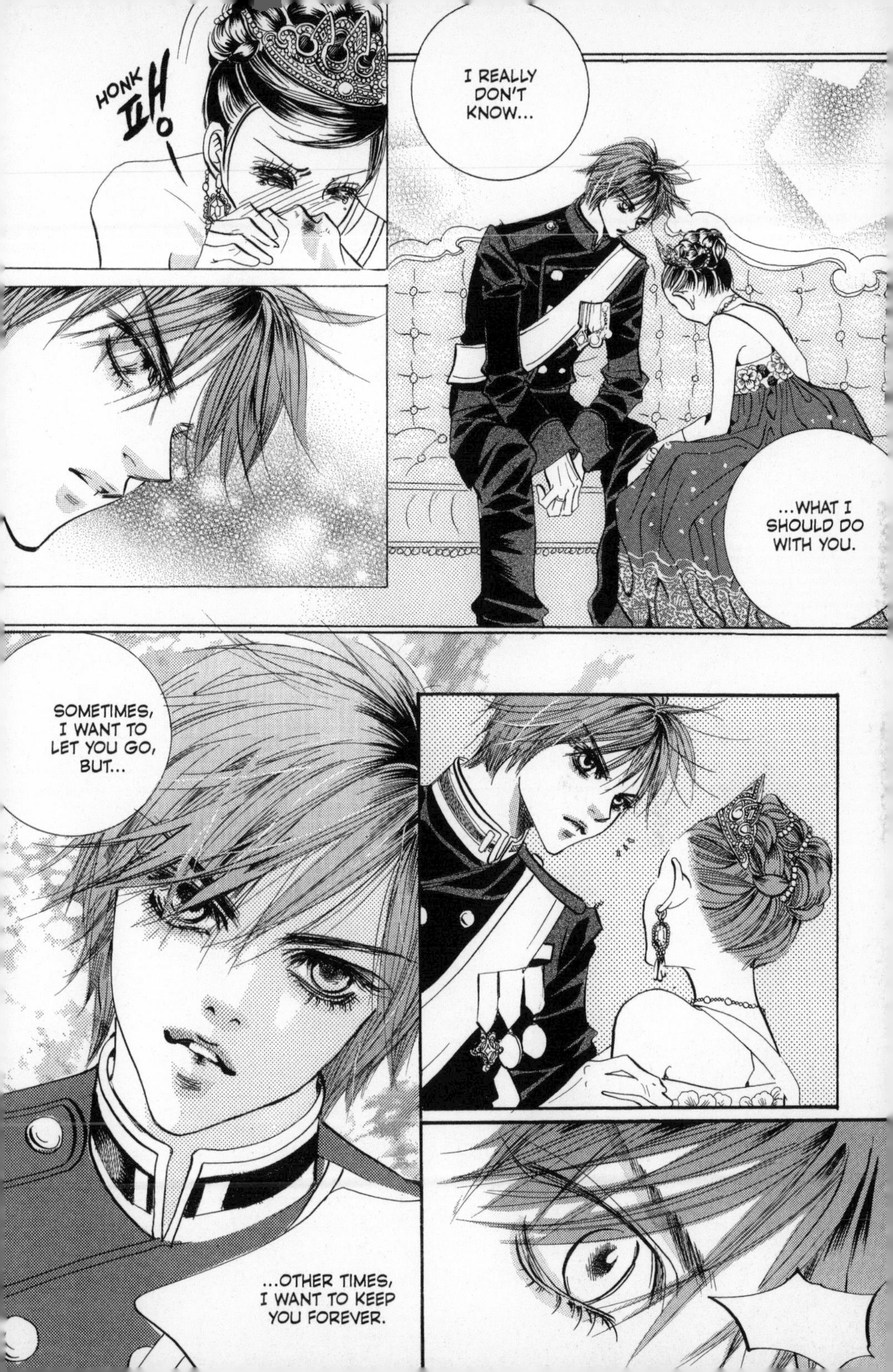
HONK
I REALLY DON'T KNOW...
...WHAT I SHOULD DO WITH YOU.
SOMETIMES, I WANT TO LET YOU GO, BUT...
...OTHER TIMES, I WANT TO KEEP YOU FOREVER.

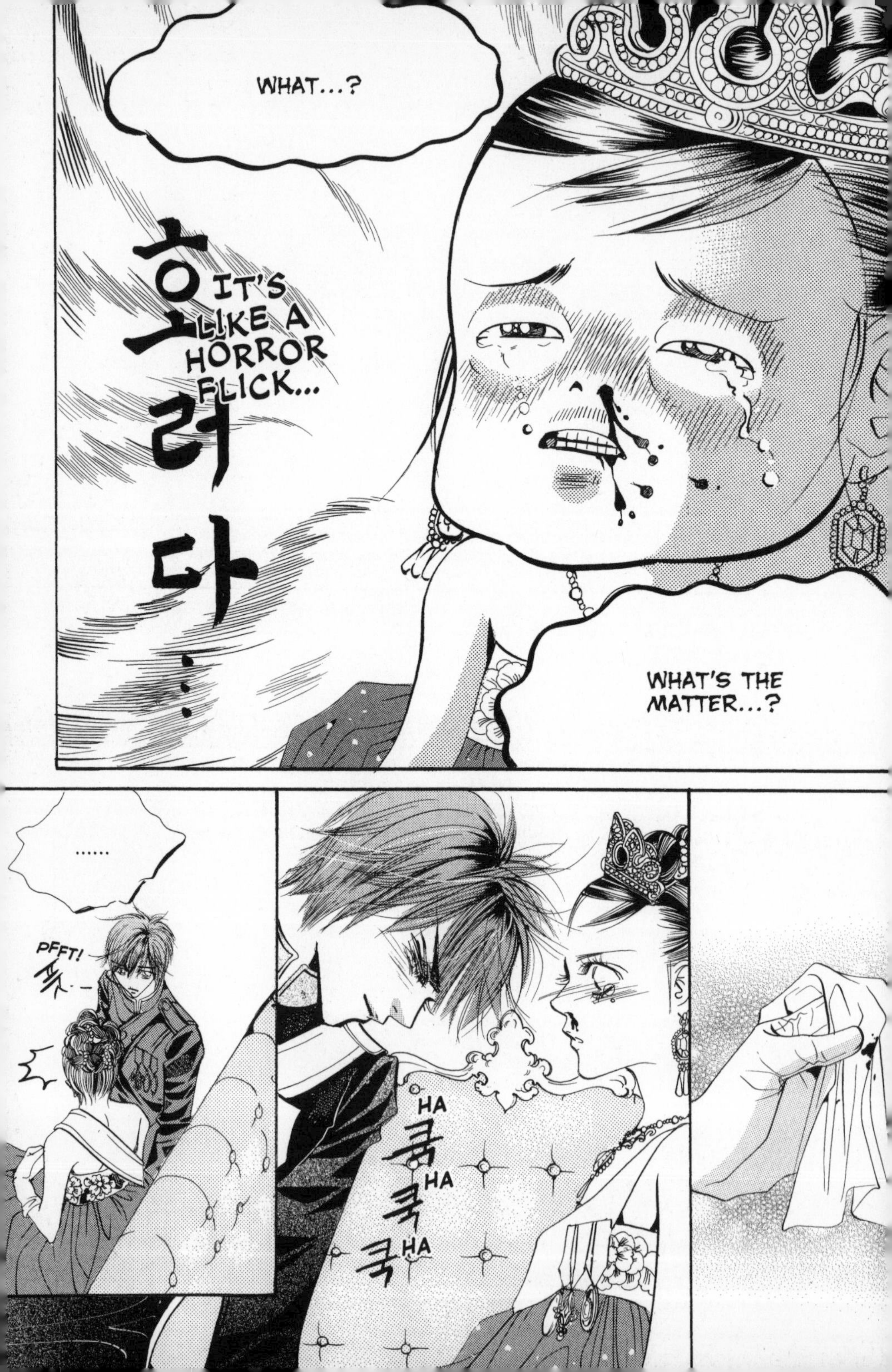
WHAT...?
호러다...
IT'S LIKE A HORROR FLICK...
WHAT'S THE MATTER...?
......
PFFT!
HA
HA
HA

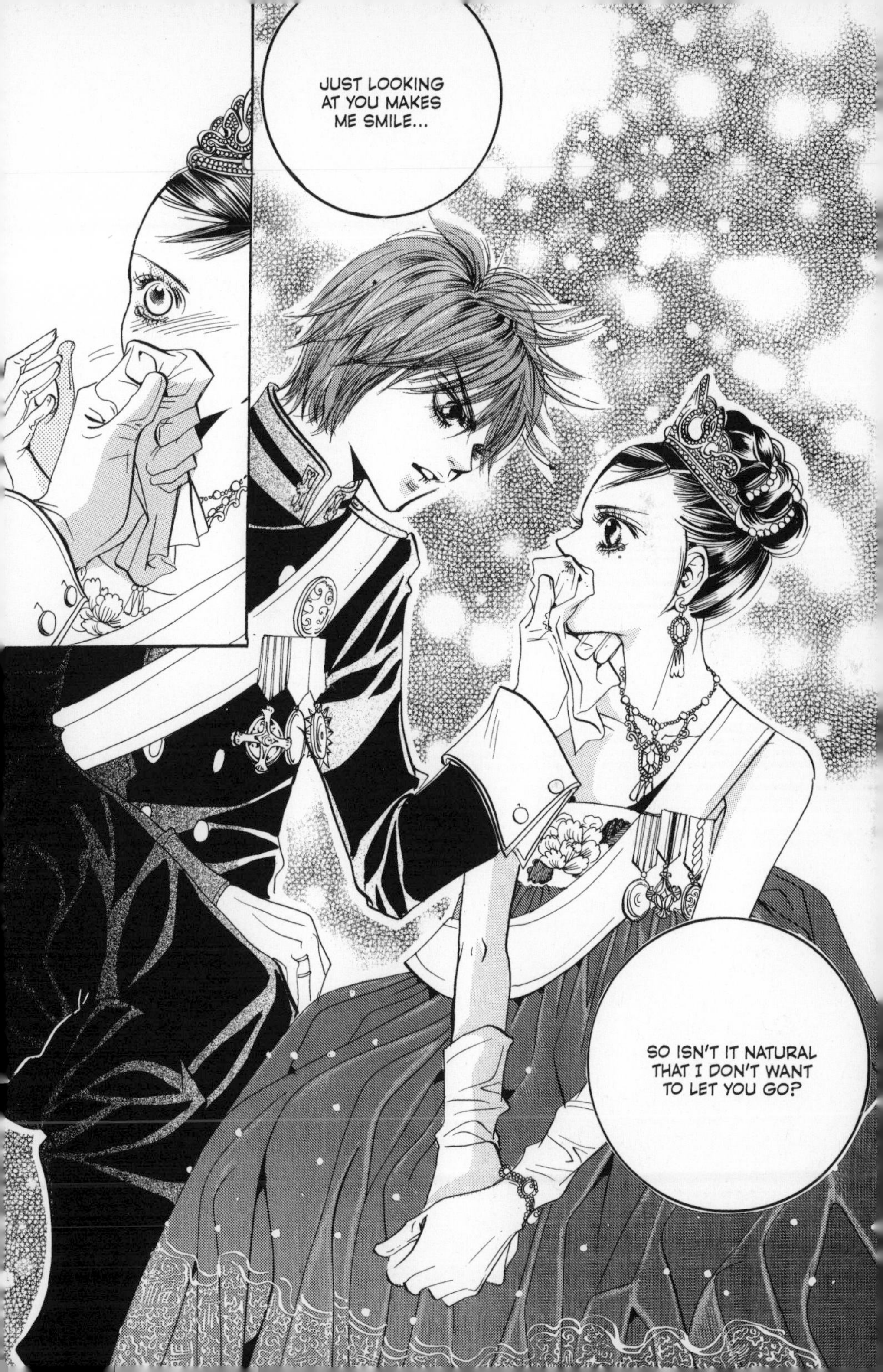
JUST LOOKING AT YOU MAKES ME SMILE...
SO ISN'T IT NATURAL THAT I DON'T WANT TO LET YOU GO?

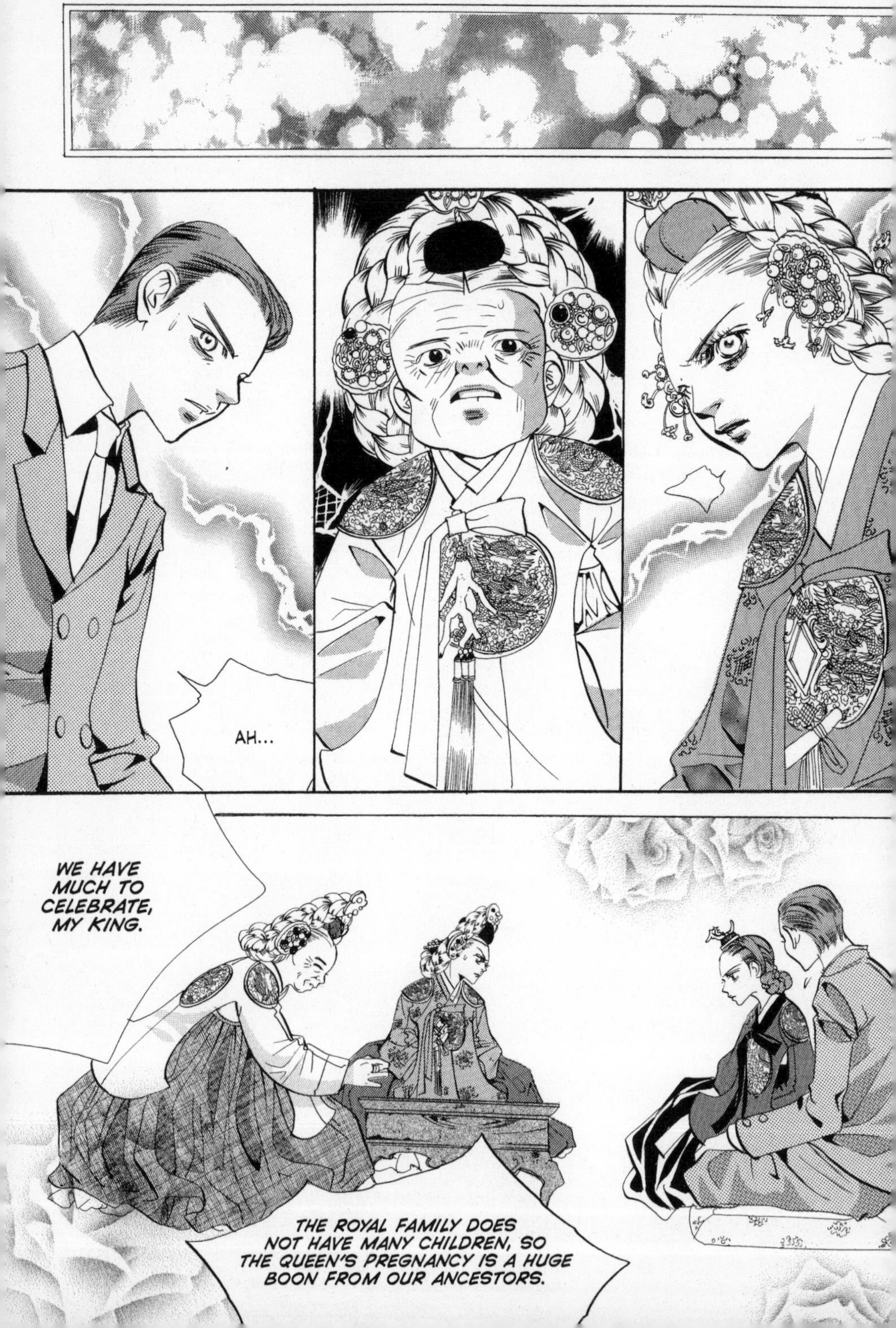
AH...
WE HAVE MUCH TO CELEBRATE, MY KING.
THE ROYAL FAMILY DOES NOT HAVE MANY CHILDREN, SO THE QUEEN'S PREGNANCY IS A HUGE BOON FROM OUR ANCESTORS.

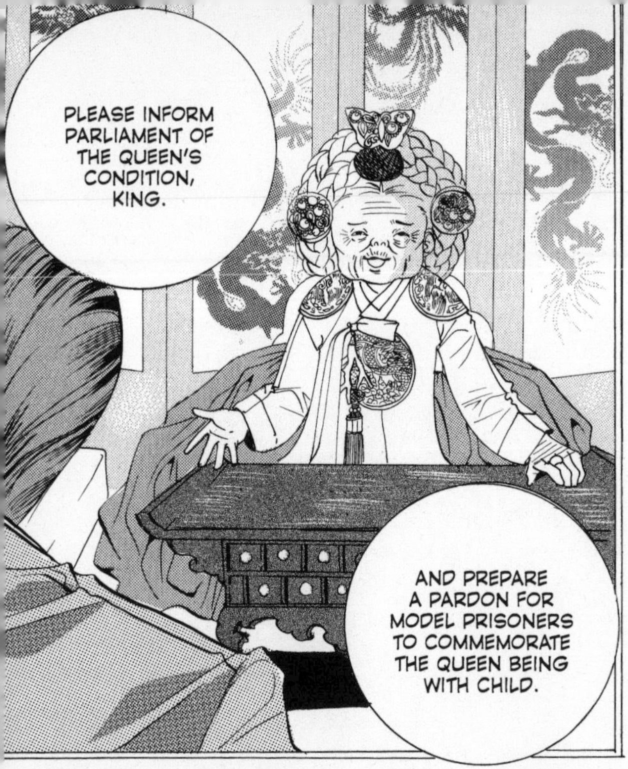
PLEASE INFORM PARLIAMENT OF THE QUEEN'S CONDITION, KING.
AND PREPARE A PARDON FOR MODEL PRISONERS TO COMMEMORATE THE QUEEN BEING WITH CHILD.

LABOR IN THE PALACE

WHEN A WOMAN IN THE PALACE BECOMES PREGNANT, THE COURT LADIES AND MAIDS WHO SERVE IN HER QUARTERS RECEIVE GENEROUS REWARDS. WHEN A QUEEN OR A CROWN PRINCESS IS WITH CHILD, A NEW AREA KNOWN AS THE SANSHIL-CHUNG IS PUT TOGETHER TO CREATE A PEACEFUL ENVIRONMENT WHERE SHE WILL CARRY THE CHILD TO TERM. HIGH GOVERNMENT OFFICIALS WORK IN SERVICE AT THE SANSHIL-CHUNG. WHEN A CONCUBINE BECOMES PREGNANT, THE SAME PLACE IS CALLED HOSAN-CHUNG.

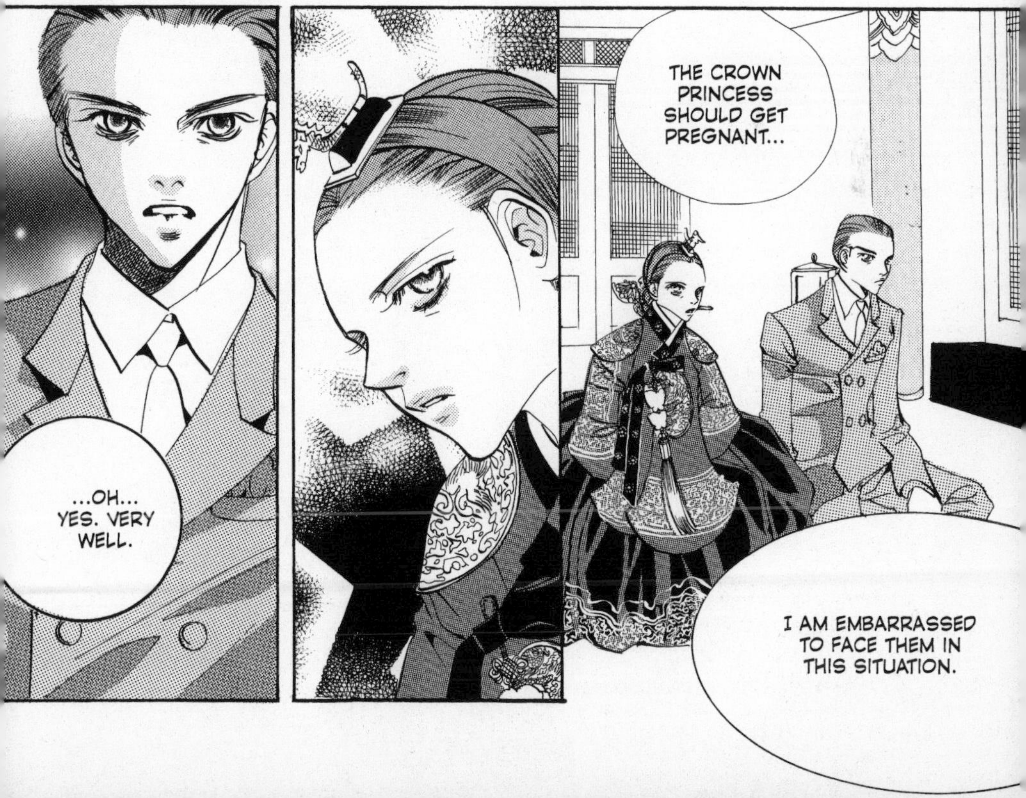
...OH... YES. VERY WELL.
THE CROWN PRINCESS SHOULD GET PREGNANT...
I AM EMBARRASSED TO FACE THEM IN THIS SITUATION.

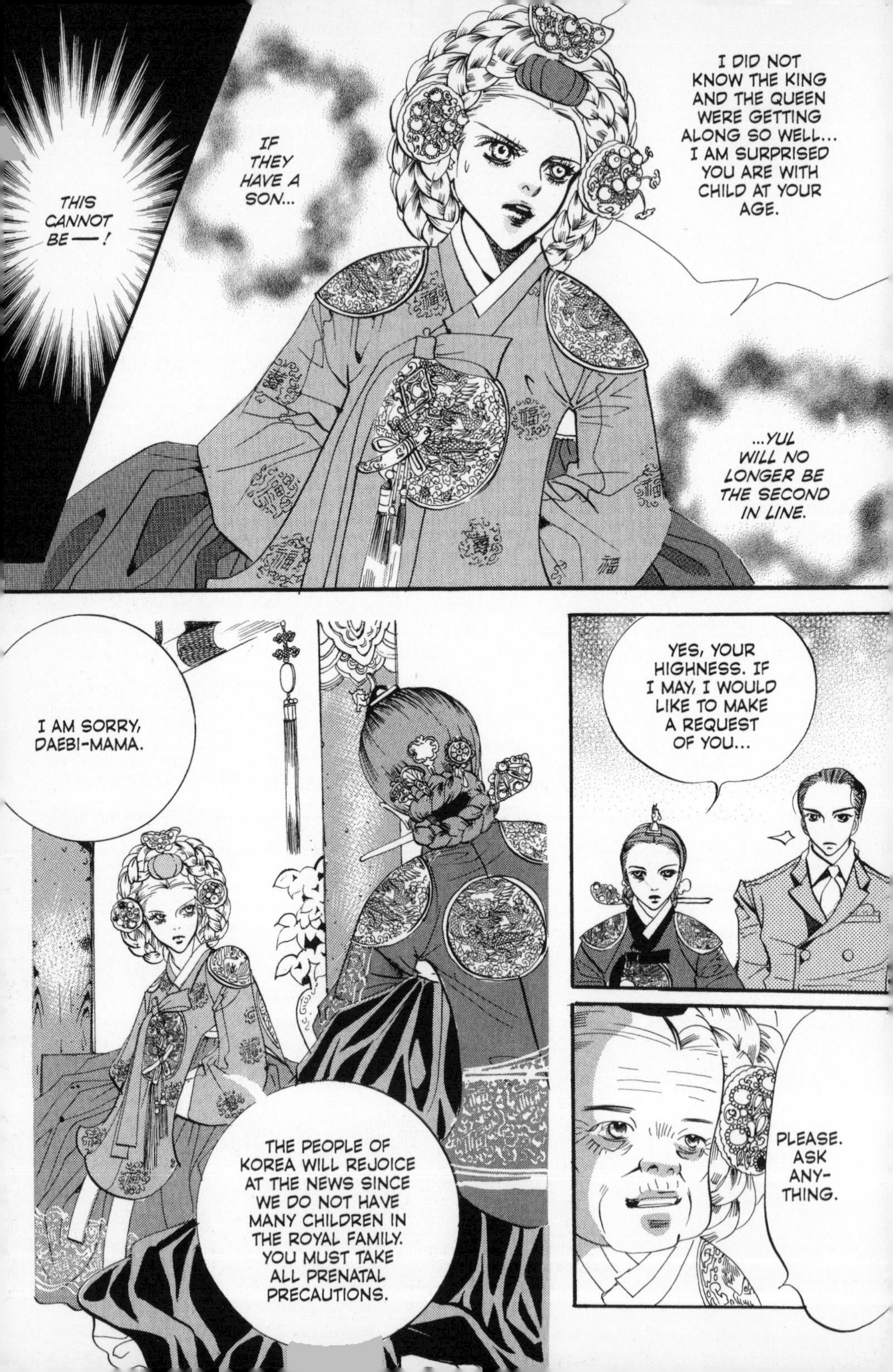
THIS CANNOT BE—!
IF THEY HAVE A SON...
I DID NOT KNOW THE KING AND THE QUEEN WERE GETTING ALONG SO WELL... I AM SURPRISED YOU ARE WITH CHILD AT YOUR AGE.
...YUL WILL NO LONGER BE THE SECOND IN LINE.
I AM SORRY, DAEBI-MAMA.
THE PEOPLE OF KOREA WILL REJOICE AT THE NEWS SINCE WE DO NOT HAVE MANY CHILDREN IN THE ROYAL FAMILY. YOU MUST TAKE ALL PRENATAL PRECAUTIONS.
YES, YOUR HIGHNESS. IF I MAY, I WOULD LIKE TO MAKE A REQUEST OF YOU...
PLEASE. ASK ANY-THING.

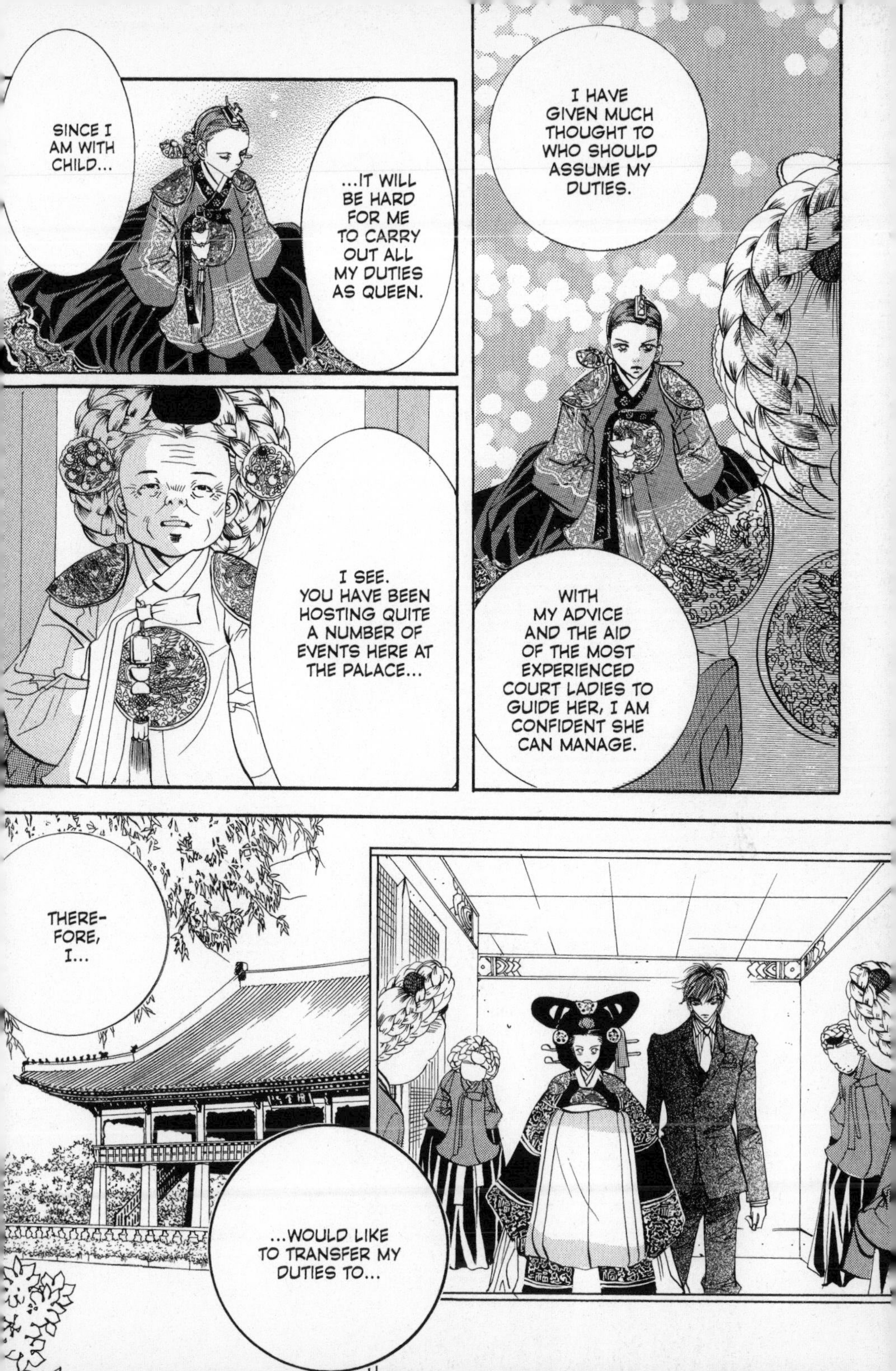
SINCE I AM WITH CHILD...
...IT WILL BE HARD FOR ME TO CARRY OUT ALL MY DUTIES AS QUEEN.
I SEE. YOU HAVE BEEN HOSTING QUITE A NUMBER OF EVENTS HERE AT THE PALACE...
I HAVE GIVEN MUCH THOUGHT TO WHO SHOULD ASSUME MY DUTIES.
WITH MY ADVICE AND THE AID OF THE MOST EXPERIENCED COURT LADIES TO GUIDE HER, I AM CONFIDENT SHE CAN MANAGE.
THERE-FORE, I...
...WOULD LIKE TO TRANSFER MY DUTIES TO...

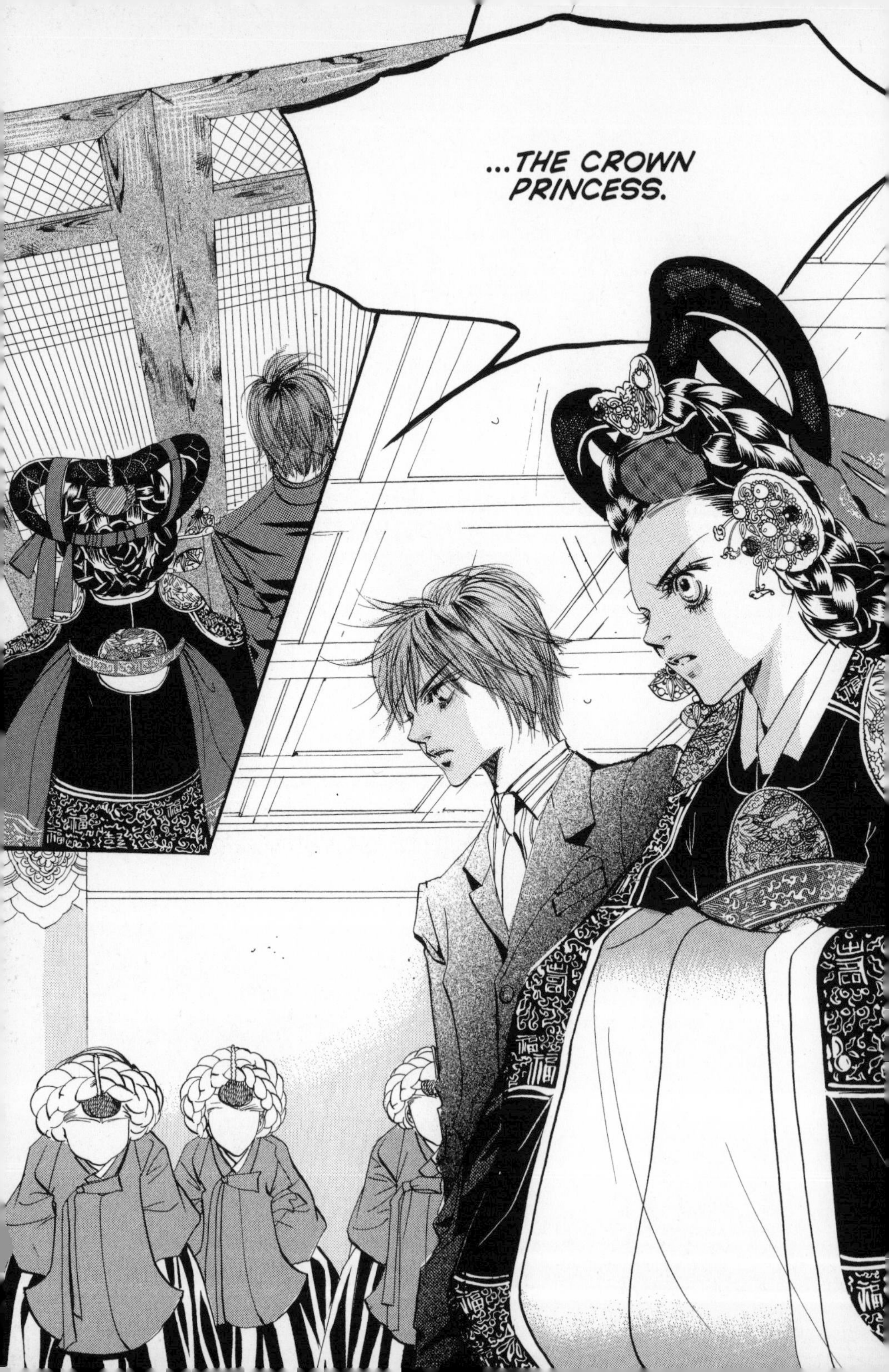
...THE CROWN PRINCESS.

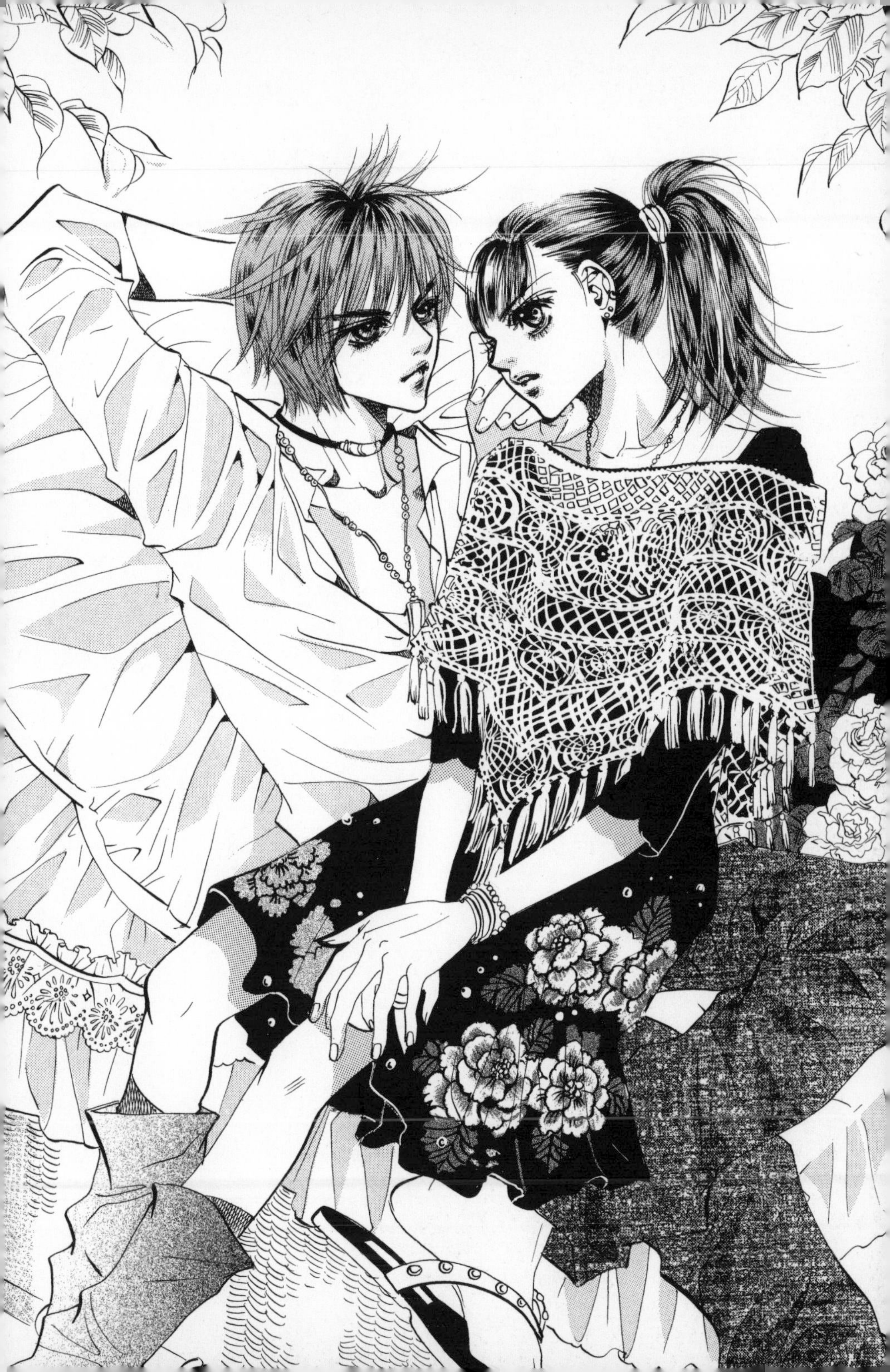

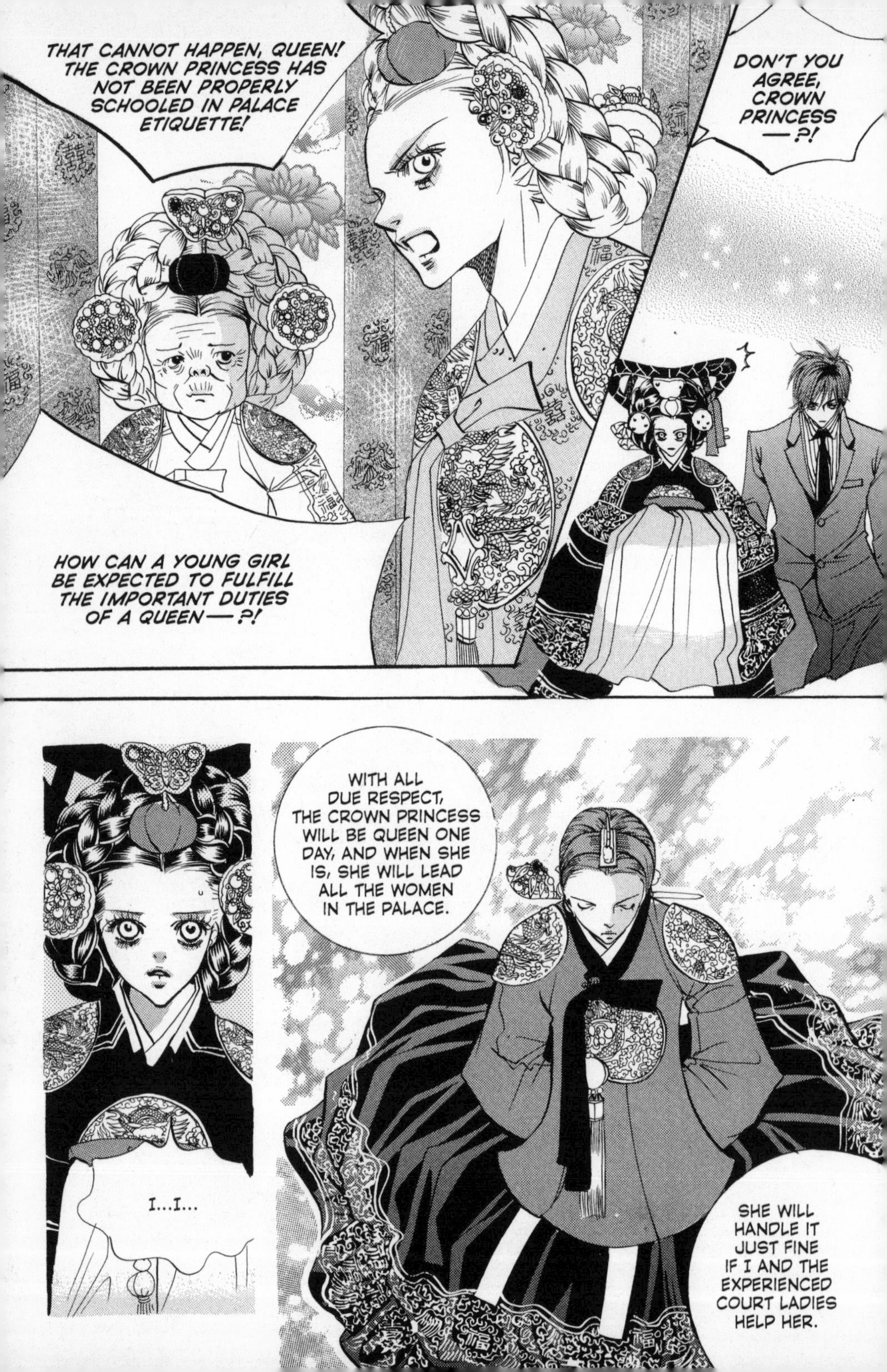
THAT CANNOT HAPPEN, QUEEN! THE CROWN PRINCESS HAS NOT BEEN PROPERLY SCHOOLED IN PALACE ETIQUETTE!
HOW CAN A YOUNG GIRL BE EXPECTED TO FULFILL THE IMPORTANT DUTIES OF A QUEEN—?!
DON'T YOU AGREE, CROWN PRINCESS —?!
I...I...
WITH ALL DUE RESPECT, THE CROWN PRINCESS WILL BE QUEEN ONE DAY, AND WHEN SHE IS, SHE WILL LEAD ALL THE WOMEN IN THE PALACE.
SHE WILL HANDLE IT JUST FINE IF I AND THE EXPERIENCED COURT LADIES HELP HER.

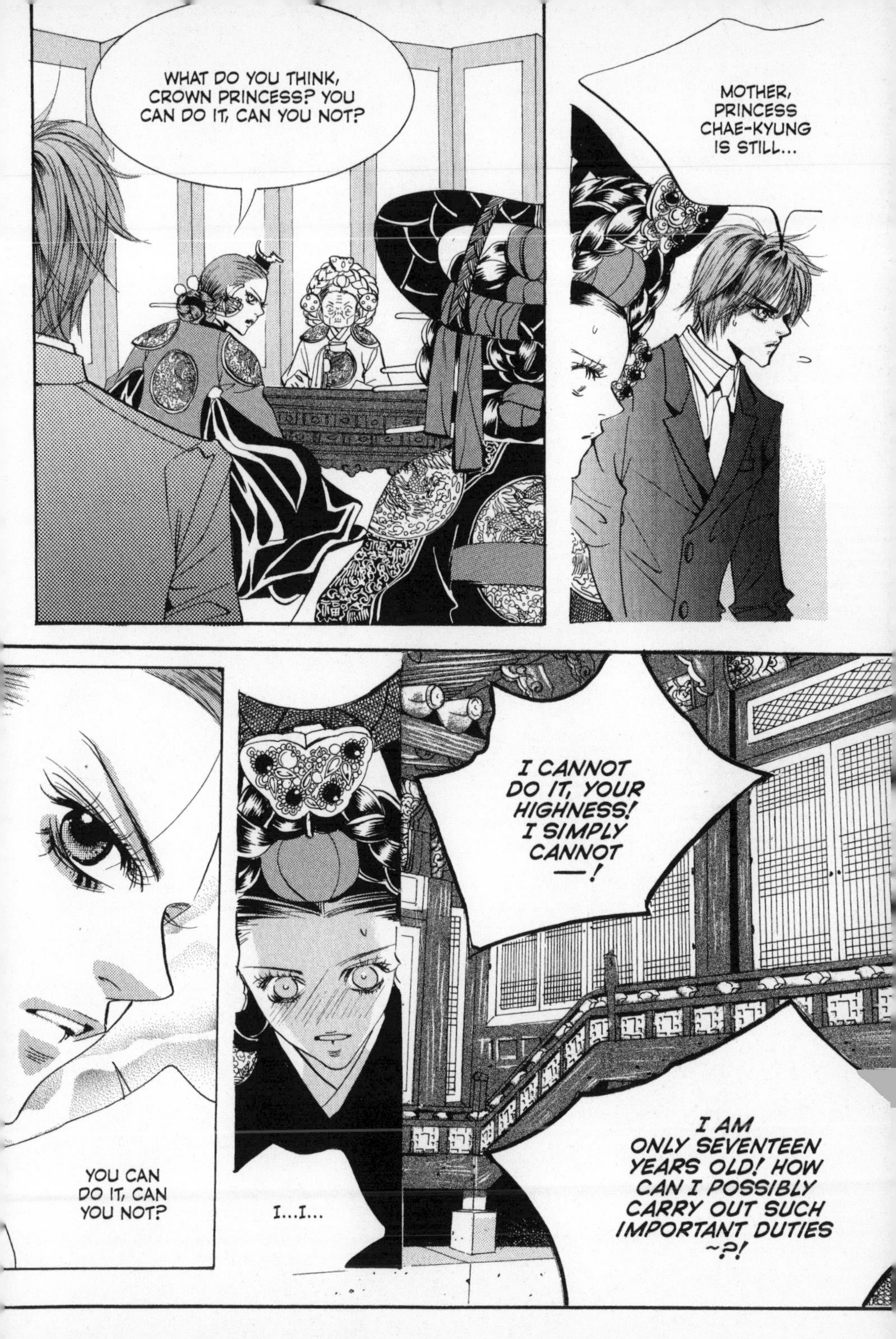
WHAT DO YOU THINK, CROWN PRINCESS? YOU CAN DO IT, CAN YOU NOT?
MOTHER, PRINCESS CHAE-KYUNG IS STILL...
YOU CAN DO IT, CAN YOU NOT?
I...I...
I CANNOT DO IT, YOUR HIGHNESS! I SIMPLY CANNOT —!
I AM ONLY SEVENTEEN YEARS OLD! HOW CAN I POSSIBLY CARRY OUT SUCH IMPORTANT DUTIES ~?!

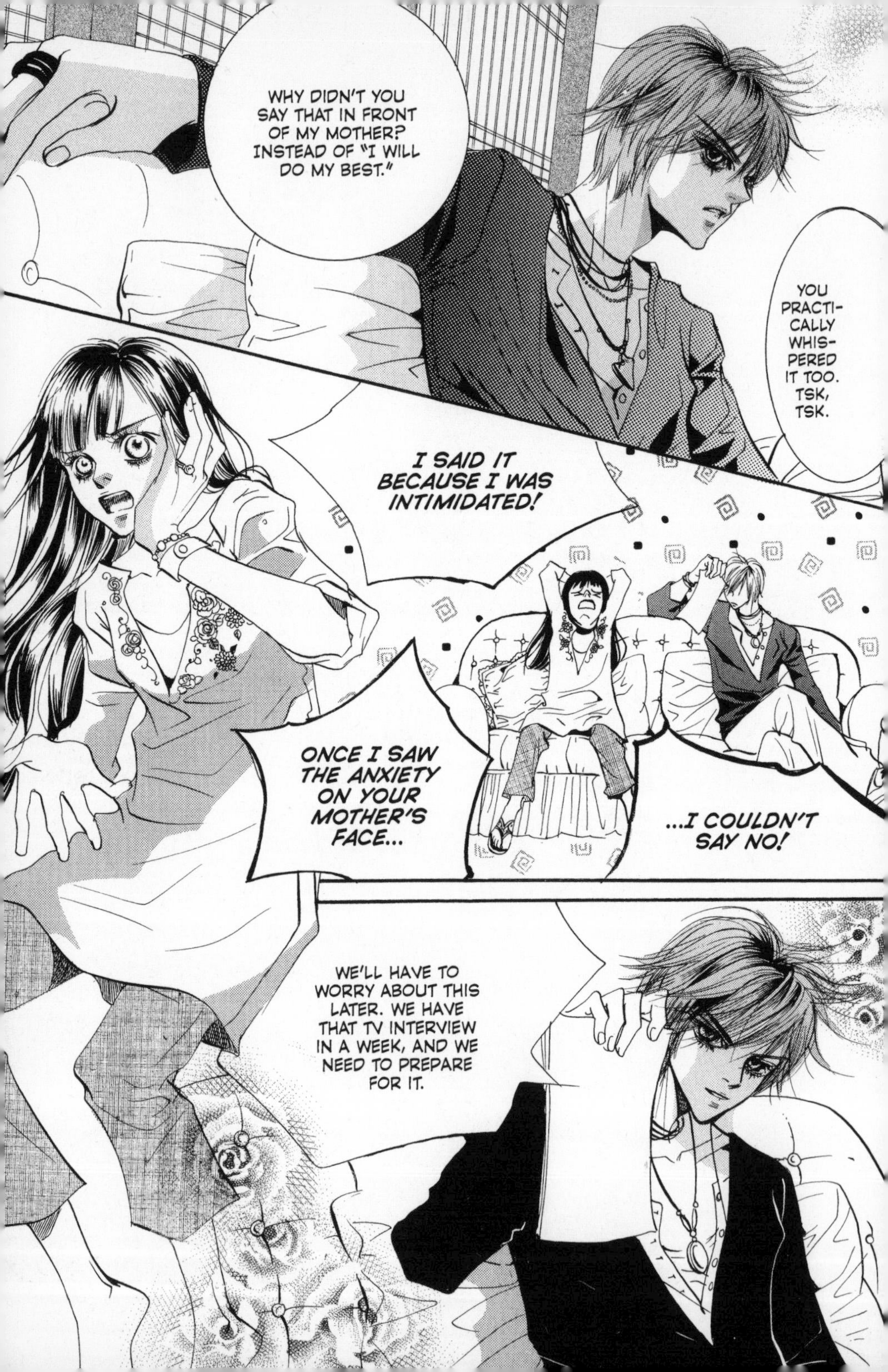
WHY DIDN'T YOU SAY THAT IN FRONT OF MY MOTHER? INSTEAD OF "I WILL DO MY BEST."
YOU PRACTI-CALLY WHIS-PERED IT TOO. TSK, TSK.
I SAID IT BECAUSE I WAS INTIMIDATED!
ONCE I SAW THE ANXIETY ON YOUR MOTHER'S FACE...
...I COULDN'T SAY NO!
WE'LL HAVE TO WORRY ABOUT THIS LATER. WE HAVE THAT TV INTERVIEW IN A WEEK, AND WE NEED TO PREPARE FOR IT.

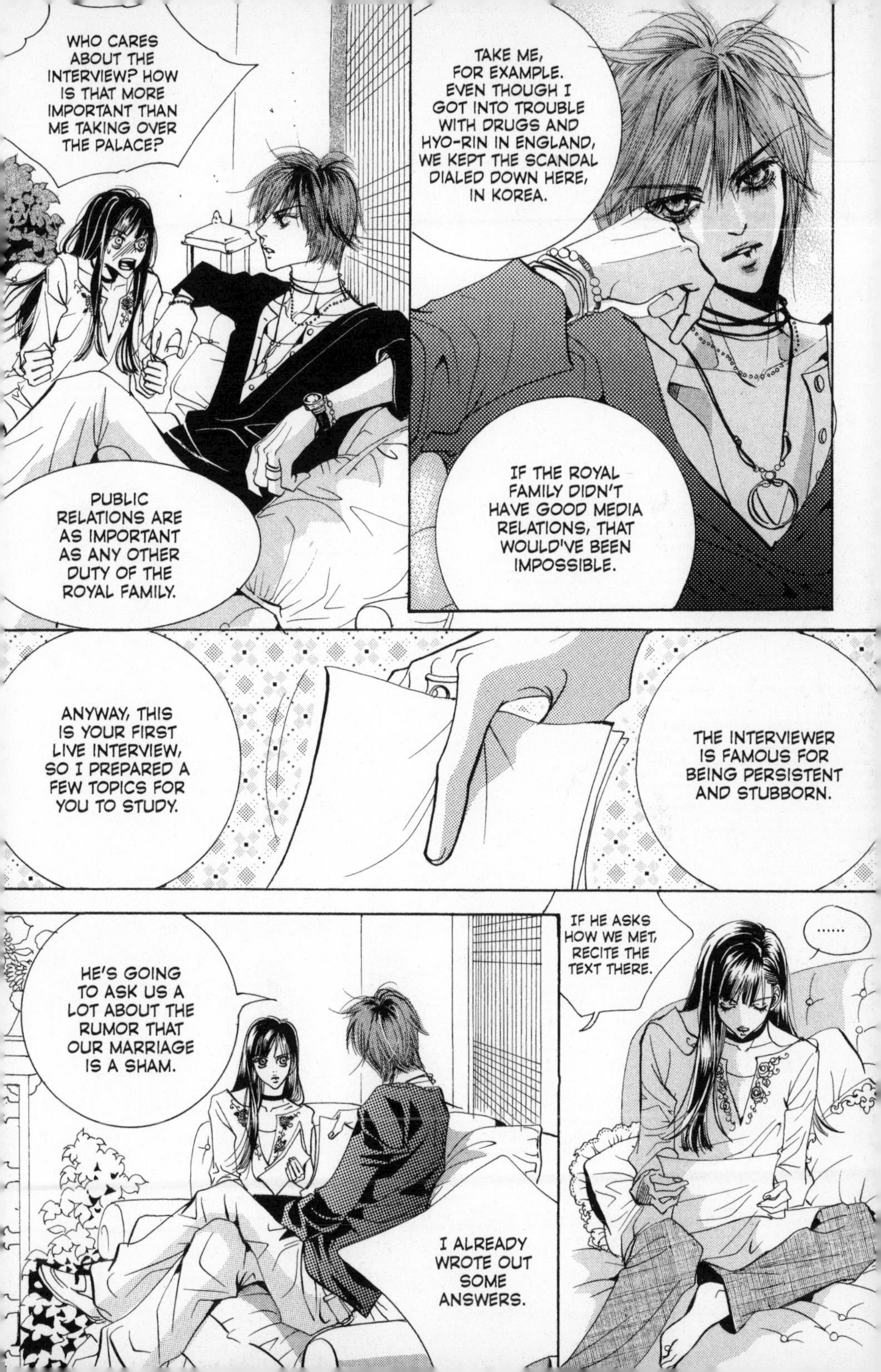
WHO CARES ABOUT THE INTERVIEW? HOW IS THAT MORE IMPORTANT THAN ME TAKING OVER THE PALACE?
PUBLIC RELATIONS ARE AS IMPORTANT AS ANY OTHER DUTY OF THE ROYAL FAMILY.
TAKE ME, FOR EXAMPLE. EVEN THOUGH I GOT INTO TROUBLE WITH DRUGS AND HYO-RIN IN ENGLAND, WE KEPT THE SCANDAL DIALED DOWN HERE, IN KOREA.
IF THE ROYAL FAMILY DIDN'T HAVE GOOD MEDIA RELATIONS, THAT WOULD'VE BEEN IMPOSSIBLE.
ANYWAY, THIS IS YOUR FIRST LIVE INTERVIEW, SO I PREPARED A FEW TOPICS FOR YOU TO STUDY.
THE INTERVIEWER IS FAMOUS FOR BEING PERSISTENT AND STUBBORN.
HE'S GOING TO ASK US A LOT ABOUT THE RUMOR THAT OUR MARRIAGE IS A SHAM.
I ALREADY WROTE OUT SOME ANSWERS.
IF HE ASKS HOW WE MET, RECITE THE TEXT THERE.
......

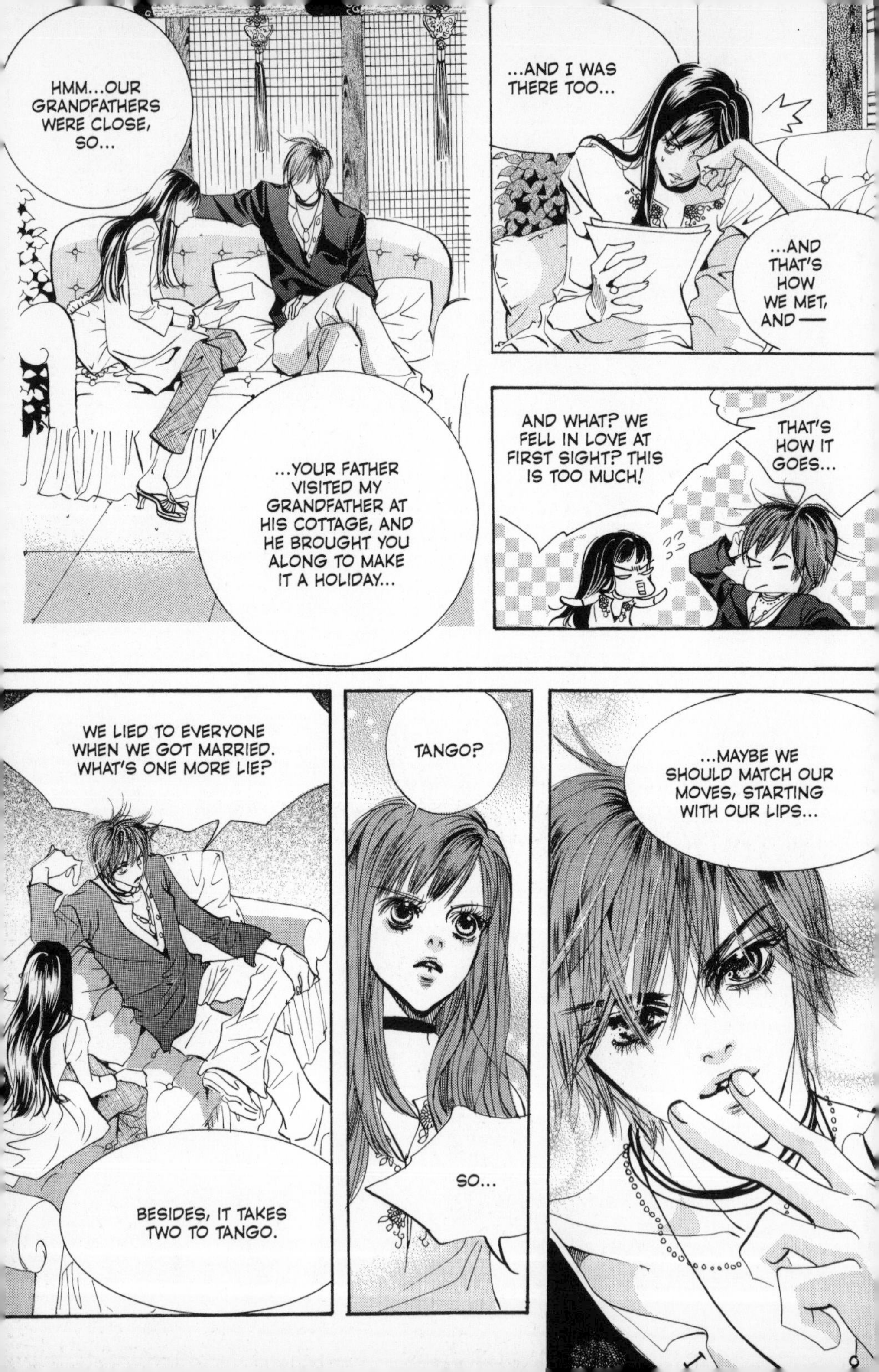
HMM...OUR GRANDFATHERS WERE CLOSE, SO...
...YOUR FATHER VISITED MY GRANDFATHER AT HIS COTTAGE, AND HE BROUGHT YOU ALONG TO MAKE IT A HOLIDAY...
...AND I WAS THERE TOO...
...AND THAT'S HOW WE MET, AND—
AND WHAT? WE FELL IN LOVE AT FIRST SIGHT? THIS IS TOO MUCH!
THAT'S HOW IT GOES...
WE LIED TO EVERYONE WHEN WE GOT MARRIED. WHAT'S ONE MORE LIE?
BESIDES, IT TAKES TWO TO TANGO.
TANGO?
SO...
...MAYBE WE SHOULD MATCH OUR MOVES, STARTING WITH OUR LIPS...

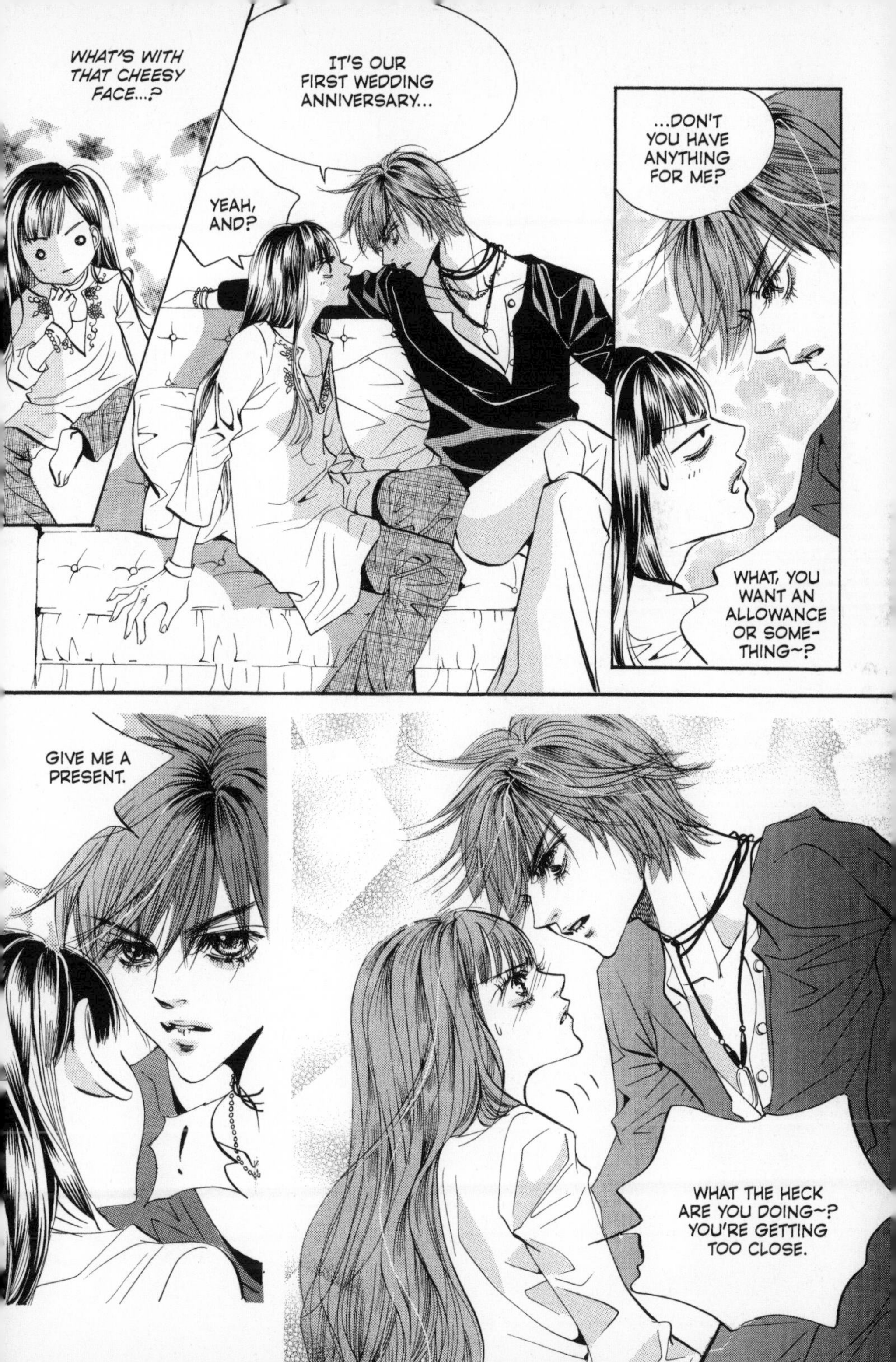
WHAT'S WITH THAT CHEESY FACE...?
IT'S OUR FIRST WEDDING ANNIVERSARY...
YEAH, AND?
...DON'T YOU HAVE ANYTHING FOR ME?
WHAT, YOU WANT AN ALLOWANCE OR SOME-THING~?
GIVE ME A PRESENT.
!
WHAT THE HECK ARE YOU DOING~? YOU'RE GETTING TOO CLOSE.

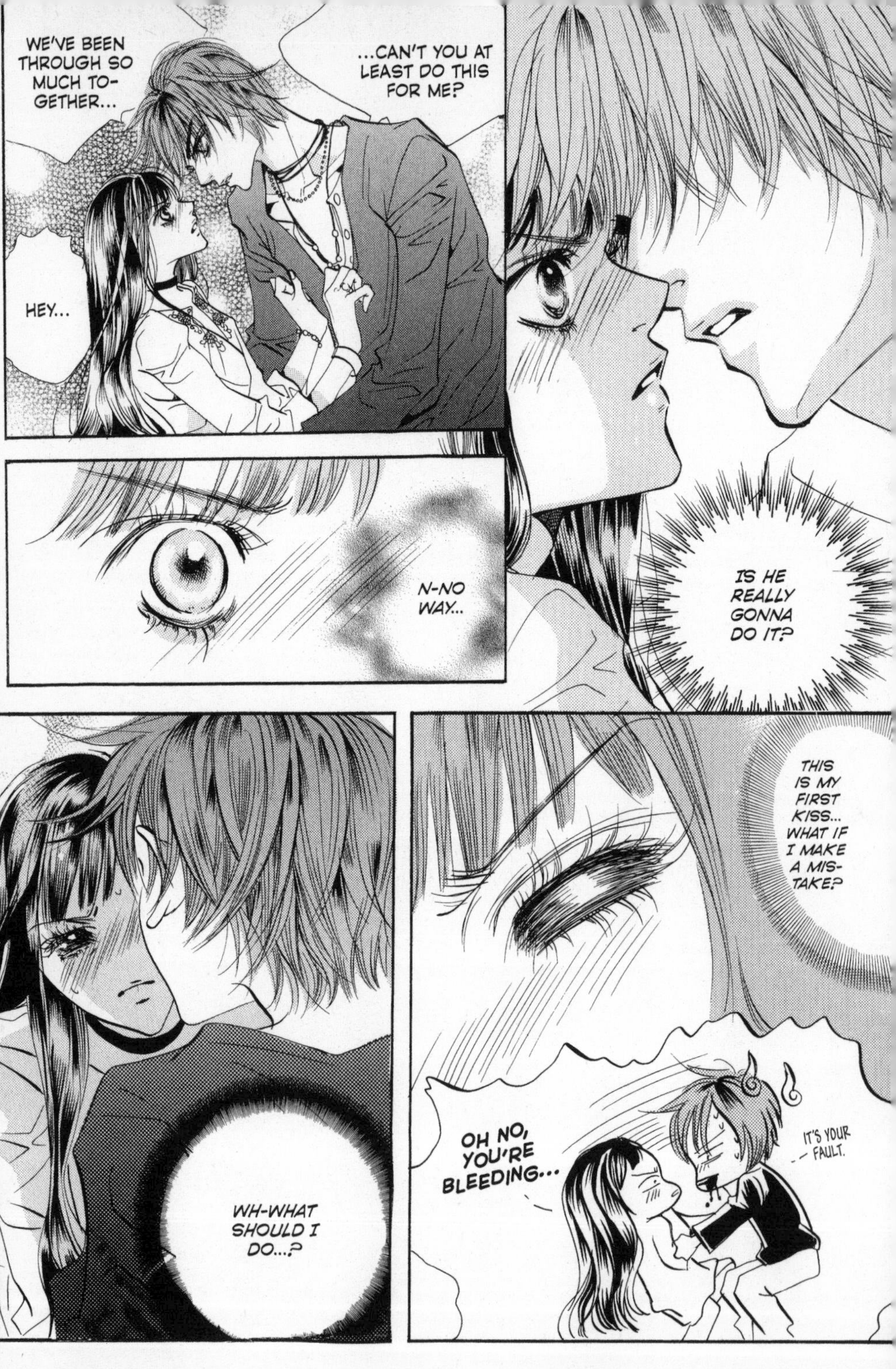
WE'VE BEEN THROUGH SO MUCH TOGETHER...
...CAN'T YOU AT LEAST DO THIS FOR ME?
HEY...
N-NO WAY...
IS HE REALLY GONNA DO IT?
WH-WHAT SHOULD I DO...?
THIS IS MY FIRST KISS... WHAT IF I MAKE A MISTAKE?
OH NO, YOU'RE BLEEDING...
IT'S YOUR FAULT.

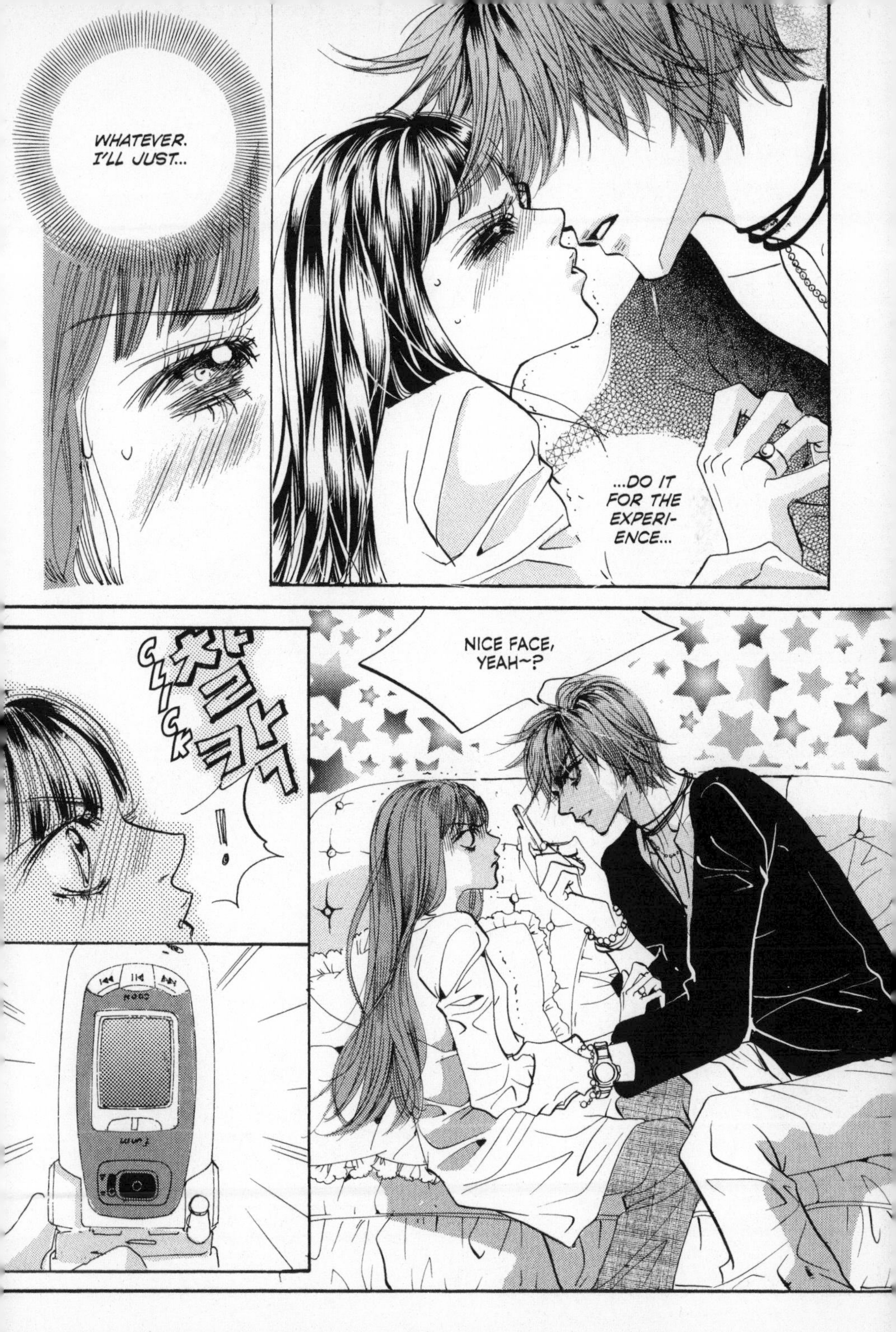
WHATEVER. I'LL JUST...
...DO IT FOR THE EXPERIENCE...
CLICK
!
NICE FACE, YEAH~?

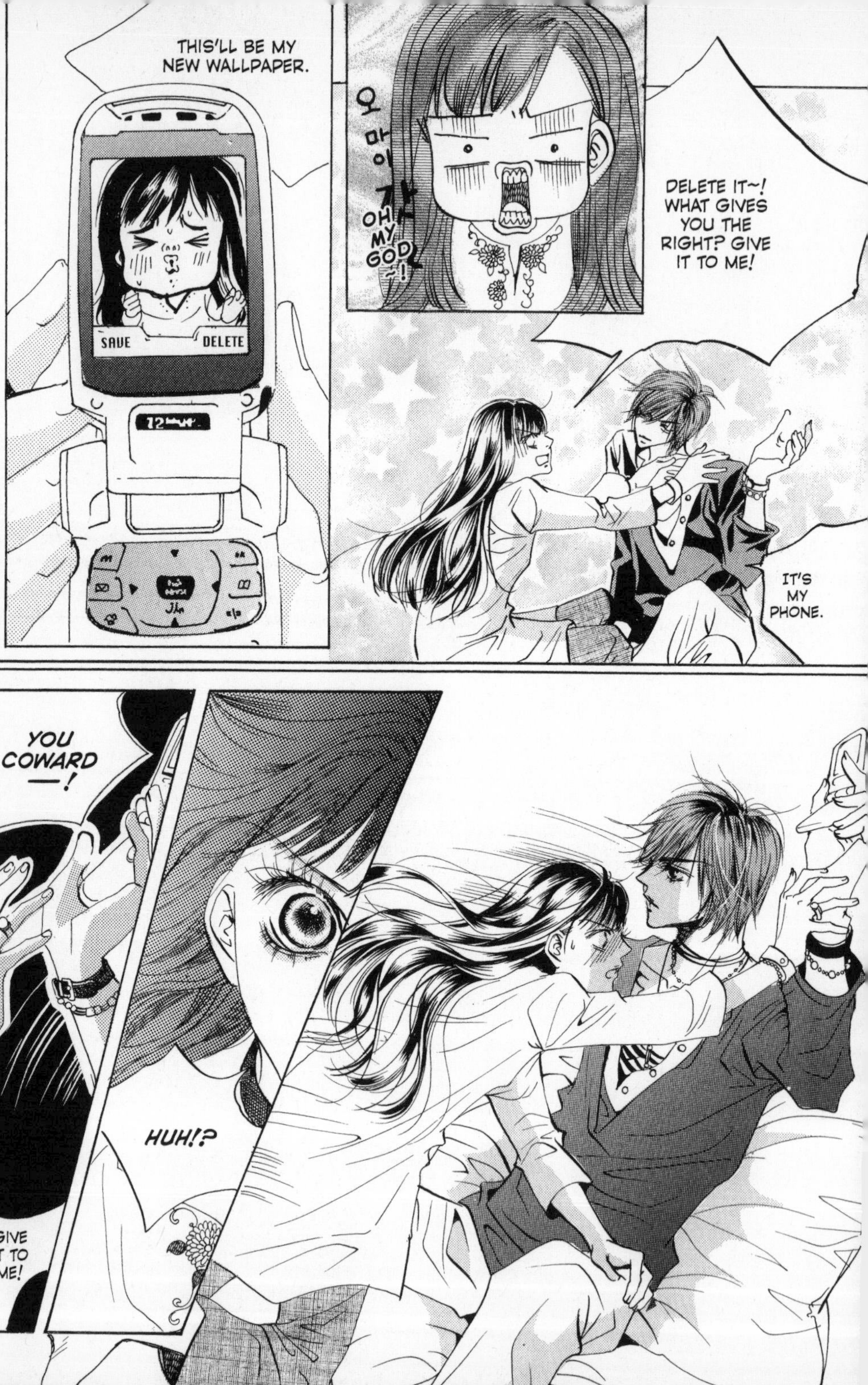
THIS'LL BE MY NEW WALLPAPER.
SAVE
DELETE
오마이갓
OH MY GOD~!
DELETE IT~! WHAT GIVES YOU THE RIGHT? GIVE IT TO ME!
IT'S MY PHONE.
YOU COWARD—!
GIVE IT TO ME!
HUH!?

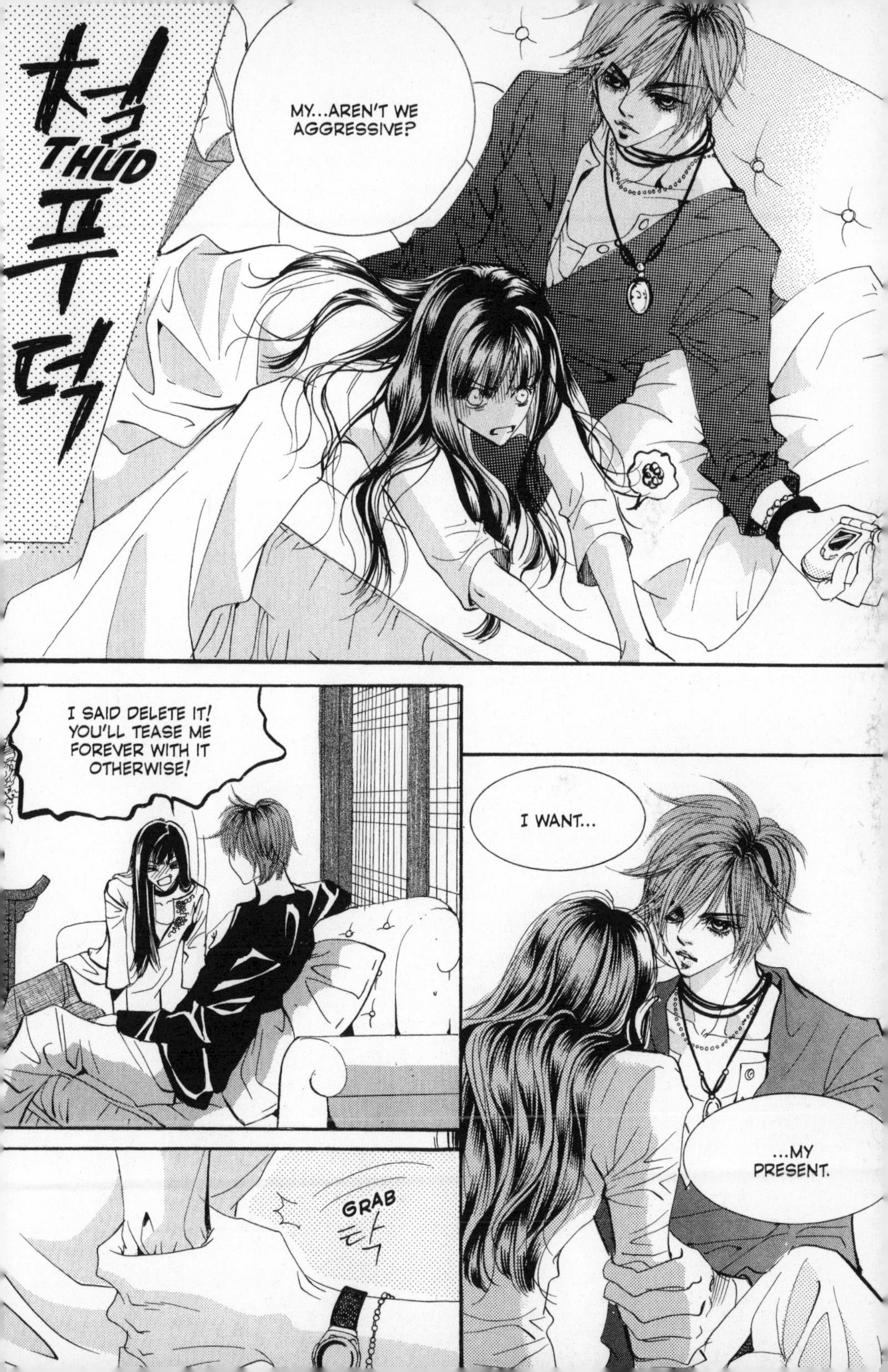
THUD
MY...AREN'T WE AGGRESSIVE?
I SAID DELETE IT! YOU'LL TEASE ME FOREVER WITH IT OTHERWISE!
GRAB
I WANT...
...MY PRESENT.

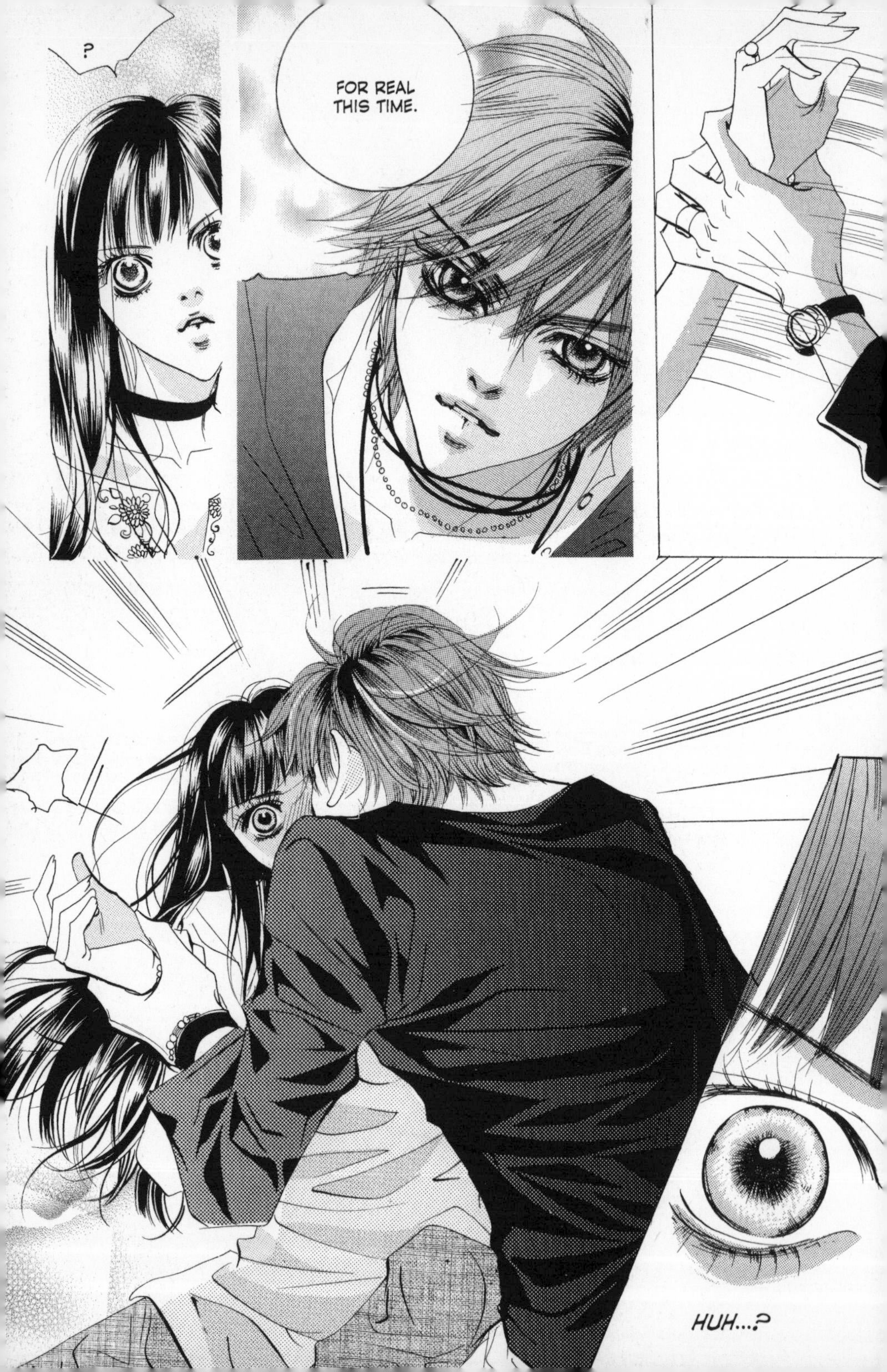
?
FOR REAL THIS TIME.
HUH...?

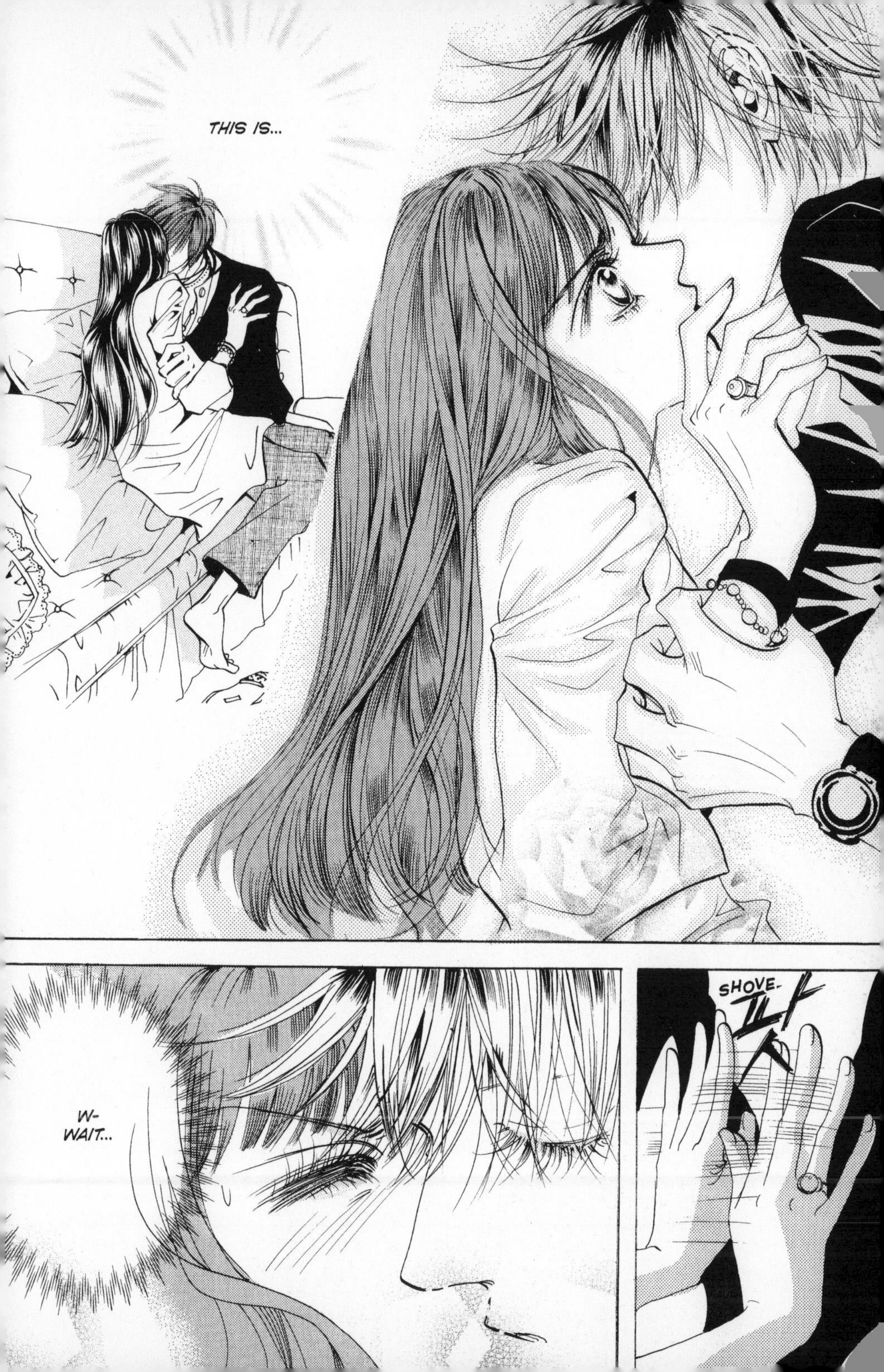
THIS IS...
W-
WAIT...
SHOVE

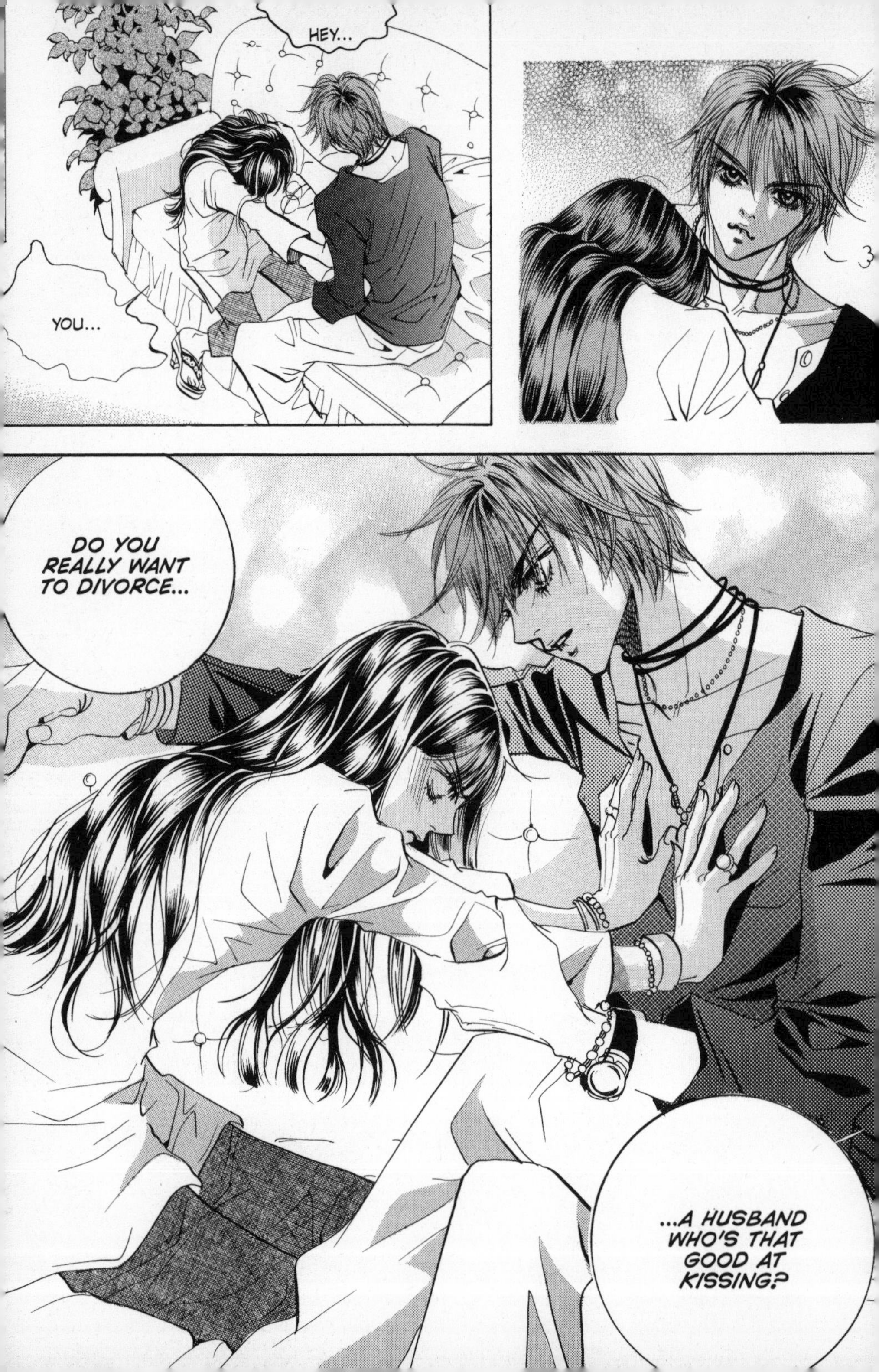
HEY...
YOU...
DO YOU REALLY WANT TO DIVORCE...
...A HUSBAND WHO'S THAT GOOD AT KISSING?

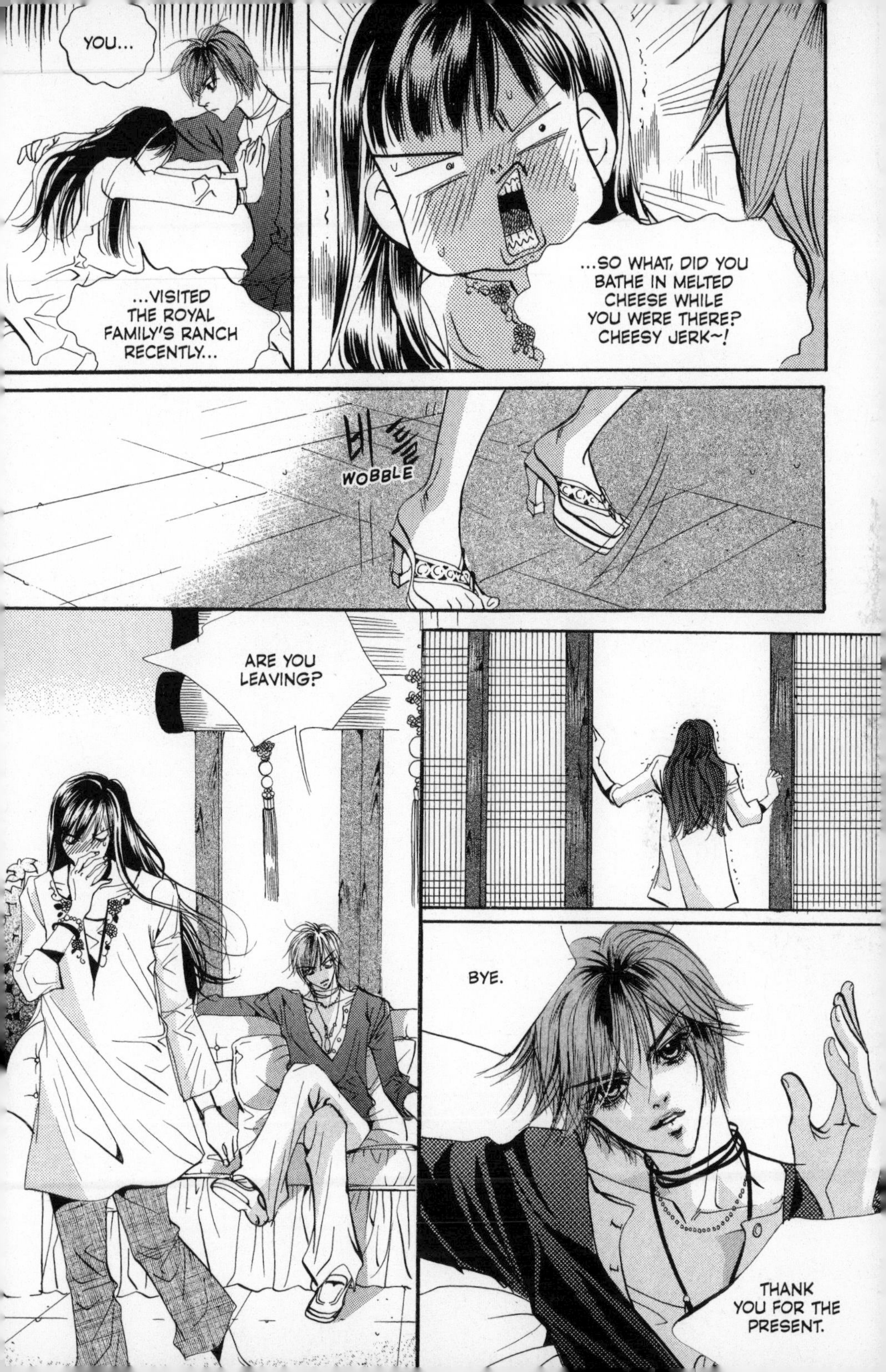
YOU...
...VISITED THE ROYAL FAMILY'S RANCH RECENTLY...
...SO WHAT, DID YOU BATHE IN MELTED CHEESE WHILE YOU WERE THERE? CHEESY JERK~!
비칠
WOBBLE
ARE YOU LEAVING?
BYE.
THANK YOU FOR THE PRESENT.

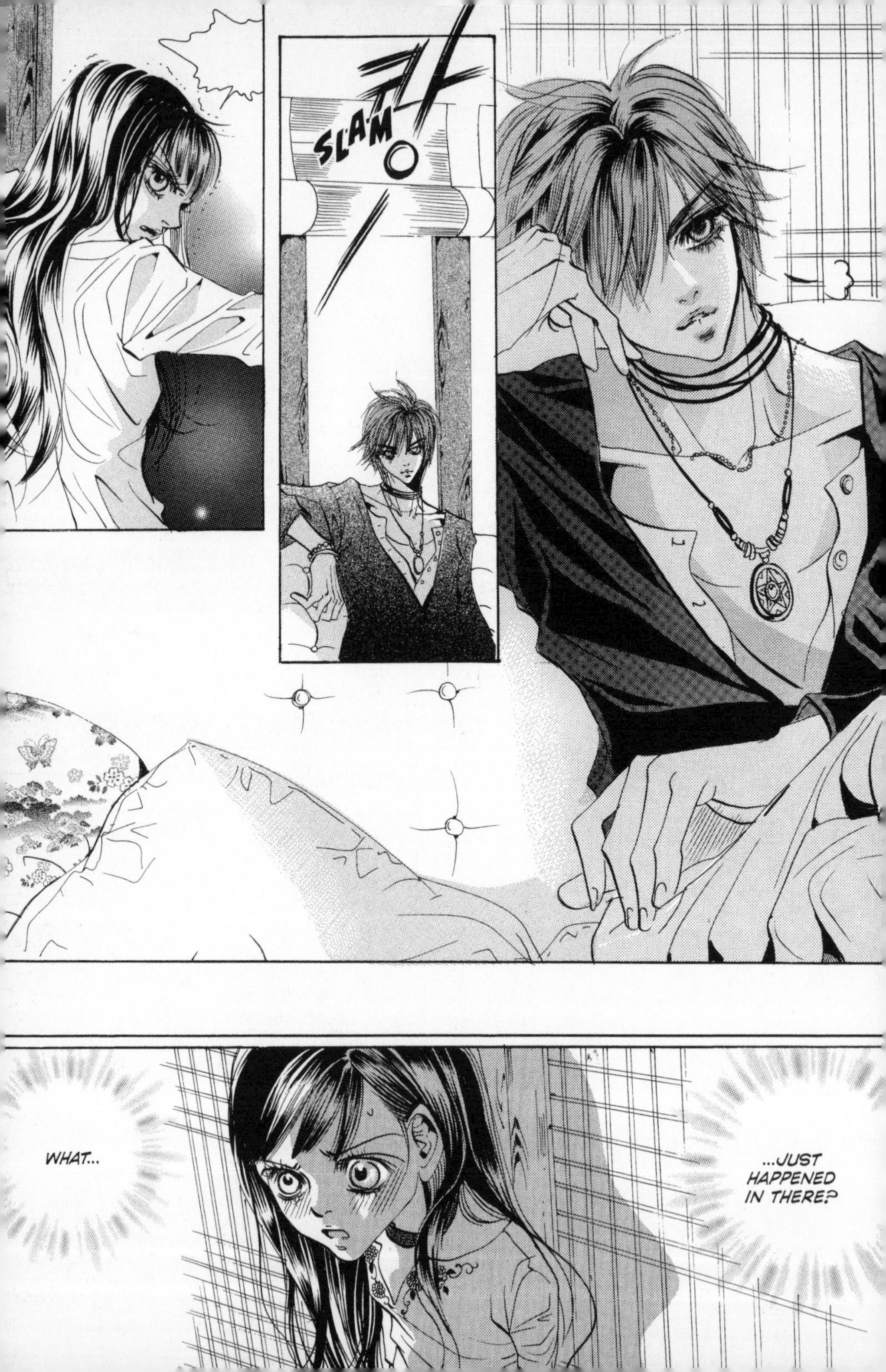
SLAM
WHAT...
...JUST HAPPENED IN THERE?

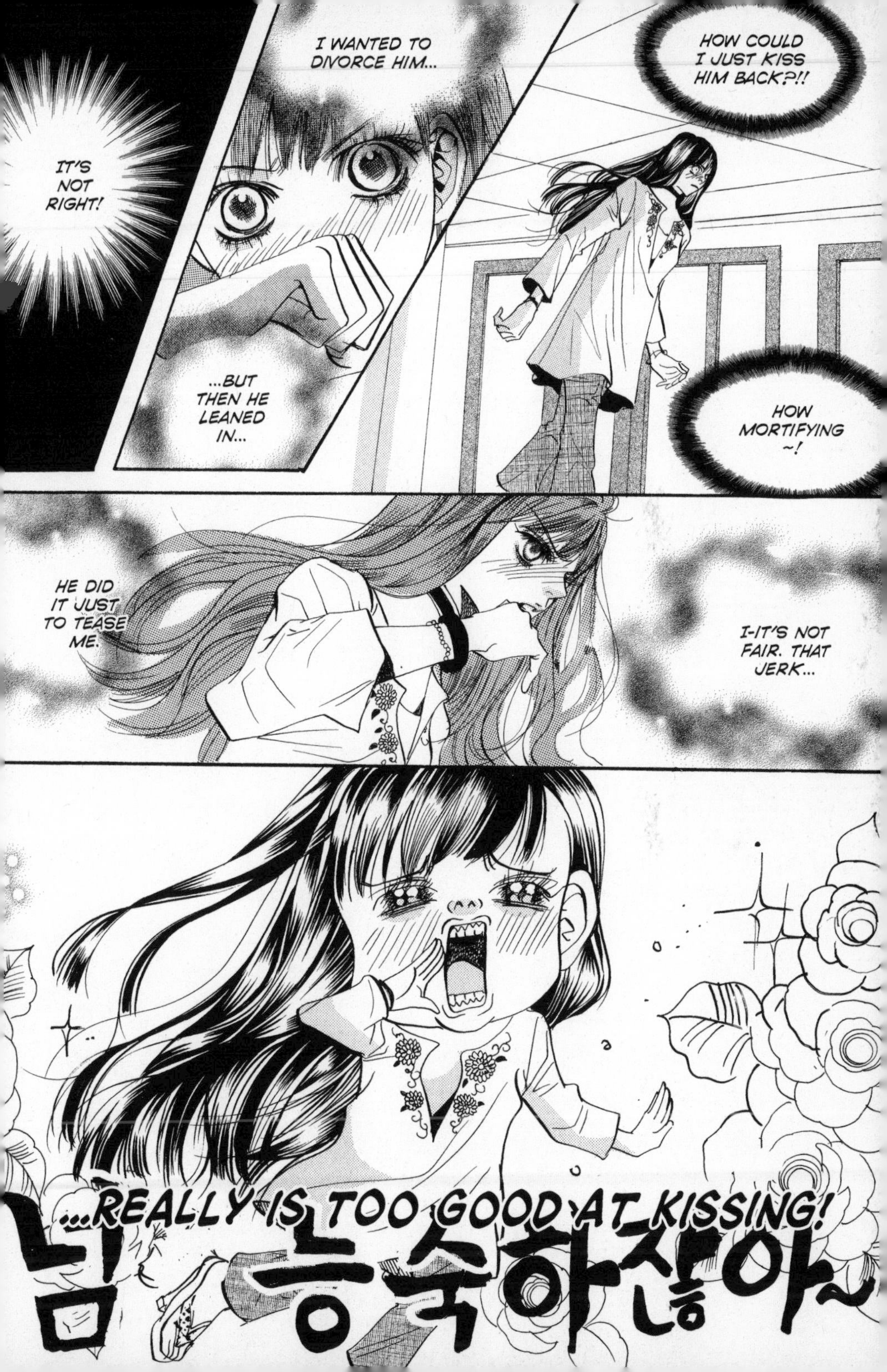
IT'S NOT RIGHT!
I WANTED TO DIVORCE HIM...
...BUT THEN HE LEANED IN...
HOW COULD I JUST KISS HIM BACK?!!
HOW MORTIFYING ~!
HE DID IT JUST TO TEASE ME.
I-IT'S NOT FAIR. THAT JERK...
...REALLY IS TOO GOOD AT KISSING!
넘 능숙하잖아~

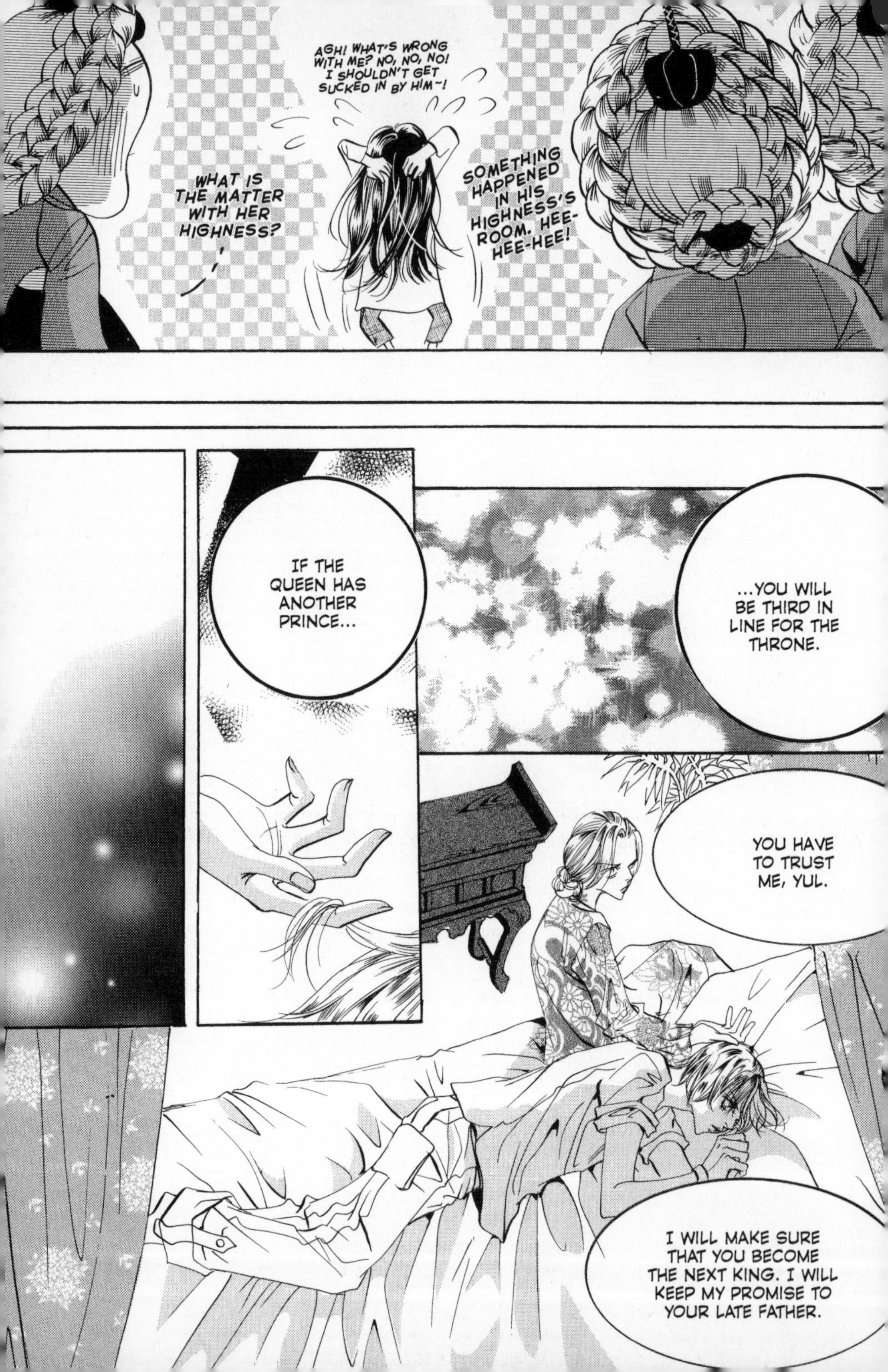
WHAT IS THE MATTER WITH HER HIGHNESS?
AGH! WHAT'S WRONG WITH ME? NO, NO, NO! I SHOULDN'T GET SUCKED IN BY HIM~!
SOMETHING HAPPENED IN HIS HIGHNESS'S ROOM. HEE-HEE-HEE!
IF THE QUEEN HAS ANOTHER PRINCE...
...YOU WILL BE THIRD IN LINE FOR THE THRONE.
YOU HAVE TO TRUST ME, YUL.
I WILL MAKE SURE THAT YOU BECOME THE NEXT KING. I WILL KEEP MY PROMISE TO YOUR LATE FATHER.

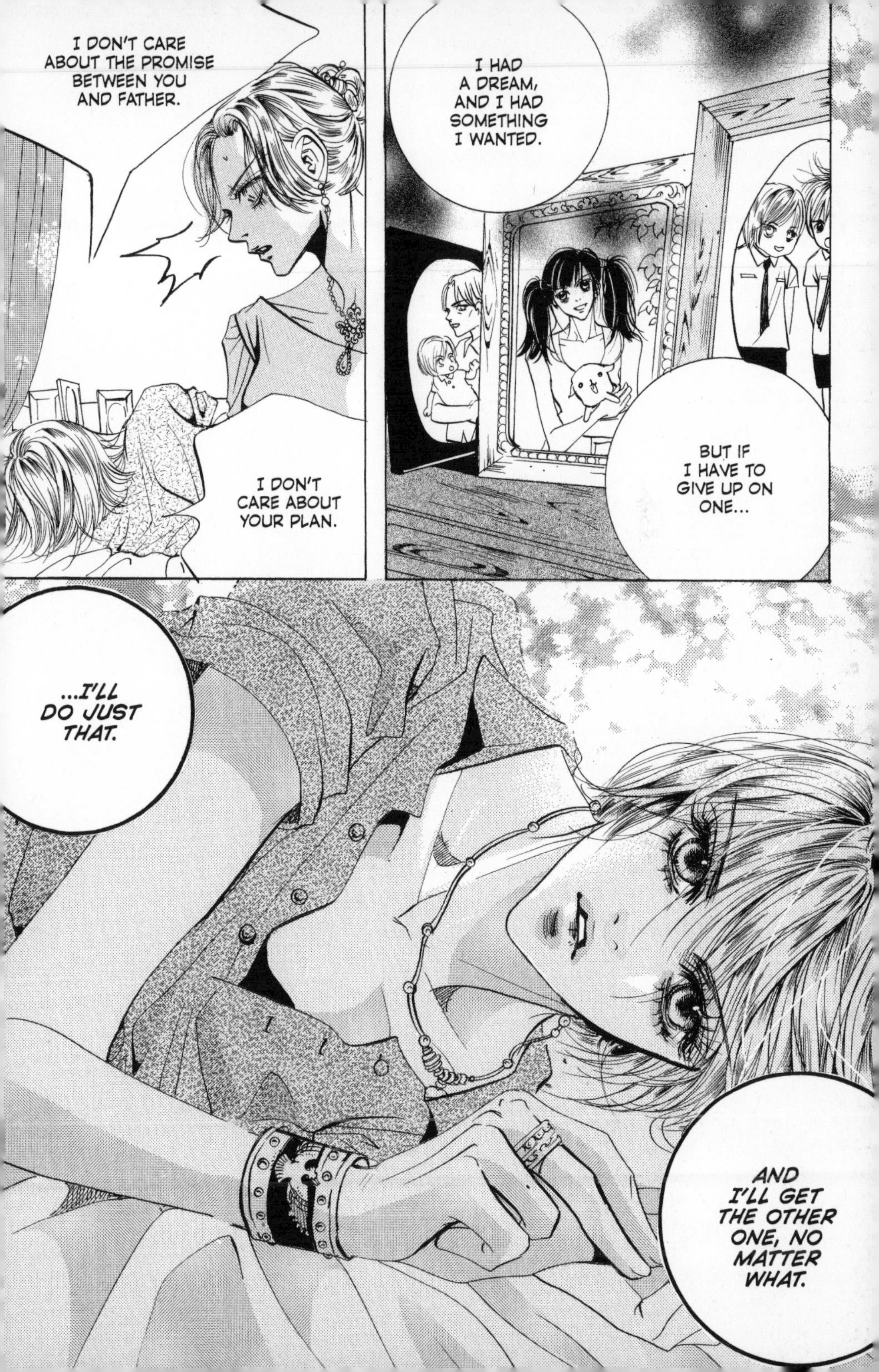
I DON'T CARE ABOUT THE PROMISE BETWEEN YOU AND FATHER.
I DON'T CARE ABOUT YOUR PLAN.
I HAD A DREAM, AND I HAD SOMETHING I WANTED.
BUT IF I HAVE TO GIVE UP ON ONE...
...I'LL DO JUST THAT.
AND I'LL GET THE OTHER ONE, NO MATTER WHAT.

THE ROYAL PALACE
Goong

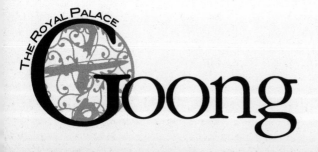

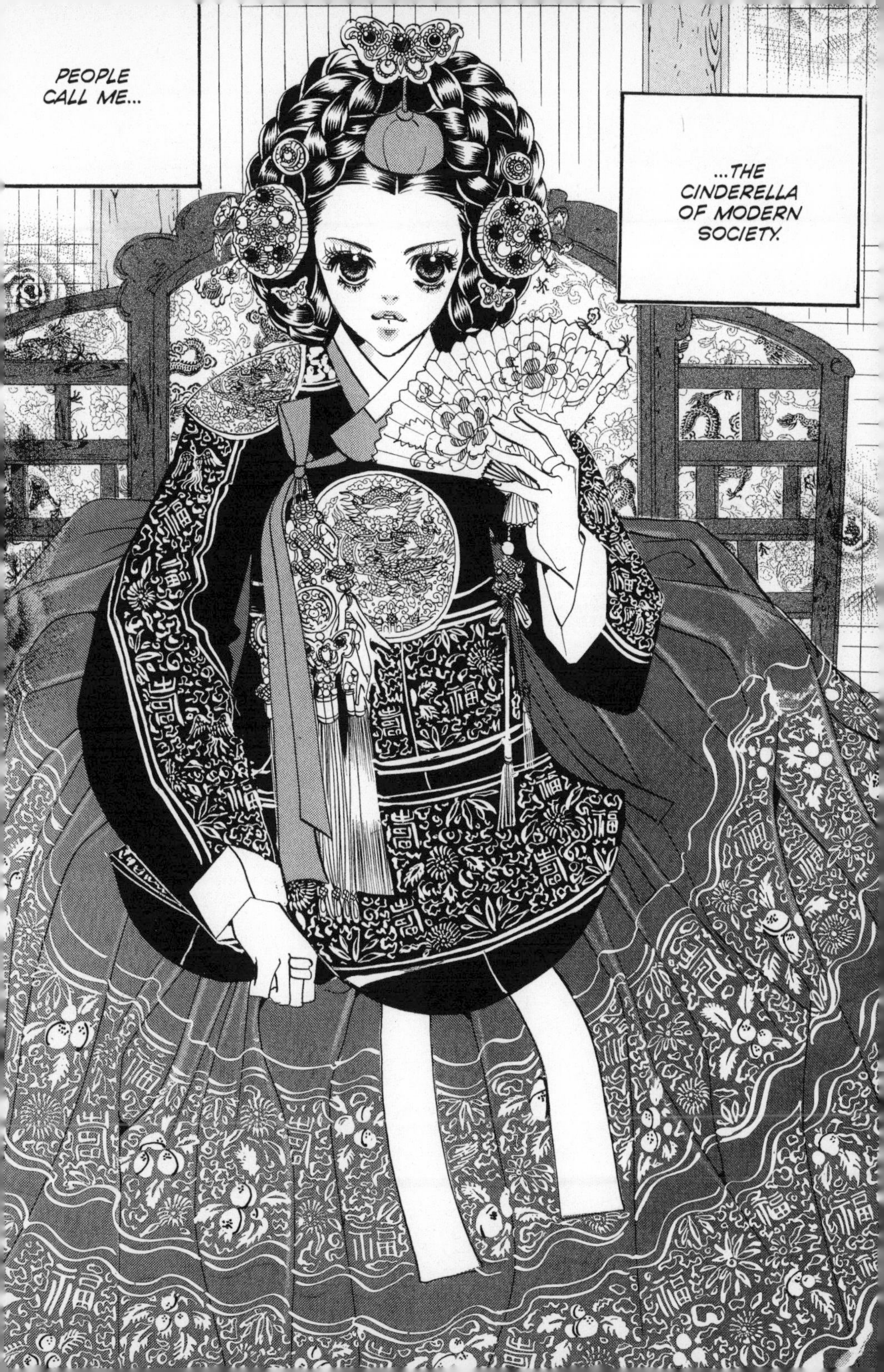
PEOPLE CALL ME...
...THE CINDERELLA OF MODERN SOCIETY.

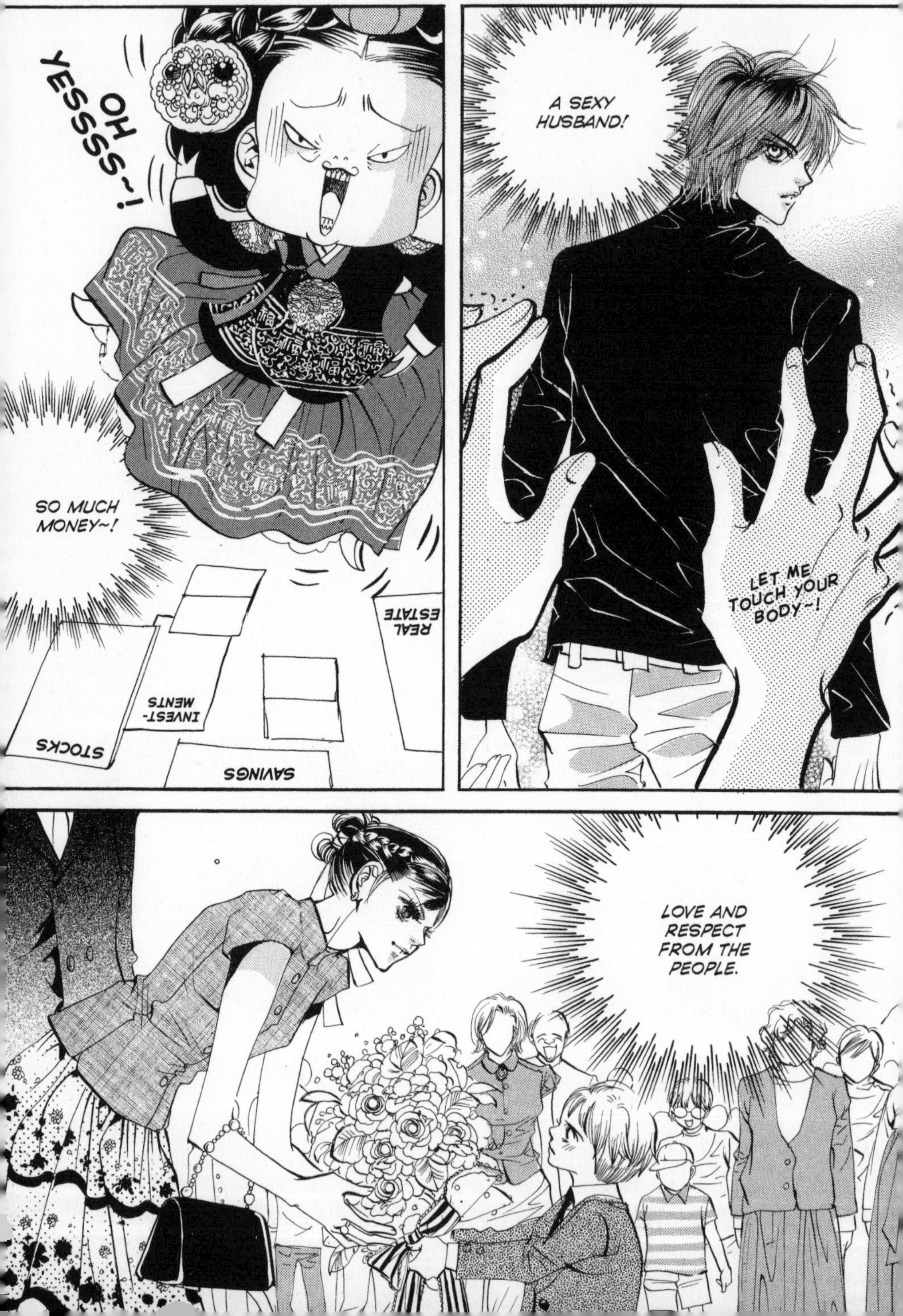
OH YESSSS~!
SO MUCH MONEY~!
REAL ESTATE
INVEST-MENTS
STOCKS
SAVINGS
A SEXY HUSBAND!
LET ME TOUCH YOUR BODY~!
LOVE AND RESPECT FROM THE PEOPLE.

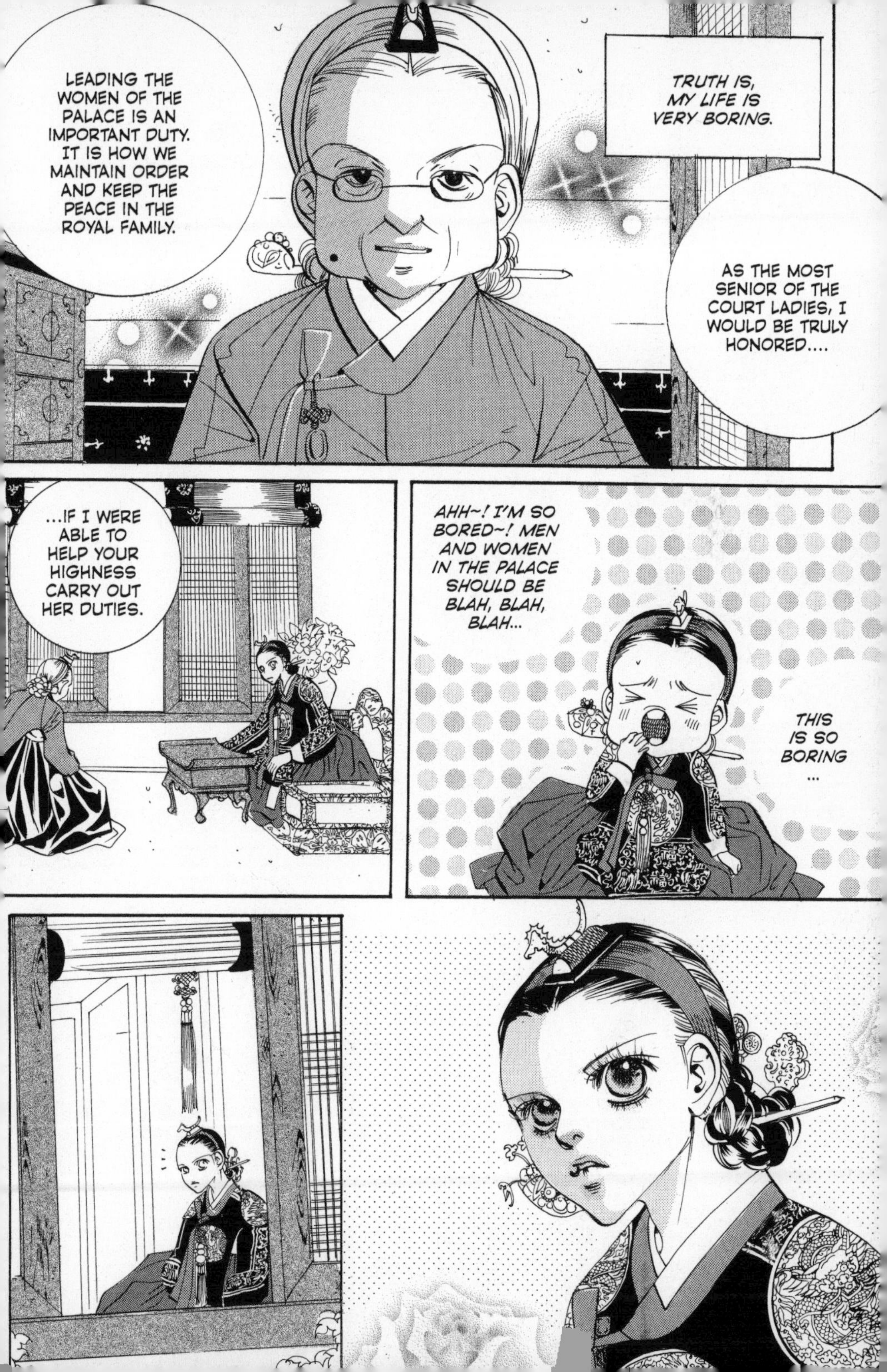
LEADING THE WOMEN OF THE PALACE IS AN IMPORTANT DUTY. IT IS HOW WE MAINTAIN ORDER AND KEEP THE PEACE IN THE ROYAL FAMILY.
TRUTH IS, MY LIFE IS VERY BORING.
AS THE MOST SENIOR OF THE COURT LADIES, I WOULD BE TRULY HONORED....
...IF I WERE ABLE TO HELP YOUR HIGHNESS CARRY OUT HER DUTIES.
AHH~! I'M SO BORED~! MEN AND WOMEN IN THE PALACE SHOULD BE BLAH, BLAH, BLAH...
THIS IS SO BORING ...

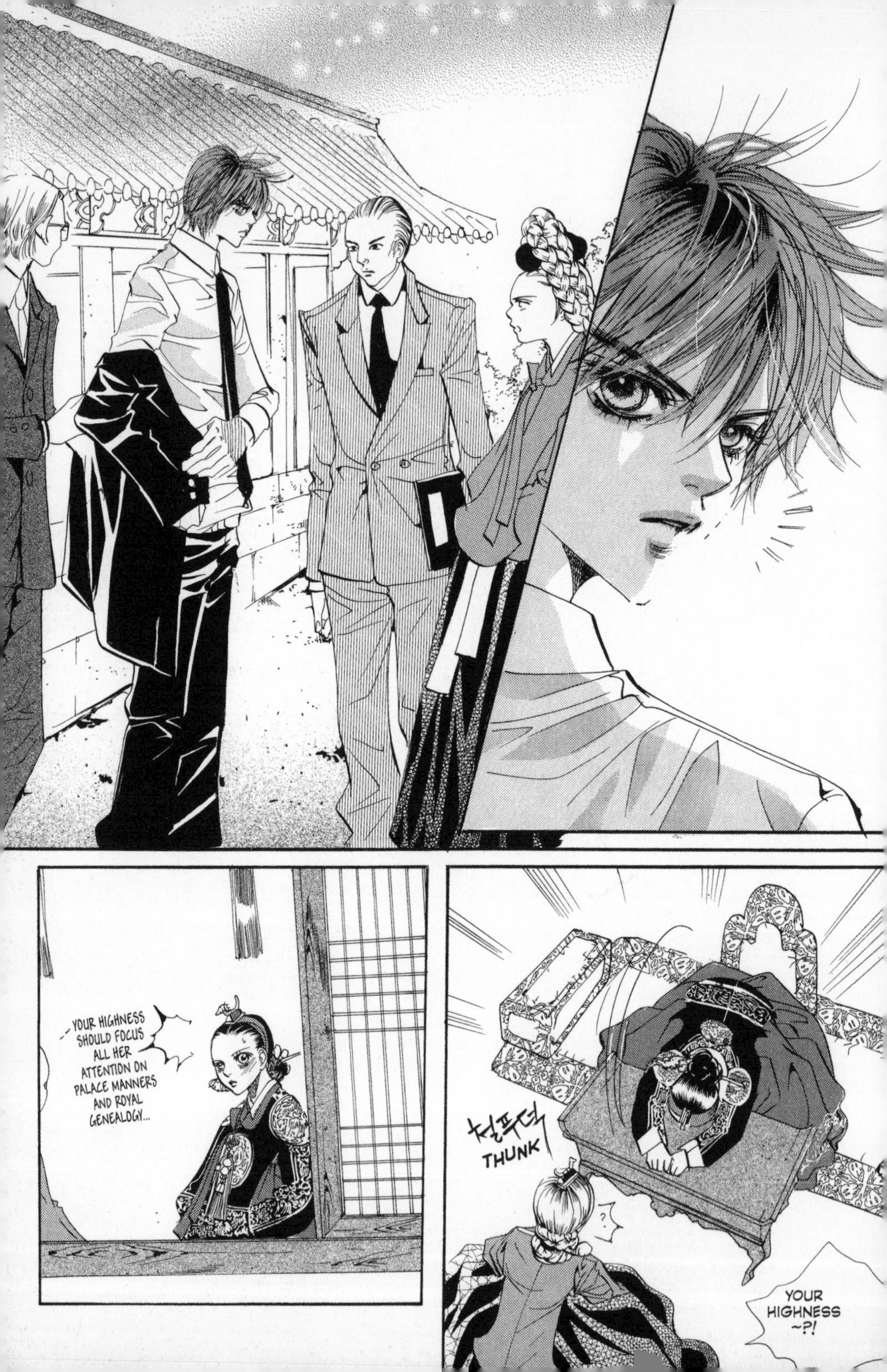
...YOUR HIGHNESS SHOULD FOCUS ALL HER ATTENTION ON PALACE MANNERS AND ROYAL GENEALOGY...
철푸덕
THUNK
?
YOUR HIGHNESS ~?!

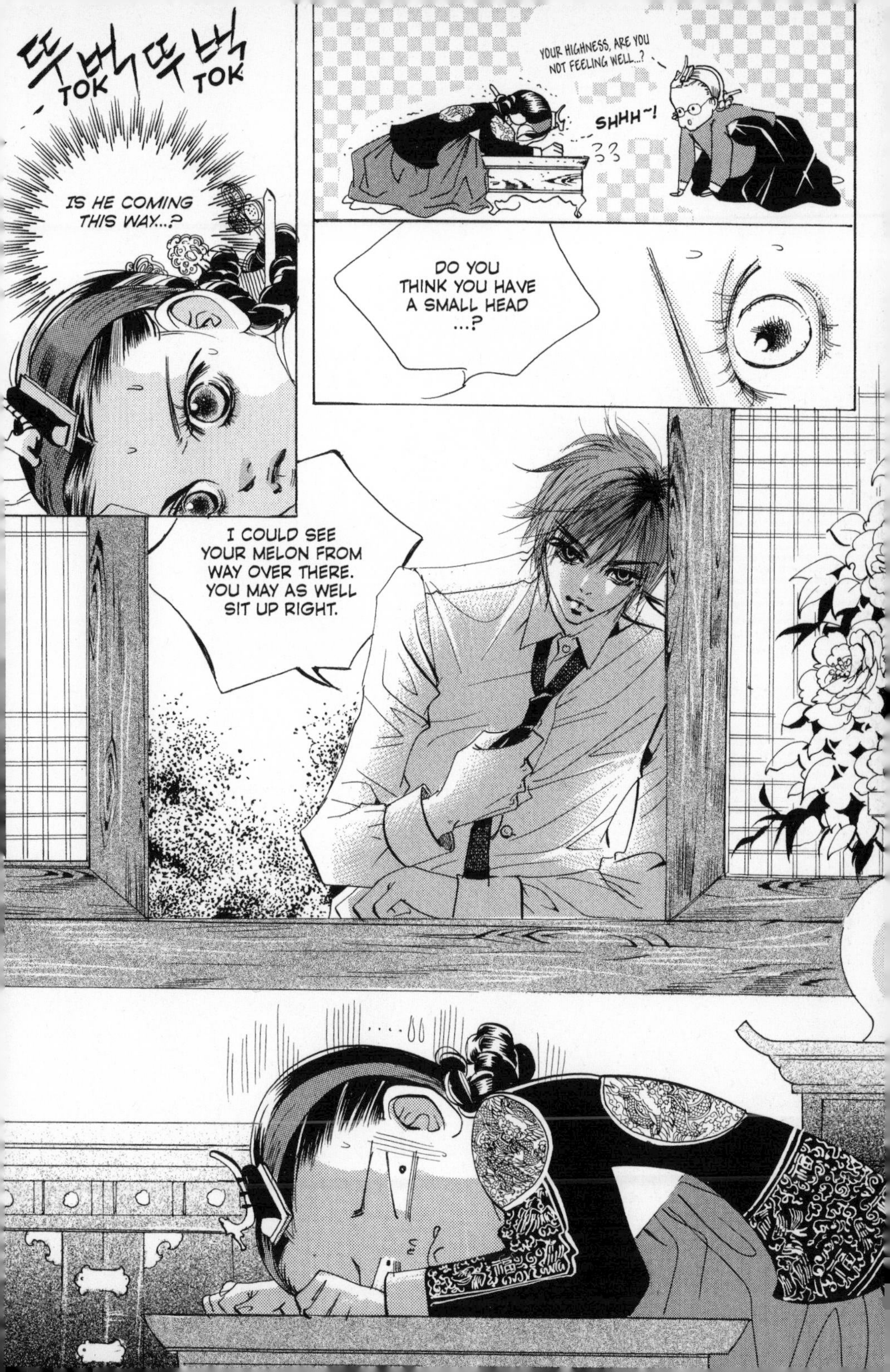
뚜벅뚜벅
TOK TOK
IS HE COMING THIS WAY...?
YOUR HIGHNESS, ARE YOU NOT FEELING WELL...?
SHHH~!
DO YOU THINK YOU HAVE A SMALL HEAD ...?
I COULD SEE YOUR MELON FROM WAY OVER THERE. YOU MAY AS WELL SIT UP RIGHT.
....

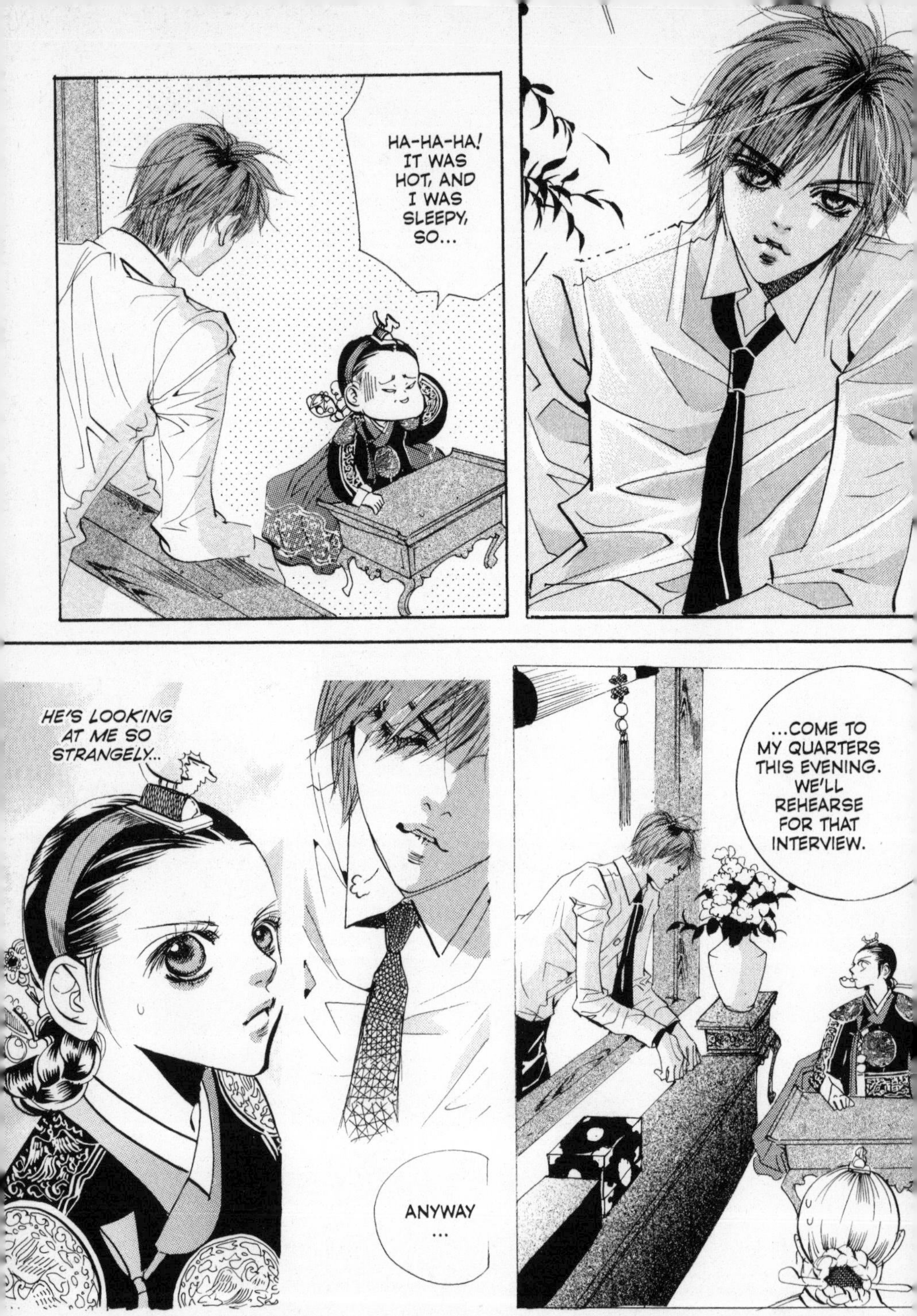
HA-HA-HA! IT WAS HOT, AND I WAS SLEEPY, SO...
HE'S LOOKING AT ME SO STRANGELY...
ANYWAY ...
...COME TO MY QUARTERS THIS EVENING. WE'LL REHEARSE FOR THAT INTERVIEW.

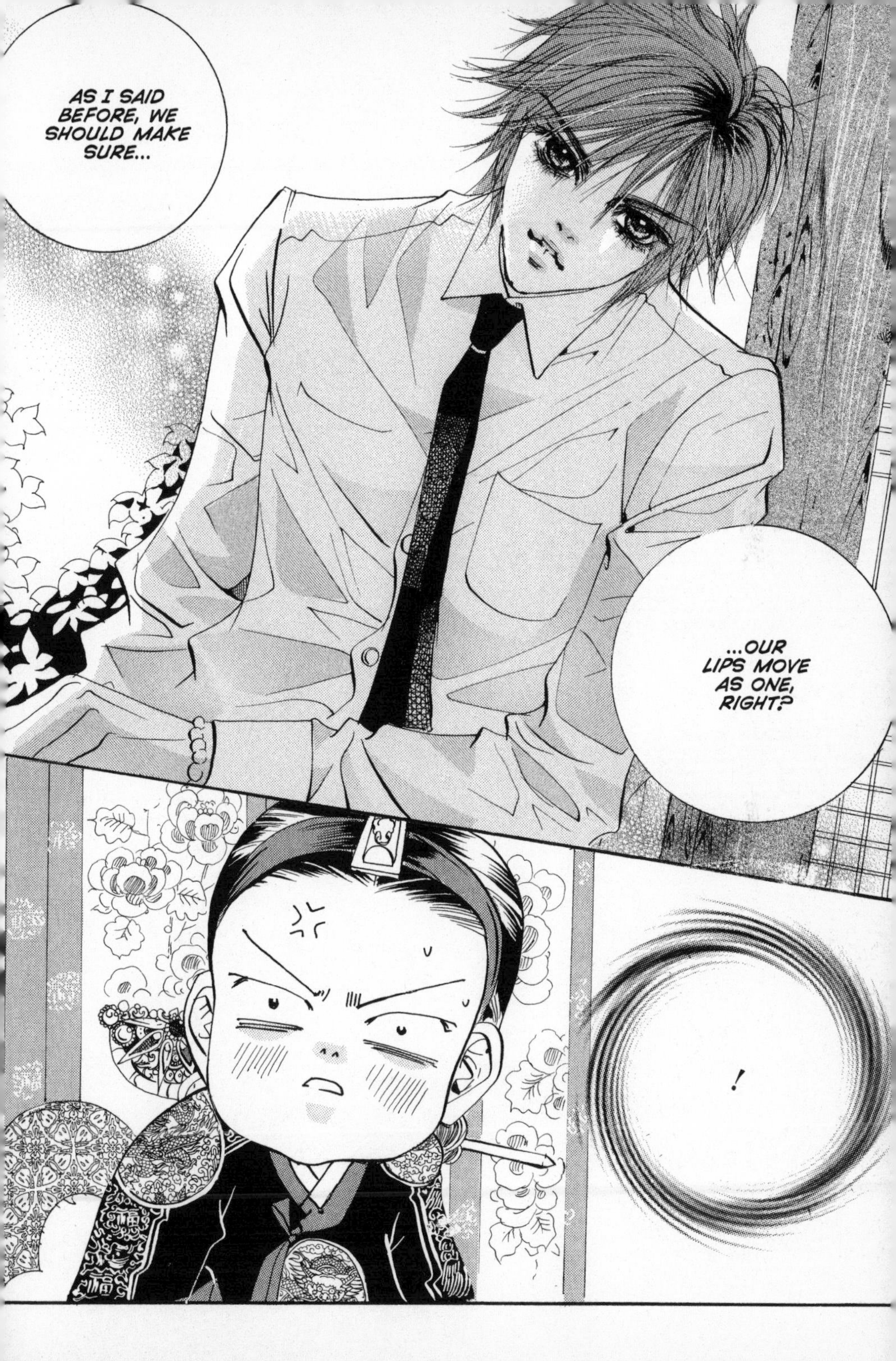
AS I SAID BEFORE, WE SHOULD MAKE SURE...
...OUR LIPS MOVE AS ONE, RIGHT?
!

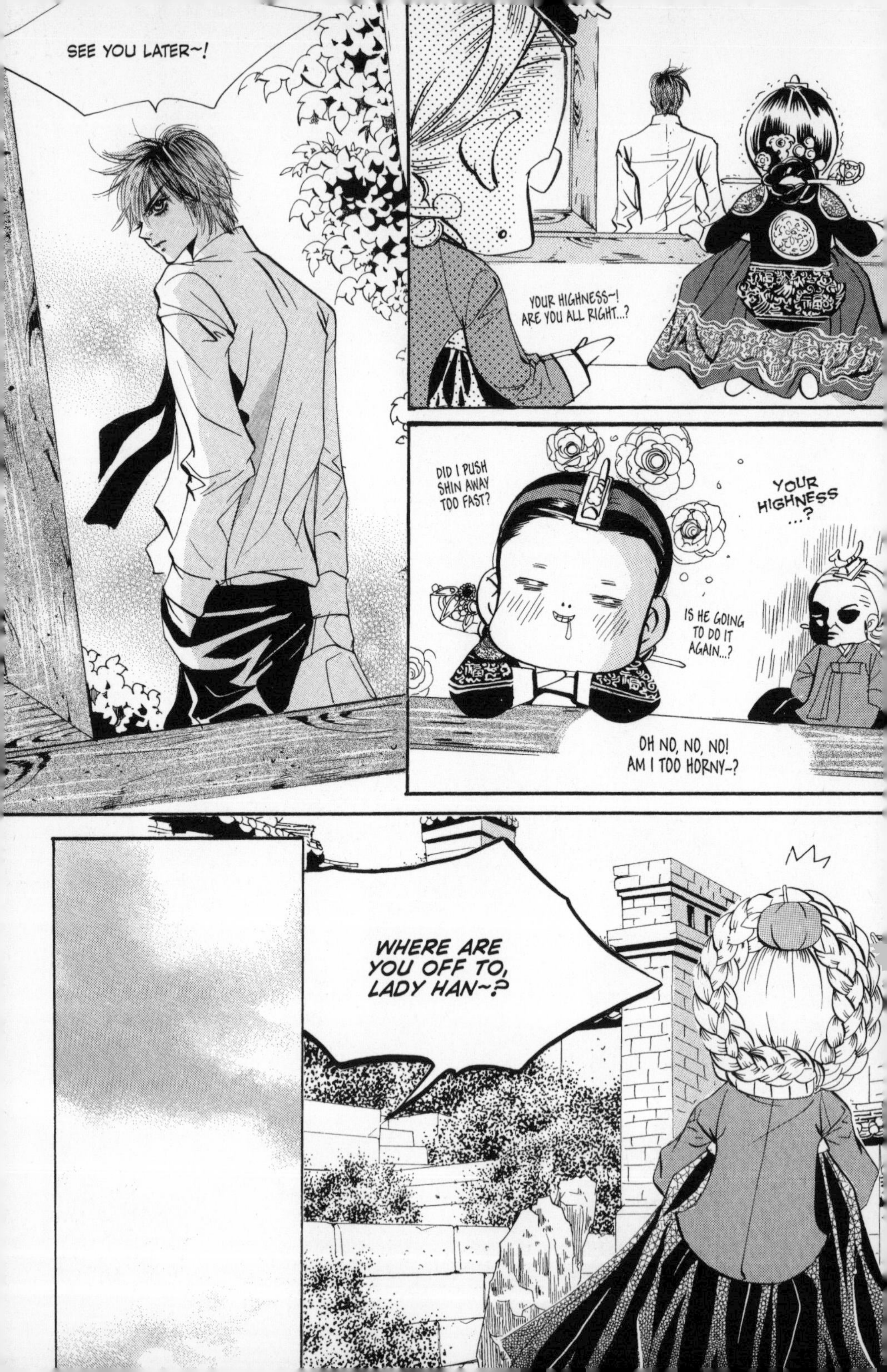
SEE YOU LATER~!
YOUR HIGHNESS~! ARE YOU ALL RIGHT...?
DID I PUSH SHIN AWAY TOO FAST?
YOUR HIGHNESS ...?
IS HE GOING TO DO IT AGAIN...?
OH NO, NO, NO! AM I TOO HORNY~?
WHERE ARE YOU OFF TO, LADY HAN~?

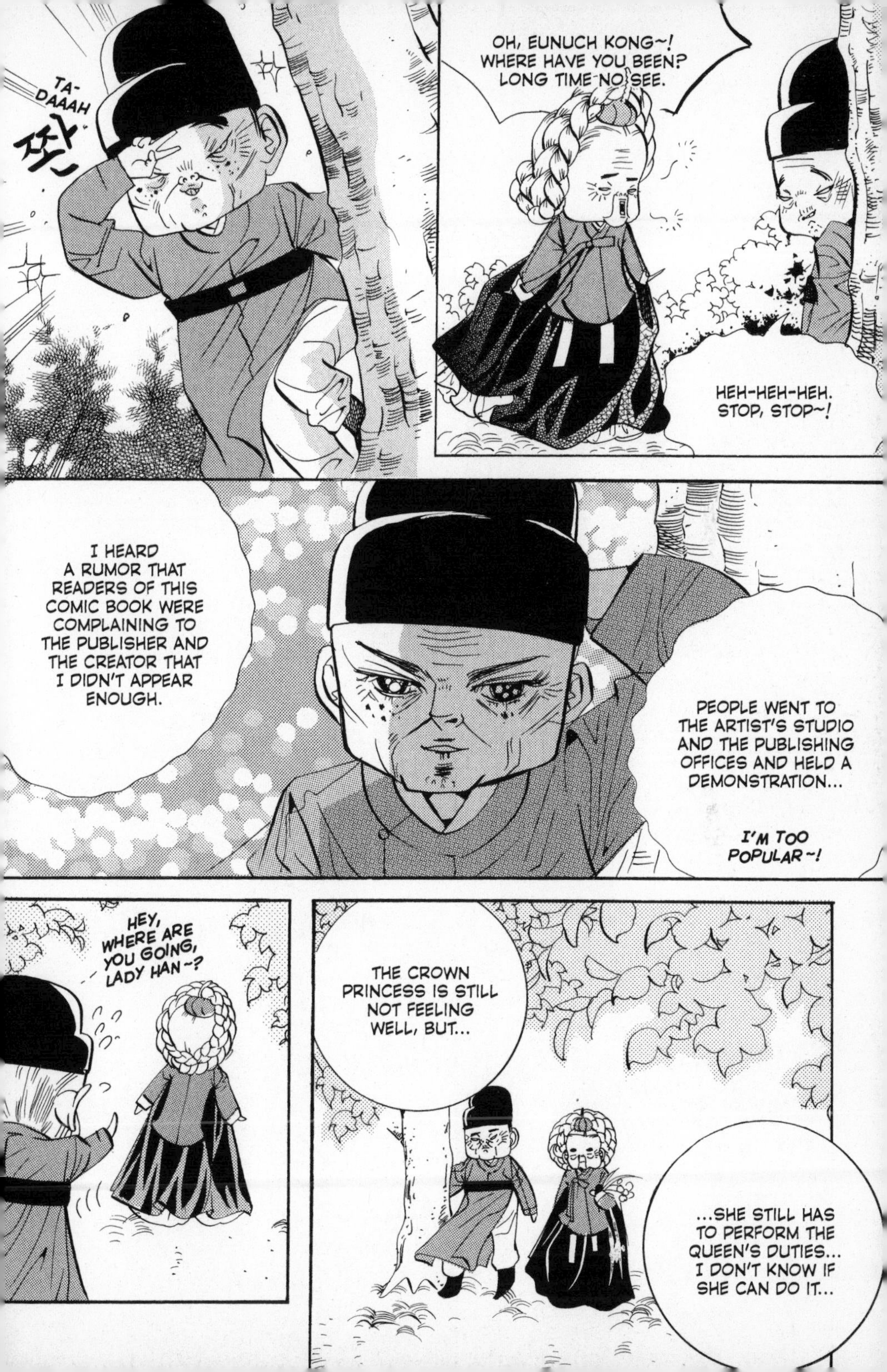

TA-DAAAH
짠
OH, EUNUCH KONG~! WHERE HAVE YOU BEEN? LONG TIME NO SEE.
HEH-HEH-HEH. STOP, STOP~!
I HEARD A RUMOR THAT READERS OF THIS COMIC BOOK WERE COMPLAINING TO THE PUBLISHER AND THE CREATOR THAT I DIDN'T APPEAR ENOUGH.
PEOPLE WENT TO THE ARTIST'S STUDIO AND THE PUBLISHING OFFICES AND HELD A DEMONSTRATION...
I'M TOO POPULAR~!
HEY, WHERE ARE YOU GOING, LADY HAN~?
THE CROWN PRINCESS IS STILL NOT FEELING WELL, BUT...
...SHE STILL HAS TO PERFORM THE QUEEN'S DUTIES... I DON'T KNOW IF SHE CAN DO IT...

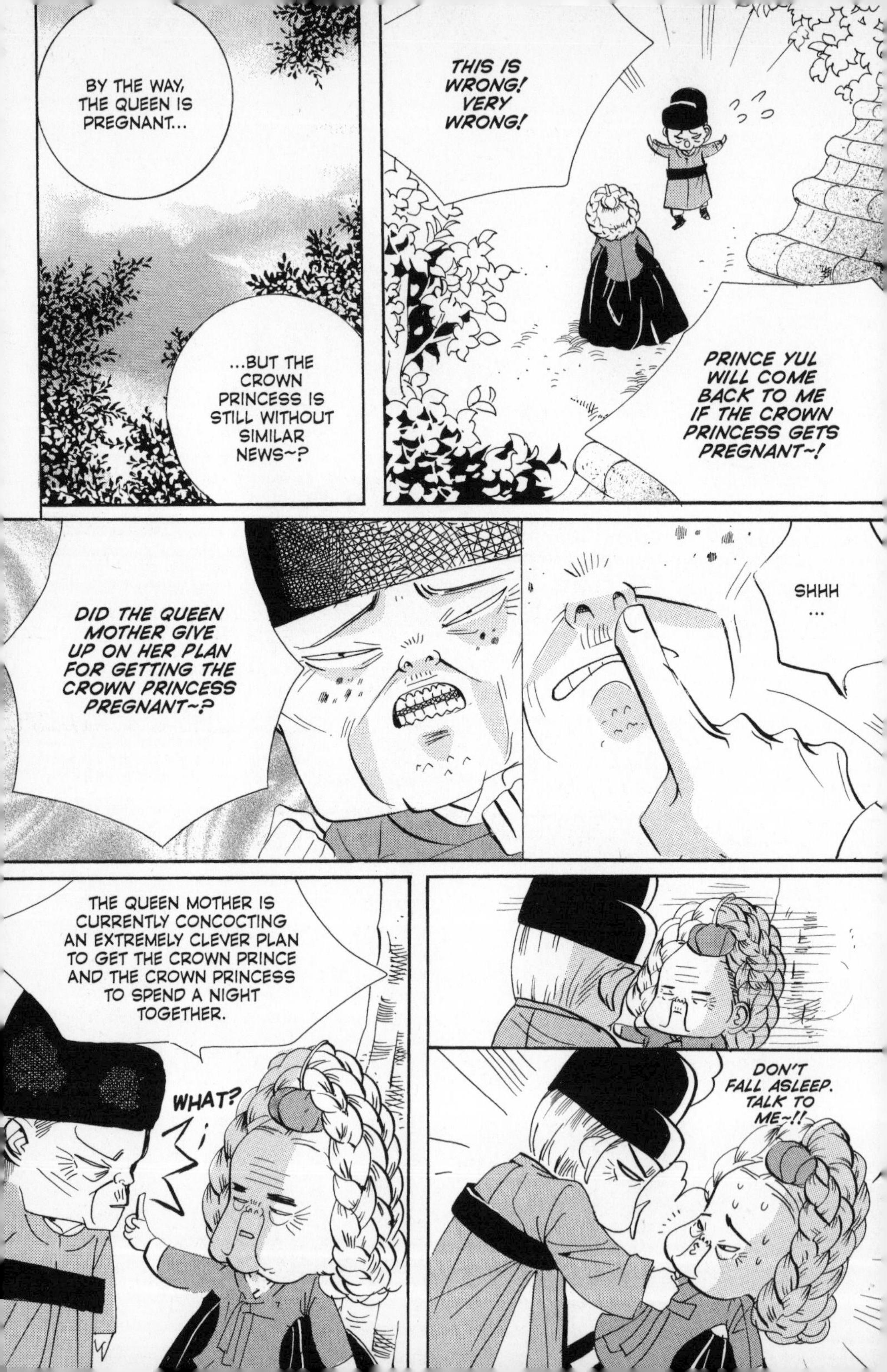
BY THE WAY, THE QUEEN IS PREGNANT...
...BUT THE CROWN PRINCESS IS STILL WITHOUT SIMILAR NEWS~?
THIS IS WRONG! VERY WRONG!
PRINCE YUL WILL COME BACK TO ME IF THE CROWN PRINCESS GETS PREGNANT~!
DID THE QUEEN MOTHER GIVE UP ON HER PLAN FOR GETTING THE CROWN PRINCESS PREGNANT~?
SHHH ...
THE QUEEN MOTHER IS CURRENTLY CONCOCTING AN EXTREMELY CLEVER PLAN TO GET THE CROWN PRINCE AND THE CROWN PRINCESS TO SPEND A NIGHT TOGETHER.
WHAT?
DON'T FALL ASLEEP. TALK TO ME~!!

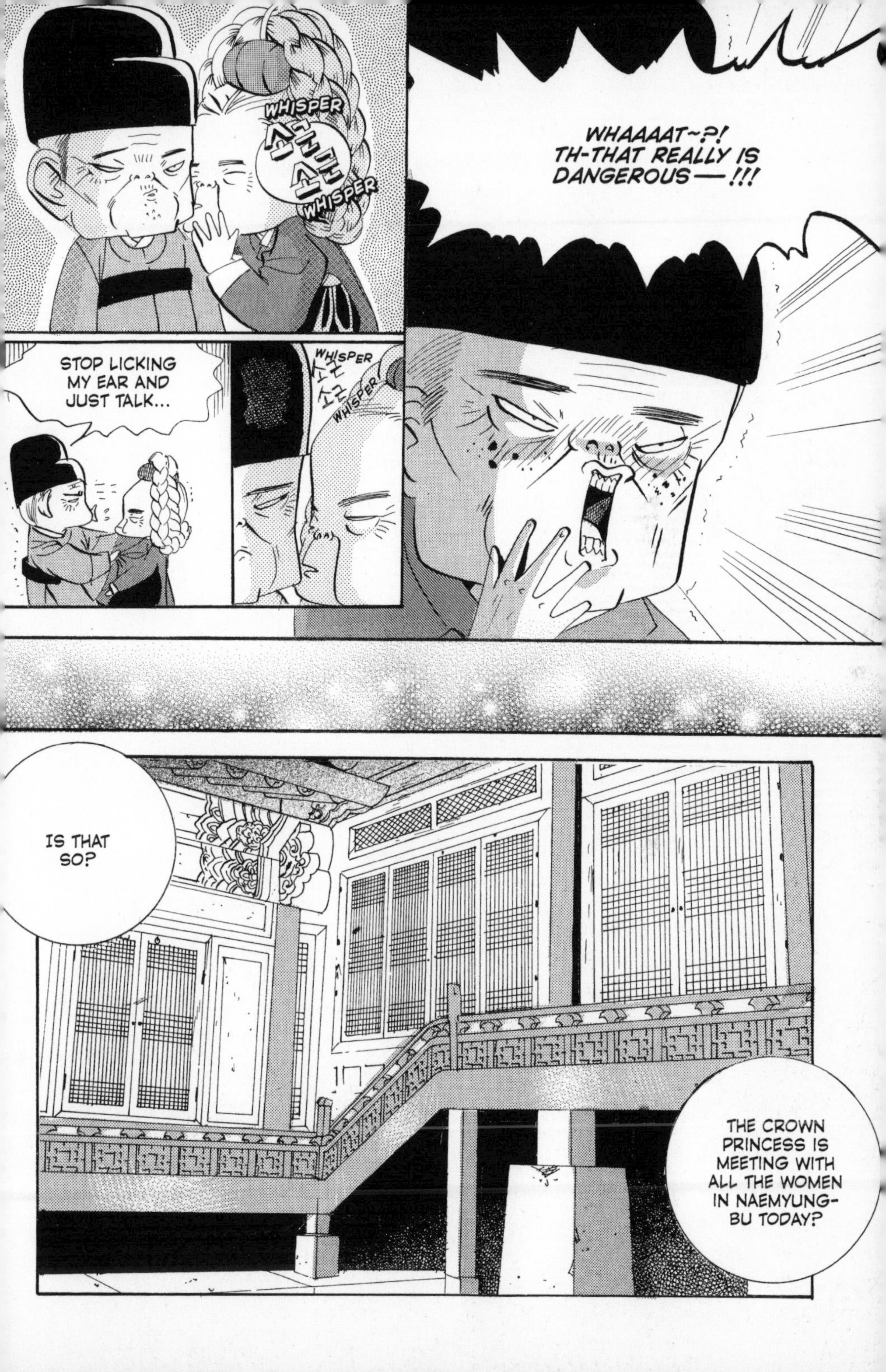
WHISPER
WHISPER
STOP LICKING MY EAR AND JUST TALK...
WHISPER
WHISPER
WHAAAAT~?! TH-THAT REALLY IS DANGEROUS—!!!
IS THAT SO?
THE CROWN PRINCESS IS MEETING WITH ALL THE WOMEN IN NAEMYUNG-BU TODAY?

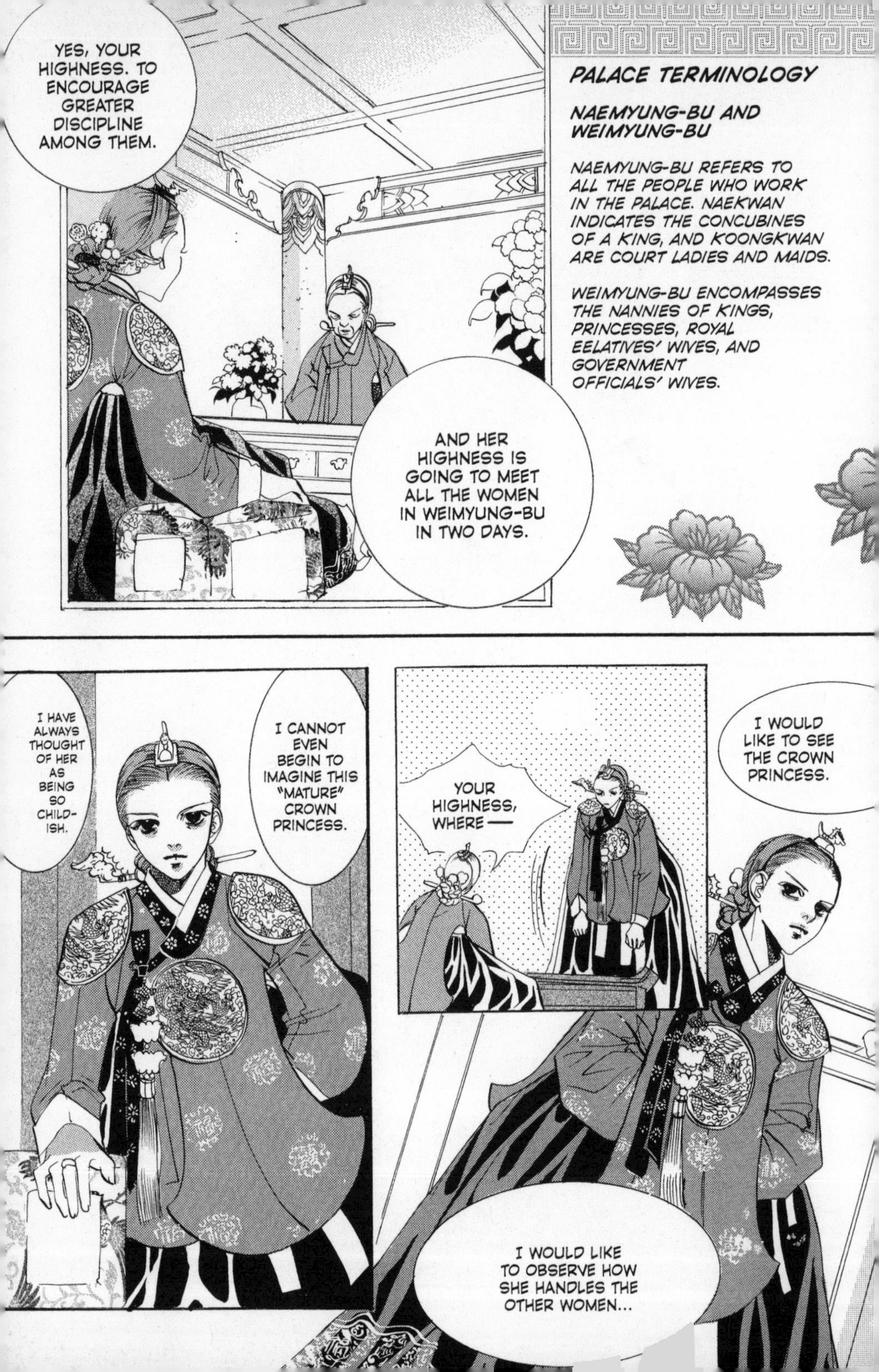
YES, YOUR HIGHNESS. TO ENCOURAGE GREATER DISCIPLINE AMONG THEM.
AND HER HIGHNESS IS GOING TO MEET ALL THE WOMEN IN WEIMYUNG-BU IN TWO DAYS.
PALACE TERMINOLOGY
NAEMYUNG-BU AND WEIMYUNG-BU
NAEMYUNG-BU REFERS TO ALL THE PEOPLE WHO WORK IN THE PALACE. NAEKWAN INDICATES THE CONCUBINES OF A KING, AND KOONGKWAN ARE COURT LADIES AND MAIDS.
WEIMYUNG-BU ENCOMPASSES THE NANNIES OF KINGS, PRINCESSES, ROYAL EELATIVES' WIVES, AND GOVERNMENT OFFICIALS' WIVES.
I HAVE ALWAYS THOUGHT OF HER AS BEING SO CHILD-ISH.
I CANNOT EVEN BEGIN TO IMAGINE THIS "MATURE" CROWN PRINCESS.
YOUR HIGHNESS, WHERE—
I WOULD LIKE TO SEE THE CROWN PRINCESS.
I WOULD LIKE TO OBSERVE HOW SHE HANDLES THE OTHER WOMEN...

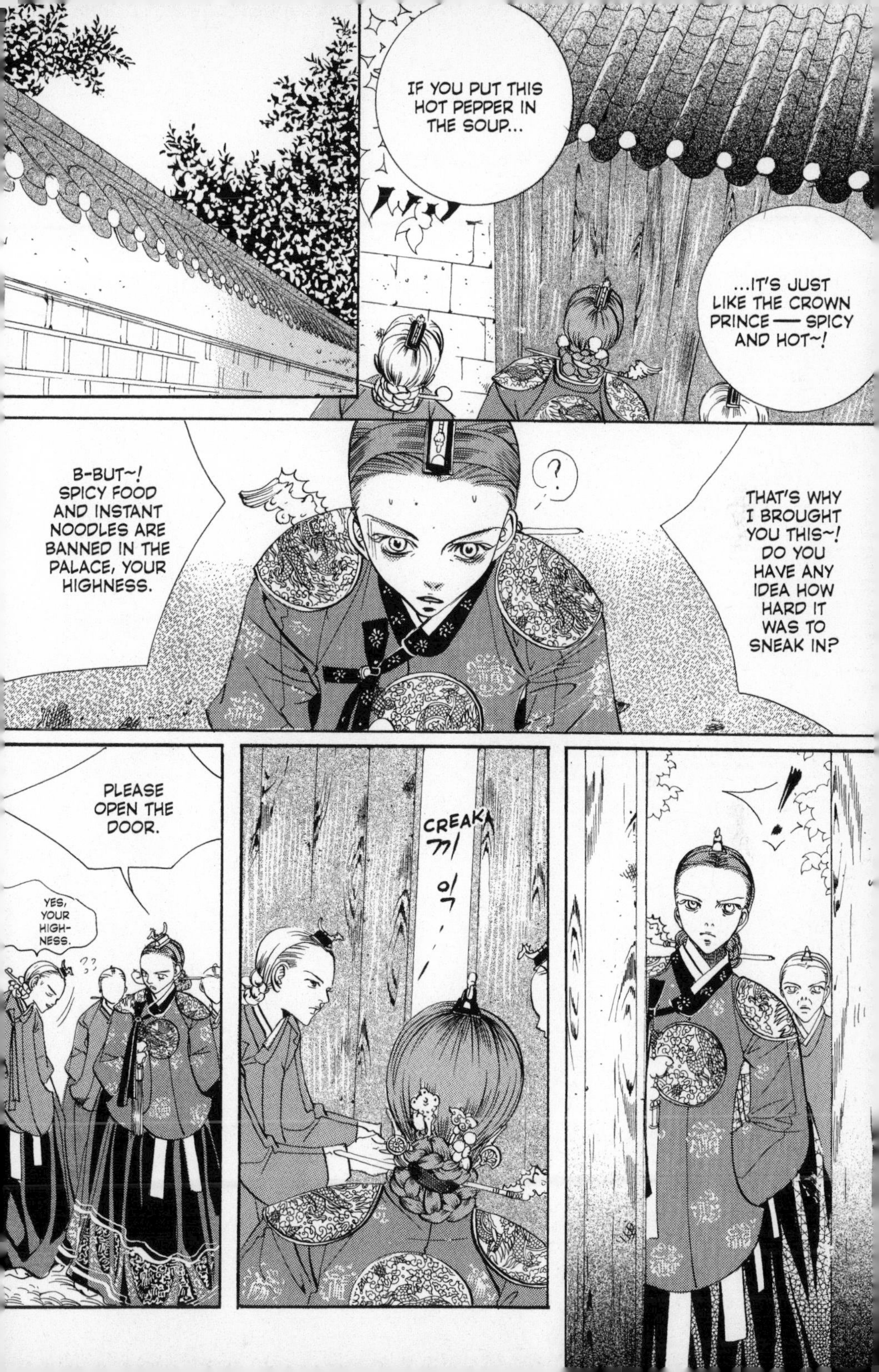
IF YOU PUT THIS HOT PEPPER IN THE SOUP...
...IT'S JUST LIKE THE CROWN PRINCE — SPICY AND HOT~!
B-BUT~! SPICY FOOD AND INSTANT NOODLES ARE BANNED IN THE PALACE, YOUR HIGHNESS.
?
THAT'S WHY I BROUGHT YOU THIS~! DO YOU HAVE ANY IDEA HOW HARD IT WAS TO SNEAK IN?
PLEASE OPEN THE DOOR.
YES, YOUR HIGH-NESS.
CREAK
끼익
!

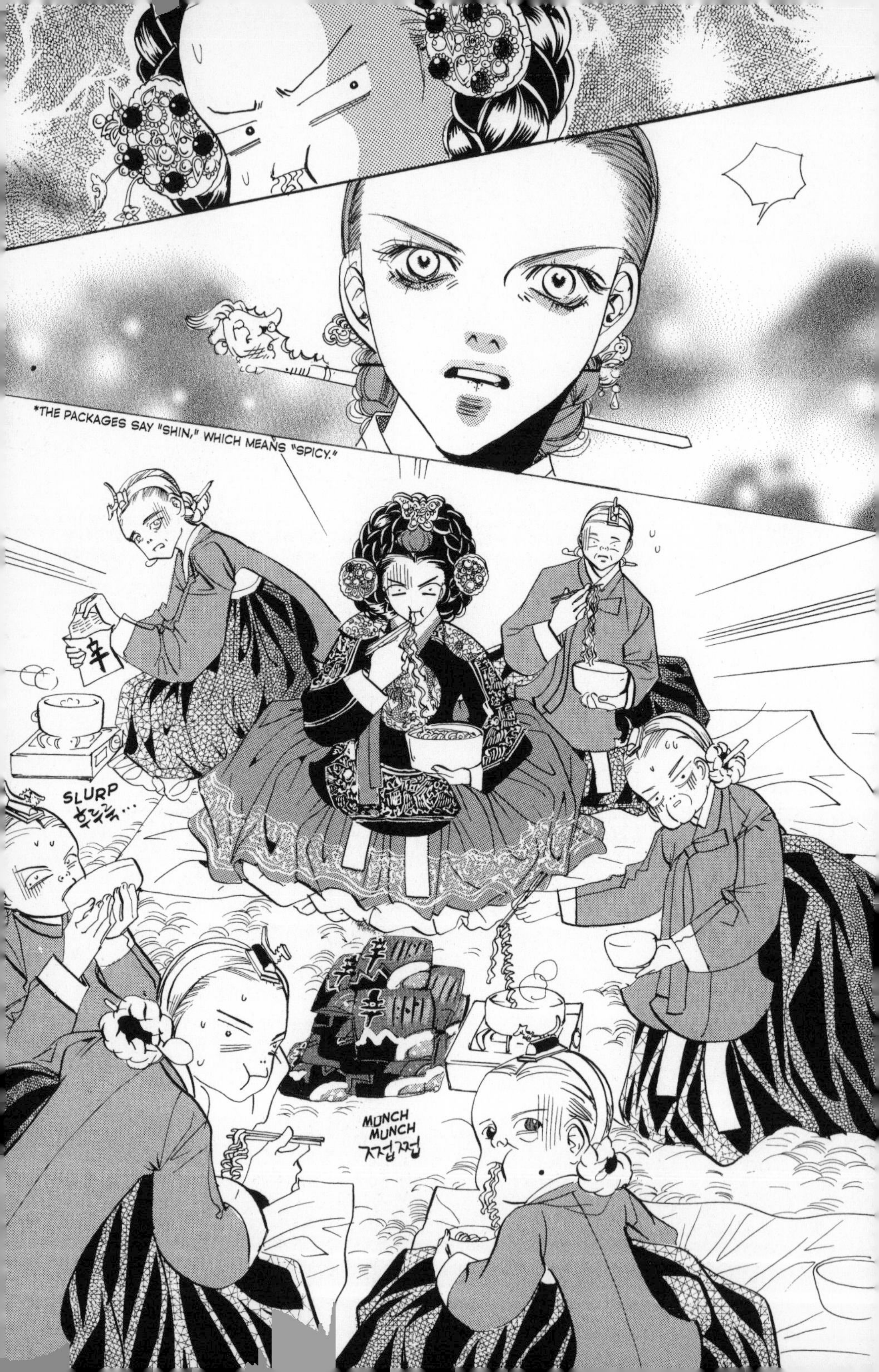
*THE PACKAGES SAY "SHIN," WHICH MEANS "SPICY."
SLURP
후르릅...
MUNCH
MUNCH
쩌접쩌접

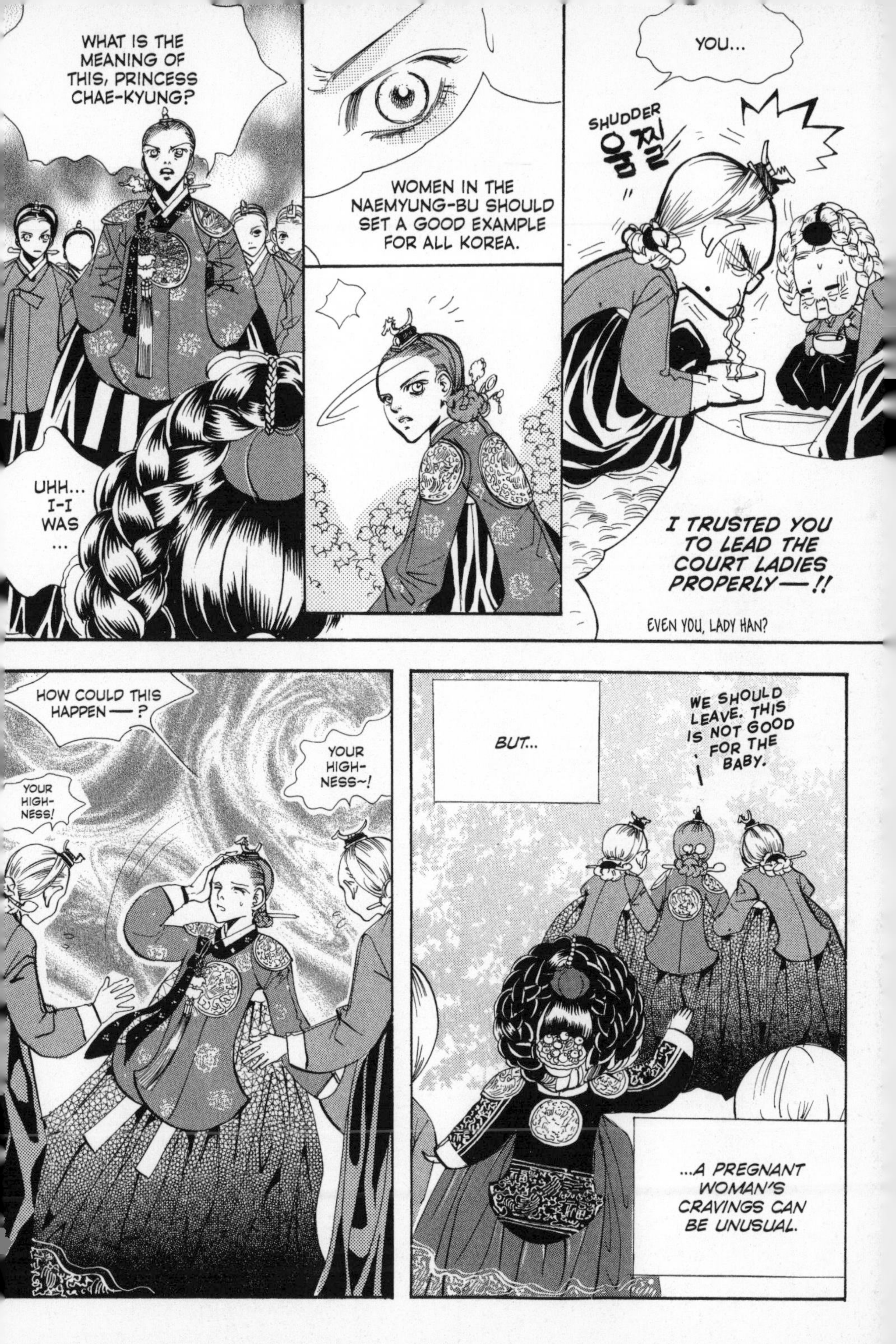
WHAT IS THE MEANING OF THIS, PRINCESS CHAE-KYUNG?
UHH... I-I WAS ...
WOMEN IN THE NAEMYUNG-BU SHOULD SET A GOOD EXAMPLE FOR ALL KOREA.
YOU...
SHUDDER
움찔
I TRUSTED YOU TO LEAD THE COURT LADIES PROPERLY—!!
EVEN YOU, LADY HAN?
HOW COULD THIS HAPPEN—?
YOUR HIGHNESS!
YOUR HIGHNESS~!
BUT...
WE SHOULD LEAVE. THIS IS NOT GOOD FOR THE BABY.
...A PREGNANT WOMAN'S CRAVINGS CAN BE UNUSUAL.

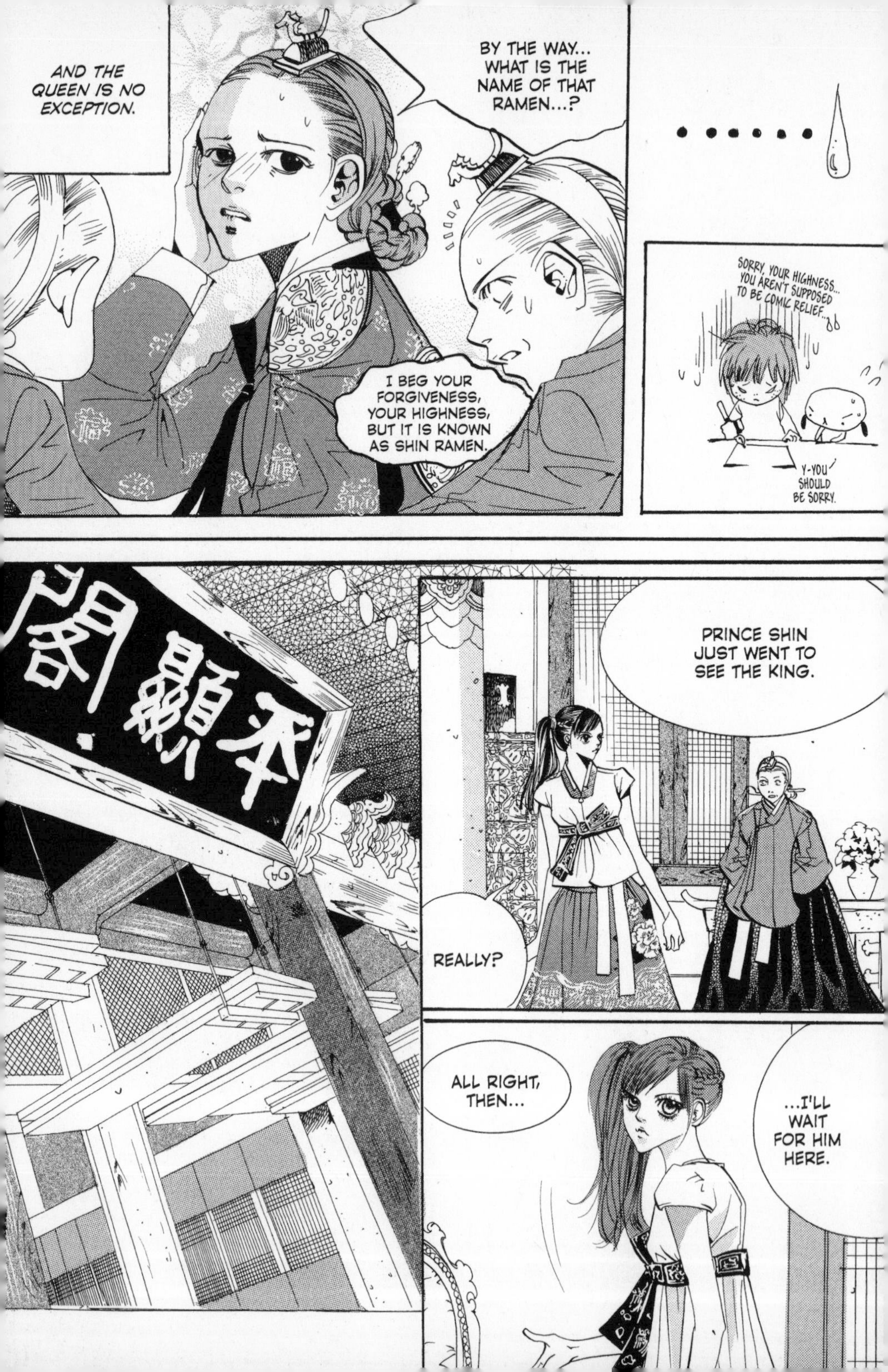
AND THE QUEEN IS NO EXCEPTION.
BY THE WAY... WHAT IS THE NAME OF THAT RAMEN...?
I BEG YOUR FORGIVENESS, YOUR HIGHNESS, BUT IT IS KNOWN AS SHIN RAMEN.
....
SORRY, YOUR HIGHNESS... YOU AREN'T SUPPOSED TO BE COMIC RELIEF...
Y-YOU SHOULD BE SORRY.
PRINCE SHIN JUST WENT TO SEE THE KING.
REALLY?
ALL RIGHT, THEN...
...I'LL WAIT FOR HIM HERE.

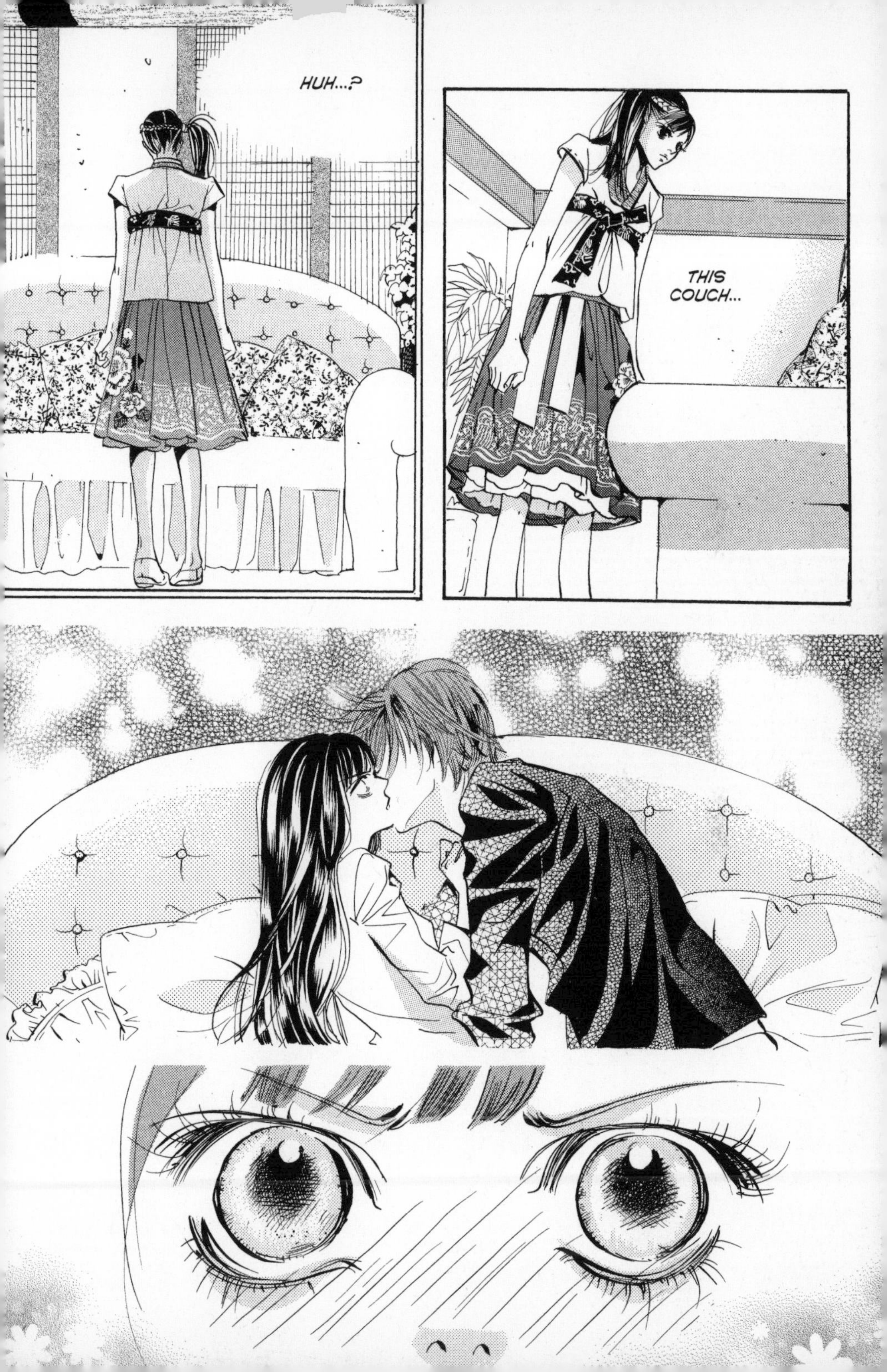
HUH...?
THIS COUCH...

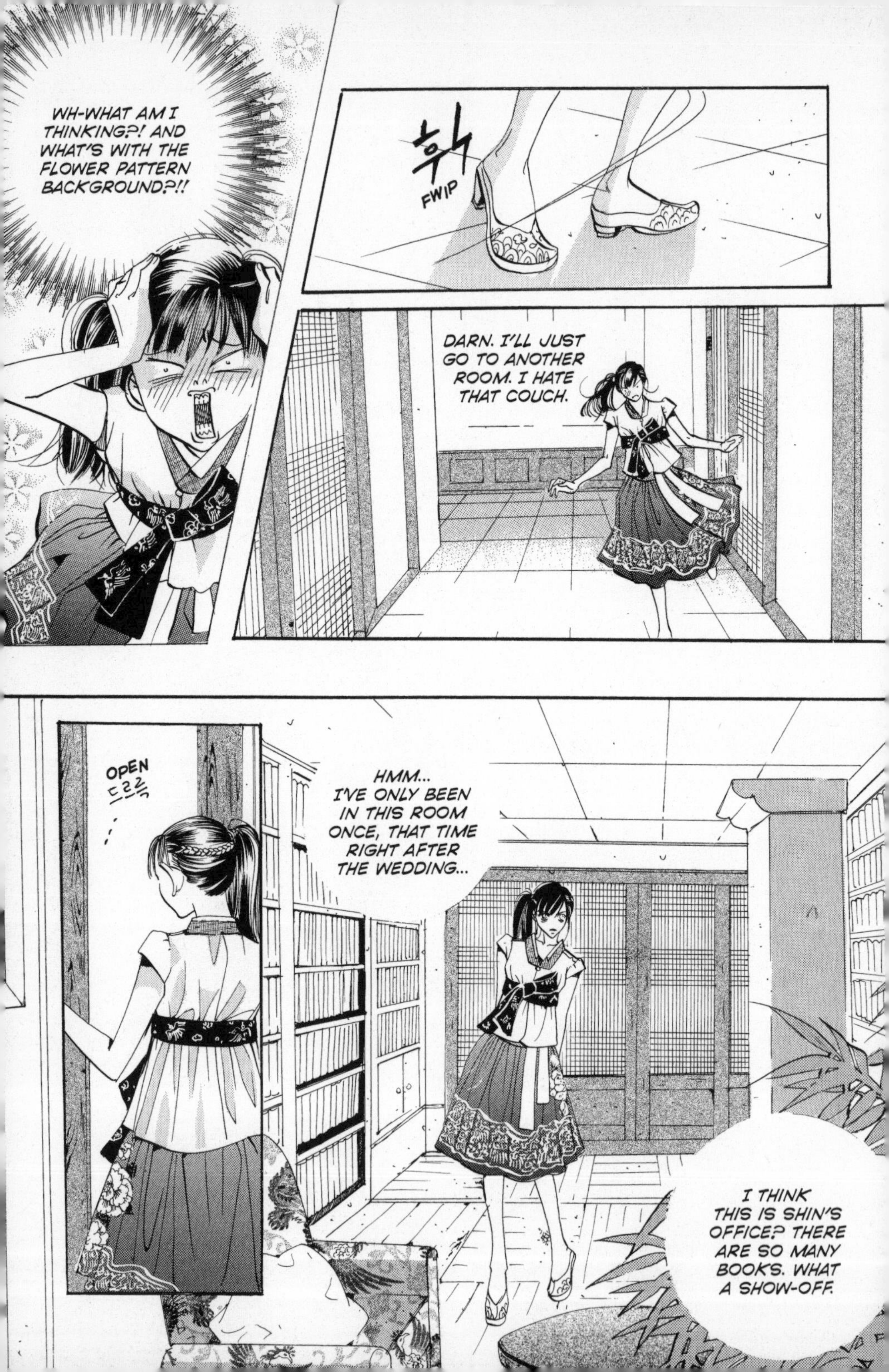
WH-WHAT AM I THINKING?! AND WHAT'S WITH THE FLOWER PATTERN BACKGROUND?!!
훽
FWIP
DARN. I'LL JUST GO TO ANOTHER ROOM. I HATE THAT COUCH.
OPEN
드르륵
HMM... I'VE ONLY BEEN IN THIS ROOM ONCE, THAT TIME RIGHT AFTER THE WEDDING...
I THINK THIS IS SHIN'S OFFICE? THERE ARE SO MANY BOOKS. WHAT A SHOW-OFF.

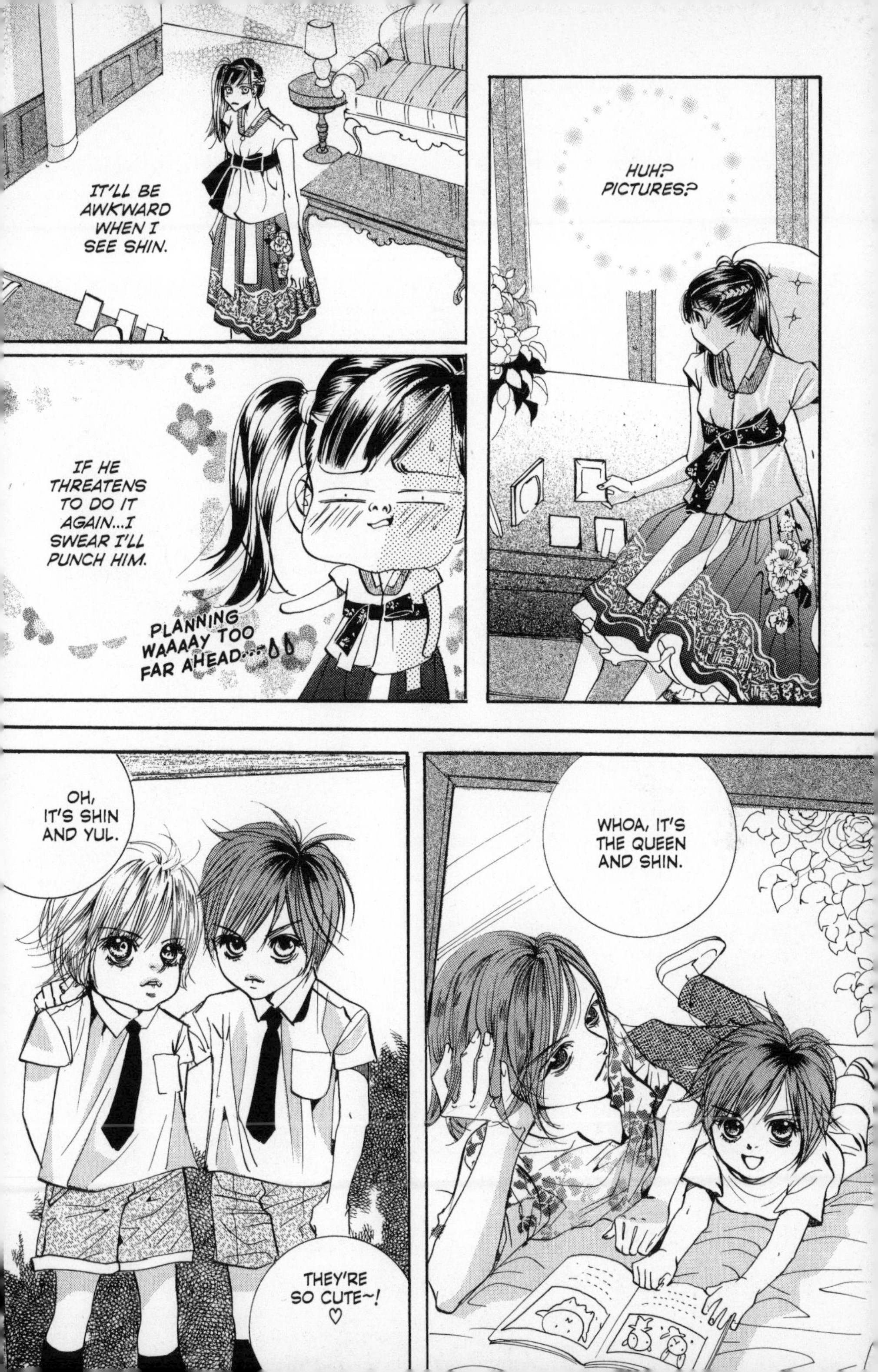
IT'LL BE AWKWARD WHEN I SEE SHIN.
IF HE THREATENS TO DO IT AGAIN...I SWEAR I'LL PUNCH HIM.
PLANNING WAAAAY TOO FAR AHEAD...
HUH? PICTURES?
OH, IT'S SHIN AND YUL.
THEY'RE SO CUTE~! ♡
WHOA, IT'S THE QUEEN AND SHIN.

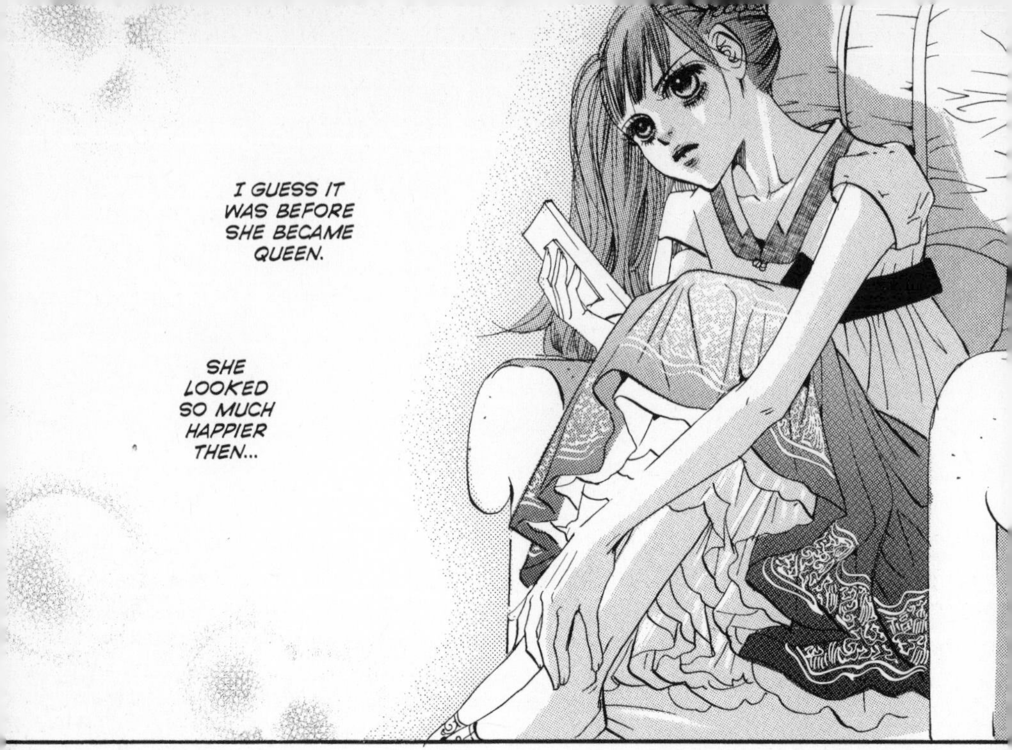
I GUESS IT WAS BEFORE SHE BECAME QUEEN.
SHE LOOKED SO MUCH HAPPIER THEN...

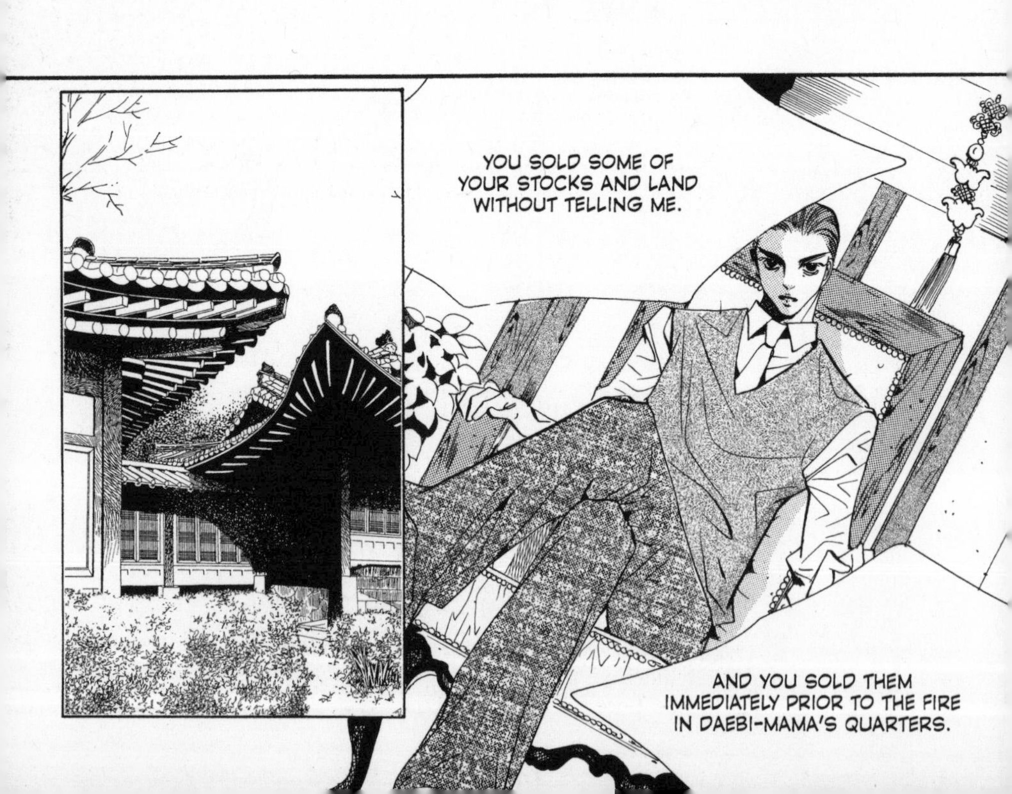
YOU SOLD SOME OF YOUR STOCKS AND LAND WITHOUT TELLING ME.
AND YOU SOLD THEM IMMEDIATELY PRIOR TO THE FIRE IN DAEBI-MAMA'S QUARTERS.

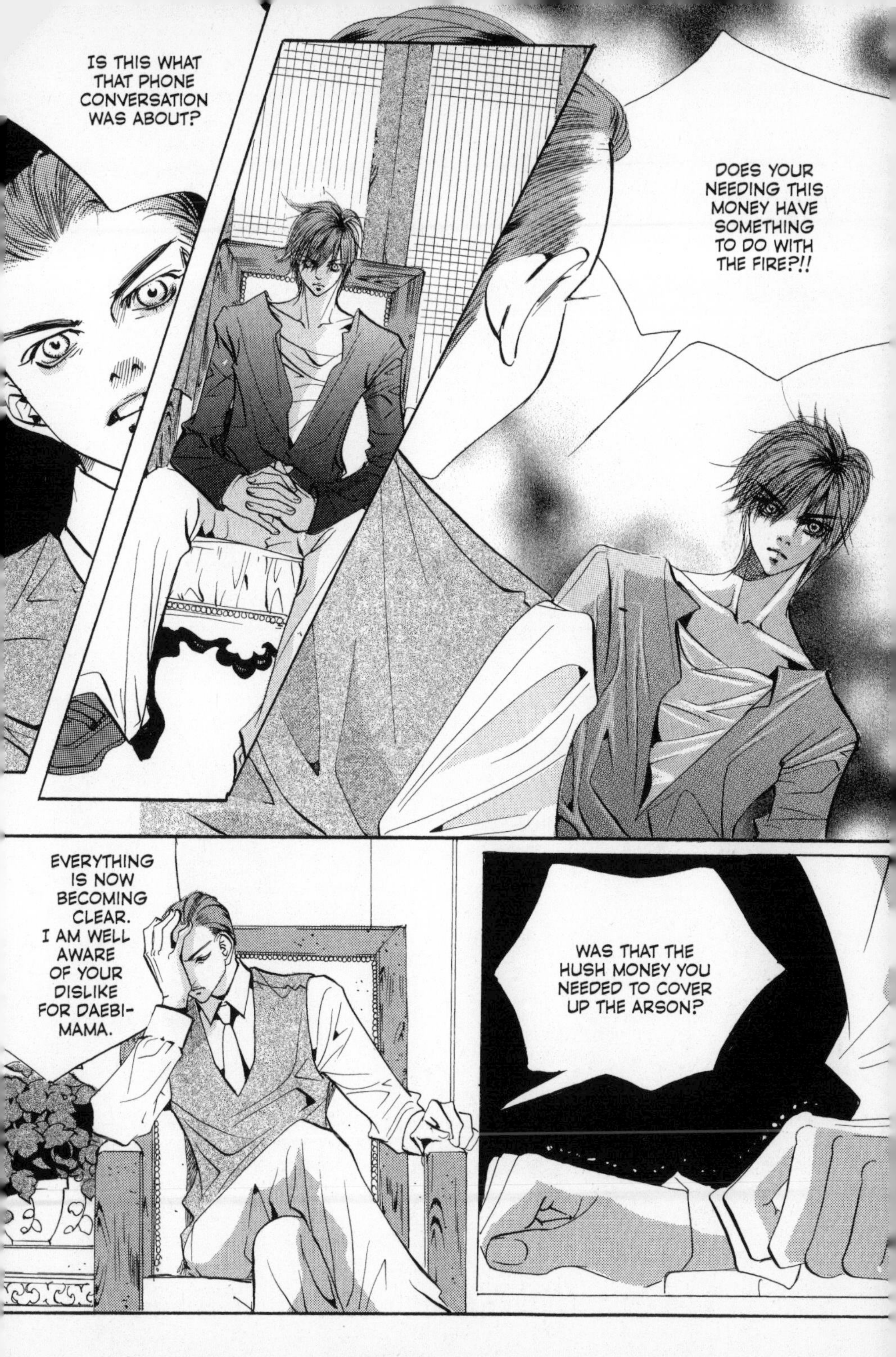
IS THIS WHAT THAT PHONE CONVERSATION WAS ABOUT?
DOES YOUR NEEDING THIS MONEY HAVE SOMETHING TO DO WITH THE FIRE?!!
EVERYTHING IS NOW BECOMING CLEAR. I AM WELL AWARE OF YOUR DISLIKE FOR DAEBI-MAMA.
WAS THAT THE HUSH MONEY YOU NEEDED TO COVER UP THE ARSON?

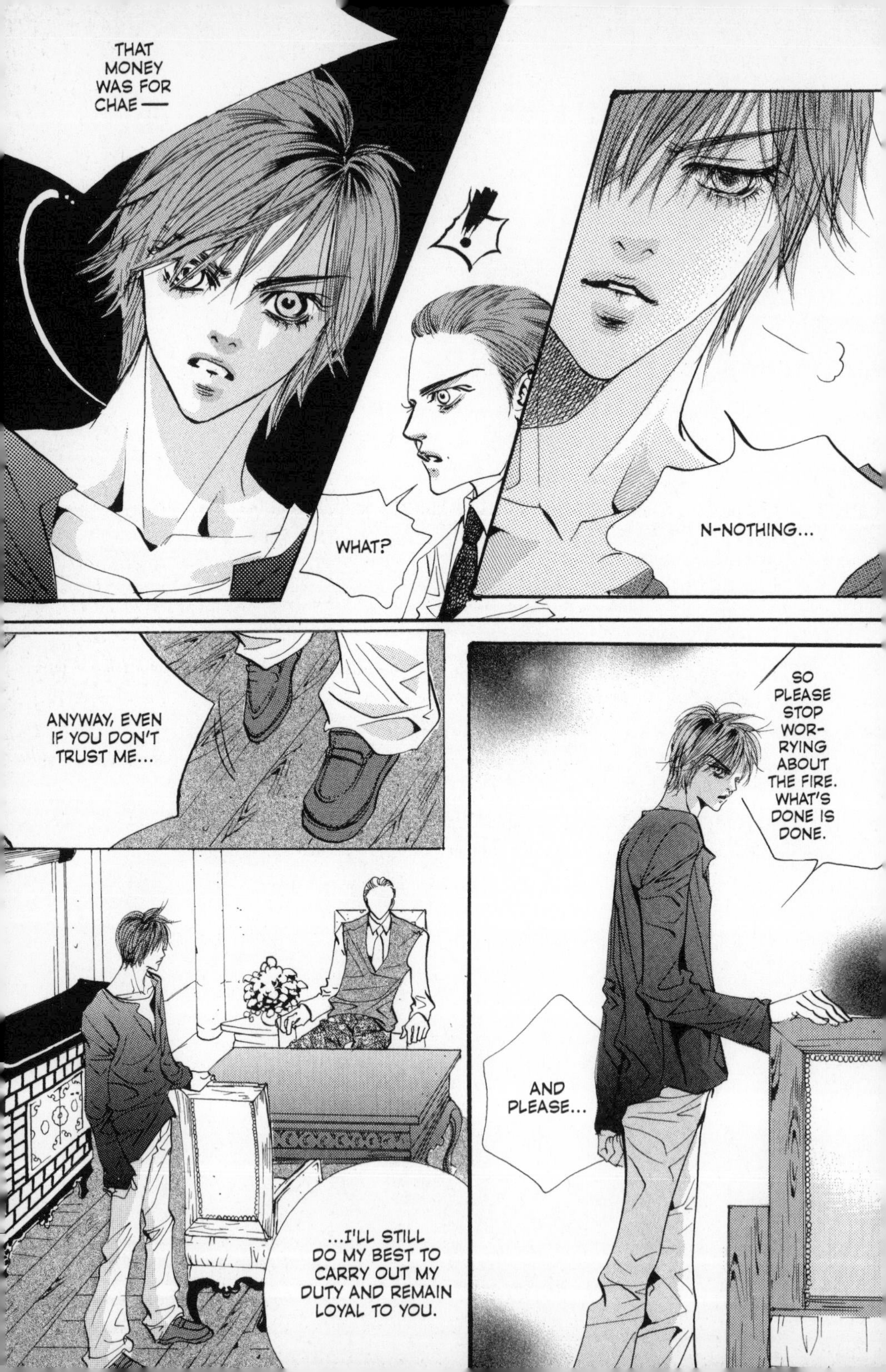
THAT MONEY WAS FOR CHAE—
!
WHAT?
N-NOTHING...
ANYWAY, EVEN IF YOU DON'T TRUST ME...
...I'LL STILL DO MY BEST TO CARRY OUT MY DUTY AND REMAIN LOYAL TO YOU.
SO PLEASE STOP WOR-RYING ABOUT THE FIRE. WHAT'S DONE IS DONE.
AND PLEASE...

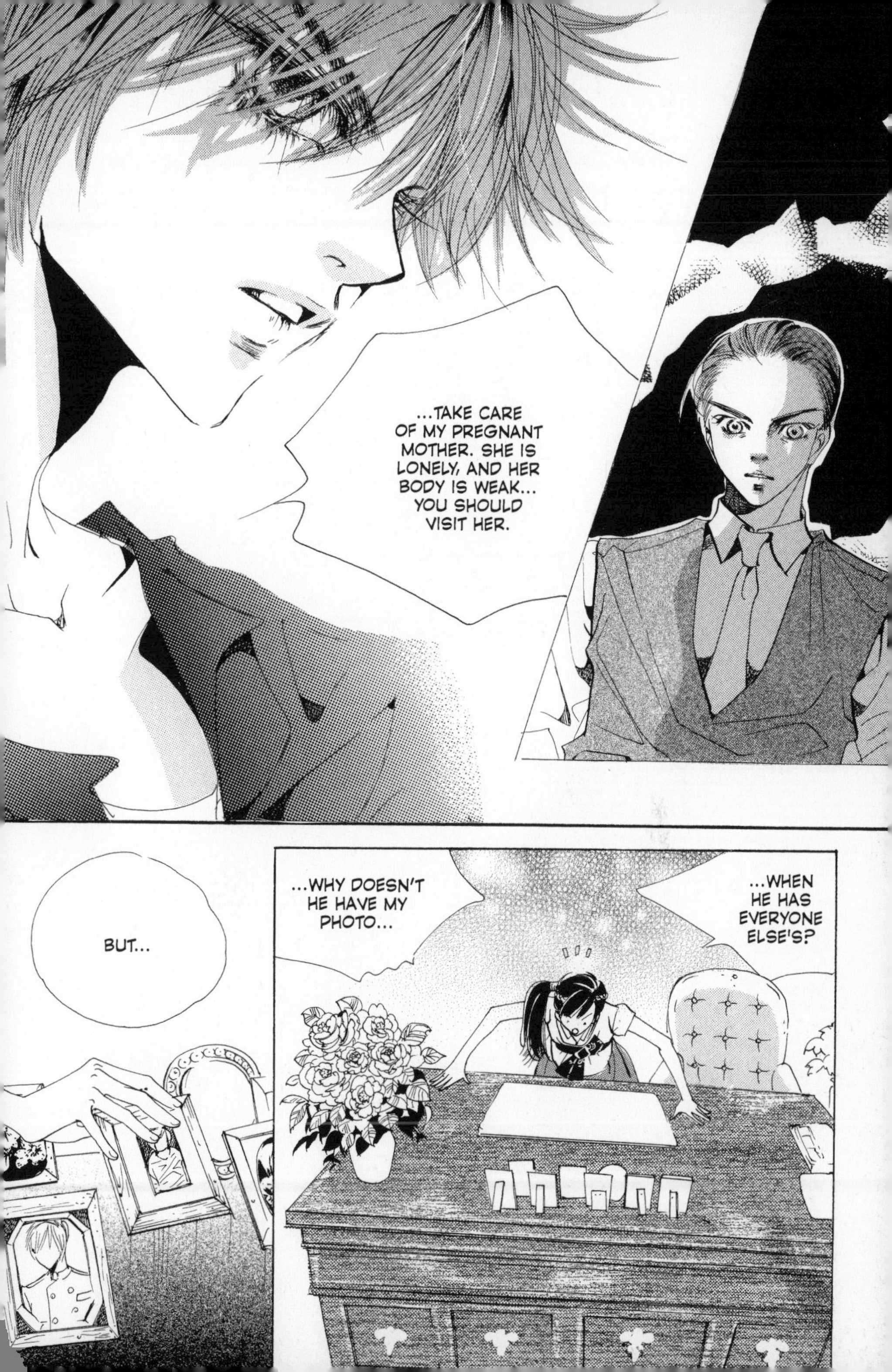
...TAKE CARE OF MY PREGNANT MOTHER. SHE IS LONELY, AND HER BODY IS WEAK... YOU SHOULD VISIT HER.
BUT...
...WHY DOESN'T HE HAVE MY PHOTO...
...WHEN HE HAS EVERYONE ELSE'S?

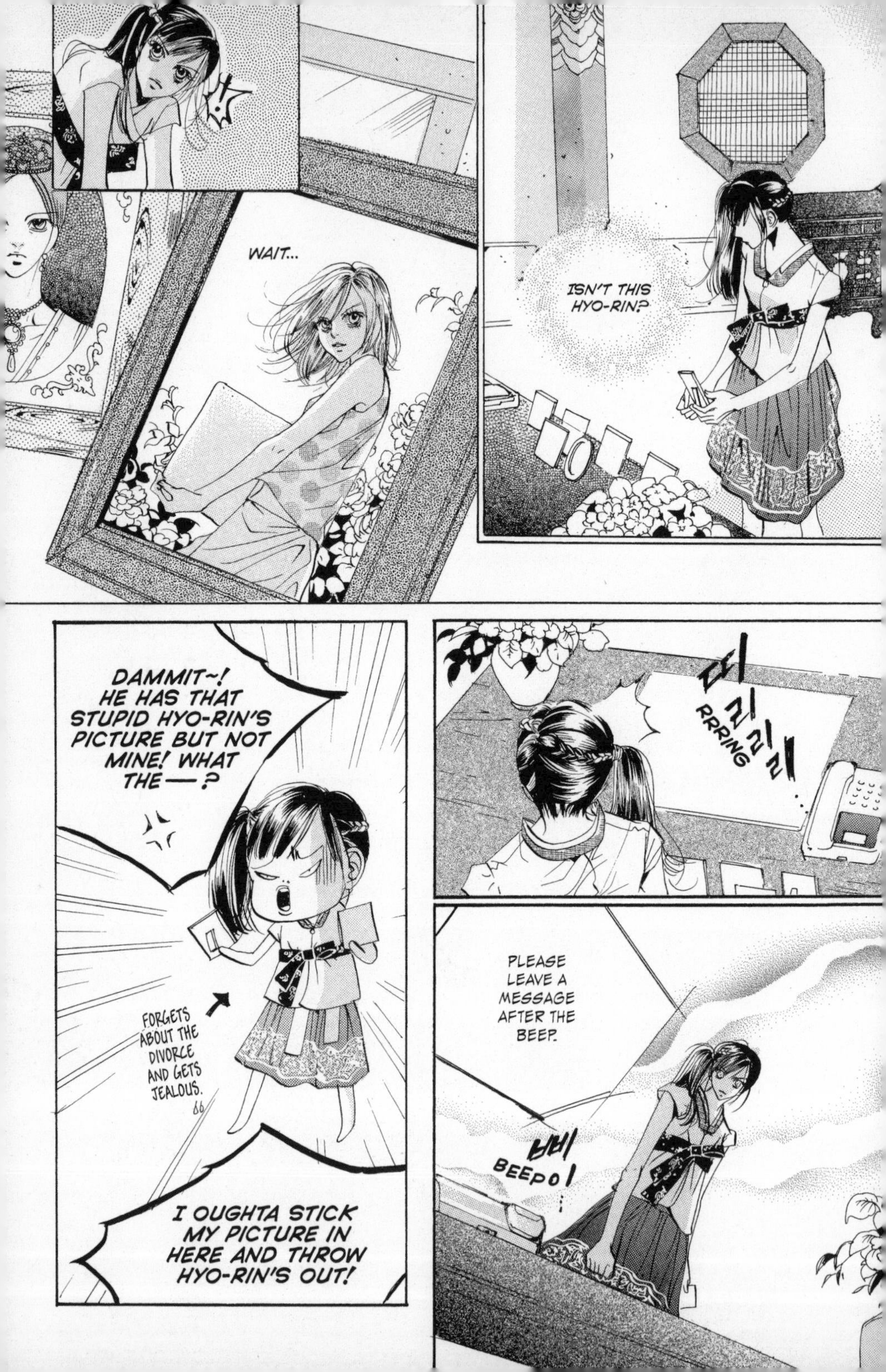

WAIT...
ISN'T THIS HYO-RIN?
DAMMIT~! HE HAS THAT STUPID HYO-RIN'S PICTURE BUT NOT MINE! WHAT THE—?
FORGETS ABOUT THE DIVORCE AND GETS JEALOUS.
I OUGHTA STICK MY PICTURE IN HERE AND THROW HYO-RIN'S OUT!
띠리리리
RRRING
PLEASE LEAVE A MESSAGE AFTER THE BEEP.
삐이
BEEP

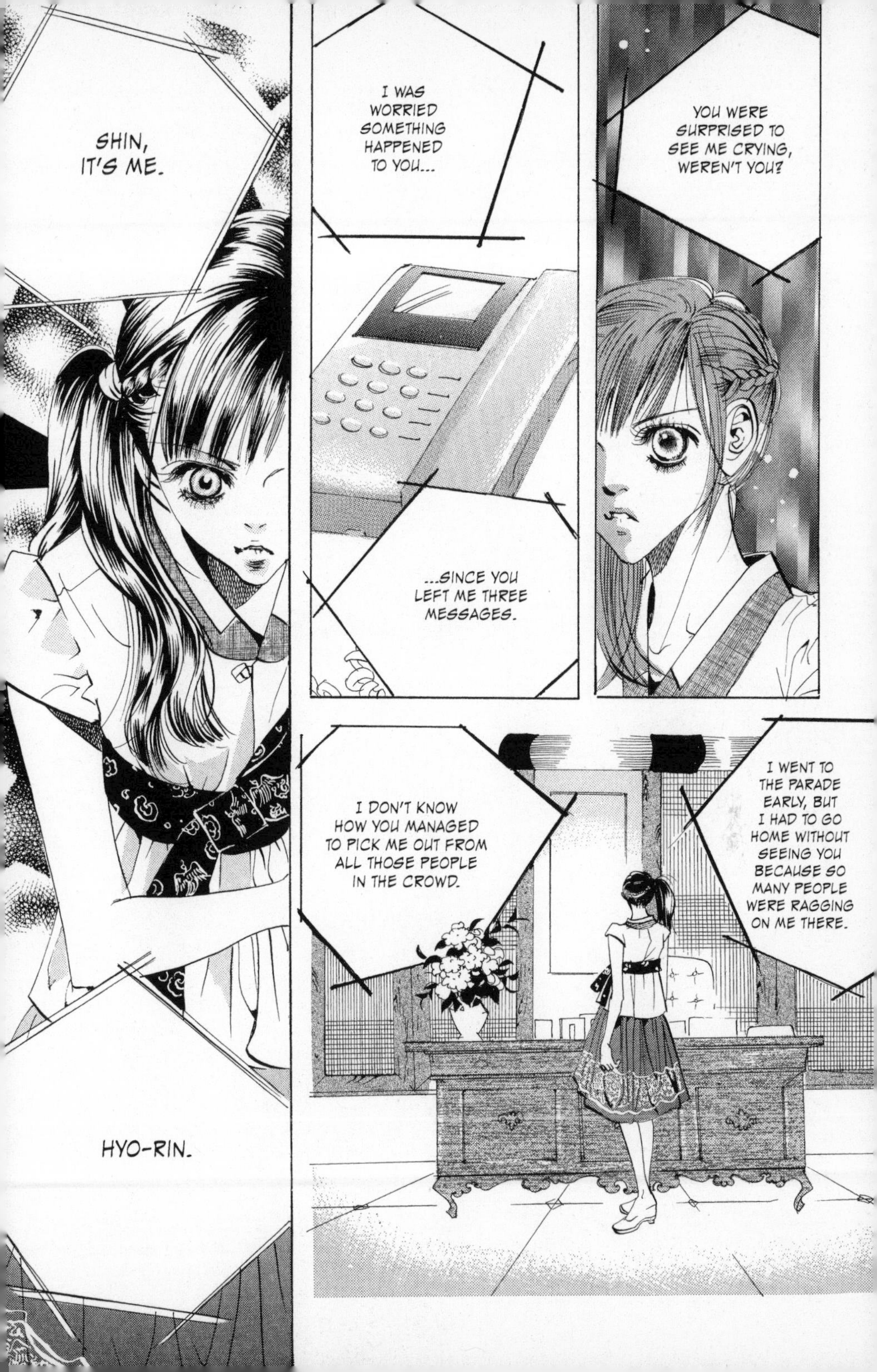
SHIN, IT'S ME.
HYO-RIN.
I WAS WORRIED SOMETHING HAPPENED TO YOU...
...SINCE YOU LEFT ME THREE MESSAGES.
YOU WERE SURPRISED TO SEE ME CRYING, WEREN'T YOU?
I DON'T KNOW HOW YOU MANAGED TO PICK ME OUT FROM ALL THOSE PEOPLE IN THE CROWD.
I WENT TO THE PARADE EARLY, BUT I HAD TO GO HOME WITHOUT SEEING YOU BECAUSE SO MANY PEOPLE WERE RAGGING ON ME THERE.

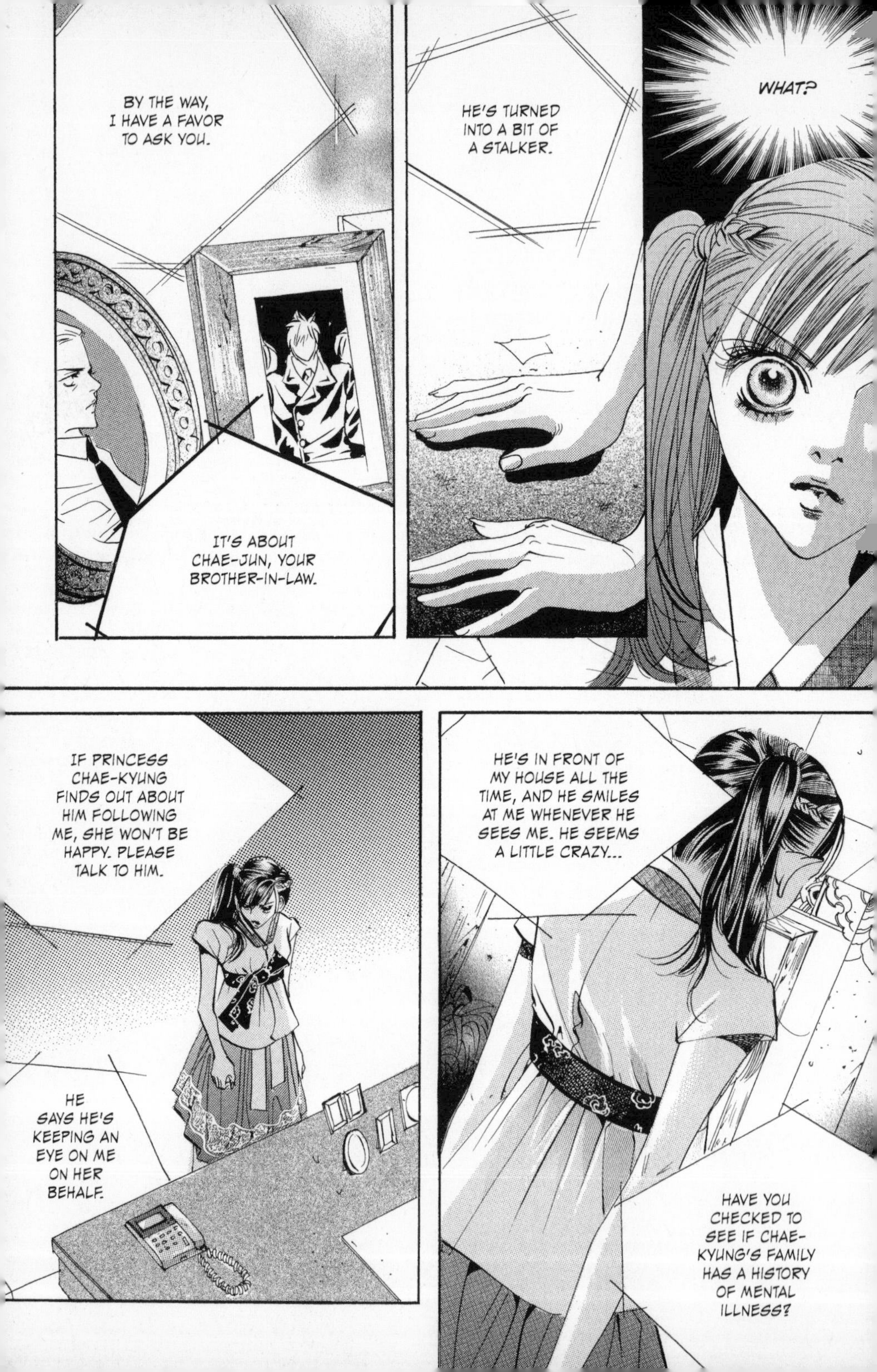
BY THE WAY, I HAVE A FAVOR TO ASK YOU.
IT'S ABOUT CHAE-JUN, YOUR BROTHER-IN-LAW.
HE'S TURNED INTO A BIT OF A STALKER.
WHAT?
IF PRINCESS CHAE-KYUNG FINDS OUT ABOUT HIM FOLLOWING ME, SHE WON'T BE HAPPY. PLEASE TALK TO HIM.
HE SAYS HE'S KEEPING AN EYE ON ME ON HER BEHALF.
HE'S IN FRONT OF MY HOUSE ALL THE TIME, AND HE SMILES AT ME WHENEVER HE SEES ME. HE SEEMS A LITTLE CRAZY...
HAVE YOU CHECKED TO SEE IF CHAE-KYUNG'S FAMILY HAS A HISTORY OF MENTAL ILLNESS?

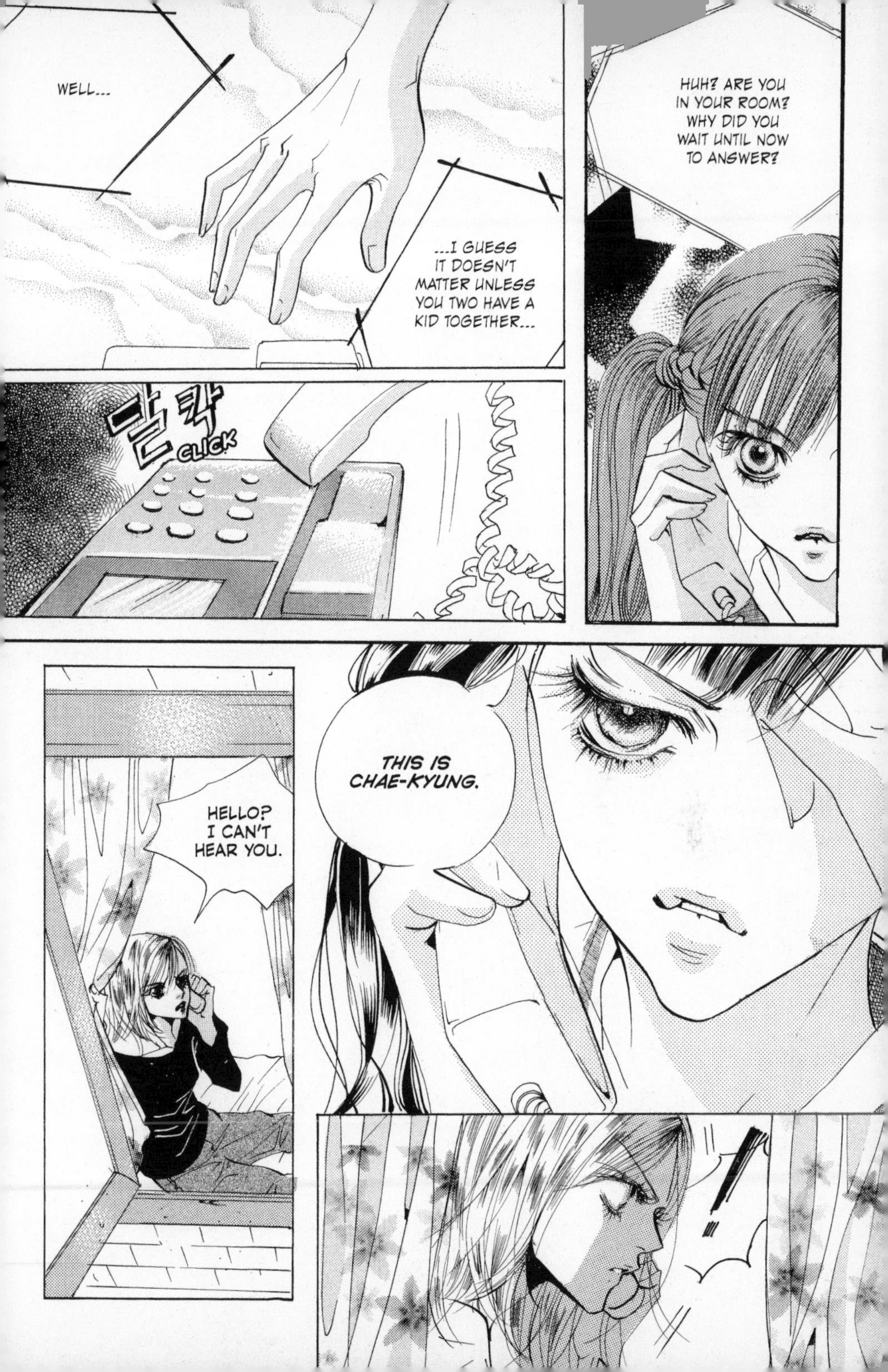
WELL...
...I GUESS IT DOESN'T MATTER UNLESS YOU TWO HAVE A KID TOGETHER...
달칵
CLICK
HUH? ARE YOU IN YOUR ROOM? WHY DID YOU WAIT UNTIL NOW TO ANSWER?
HELLO? I CAN'T HEAR YOU.
THIS IS CHAE-KYUNG.
!!

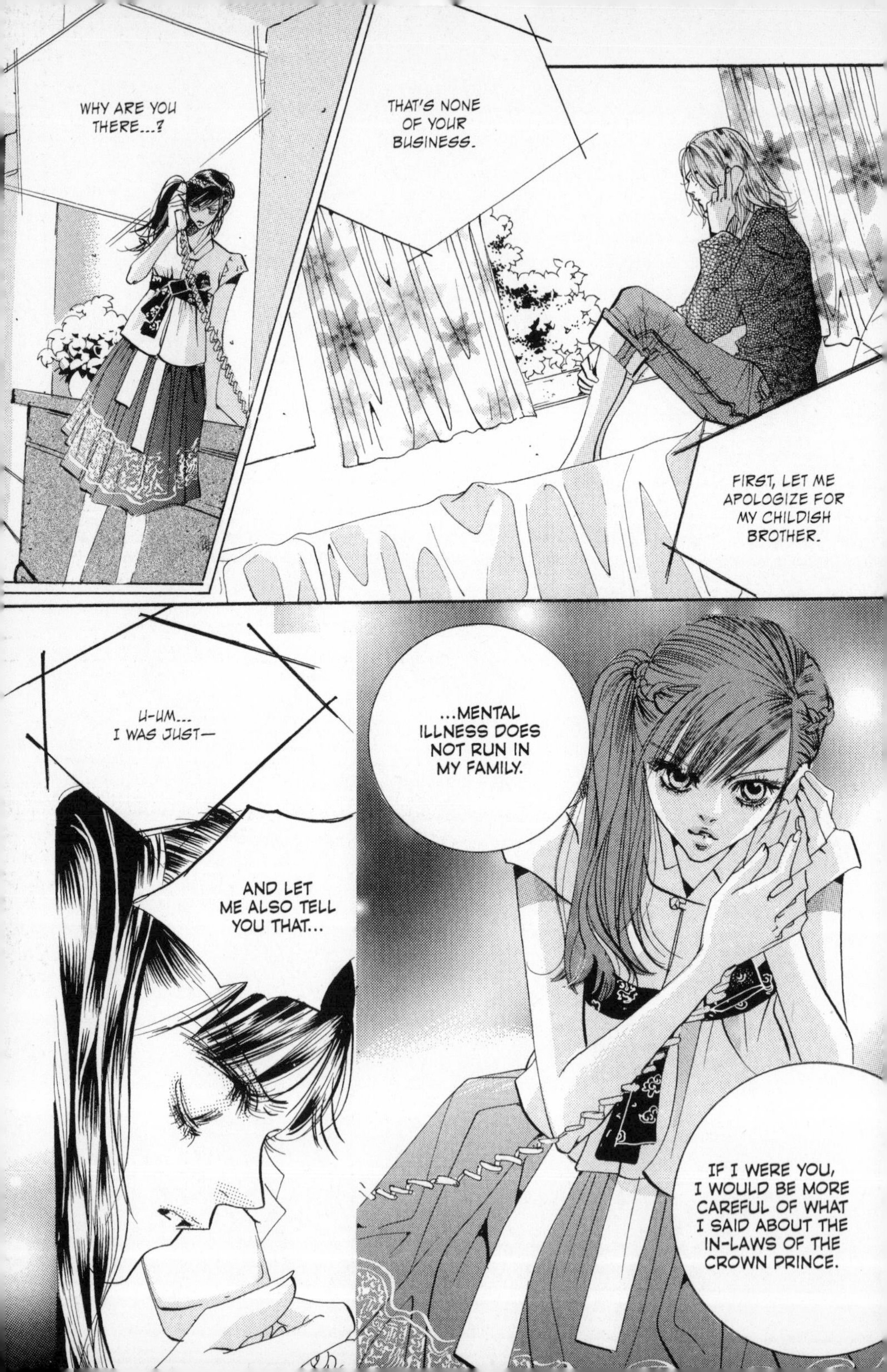
WHY ARE YOU THERE...?
THAT'S NONE OF YOUR BUSINESS.
FIRST, LET ME APOLOGIZE FOR MY CHILDISH BROTHER.
U-UM... I WAS JUST—
AND LET ME ALSO TELL YOU THAT...
...MENTAL ILLNESS DOES NOT RUN IN MY FAMILY.
IF I WERE YOU, I WOULD BE MORE CAREFUL OF WHAT I SAID ABOUT THE IN-LAWS OF THE CROWN PRINCE.

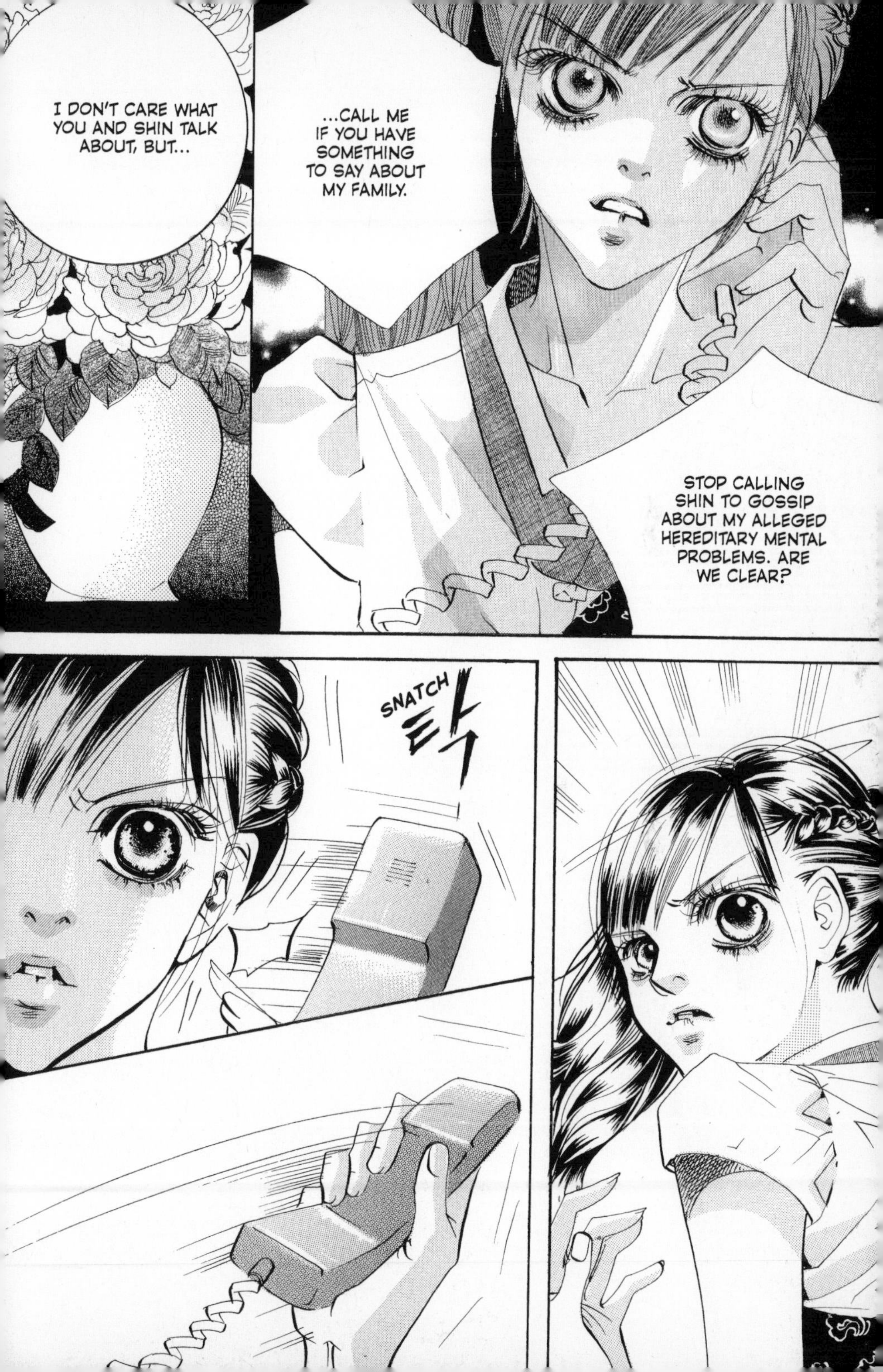
I DON'T CARE WHAT YOU AND SHIN TALK ABOUT, BUT...
...CALL ME IF YOU HAVE SOMETHING TO SAY ABOUT MY FAMILY.
STOP CALLING SHIN TO GOSSIP ABOUT MY ALLEGED HEREDITARY MENTAL PROBLEMS. ARE WE CLEAR?
SNATCH
탁

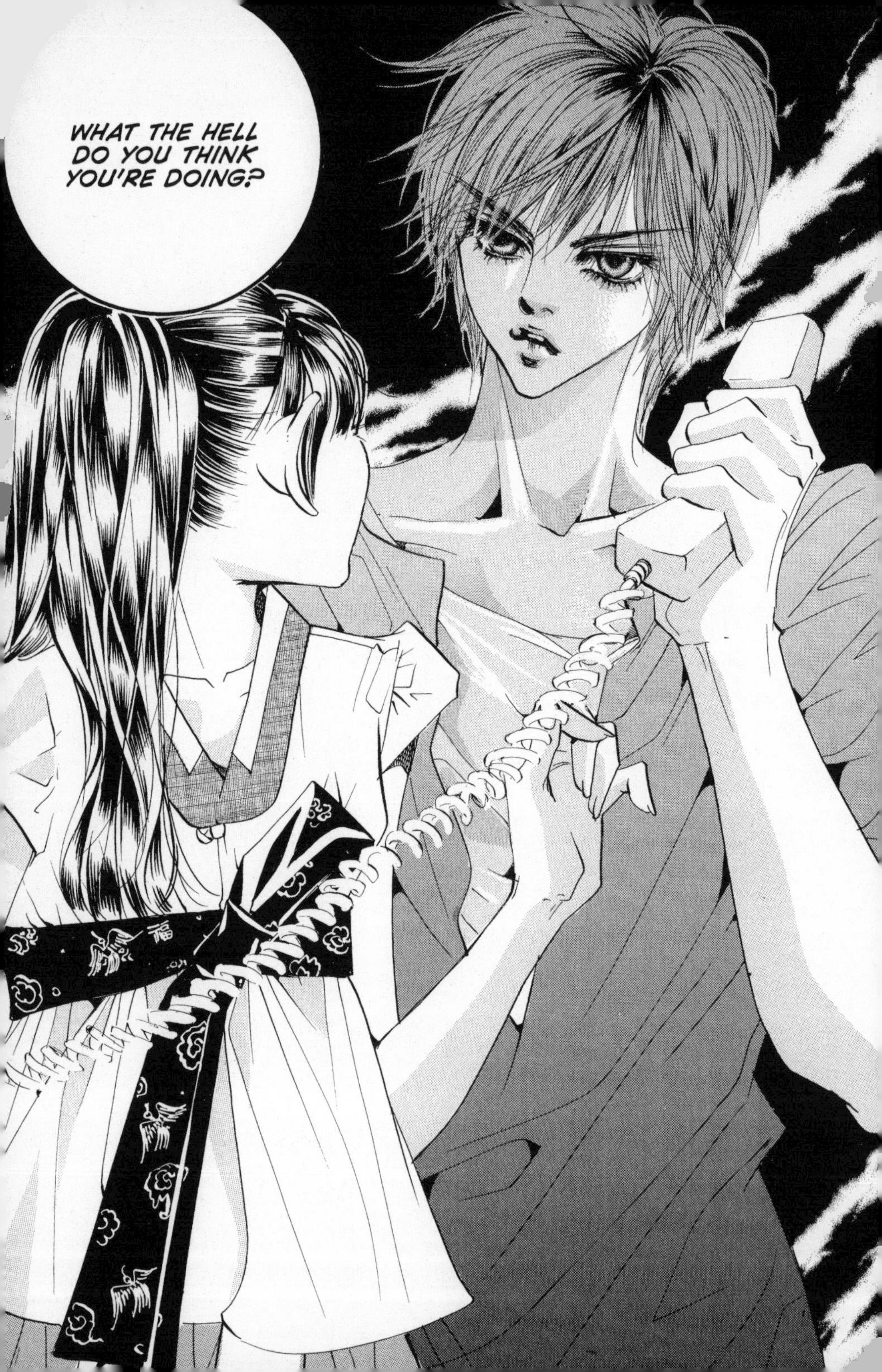
WHAT THE HELL
DO YOU THINK
YOU'RE DOING?

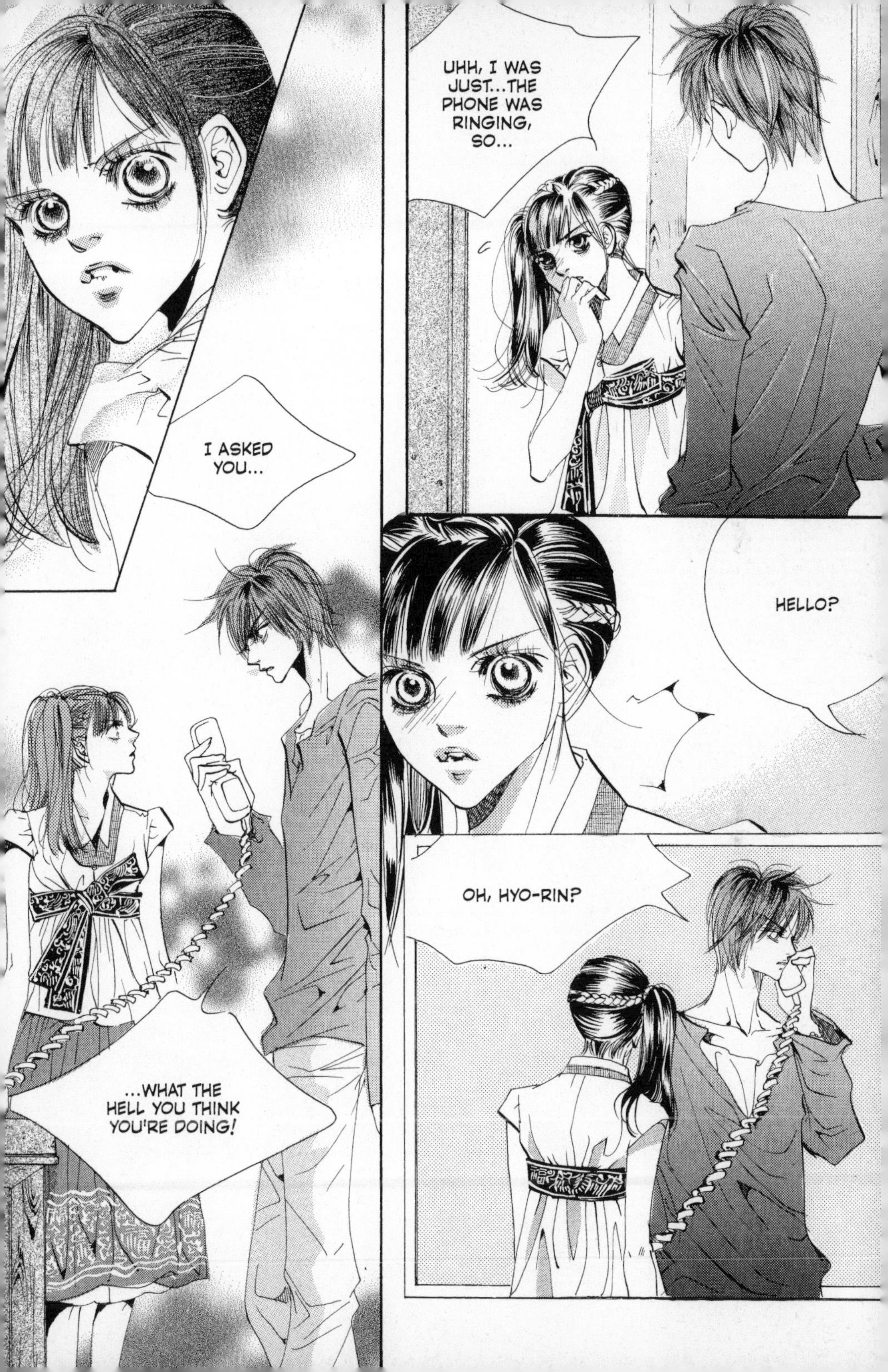
I ASKED YOU...
...WHAT THE HELL YOU THINK YOU'RE DOING!
UHH, I WAS JUST...THE PHONE WAS RINGING, SO...
HELLO?
OH, HYO-RIN?

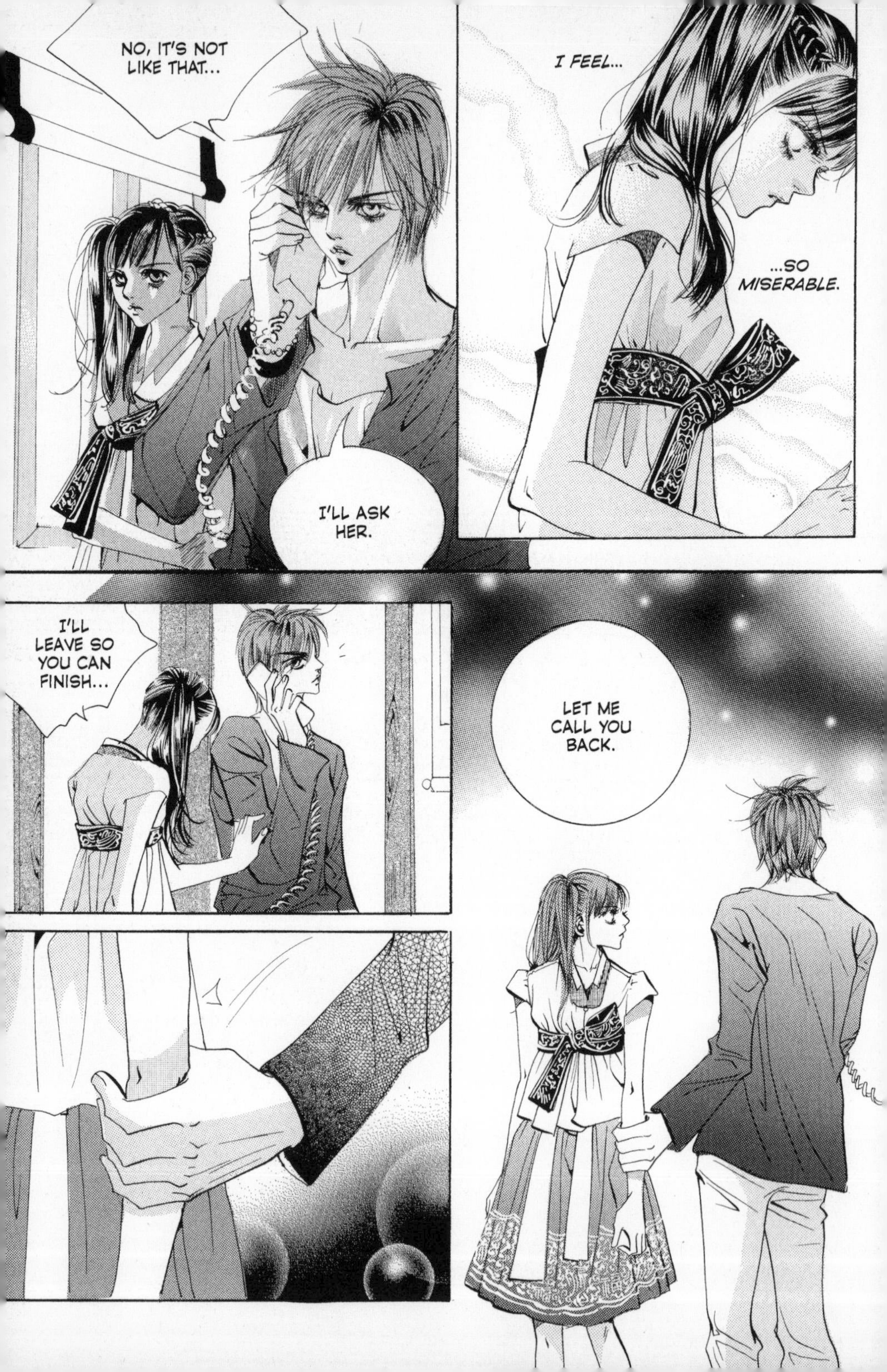
NO, IT'S NOT LIKE THAT...
I'LL ASK HER.
I FEEL...
...SO MISERABLE.
I'LL LEAVE SO YOU CAN FINISH...
LET ME CALL YOU BACK.

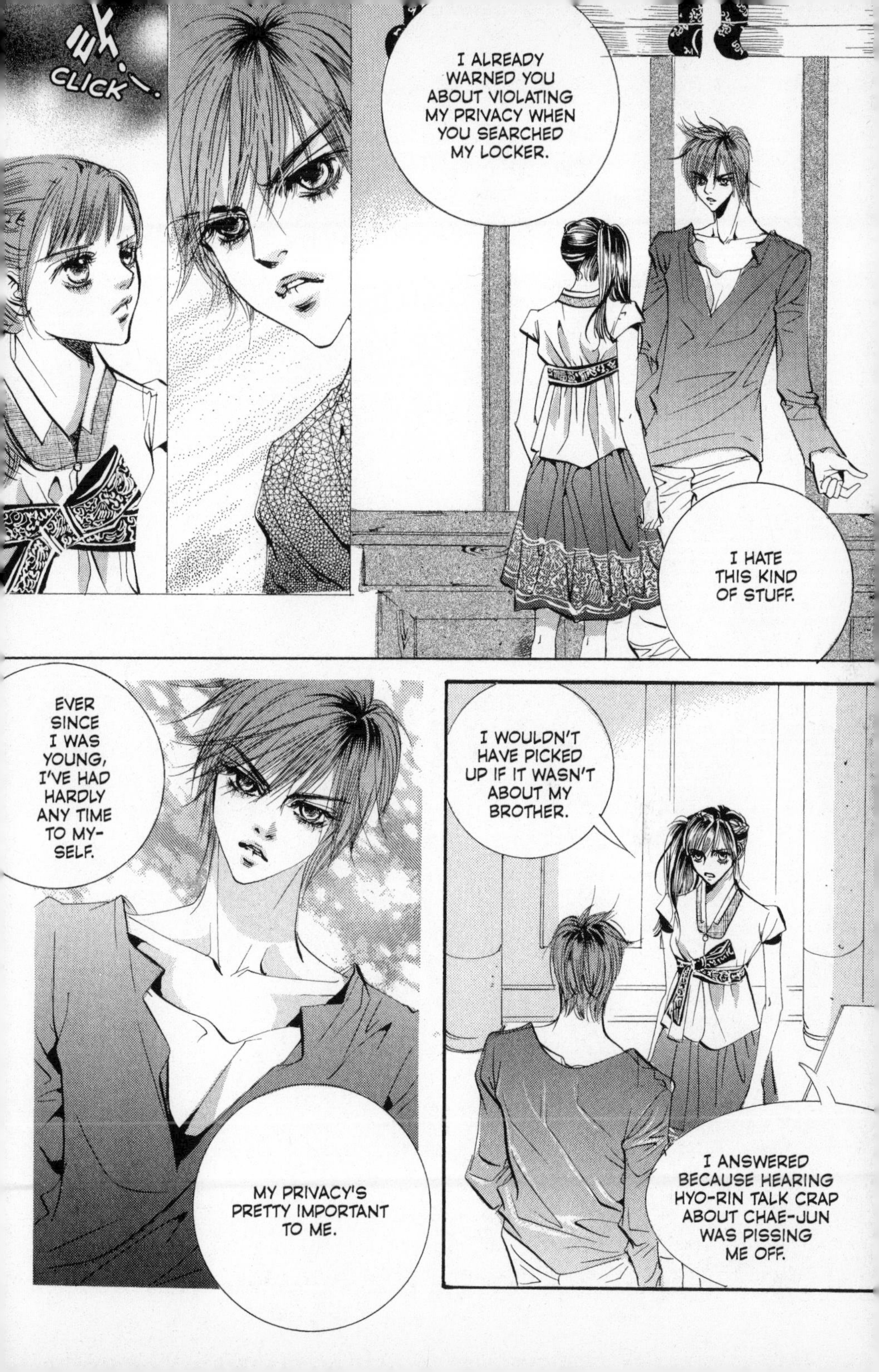
CLICK
I ALREADY WARNED YOU ABOUT VIOLATING MY PRIVACY WHEN YOU SEARCHED MY LOCKER.
I HATE THIS KIND OF STUFF.
EVER SINCE I WAS YOUNG, I'VE HAD HARDLY ANY TIME TO MY-SELF.
MY PRIVACY'S PRETTY IMPORTANT TO ME.
I WOULDN'T HAVE PICKED UP IF IT WASN'T ABOUT MY BROTHER.
I ANSWERED BECAUSE HEARING HYO-RIN TALK CRAP ABOUT CHAE-JUN WAS PISSING ME OFF.

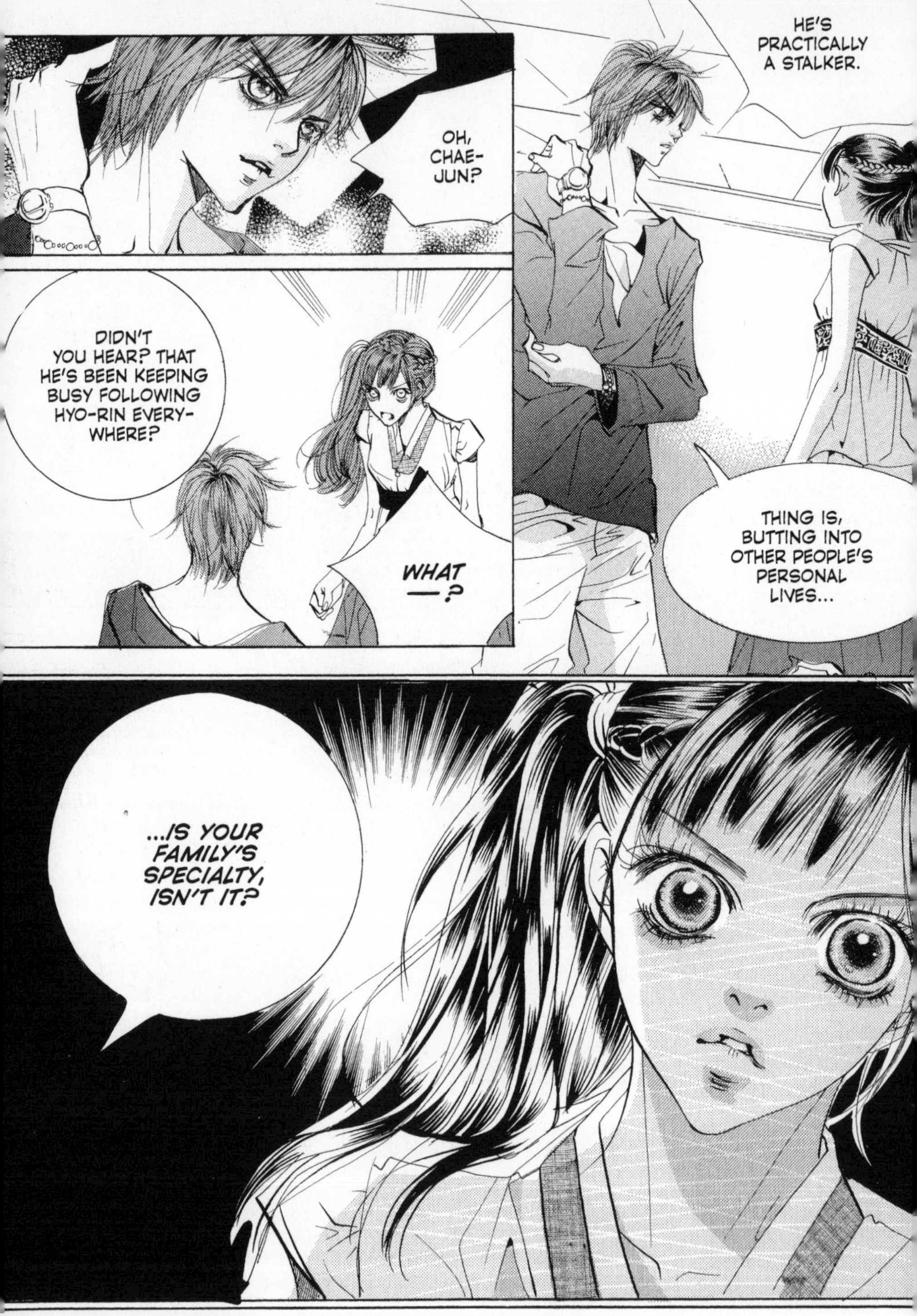
OH, CHAE-JUN?
DIDN'T YOU HEAR? THAT HE'S BEEN KEEPING BUSY FOLLOWING HYO-RIN EVERY-WHERE?
WHAT—?
HE'S PRACTICALLY A STALKER.
THING IS, BUTTING INTO OTHER PEOPLE'S PERSONAL LIVES...
...IS YOUR FAMILY'S SPECIALTY, ISN'T IT?

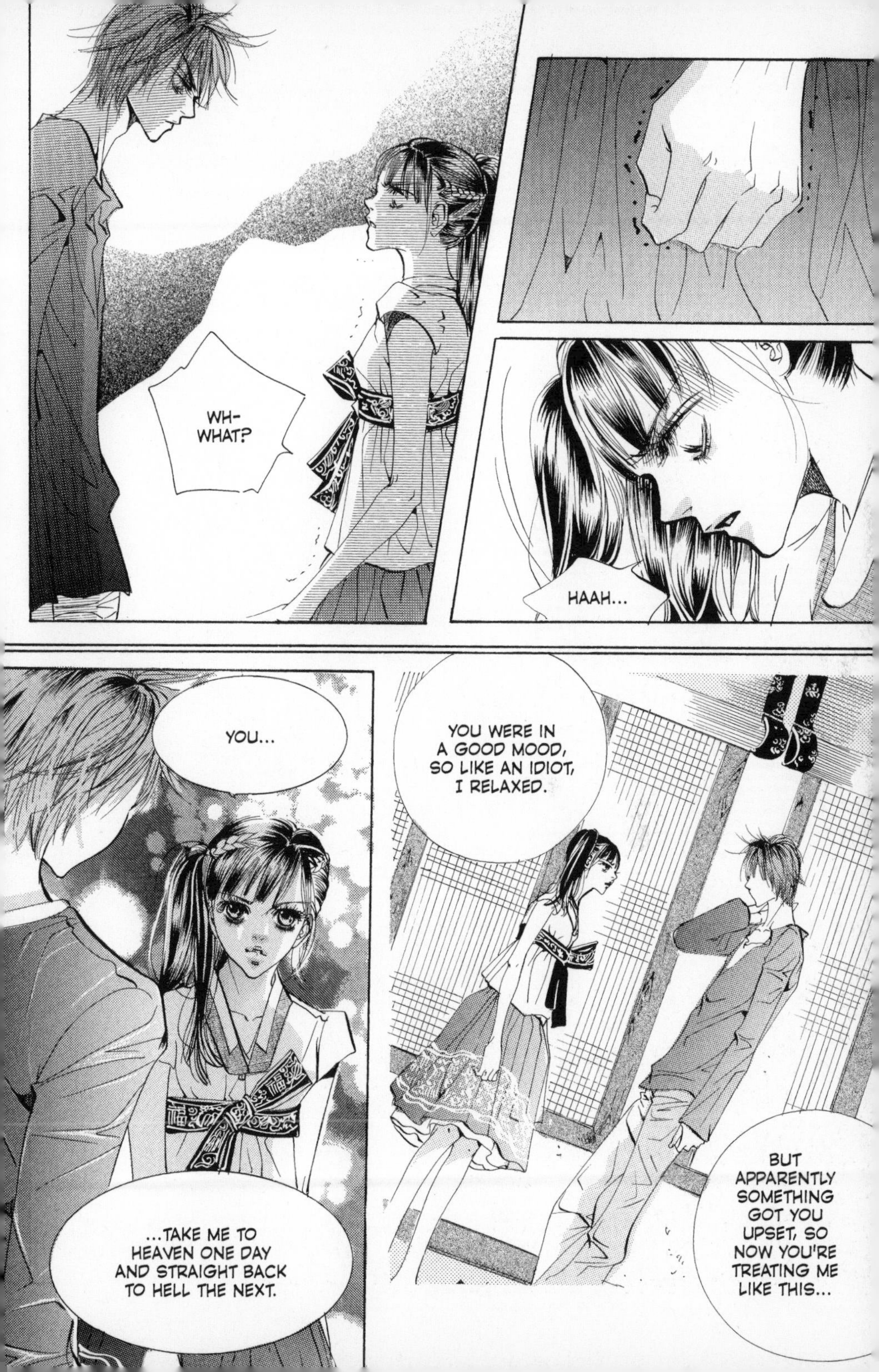
WH-
WHAT?
HAAH...
YOU...
...TAKE ME TO
HEAVEN ONE DAY
AND STRAIGHT BACK
TO HELL THE NEXT.
YOU WERE IN
A GOOD MOOD,
SO LIKE AN IDIOT,
I RELAXED.
BUT
APPARENTLY
SOMETHING
GOT YOU
UPSET, SO
NOW YOU'RE
TREATING ME
LIKE THIS...

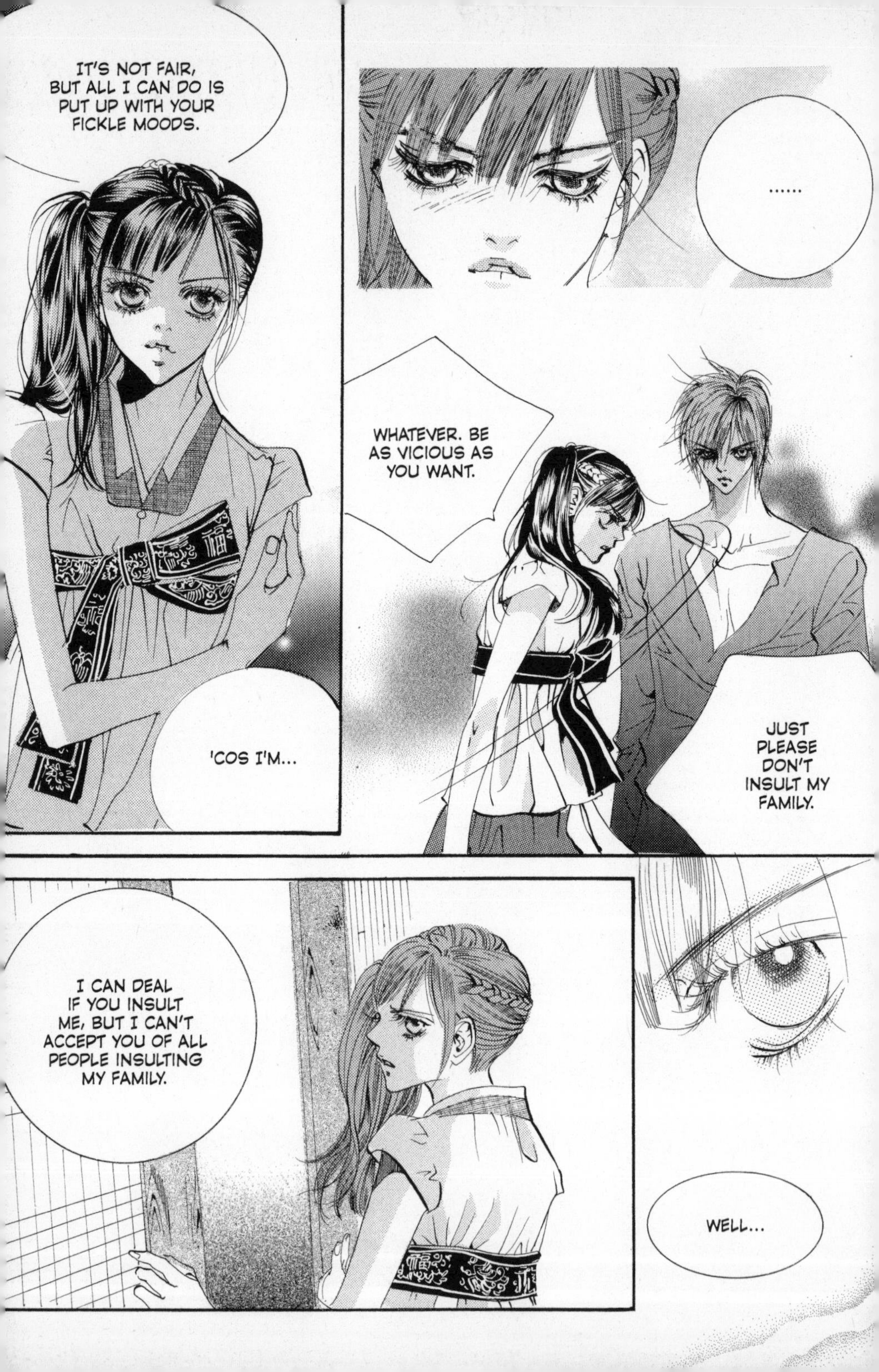
IT'S NOT FAIR, BUT ALL I CAN DO IS PUT UP WITH YOUR FICKLE MOODS.
'COS I'M...
......
WHATEVER. BE AS VICIOUS AS YOU WANT.
JUST PLEASE DON'T INSULT MY FAMILY.
I CAN DEAL IF YOU INSULT ME, BUT I CAN'T ACCEPT YOU OF ALL PEOPLE INSULTING MY FAMILY.
WELL...

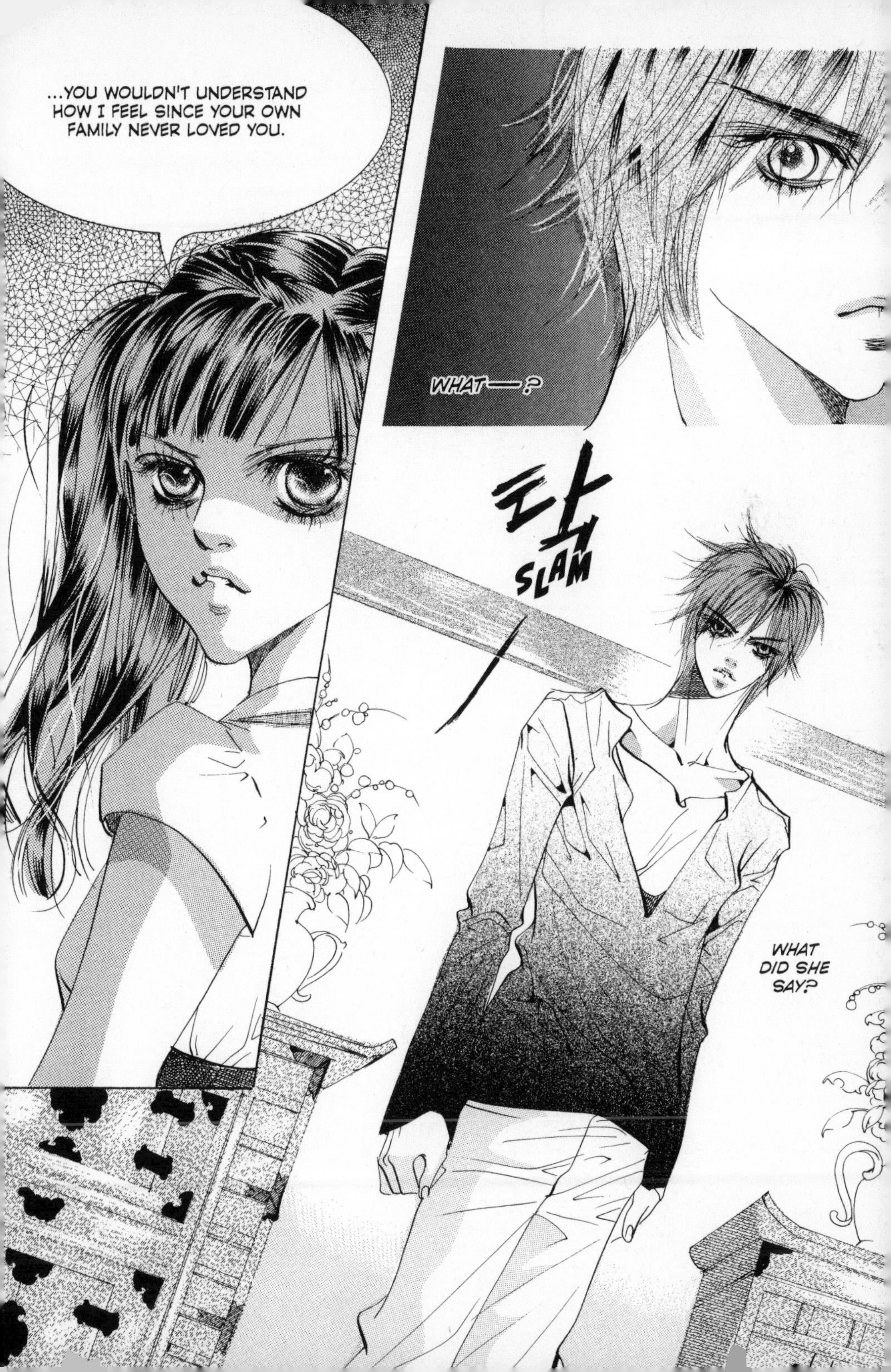
...YOU WOULDN'T UNDERSTAND HOW I FEEL SINCE YOUR OWN FAMILY NEVER LOVED YOU.
WHAT—?
탁
SLAM
WHAT DID SHE SAY?

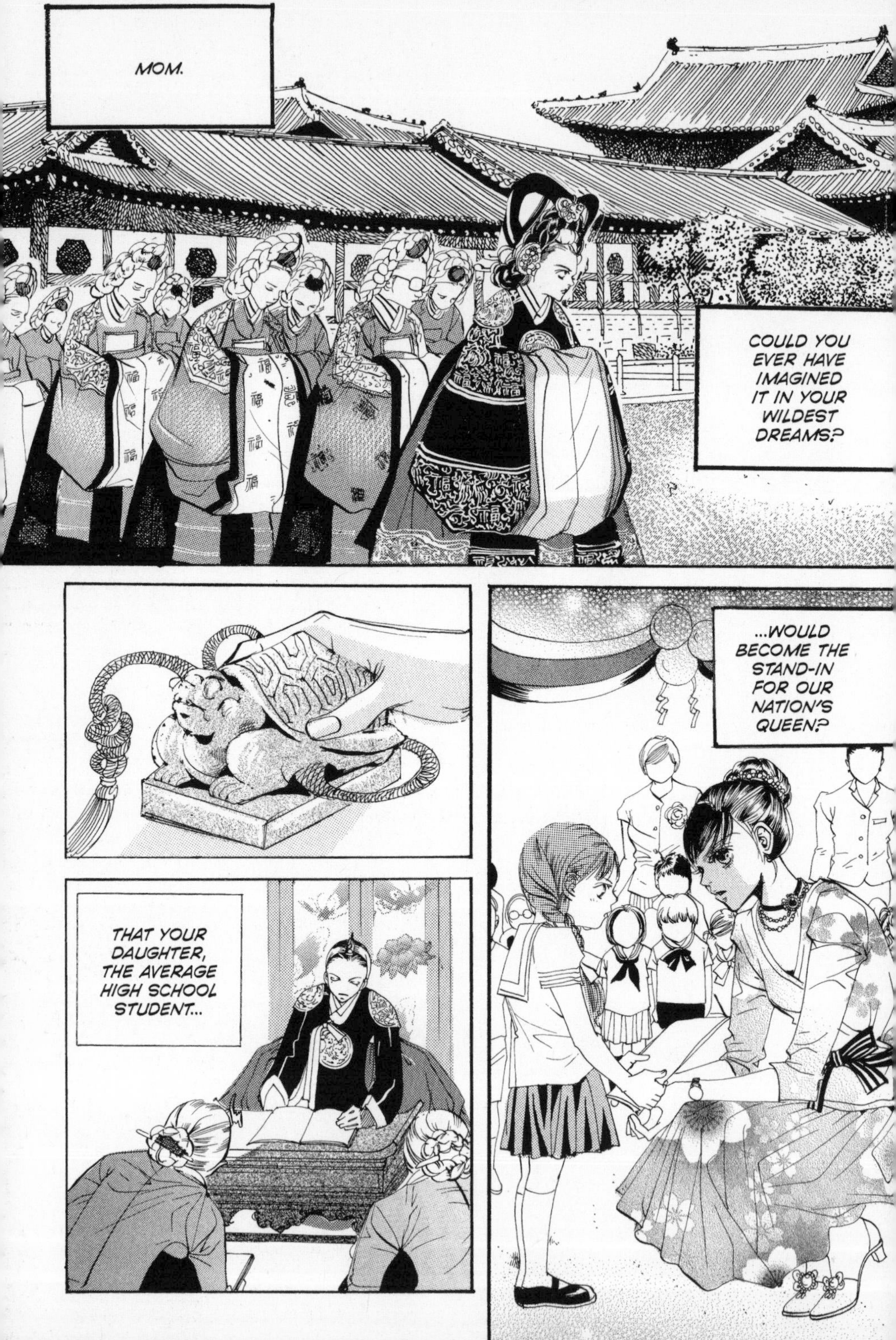
MOM.
COULD YOU EVER HAVE IMAGINED IT IN YOUR WILDEST DREAMS?
THAT YOUR DAUGHTER, THE AVERAGE HIGH SCHOOL STUDENT...
...WOULD BECOME THE STAND-IN FOR OUR NATION'S QUEEN?

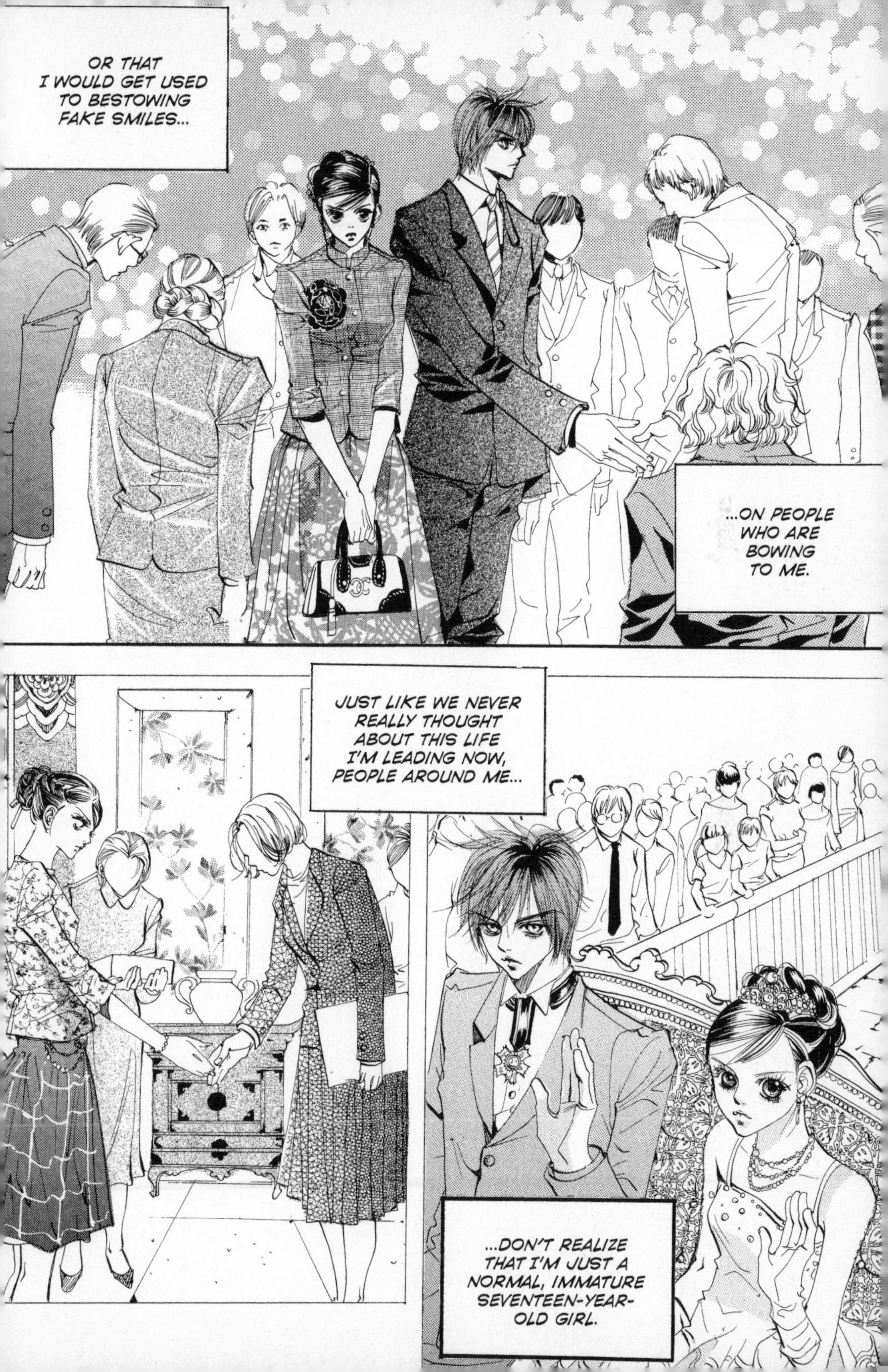
OR THAT I WOULD GET USED TO BESTOWING FAKE SMILES...
...ON PEOPLE WHO ARE BOWING TO ME.
JUST LIKE WE NEVER REALLY THOUGHT ABOUT THIS LIFE I'M LEADING NOW, PEOPLE AROUND ME...
...DON'T REALIZE THAT I'M JUST A NORMAL, IMMATURE SEVENTEEN-YEAR-OLD GIRL.

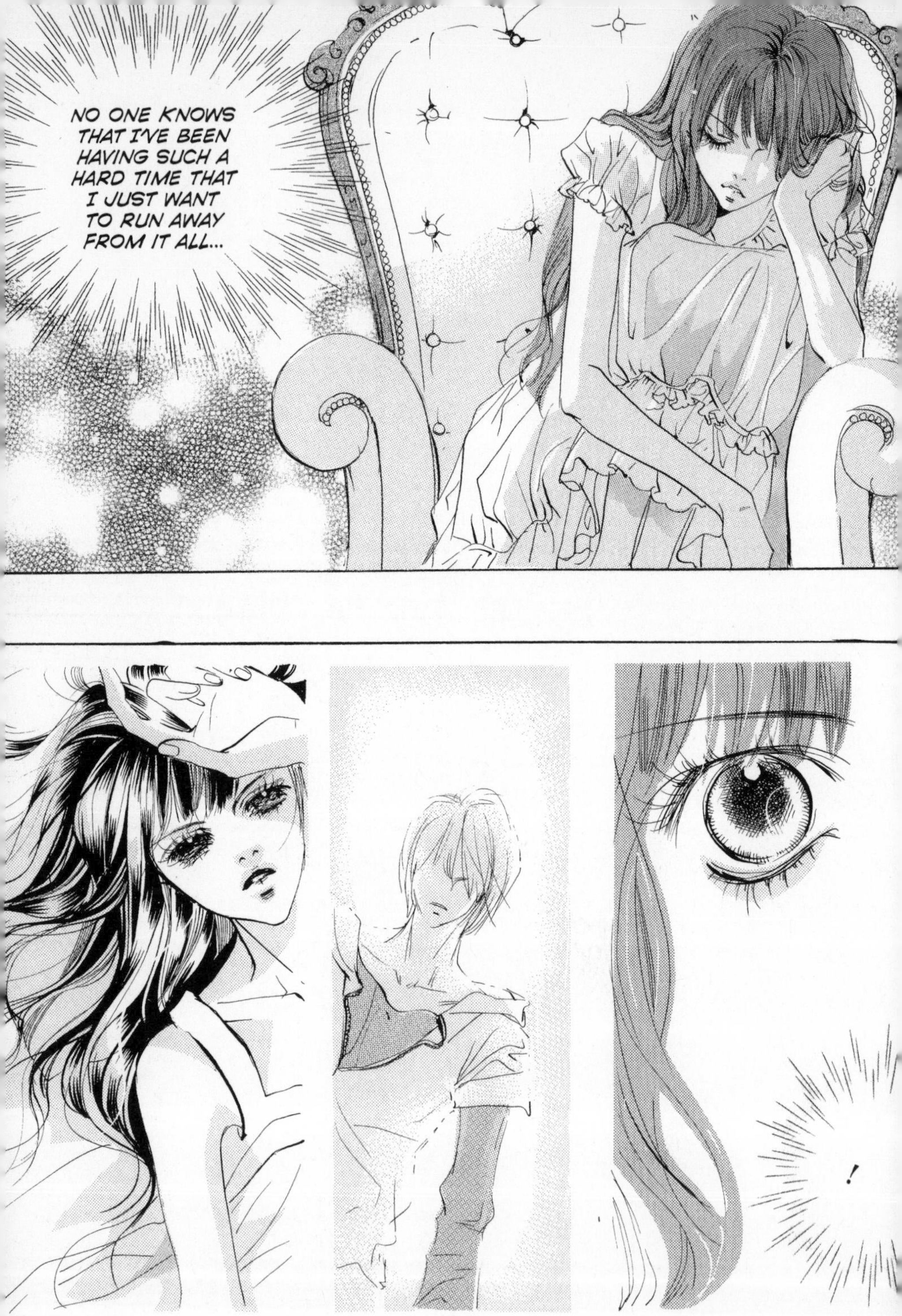
NO ONE KNOWS THAT I'VE BEEN HAVING SUCH A HARD TIME THAT I JUST WANT TO RUN AWAY FROM IT ALL...
!

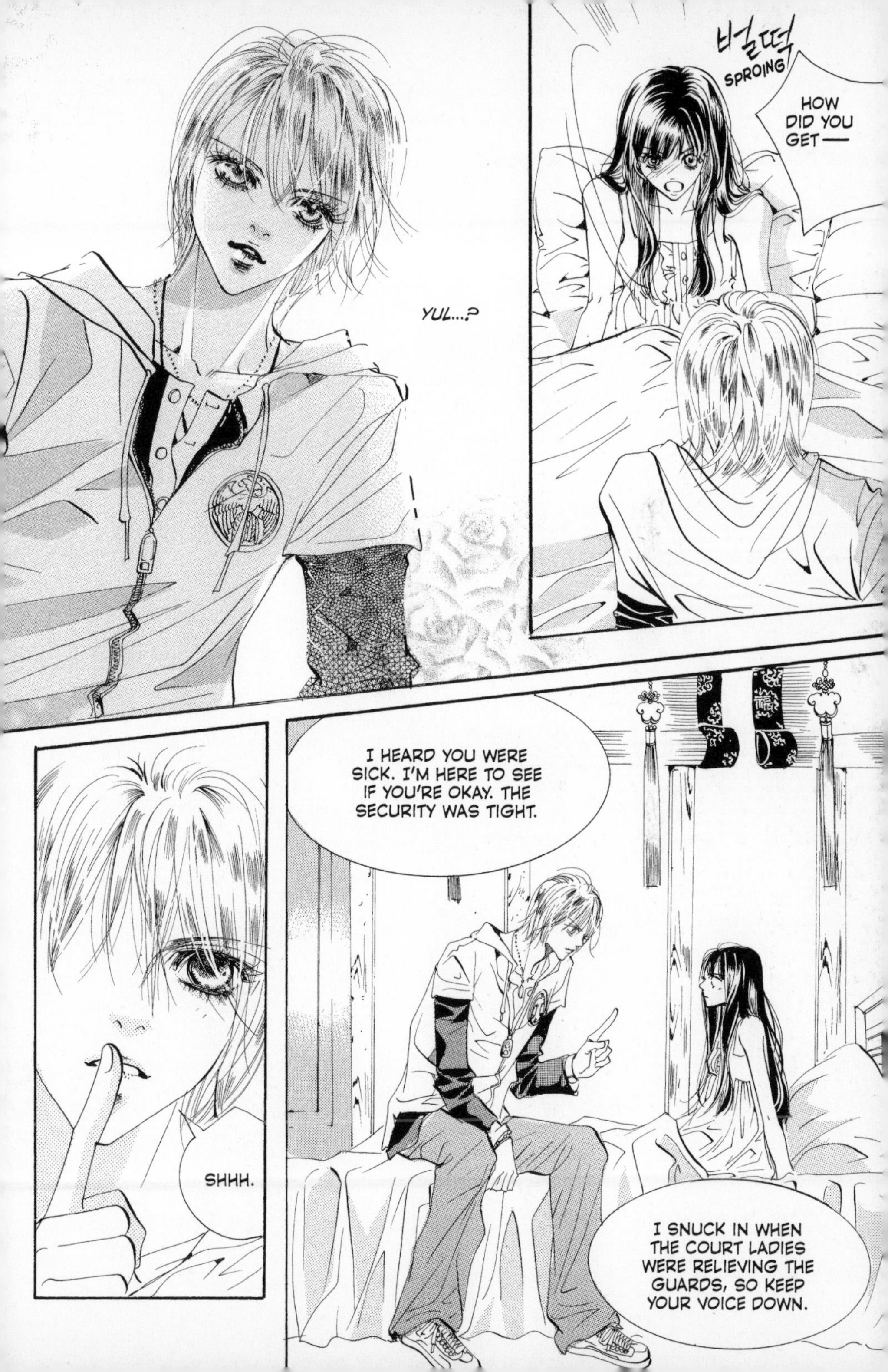
YUL...?
비걸떡
SPROING
HOW DID YOU GET—
SHHH.
I HEARD YOU WERE SICK. I'M HERE TO SEE IF YOU'RE OKAY. THE SECURITY WAS TIGHT.
I SNUCK IN WHEN THE COURT LADIES WERE RELIEVING THE GUARDS, SO KEEP YOUR VOICE DOWN.

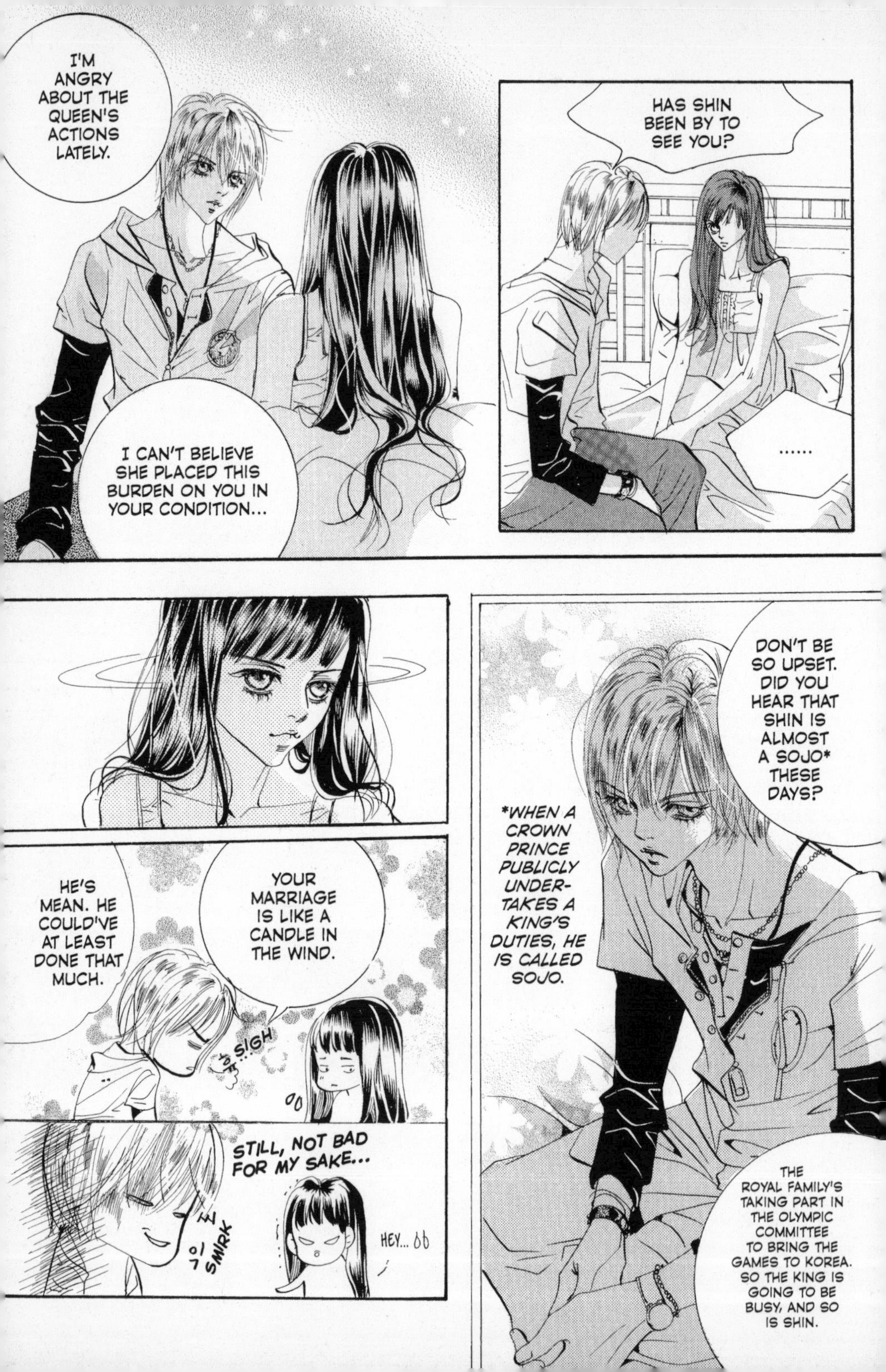
I'M ANGRY ABOUT THE QUEEN'S ACTIONS LATELY.
I CAN'T BELIEVE SHE PLACED THIS BURDEN ON YOU IN YOUR CONDITION...
HAS SHIN BEEN BY TO SEE YOU?
......
HE'S MEAN. HE COULD'VE AT LEAST DONE THAT MUCH.
YOUR MARRIAGE IS LIKE A CANDLE IN THE WIND.
SIGH
STILL, NOT BAD FOR MY SAKE...
SMIRK
HEY...
DON'T BE SO UPSET. DID YOU HEAR THAT SHIN IS ALMOST A SOJO* THESE DAYS?
*WHEN A CROWN PRINCE PUBLICLY UNDER-TAKES A KING'S DUTIES, HE IS CALLED SOJO.
THE ROYAL FAMILY'S TAKING PART IN THE OLYMPIC COMMITTEE TO BRING THE GAMES TO KOREA. SO THE KING IS GOING TO BE BUSY, AND SO IS SHIN.

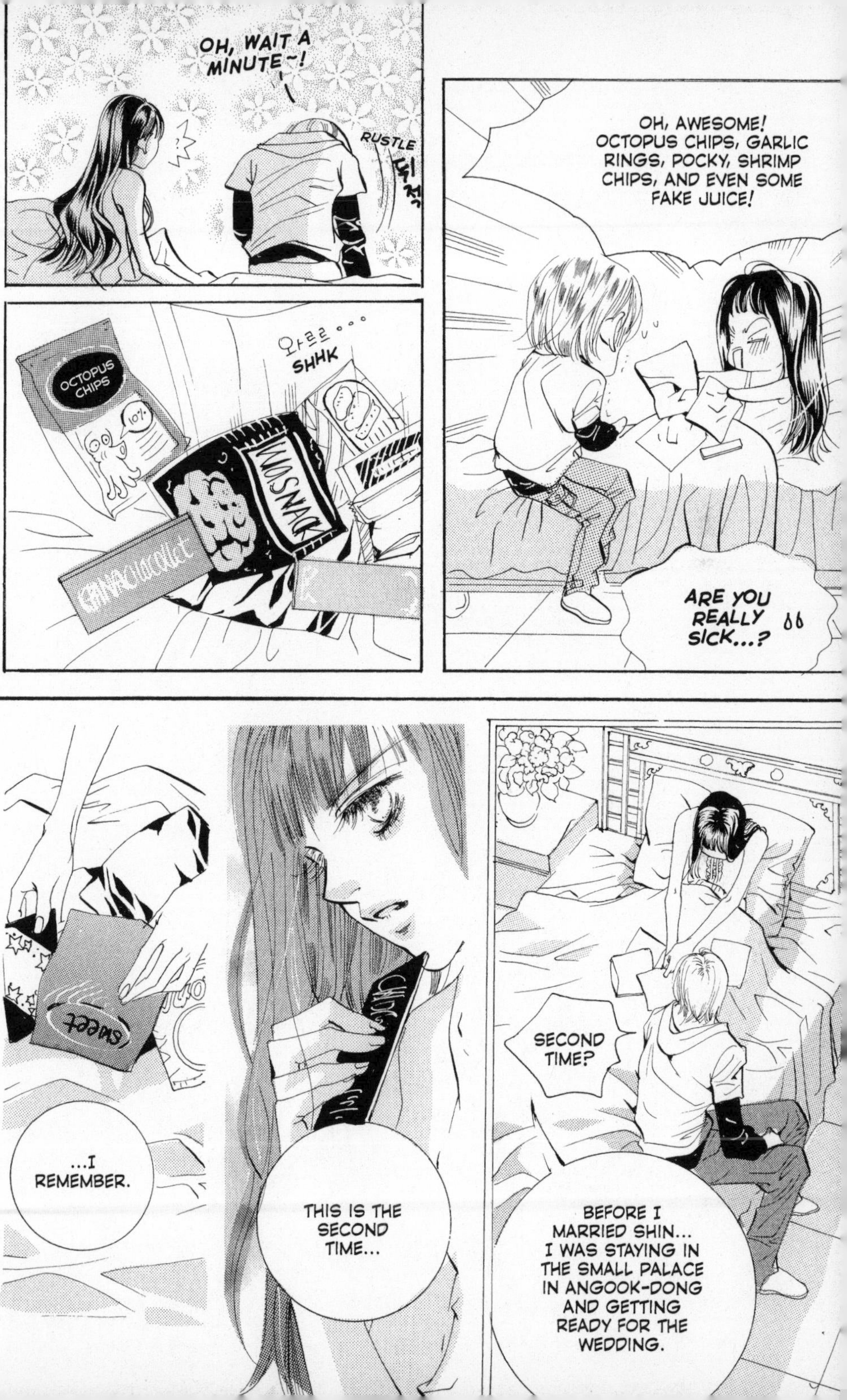
OH, WAIT A MINUTE~!
RUSTLE
뒤적
와르르
SHHK
OCTOPUS CHIPS
OH, AWESOME! OCTOPUS CHIPS, GARLIC RINGS, POCKY, SHRIMP CHIPS, AND EVEN SOME FAKE JUICE!
ARE YOU REALLY SICK...?
...I REMEMBER.
THIS IS THE SECOND TIME...
SECOND TIME?
BEFORE I MARRIED SHIN... I WAS STAYING IN THE SMALL PALACE IN ANGOOK-DONG AND GETTING READY FOR THE WEDDING.

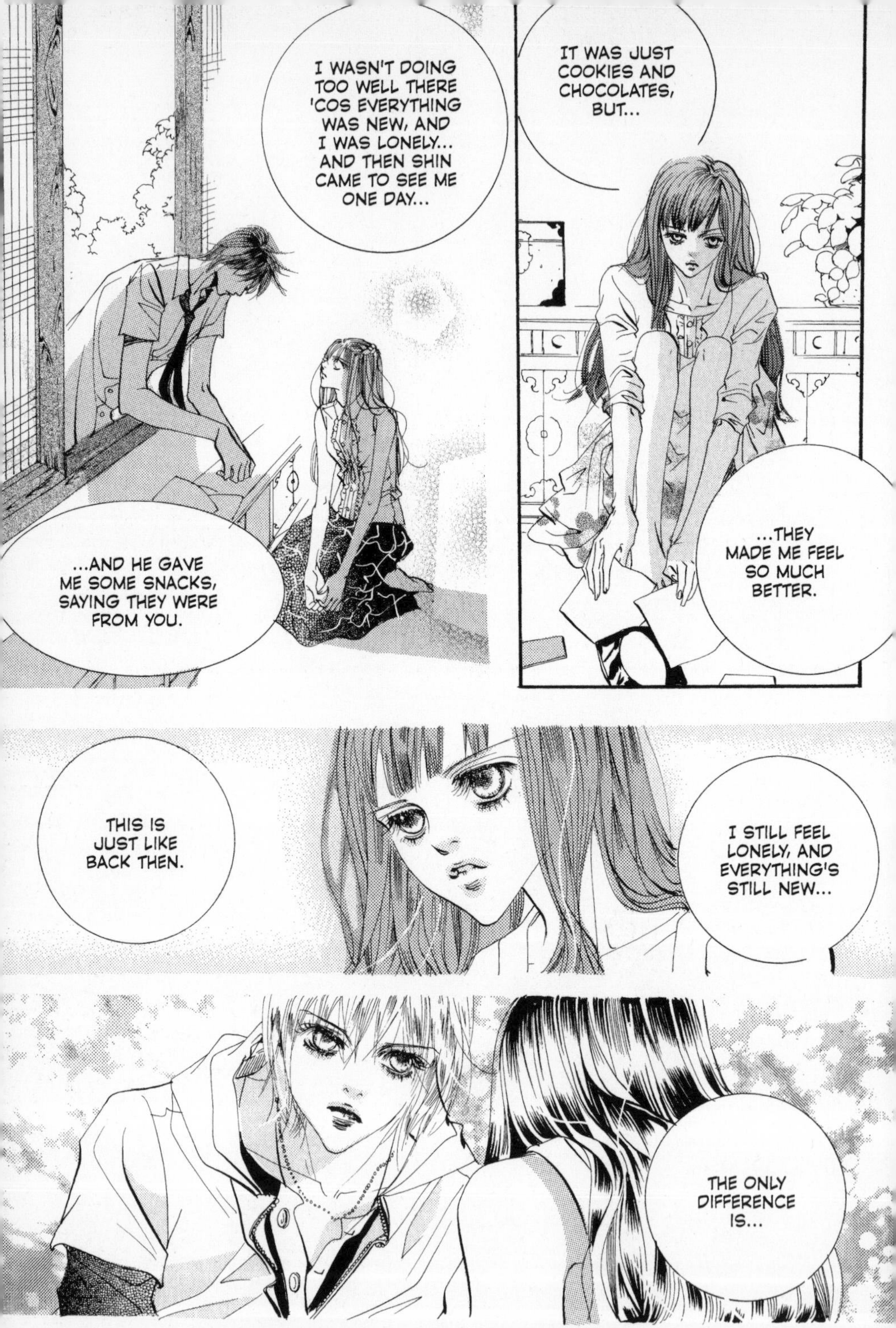
I WASN'T DOING TOO WELL THERE 'COS EVERYTHING WAS NEW, AND I WAS LONELY... AND THEN SHIN CAME TO SEE ME ONE DAY...
...AND HE GAVE ME SOME SNACKS, SAYING THEY WERE FROM YOU.
IT WAS JUST COOKIES AND CHOCOLATES, BUT...
...THEY MADE ME FEEL SO MUCH BETTER.
THIS IS JUST LIKE BACK THEN.
I STILL FEEL LONELY, AND EVERYTHING'S STILL NEW...
THE ONLY DIFFERENCE IS...

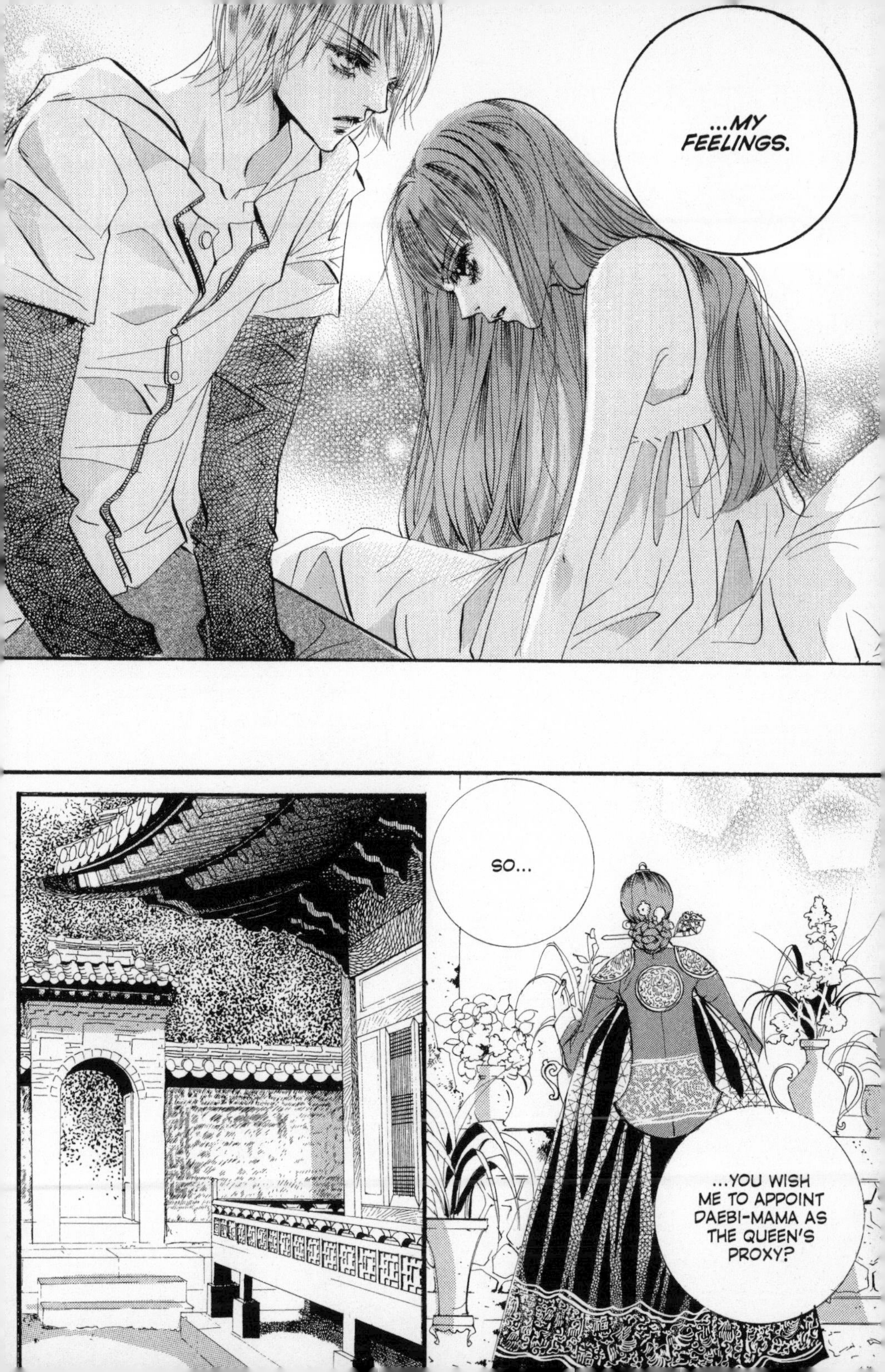
...MY FEELINGS.
SO...
...YOU WISH ME TO APPOINT DAEBI-MAMA AS THE QUEEN'S PROXY?

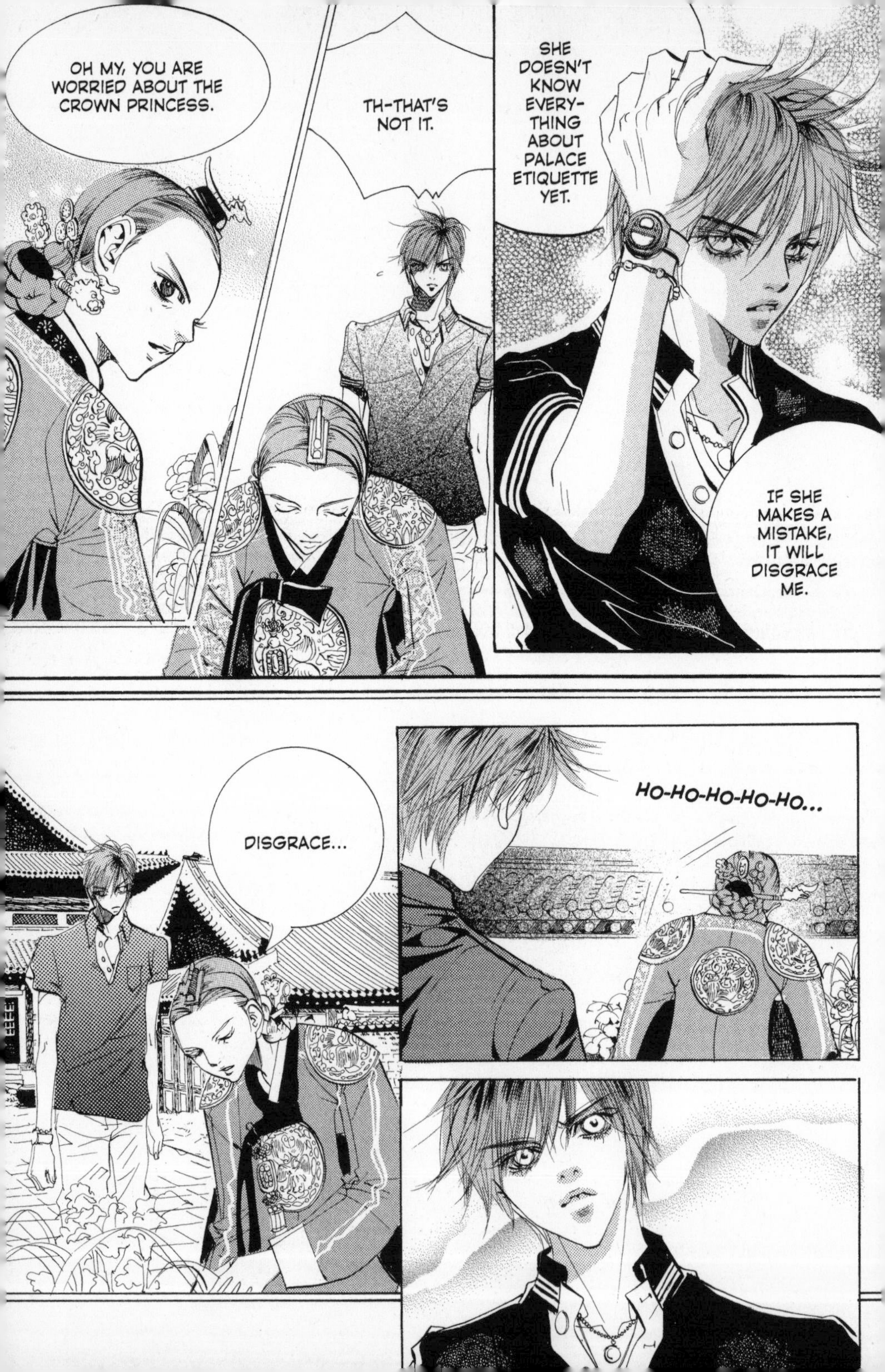
OH MY, YOU ARE WORRIED ABOUT THE CROWN PRINCESS.
TH-THAT'S NOT IT.
SHE DOESN'T KNOW EVERY-THING ABOUT PALACE ETIQUETTE YET.
IF SHE MAKES A MISTAKE, IT WILL DISGRACE ME.
DISGRACE...
HO-HO-HO-HO-HO...

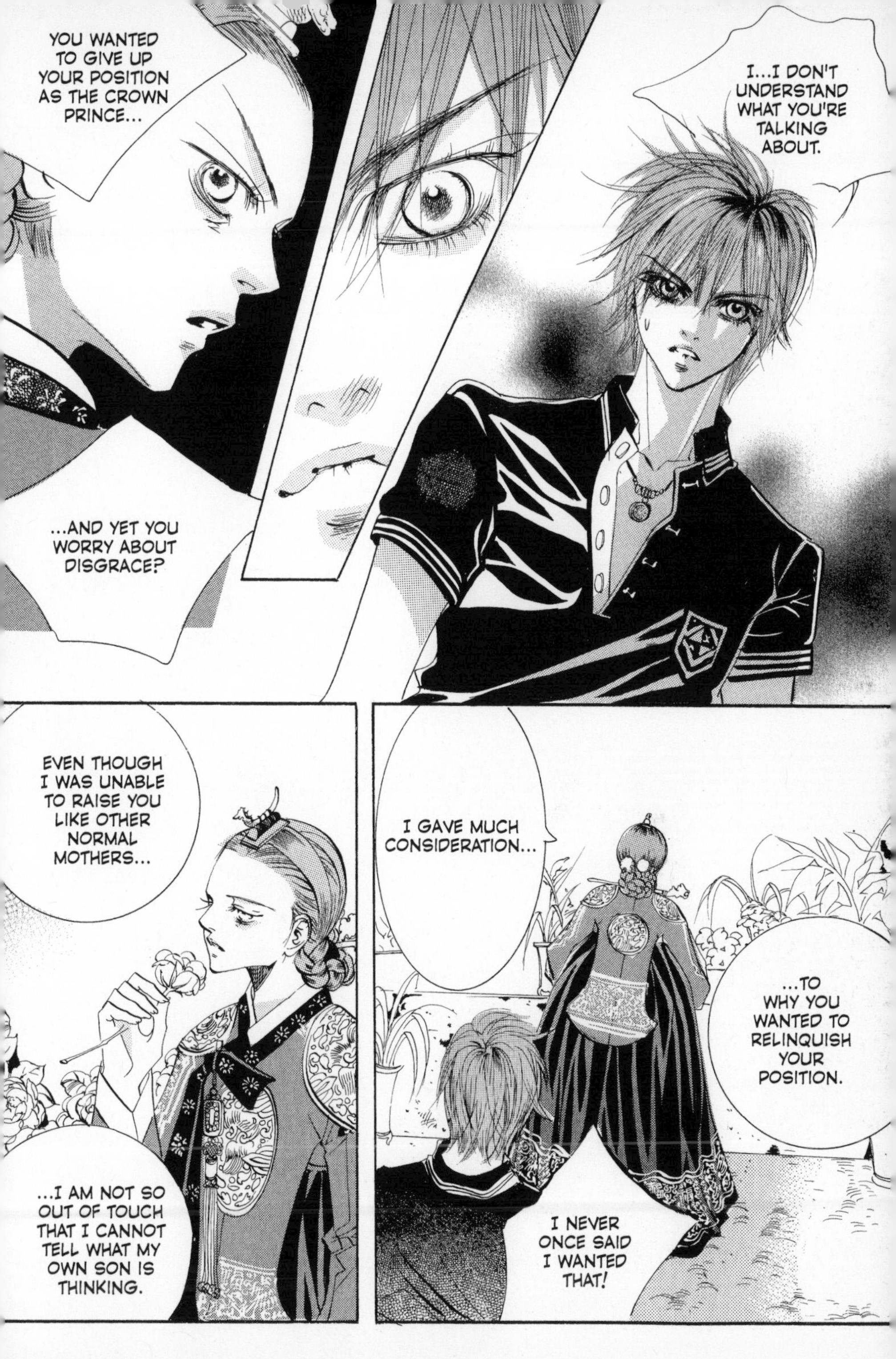
YOU WANTED TO GIVE UP YOUR POSITION AS THE CROWN PRINCE...
...AND YET YOU WORRY ABOUT DISGRACE?
I...I DON'T UNDERSTAND WHAT YOU'RE TALKING ABOUT.
EVEN THOUGH I WAS UNABLE TO RAISE YOU LIKE OTHER NORMAL MOTHERS...
...I AM NOT SO OUT OF TOUCH THAT I CANNOT TELL WHAT MY OWN SON IS THINKING.
I GAVE MUCH CONSIDERATION...
...TO WHY YOU WANTED TO RELINQUISH YOUR POSITION.
I NEVER ONCE SAID I WANTED THAT!

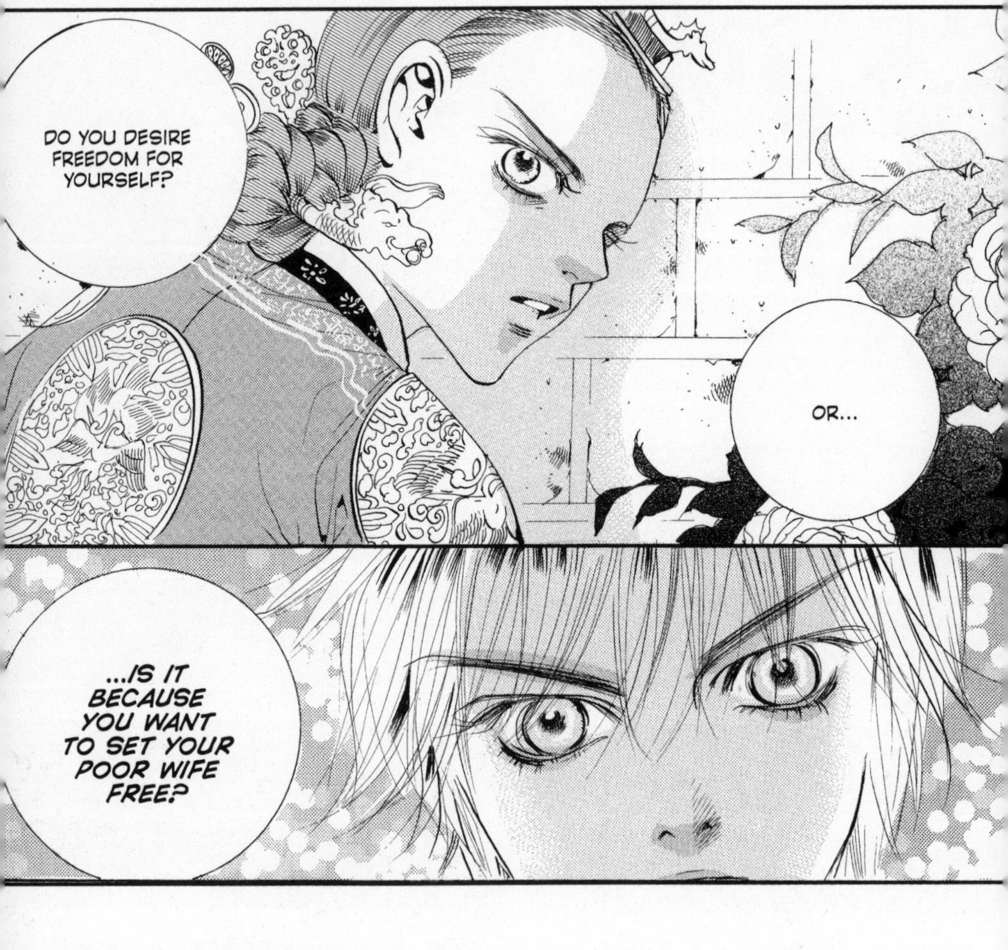
DO YOU DESIRE FREEDOM FOR YOURSELF?
OR...
...IS IT BECAUSE YOU WANT TO SET YOUR POOR WIFE FREE?

WEIMYUNG-BU

LET'S LEARN SOME MORE ABOUT THE RANKS OF WEIMYUNG-BU. WOMEN OF NAEMYUNG-BU GET RANKED IN THE PALACE, BUT WOMEN OF WEIMYUNG-BU ARE RANKED OUTSIDE THE PALACE. EVEN IF TWO WOMEN HAVE THE SAME POSITION, THEY WILL BE EITHER JONG OR JUNG, DEPENDING ON THEIR HUSBAND'S RANK.

1. WIVES OF THE ROYAL RELATIVES
JUNG-POOM 1: BUBUIN AND GUNBUIN
JONG-POOM 1: GUNBUIN
JUNG-POOM 2: HYUNBUIN
JONG-POOM 2: HYUNBUIN
JUNG-POOM 3: SHINBUIN
JONG-POOM 3: SHININ
JUNG-POOM 4: HYEIN
JONG-POOM 4: HYEIN
JUNG-POOM 5: ONIN
JONG-POOM 5: ONIN
JUNG-POOM 6: SOONIN

2. WIVES OF GOVERNMENT OFFICIALS
JUNG-POOM 1: JUNGKYUNGBUIN
JONG-POOM 1: JUNGKYUNGBUIN
JUNG-POOM 2: JUNGBUIN
JONG-POOM 2: JUNGBUIN
JUNG-POOM 3 (HIGHER): SOOKBUIN
JUNG-POOM 3 (LOWER): SOOKIN
JONG-POOM 3: SOOKIN
JUNG-POOM 4: YOUNGIN
JONG-POOM 4: YOUNGIN
JUNG-POOM 5: GONGIN
JONG-POOM 5: GONGIN
JUNG-POOM 6: YUIIN
JONG-POOM 6: YUIIN
JUNG-POOM 7: ANIN
JONG-POOM 7: ANIN
JUNG-POOM 8: DANIN
JONG-POOM 8: DANIN
JUNG-POOM 9: YOOIN
JONG-POOM 9: YOOIN

THE KING'S DAUGHTERS (PRINCESSES) DIDN'T HAVE RANKS, WHETHER THEIR MOTHER WAS A QUEEN OR A CONCUBINE. THEY WERE ABOVE SUCH CATEGORIZATION. A KING'S NANNY WAS CALLED BONGBUIN, AND HER RANK WAS JONG-POOM 1. A MOTHER OF A QUEEN WAS CALLED BUBUIN, AND HER RANK WAS JUNG-POOM 1. IF A CROWN PRINCE HAD A DAUGHTER WITH HIS WIFE, SHE WAS KNOWN AS GUNJU, AND HER RANK WAS JUNG-POOM 2, WHEREAS HIS DAUGHTER WITH A CONCUBINE WAS CALLED HYUNJU, AND HER RANK WAS JUNG-POOM 3.

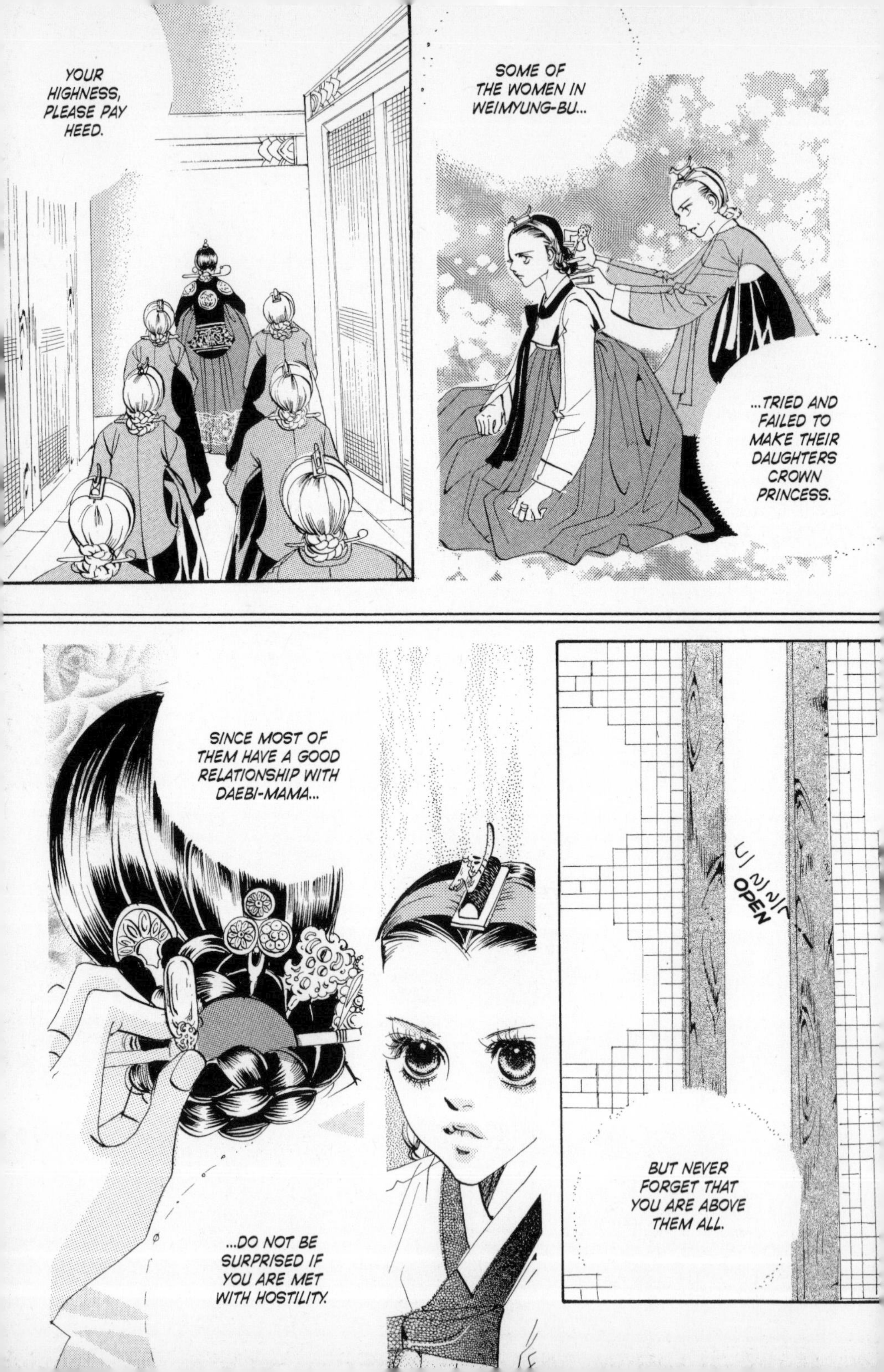
YOUR HIGHNESS, PLEASE PAY HEED.
SOME OF THE WOMEN IN WEIMYUNG-BU...
...TRIED AND FAILED TO MAKE THEIR DAUGHTERS CROWN PRINCESS.
SINCE MOST OF THEM HAVE A GOOD RELATIONSHIP WITH DAEBI-MAMA...
...DO NOT BE SURPRISED IF YOU ARE MET WITH HOSTILITY.
OPEN
BUT NEVER FORGET THAT YOU ARE ABOVE THEM ALL.

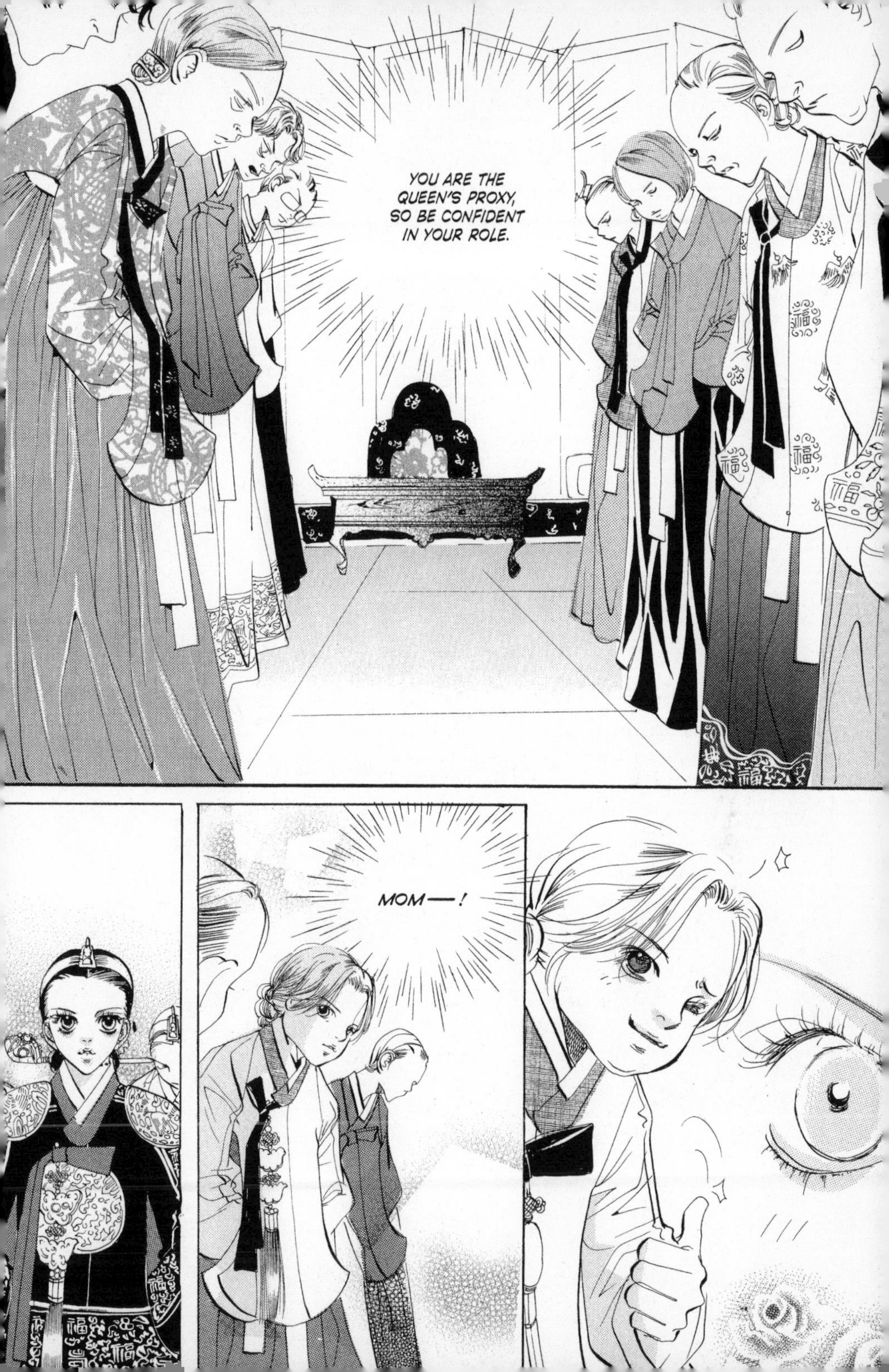
YOU ARE THE QUEEN'S PROXY, SO BE CONFIDENT IN YOUR ROLE.
MOM—!

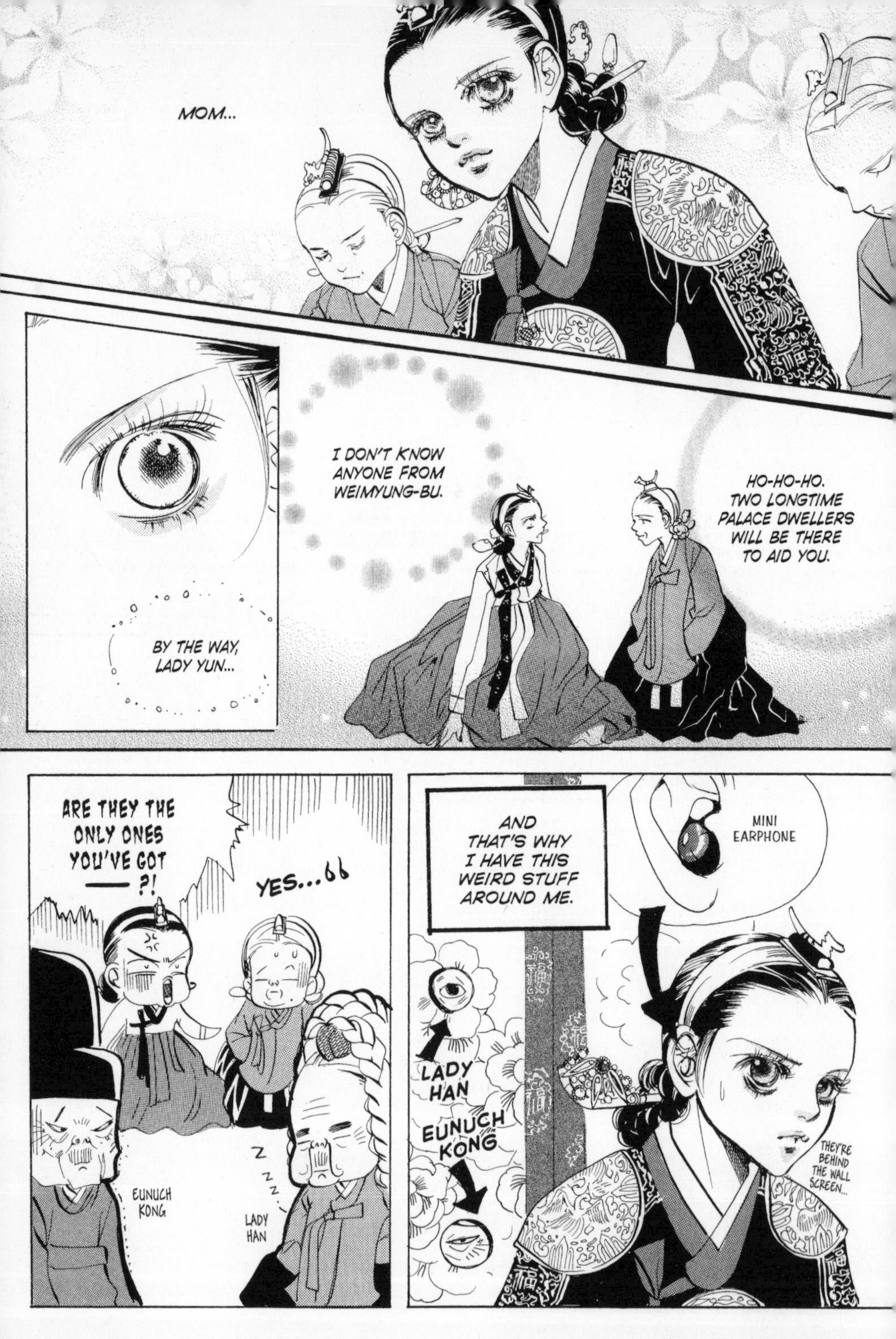
MOM...
BY THE WAY, LADY YUN...
I DON'T KNOW ANYONE FROM WEIMYUNG-BU.
HO-HO-HO. TWO LONGTIME PALACE DWELLERS WILL BE THERE TO AID YOU.
ARE THEY THE ONLY ONES YOU'VE GOT —— ?!
YES...
EUNUCH KONG
Z Z Z
LADY HAN
AND THAT'S WHY I HAVE THIS WEIRD STUFF AROUND ME.
MINI EARPHONE
LADY HAN
EUNUCH KONG
THEY'RE BEHIND THE WALL SCREEN...

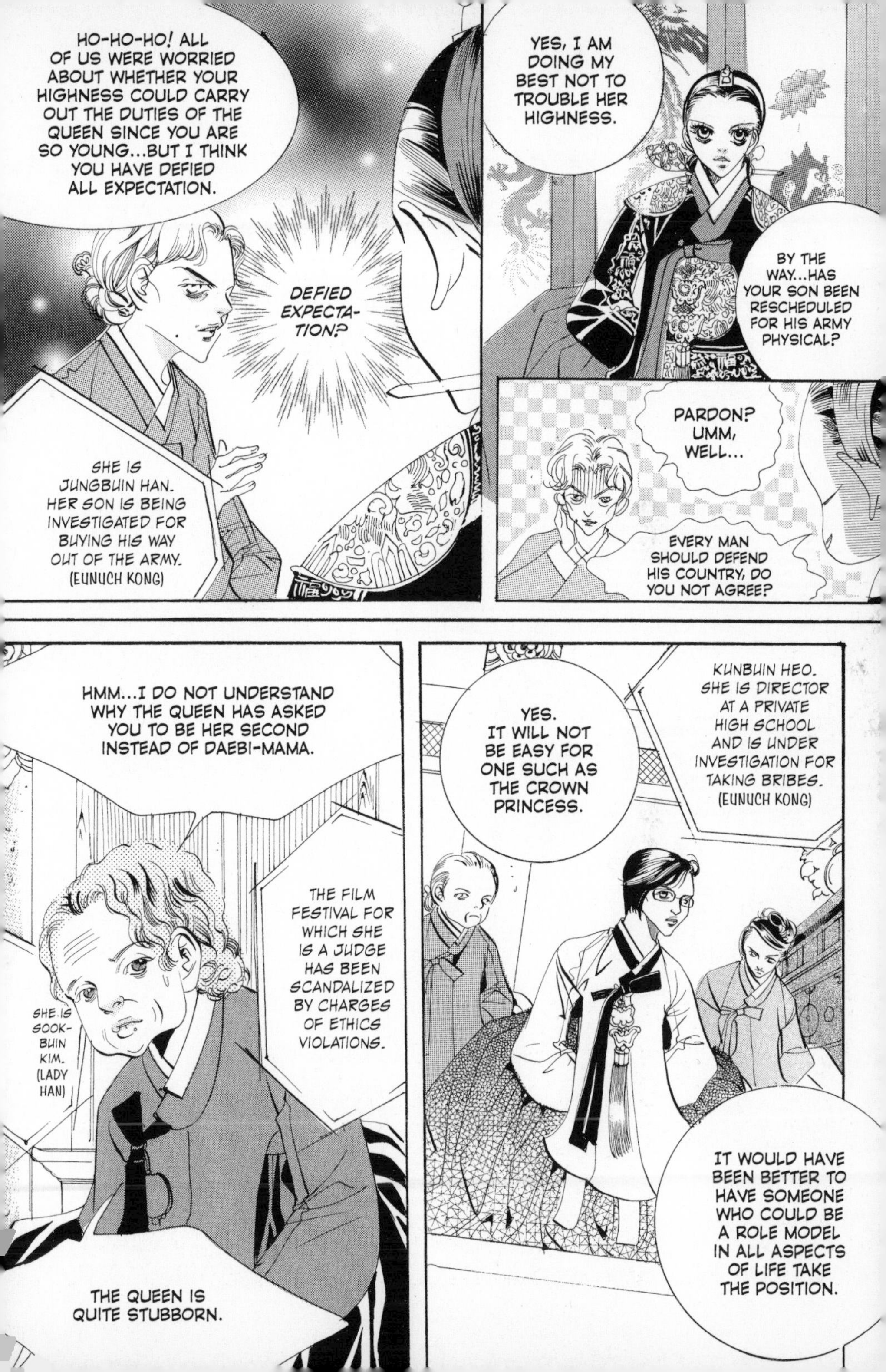
HO-HO-HO! ALL OF US WERE WORRIED ABOUT WHETHER YOUR HIGHNESS COULD CARRY OUT THE DUTIES OF THE QUEEN SINCE YOU ARE SO YOUNG...BUT I THINK YOU HAVE DEFIED ALL EXPECTATION.
DEFIED EXPECTATION?
SHE IS JUNGBUIN HAN. HER SON IS BEING INVESTIGATED FOR BUYING HIS WAY OUT OF THE ARMY. (EUNUCH KONG)
YES, I AM DOING MY BEST NOT TO TROUBLE HER HIGHNESS.
BY THE WAY...HAS YOUR SON BEEN RESCHEDULED FOR HIS ARMY PHYSICAL?
PARDON? UMM, WELL...
EVERY MAN SHOULD DEFEND HIS COUNTRY, DO YOU NOT AGREE?
HMM...I DO NOT UNDERSTAND WHY THE QUEEN HAS ASKED YOU TO BE HER SECOND INSTEAD OF DAEBI-MAMA.
SHE IS SOOK-BUIN KIM. (LADY HAN)
THE FILM FESTIVAL FOR WHICH SHE IS A JUDGE HAS BEEN SCANDALIZED BY CHARGES OF ETHICS VIOLATIONS.
THE QUEEN IS QUITE STUBBORN.
YES. IT WILL NOT BE EASY FOR ONE SUCH AS THE CROWN PRINCESS.
KUNBUIN HEO. SHE IS DIRECTOR AT A PRIVATE HIGH SCHOOL AND IS UNDER INVESTIGATION FOR TAKING BRIBES. (EUNUCH KONG)
IT WOULD HAVE BEEN BETTER TO HAVE SOMEONE WHO COULD BE A ROLE MODEL IN ALL ASPECTS OF LIFE TAKE THE POSITION.

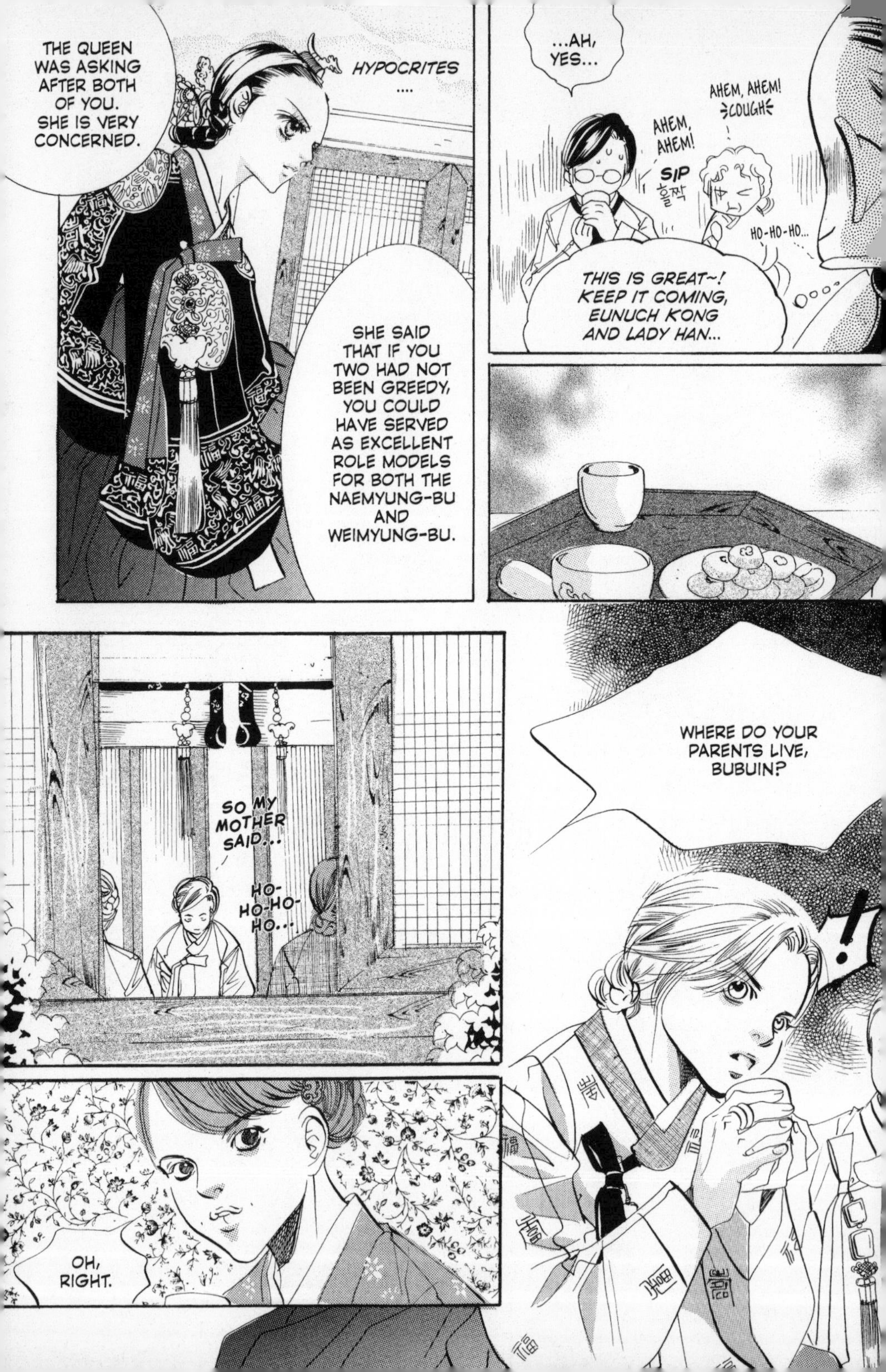
THE QUEEN WAS ASKING AFTER BOTH OF YOU. SHE IS VERY CONCERNED.
HYPOCRITES....
SHE SAID THAT IF YOU TWO HAD NOT BEEN GREEDY, YOU COULD HAVE SERVED AS EXCELLENT ROLE MODELS FOR BOTH THE NAEMYUNG-BU AND WEIMYUNG-BU.
...AH, YES...
AHEM, AHEM!
SIP
홀짝
AHEM, AHEM!
COUGH
HO-HO-HO...
THIS IS GREAT~! KEEP IT COMING, EUNUCH KONG AND LADY HAN...
SO MY MOTHER SAID...
HO-HO-HO-HO...
OH, RIGHT.
WHERE DO YOUR PARENTS LIVE, BUBUIN?
!

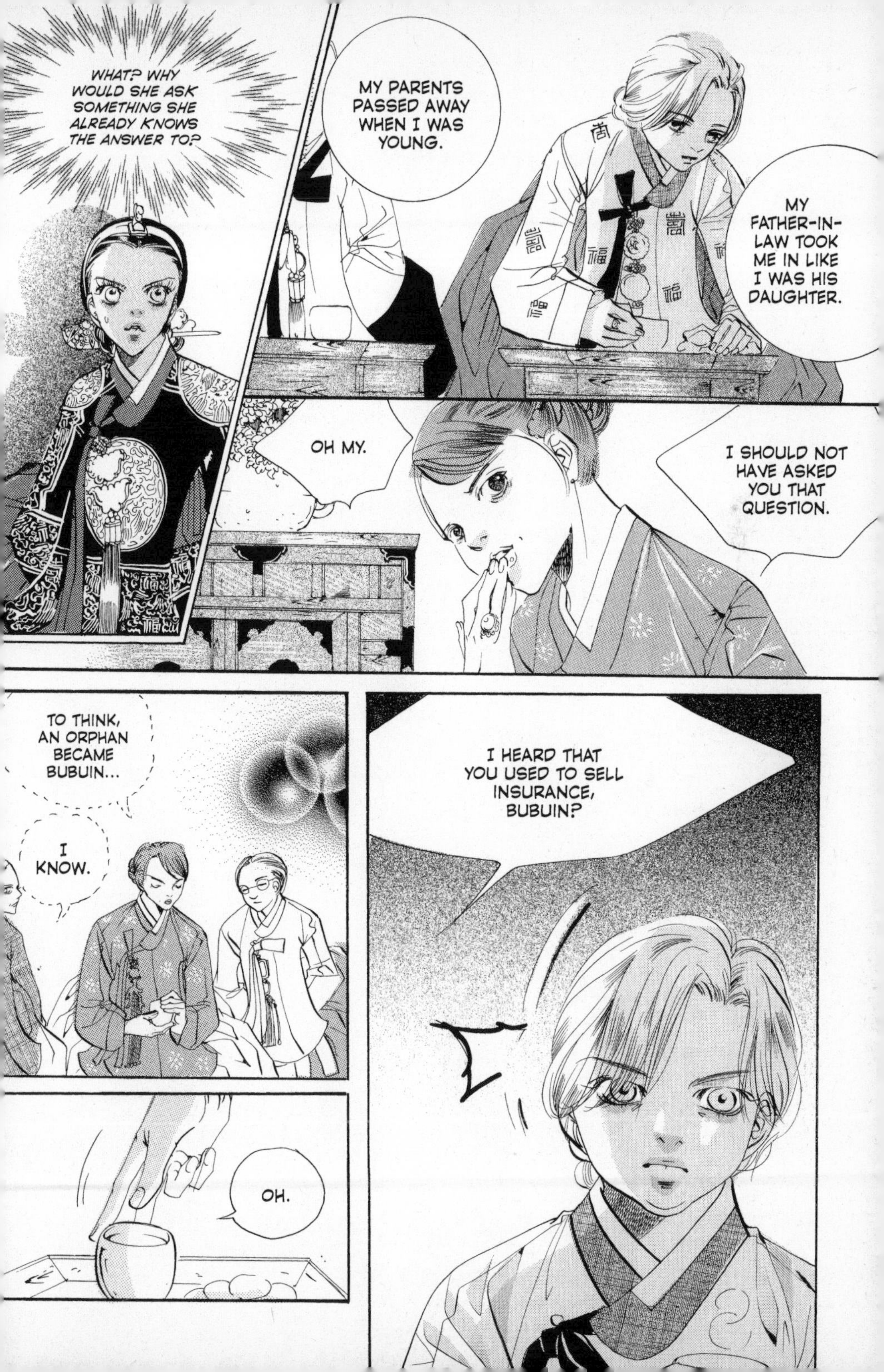
WHAT? WHY WOULD SHE ASK SOMETHING SHE ALREADY KNOWS THE ANSWER TO?
MY PARENTS PASSED AWAY WHEN I WAS YOUNG.
MY FATHER-IN-LAW TOOK ME IN LIKE I WAS HIS DAUGHTER.
OH MY.
I SHOULD NOT HAVE ASKED YOU THAT QUESTION.
TO THINK, AN ORPHAN BECAME BUBUIN...
I KNOW.
OH.
I HEARD THAT YOU USED TO SELL INSURANCE, BUBUIN?

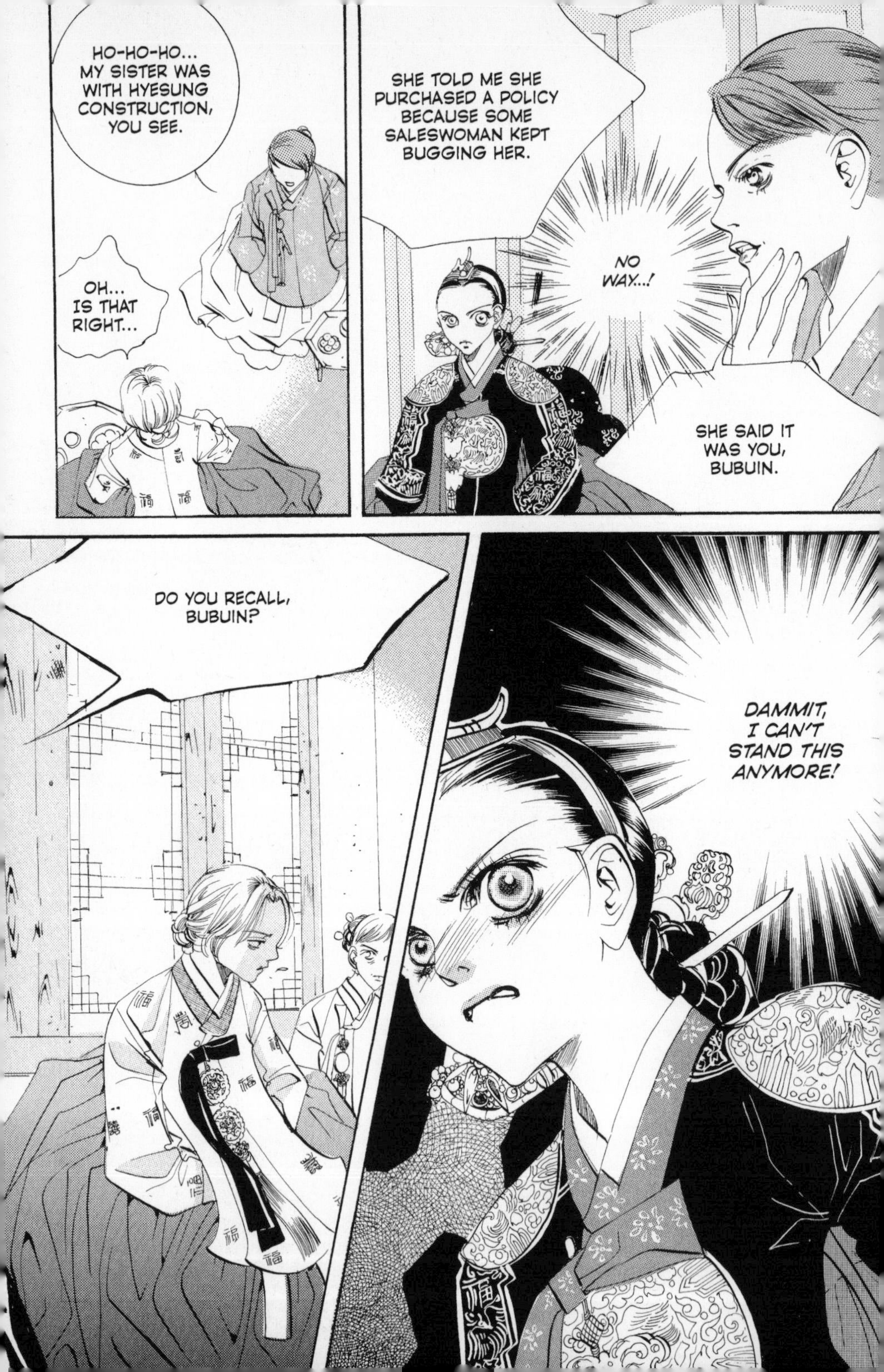
HO-HO-HO... MY SISTER WAS WITH HYESUNG CONSTRUCTION, YOU SEE.
OH... IS THAT RIGHT...
SHE TOLD ME SHE PURCHASED A POLICY BECAUSE SOME SALESWOMAN KEPT BUGGING HER.
NO WAY...!
SHE SAID IT WAS YOU, BUBUIN.
DO YOU RECALL, BUBUIN?
DAMMIT, I CAN'T STAND THIS ANYMORE!

WHOSE WISH IS THIS...? II

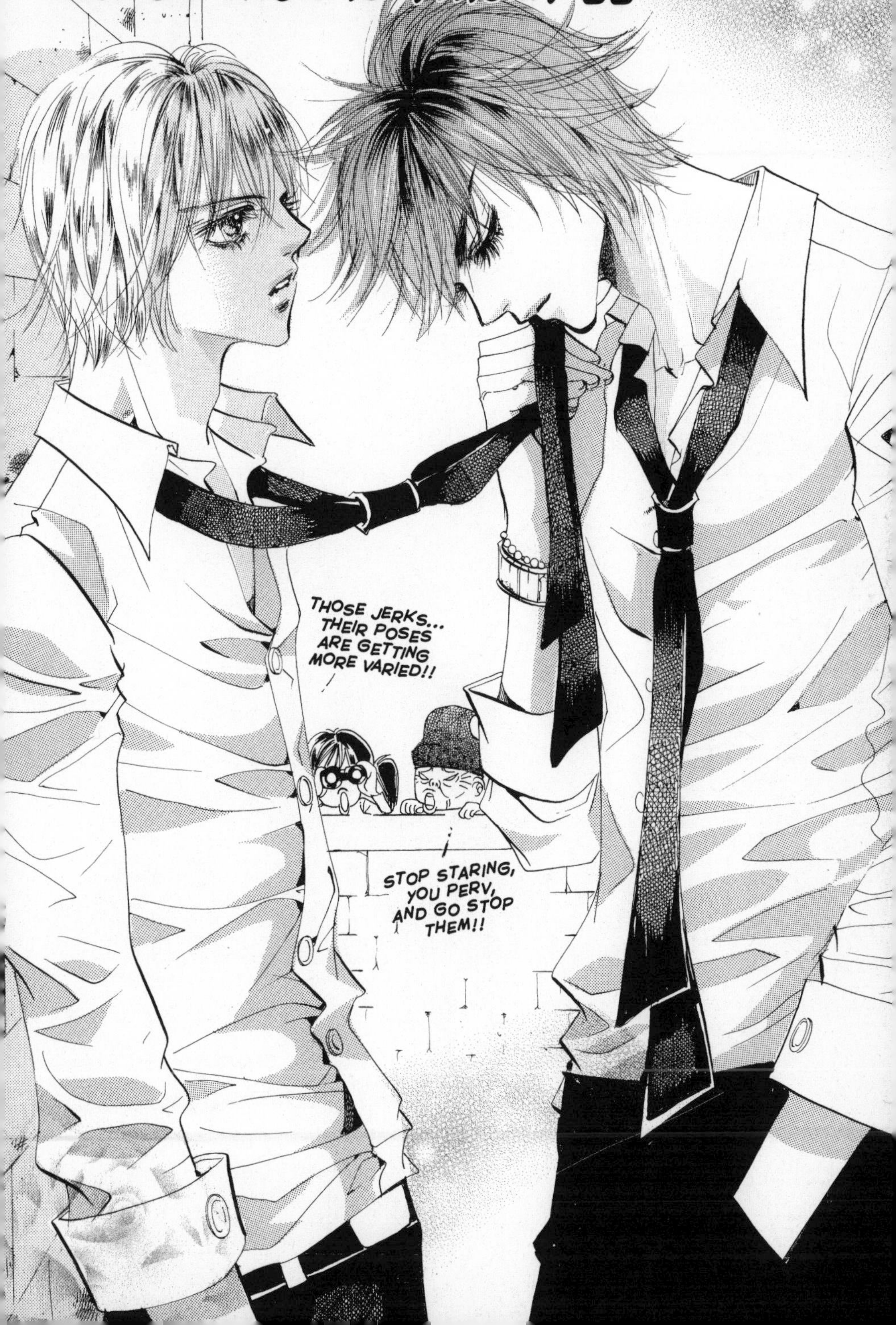
THOSE JERKS... THEIR POSES ARE GETTING MORE VARIED!!
STOP STARING, YOU PERV, AND GO STOP THEM!!

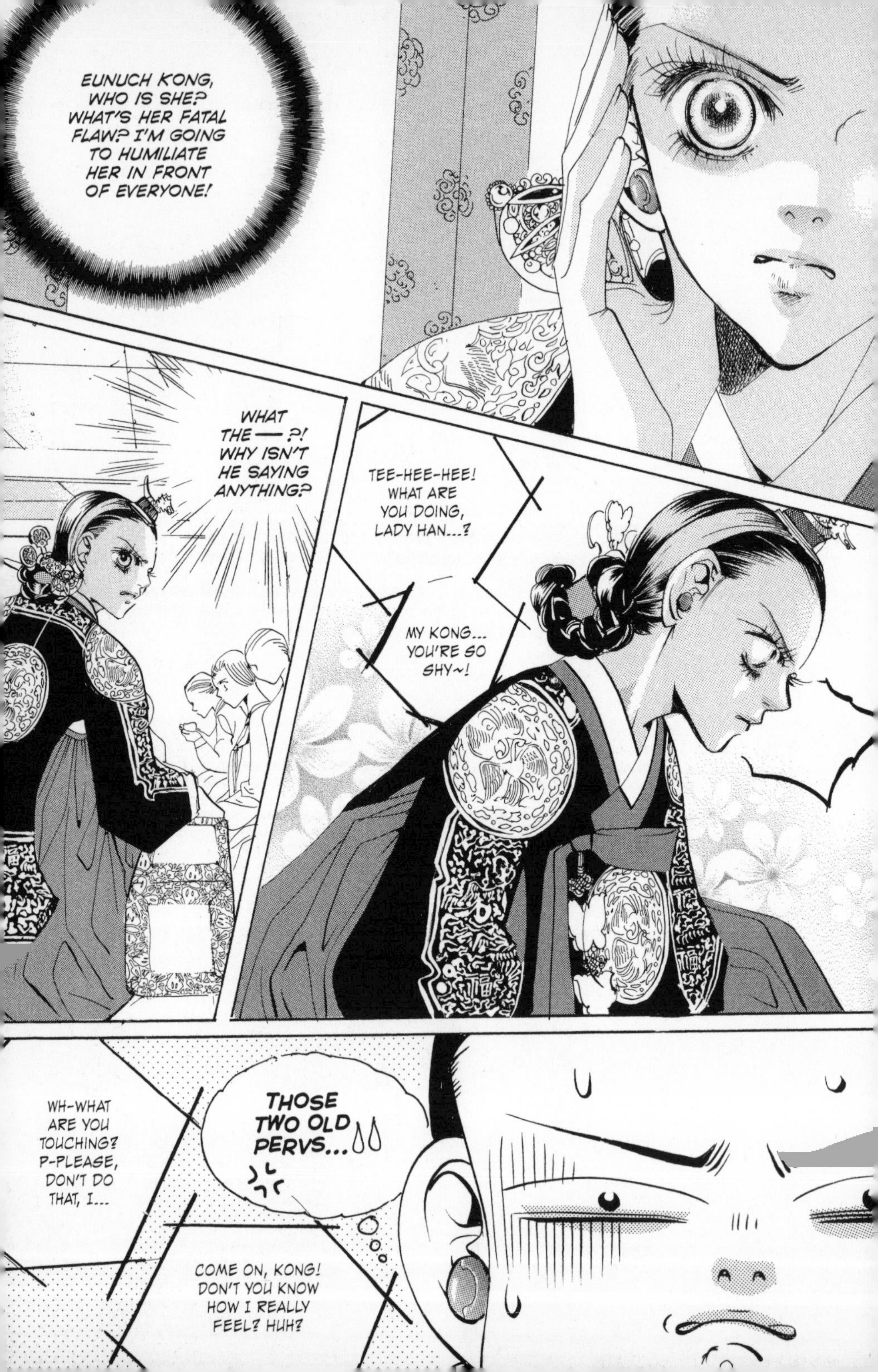
EUNUCH KONG, WHO IS SHE? WHAT'S HER FATAL FLAW? I'M GOING TO HUMILIATE HER IN FRONT OF EVERYONE!
WHAT THE— ?! WHY ISN'T HE SAYING ANYTHING?
TEE-HEE-HEE! WHAT ARE YOU DOING, LADY HAN...?
MY KONG... YOU'RE SO SHY~!
WH-WHAT ARE YOU TOUCHING? P-PLEASE, DON'T DO THAT, I...
THOSE TWO OLD PERVS...
COME ON, KONG! DON'T YOU KNOW HOW I REALLY FEEL? HUH?

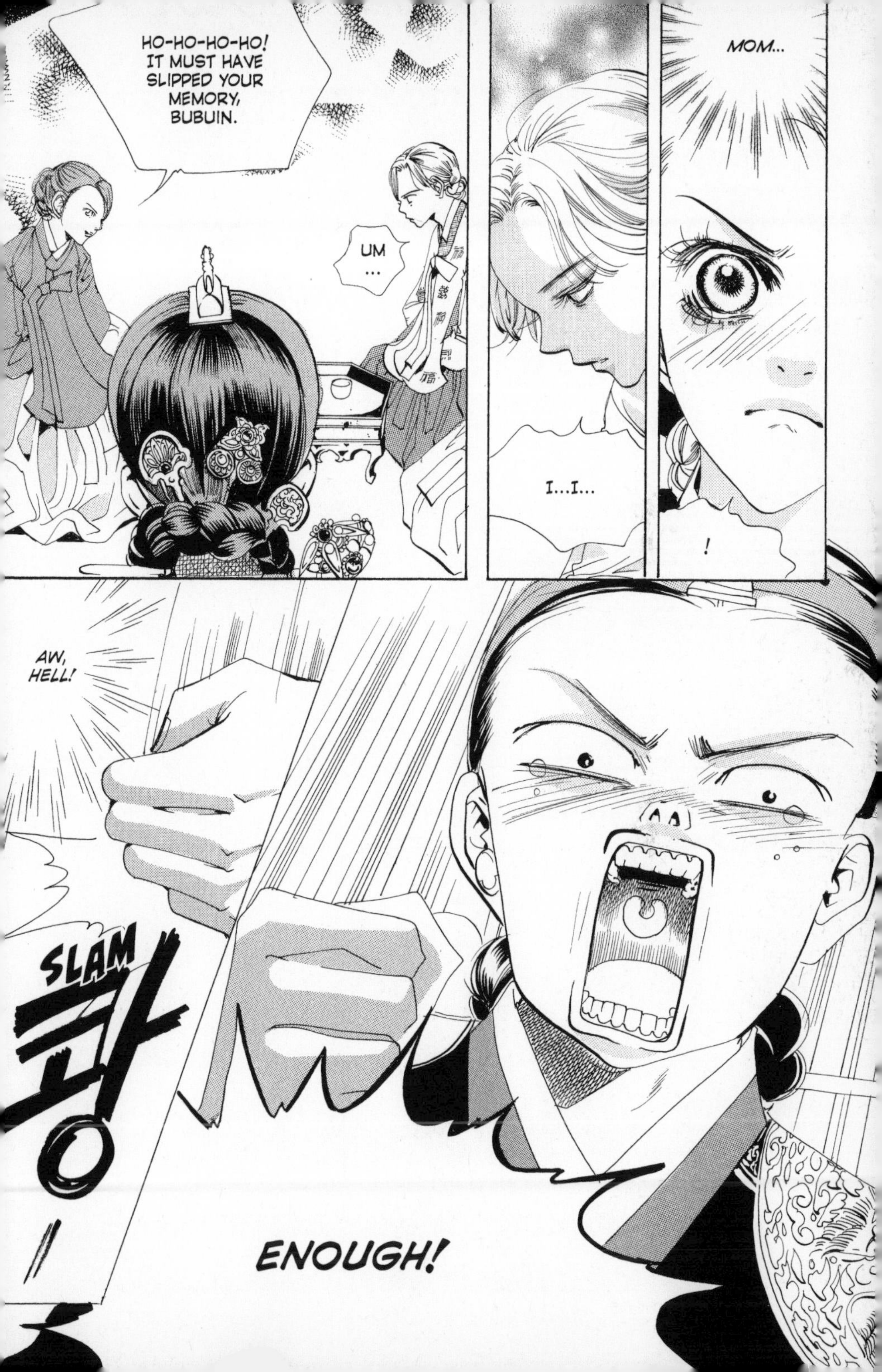
HO-HO-HO-HO! IT MUST HAVE SLIPPED YOUR MEMORY, BUBUIN.
UM ...
I...I...
MOM...
!
AW, HELL!
SLAM
콰
ENOUGH!

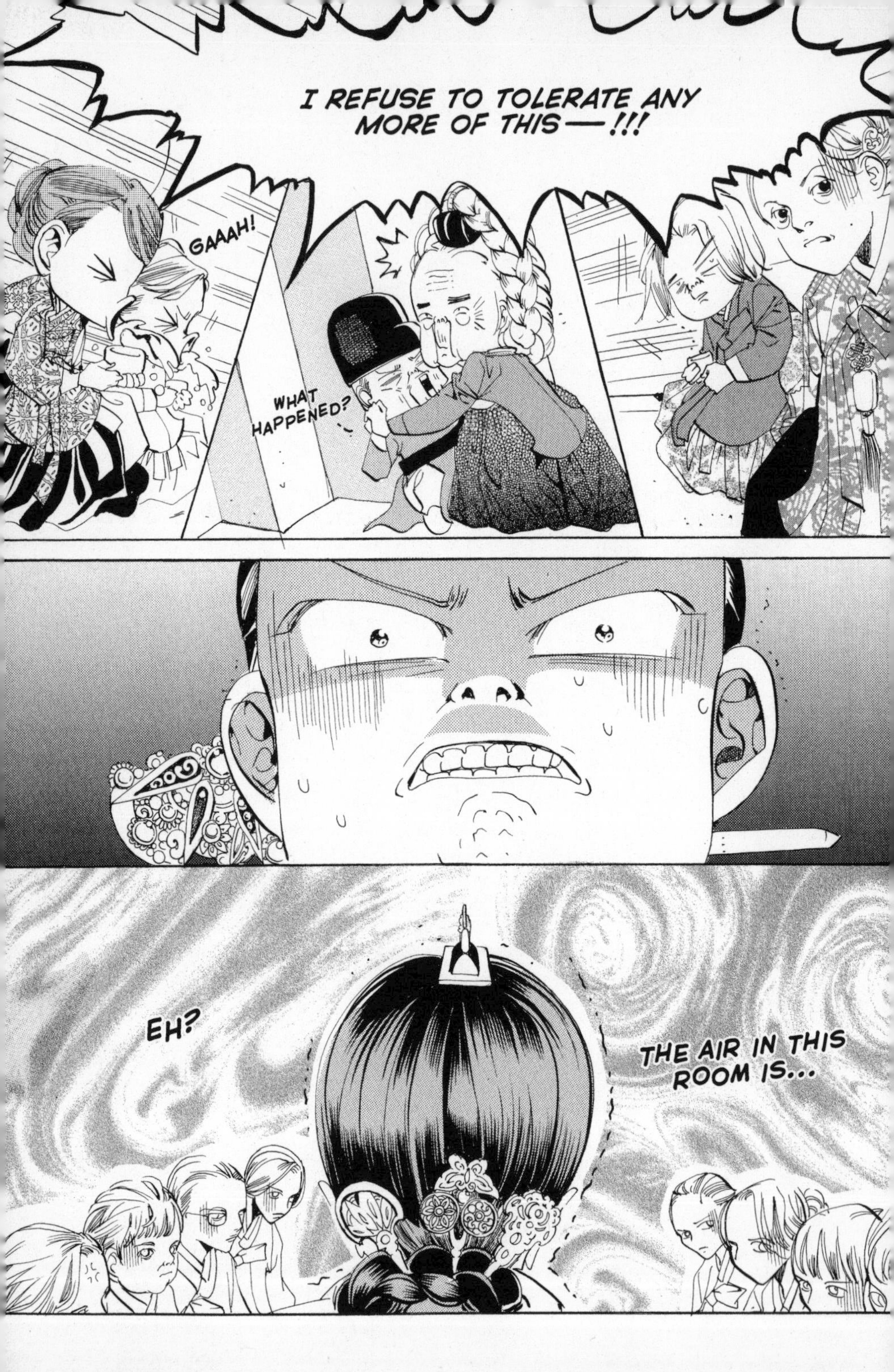
I REFUSE TO TOLERATE ANY MORE OF THIS—!!!
GAAAH!
WHAT HAPPENED?
EH?
THE AIR IN THIS ROOM IS...

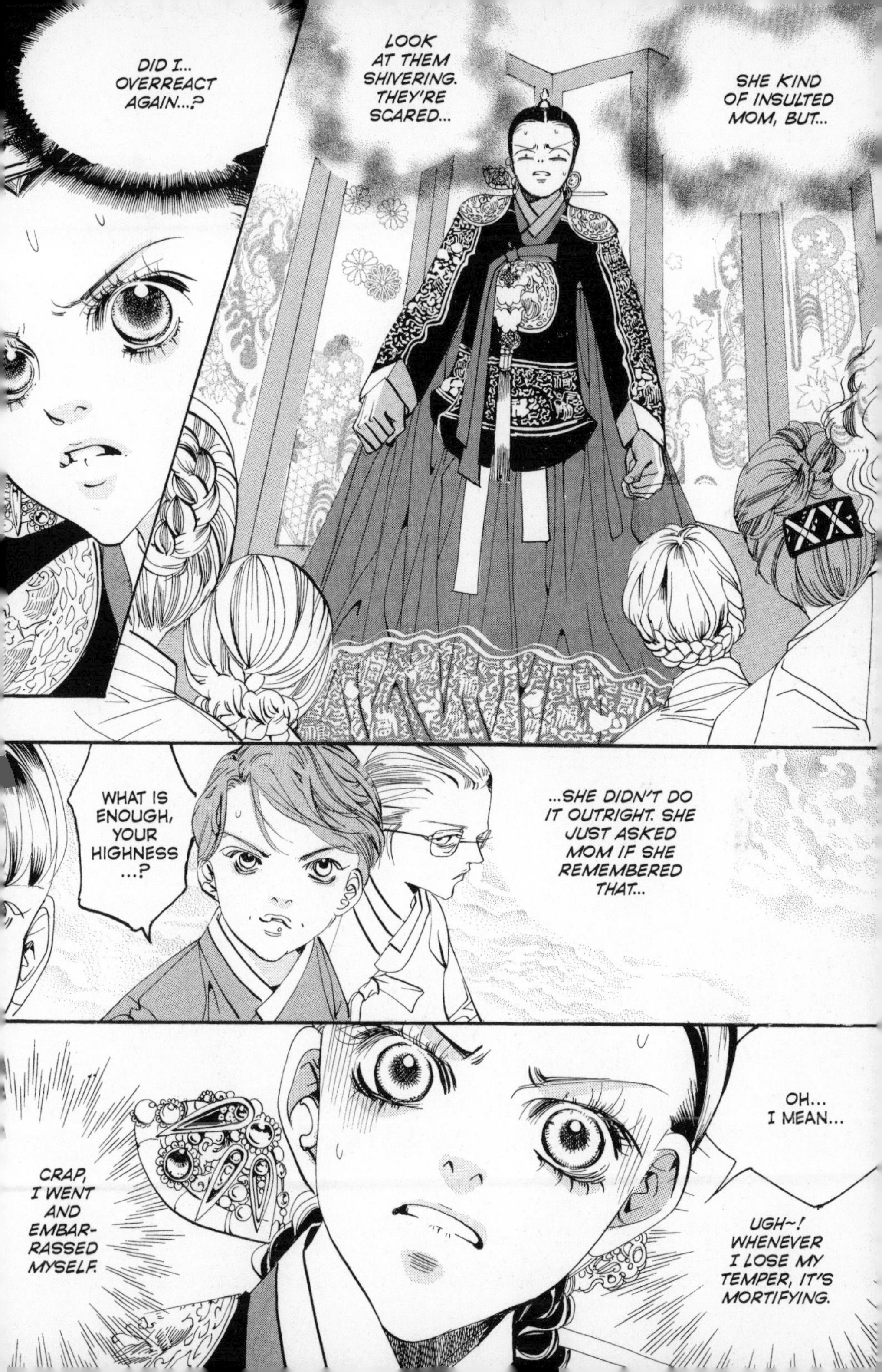
DID I... OVERREACT AGAIN...?
LOOK AT THEM SHIVERING. THEY'RE SCARED...
SHE KIND OF INSULTED MOM, BUT...
WHAT IS ENOUGH, YOUR HIGHNESS ...?
...SHE DIDN'T DO IT OUTRIGHT. SHE JUST ASKED MOM IF SHE REMEMBERED THAT...
CRAP, I WENT AND EMBAR-RASSED MYSELF.
OH... I MEAN...
UGH~! WHENEVER I LOSE MY TEMPER, IT'S MORTIFYING.

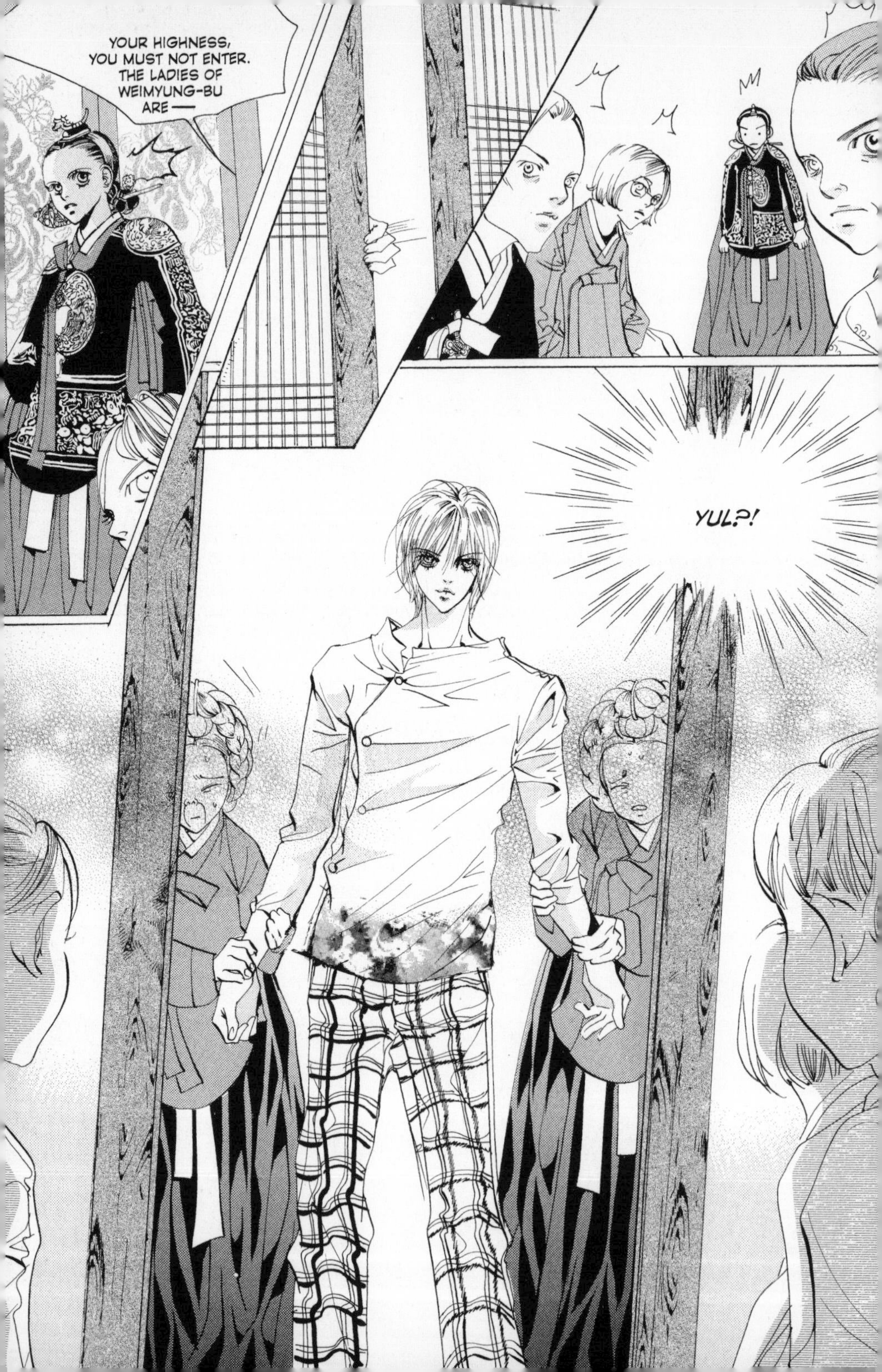
YOUR HIGHNESS, YOU MUST NOT ENTER. THE LADIES OF WEIMYUNG-BU ARE —
YUL?!

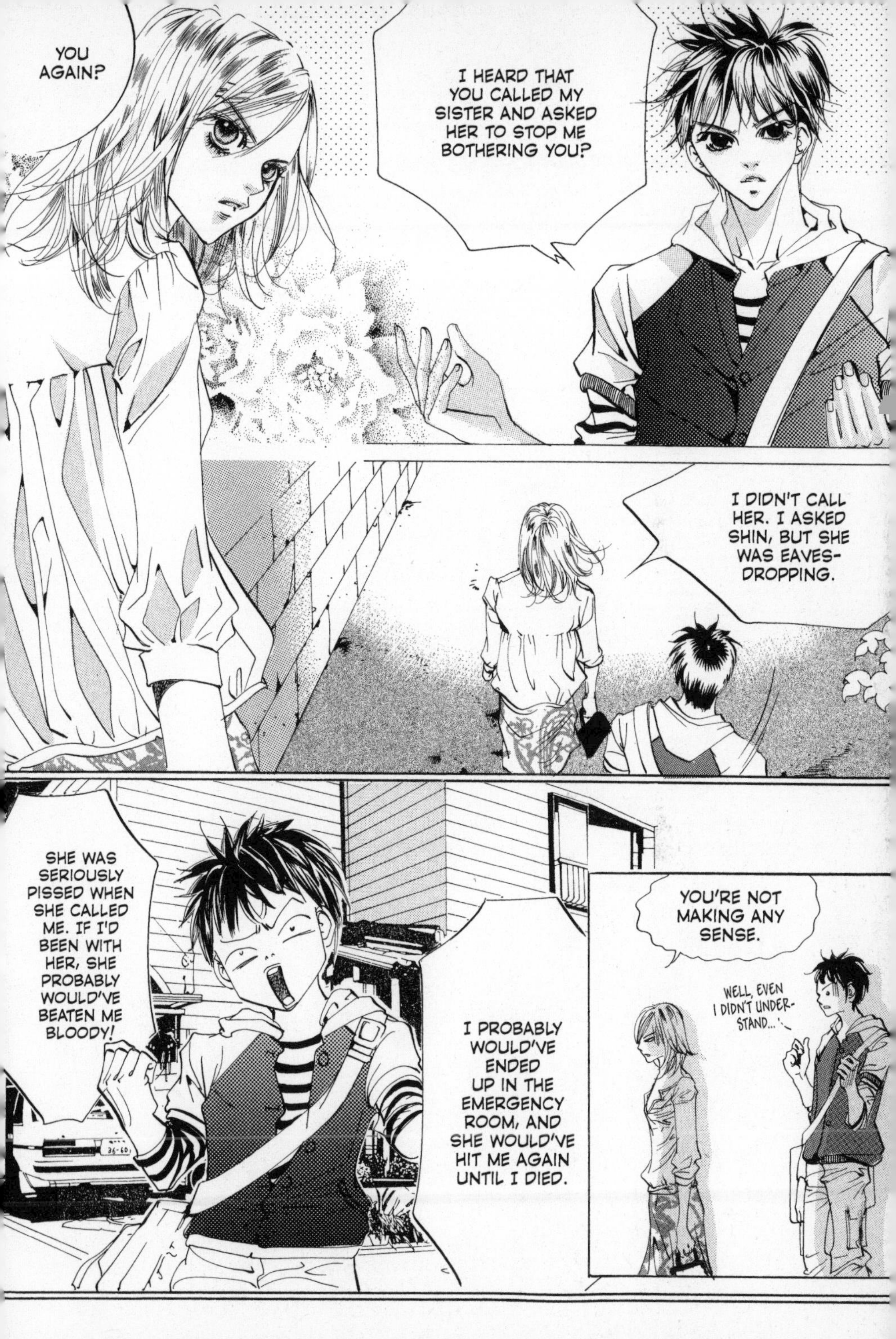
YOU AGAIN?
I HEARD THAT YOU CALLED MY SISTER AND ASKED HER TO STOP ME BOTHERING YOU?
I DIDN'T CALL HER. I ASKED SHIN, BUT SHE WAS EAVES-DROPPING.
SHE WAS SERIOUSLY PISSED WHEN SHE CALLED ME. IF I'D BEEN WITH HER, SHE PROBABLY WOULD'VE BEATEN ME BLOODY!
I PROBABLY WOULD'VE ENDED UP IN THE EMERGENCY ROOM, AND SHE WOULD'VE HIT ME AGAIN UNTIL I DIED.
YOU'RE NOT MAKING ANY SENSE.
WELL, EVEN I DIDN'T UNDER-STAND...

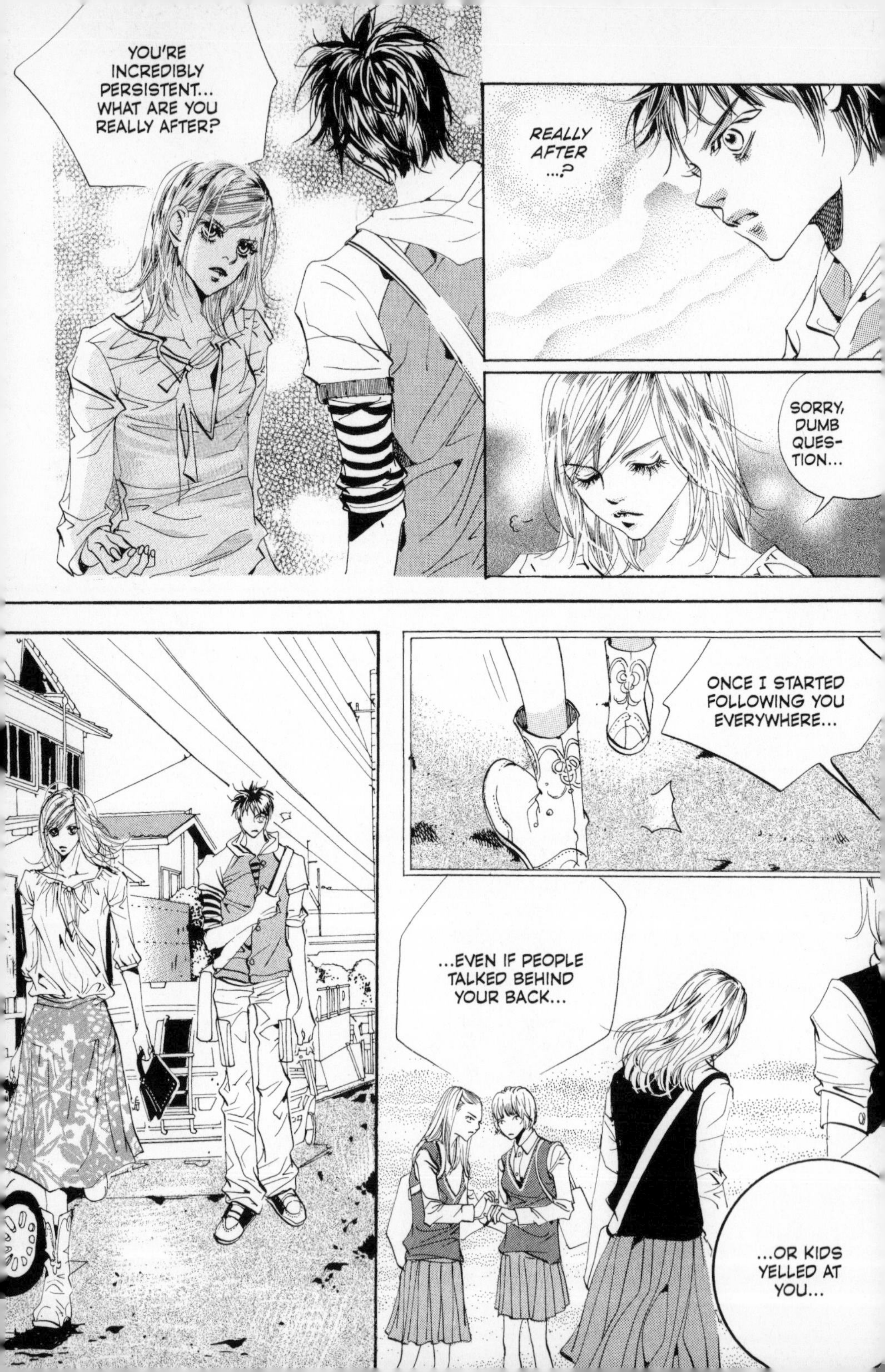
YOU'RE INCREDIBLY PERSISTENT... WHAT ARE YOU REALLY AFTER?
REALLY AFTER ...?
SORRY, DUMB QUES-TION...
ONCE I STARTED FOLLOWING YOU EVERYWHERE...
...EVEN IF PEOPLE TALKED BEHIND YOUR BACK...
...OR KIDS YELLED AT YOU...

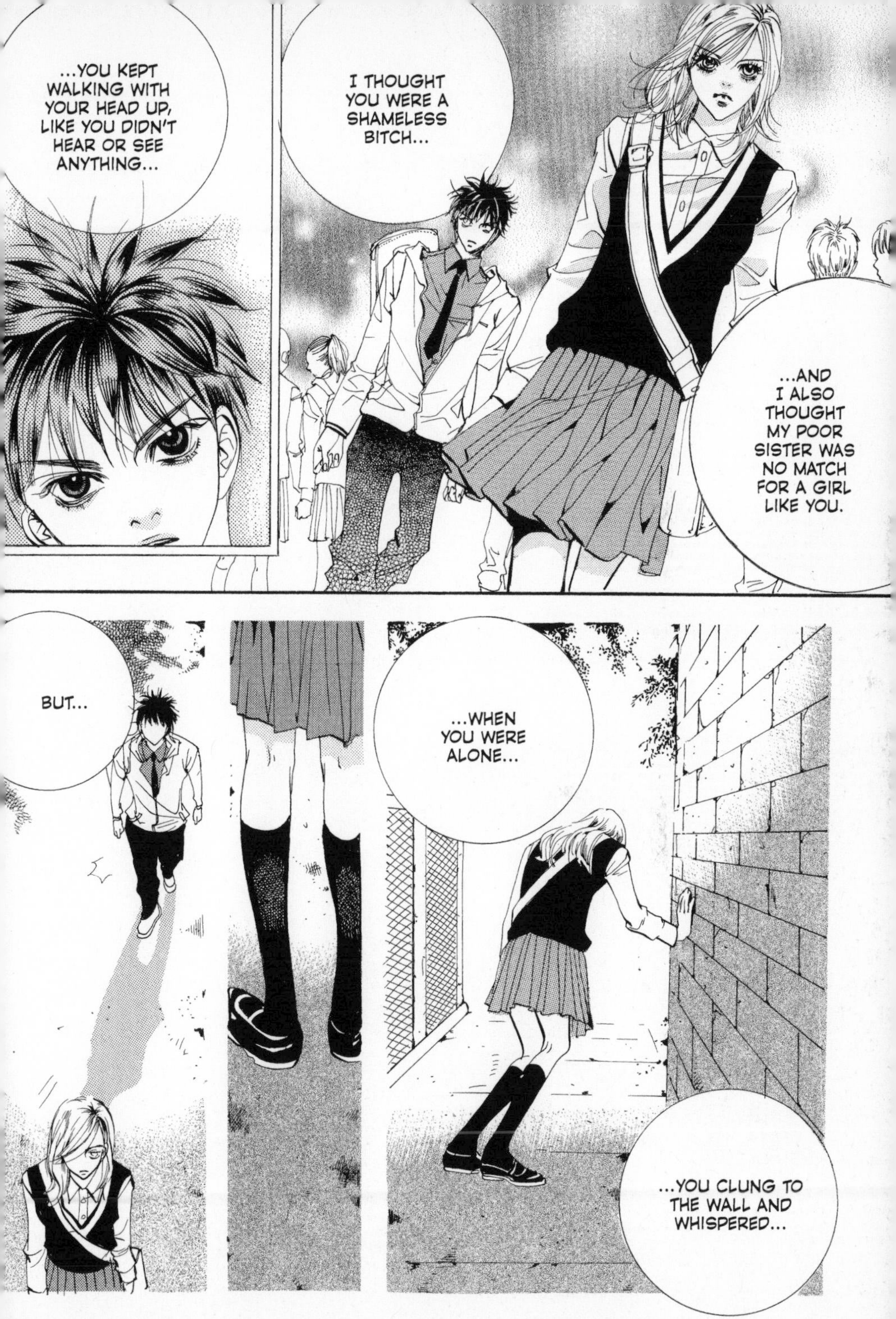
...YOU KEPT WALKING WITH YOUR HEAD UP, LIKE YOU DIDN'T HEAR OR SEE ANYTHING...
I THOUGHT YOU WERE A SHAMELESS BITCH...
...AND I ALSO THOUGHT MY POOR SISTER WAS NO MATCH FOR A GIRL LIKE YOU.
BUT...
...WHEN YOU WERE ALONE...
...YOU CLUNG TO THE WALL AND WHISPERED...

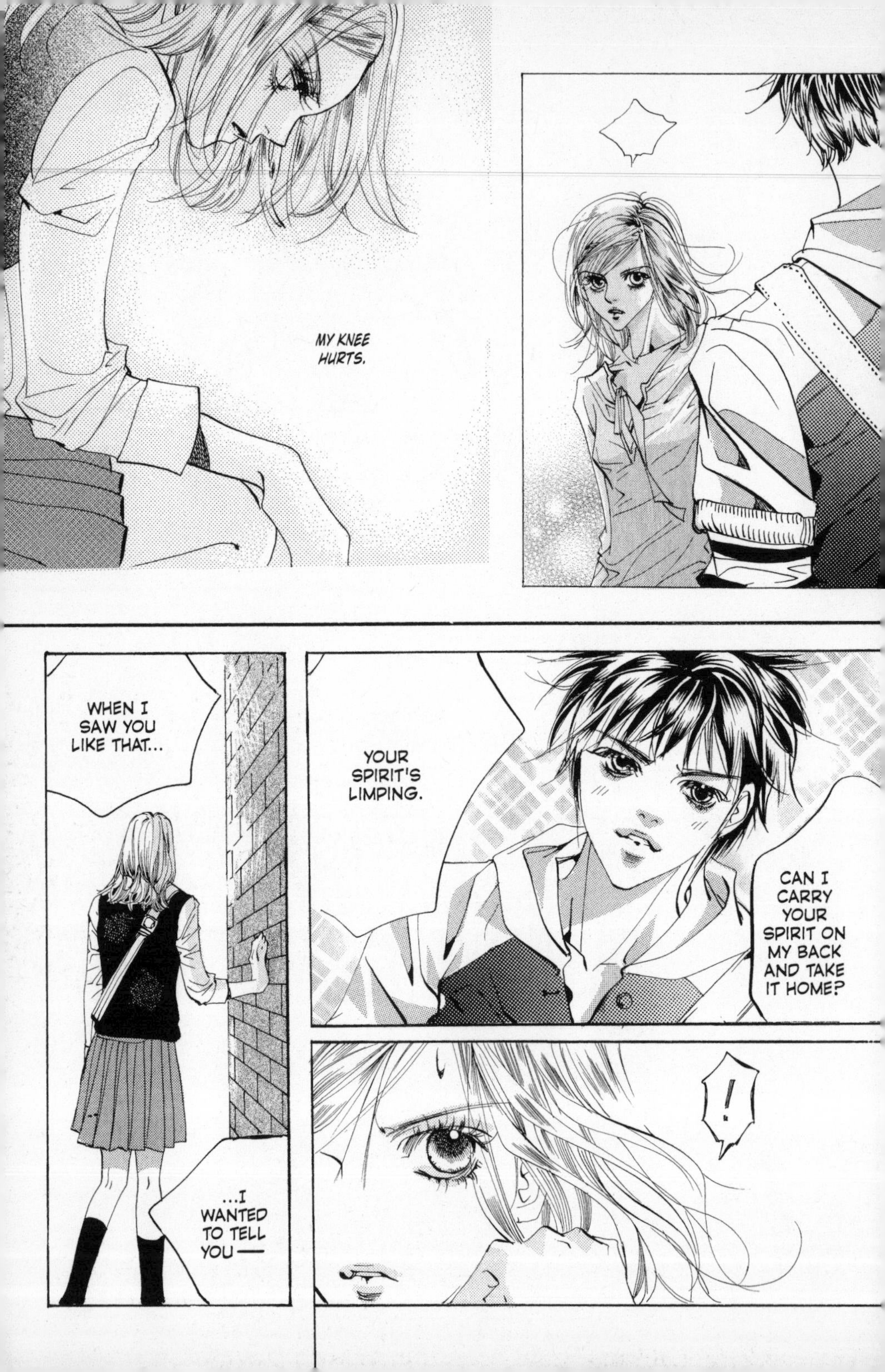
MY KNEE HURTS.
WHEN I SAW YOU LIKE THAT...
...I WANTED TO TELL YOU—
YOUR SPIRIT'S LIMPING.
CAN I CARRY YOUR SPIRIT ON MY BACK AND TAKE IT HOME?
!

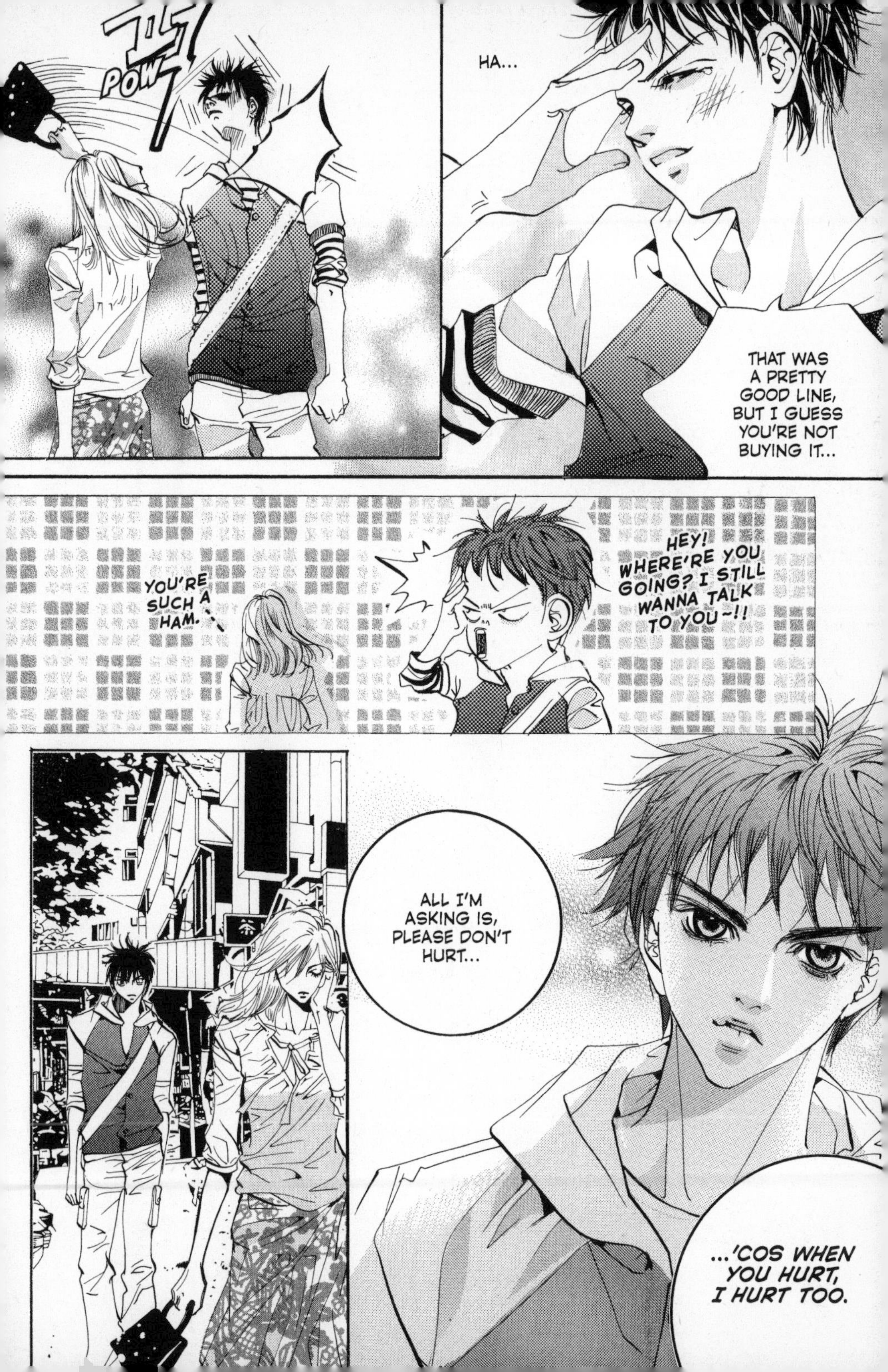
POW
HA...
THAT WAS A PRETTY GOOD LINE, BUT I GUESS YOU'RE NOT BUYING IT...
YOU'RE SUCH A HAM...
HEY! WHERE'RE YOU GOING? I STILL WANNA TALK TO YOU~!!
ALL I'M ASKING IS, PLEASE DON'T HURT...
...'COS WHEN YOU HURT, I HURT TOO.

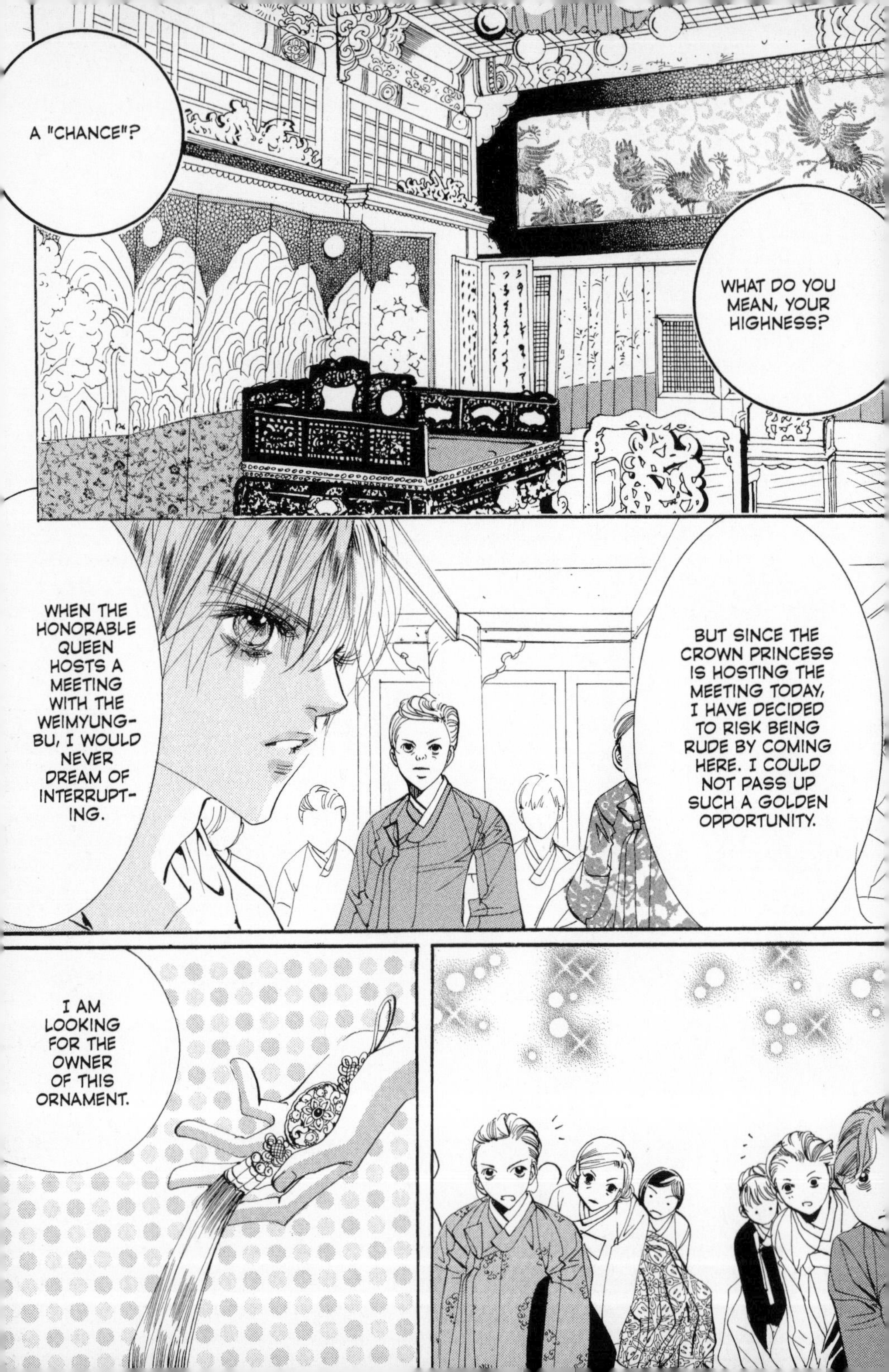
A "CHANCE"?
WHAT DO YOU MEAN, YOUR HIGHNESS?
WHEN THE HONORABLE QUEEN HOSTS A MEETING WITH THE WEIMYUNG-BU, I WOULD NEVER DREAM OF INTERRUPT-ING.
BUT SINCE THE CROWN PRINCESS IS HOSTING THE MEETING TODAY, I HAVE DECIDED TO RISK BEING RUDE BY COMING HERE. I COULD NOT PASS UP SUCH A GOLDEN OPPORTUNITY.
I AM LOOKING FOR THE OWNER OF THIS ORNAMENT.

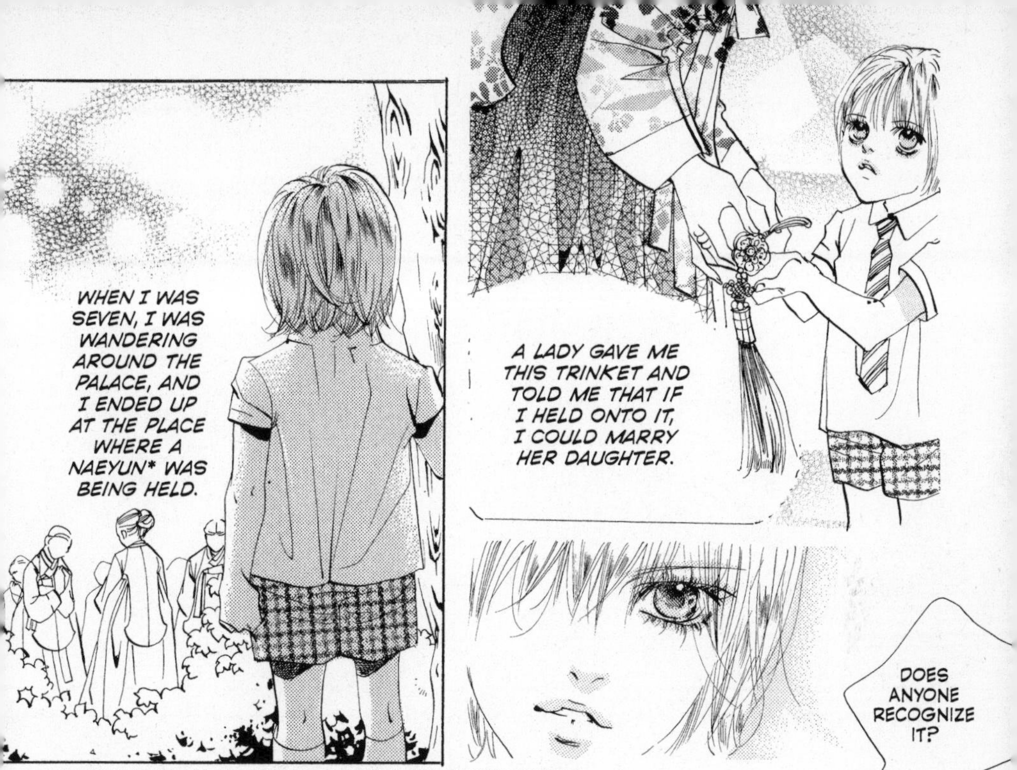
WHEN I WAS SEVEN, I WAS WANDERING AROUND THE PALACE, AND I ENDED UP AT THE PLACE WHERE A NAEYUN* WAS BEING HELD.
A LADY GAVE ME THIS TRINKET AND TOLD ME THAT IF I HELD ONTO IT, I COULD MARRY HER DAUGHTER.
DOES ANYONE RECOGNIZE IT?

*NAEYUN: ALSO CALLED NAEJINYUN. IT IS AN INVITATION-ONLY PALACE PARTY.

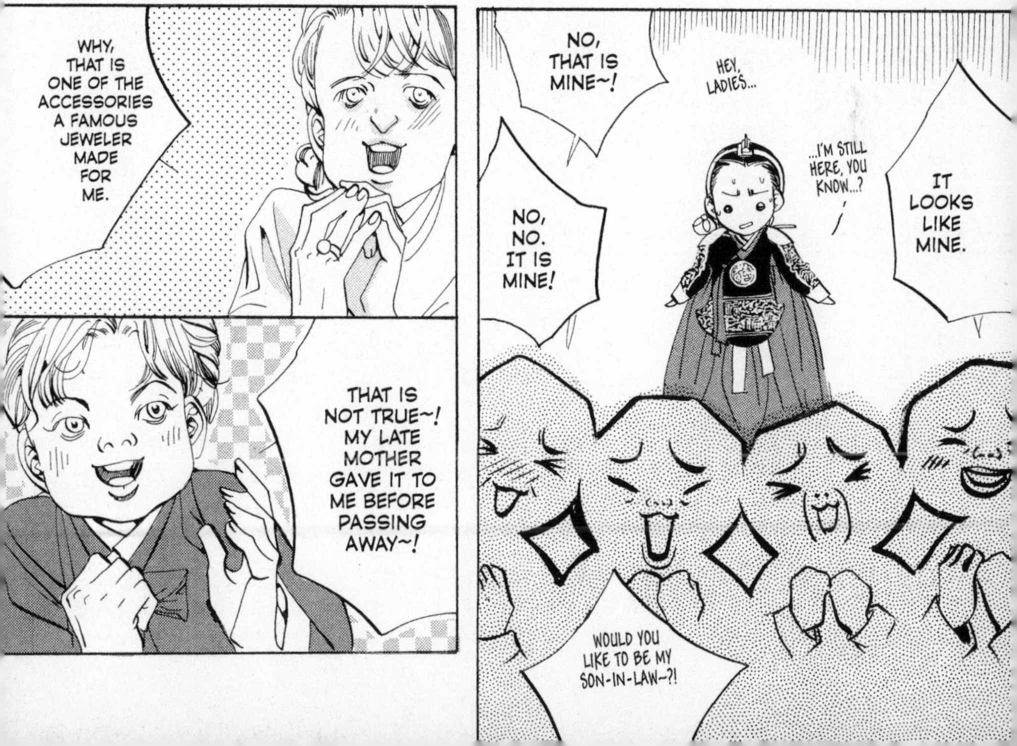
WHY, THAT IS ONE OF THE ACCESSORIES A FAMOUS JEWELER MADE FOR ME.
THAT IS NOT TRUE~! MY LATE MOTHER GAVE IT TO ME BEFORE PASSING AWAY~!
NO, THAT IS MINE~!
HEY, LADIES...
...I'M STILL HERE, YOU KNOW...?
NO, NO. IT IS MINE!
IT LOOKS LIKE MINE.
WOULD YOU LIKE TO BE MY SON-IN-LAW~?!

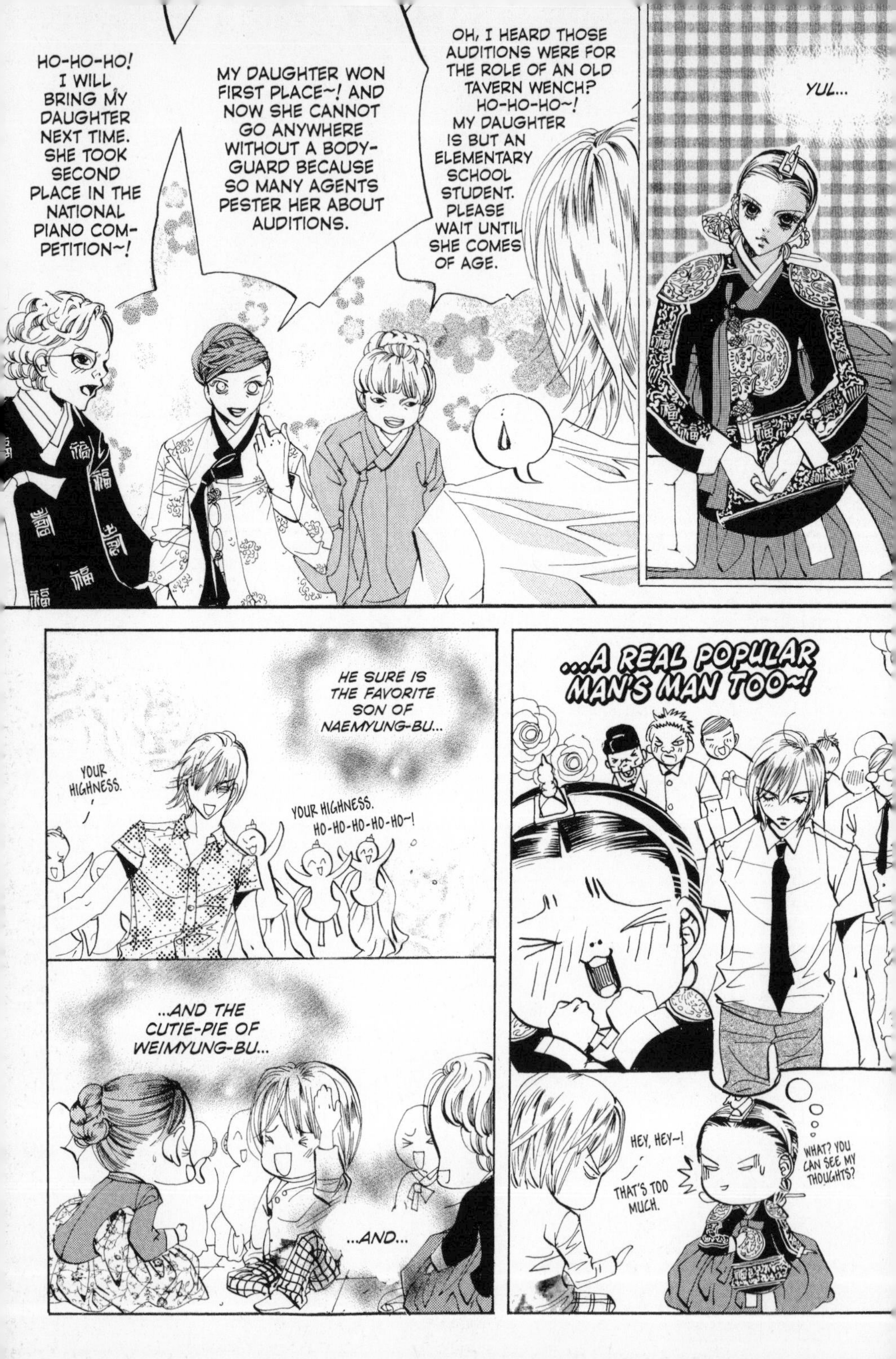
HO-HO-HO! I WILL BRING MY DAUGHTER NEXT TIME. SHE TOOK SECOND PLACE IN THE NATIONAL PIANO COMPETITION~!
MY DAUGHTER WON FIRST PLACE~! AND NOW SHE CANNOT GO ANYWHERE WITHOUT A BODY-GUARD BECAUSE SO MANY AGENTS PESTER HER ABOUT AUDITIONS.
OH, I HEARD THOSE AUDITIONS WERE FOR THE ROLE OF AN OLD TAVERN WENCH? HO-HO-HO~! MY DAUGHTER IS BUT AN ELEMENTARY SCHOOL STUDENT. PLEASE WAIT UNTIL SHE COMES OF AGE.
YUL...
HE SURE IS THE FAVORITE SON OF NAEMYUNG-BU...
YOUR HIGHNESS.
YOUR HIGHNESS. HO-HO-HO-HO-HO~!
...AND THE CUTIE-PIE OF WEIMYUNG-BU...
...AND...
...A REAL POPULAR MAN'S MAN TOO~!
HEY, HEY~!
THAT'S TOO MUCH.
WHAT? YOU CAN SEE MY THOUGHTS?

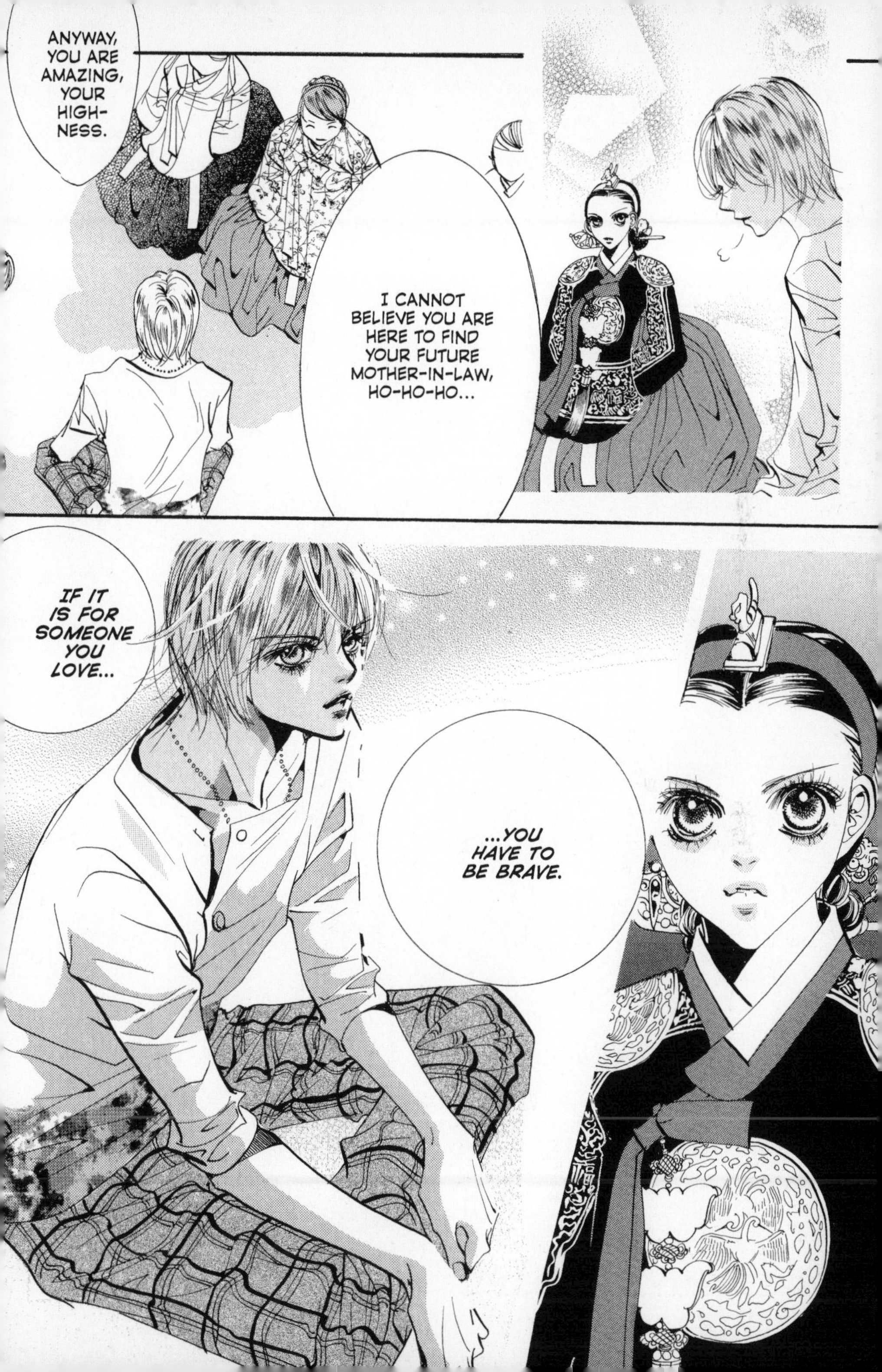
ANYWAY, YOU ARE AMAZING, YOUR HIGH-NESS.
I CANNOT BELIEVE YOU ARE HERE TO FIND YOUR FUTURE MOTHER-IN-LAW, HO-HO-HO...
IF IT IS FOR SOMEONE YOU LOVE...
...YOU HAVE TO BE BRAVE.

HEE-HEE-HEE... HE CONFESSED HIS LOVE FOR ME IN FRONT OF EVERYONE...

AHH, HIS HIGHNESS—!

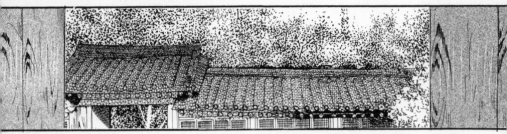

IF IT HADN'T BEEN FOR YOU, IT WOULD'VE BEEN TOTALLY EMBARRASSING.

I STOOD UP 'COS I WAS FURIOUS, BUT THEN I DIDN'T KNOW WHAT TO SAY.

THE CROWN PRINCESS WOULD HAVE BEEN IN TROUBLE IF YOU HAD NOT HELPED HER, YOUR HIGHNESS.

I WAS WORRIED THAT HER HIGHNESS WOULD LOSE HER TEMPER AND SAY SOMETHING HORRENDOUS.

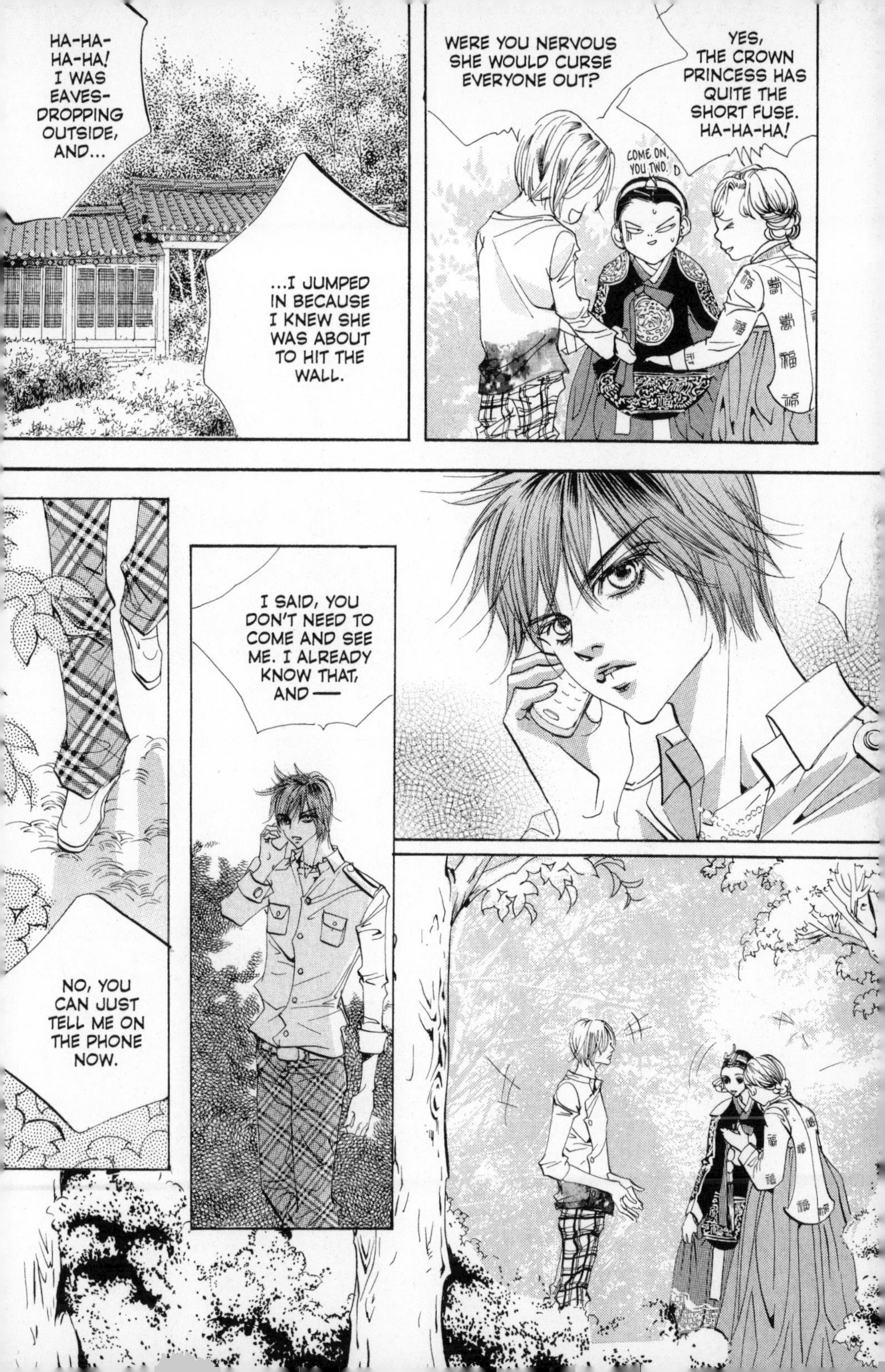
HA-HA-HA-HA! I WAS EAVES-DROPPING OUTSIDE, AND...
...I JUMPED IN BECAUSE I KNEW SHE WAS ABOUT TO HIT THE WALL.
WERE YOU NERVOUS SHE WOULD CURSE EVERYONE OUT?
YES, THE CROWN PRINCESS HAS QUITE THE SHORT FUSE. HA-HA-HA!
COME ON, YOU TWO.
I SAID, YOU DON'T NEED TO COME AND SEE ME. I ALREADY KNOW THAT, AND—
NO, YOU CAN JUST TELL ME ON THE PHONE NOW.

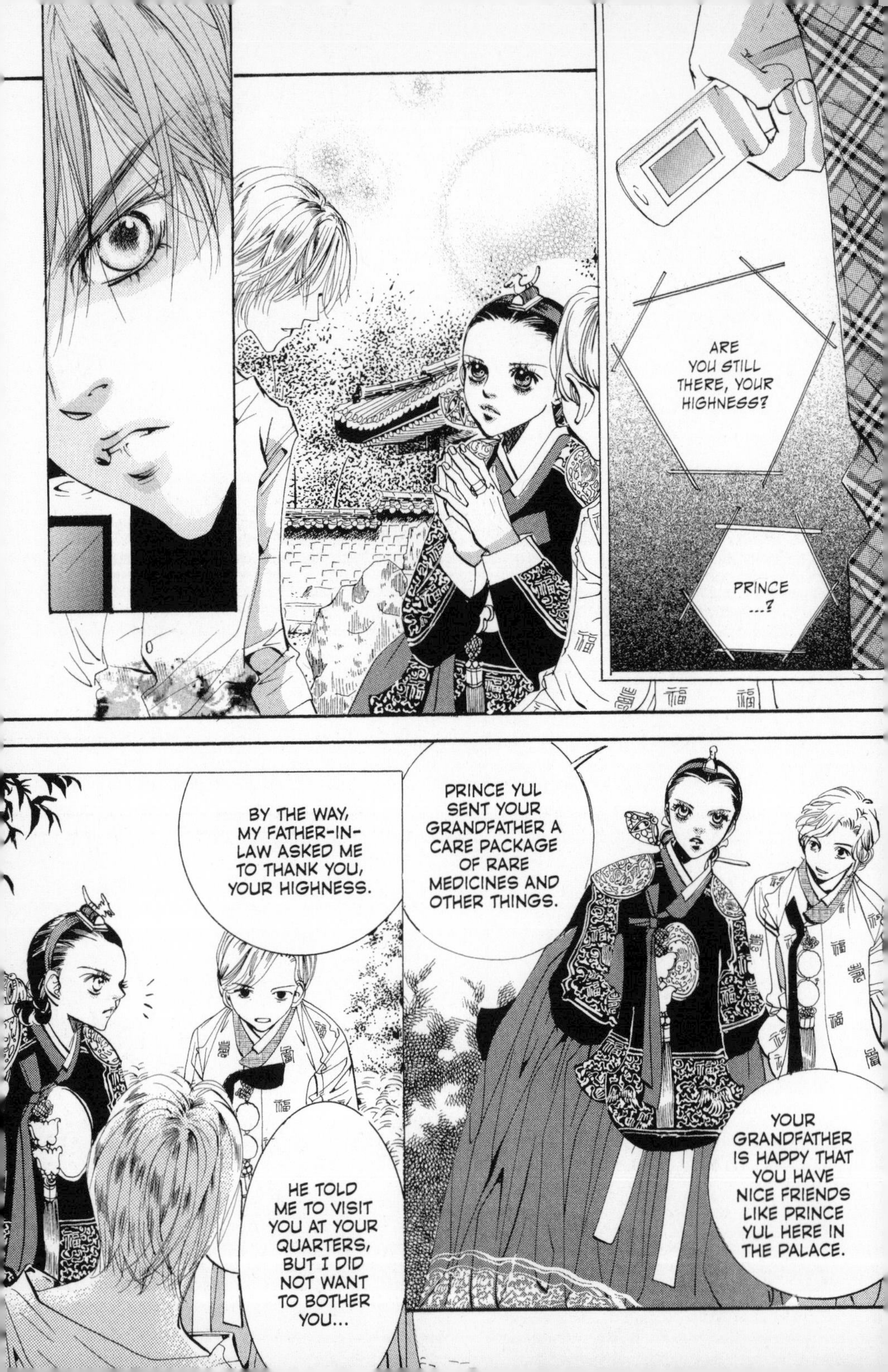
ARE YOU STILL THERE, YOUR HIGHNESS?
PRINCE ...?
BY THE WAY, MY FATHER-IN-LAW ASKED ME TO THANK YOU, YOUR HIGHNESS.
HE TOLD ME TO VISIT YOU AT YOUR QUARTERS, BUT I DID NOT WANT TO BOTHER YOU...
PRINCE YUL SENT YOUR GRANDFATHER A CARE PACKAGE OF RARE MEDICINES AND OTHER THINGS.
YOUR GRANDFATHER IS HAPPY THAT YOU HAVE NICE FRIENDS LIKE PRINCE YUL HERE IN THE PALACE.

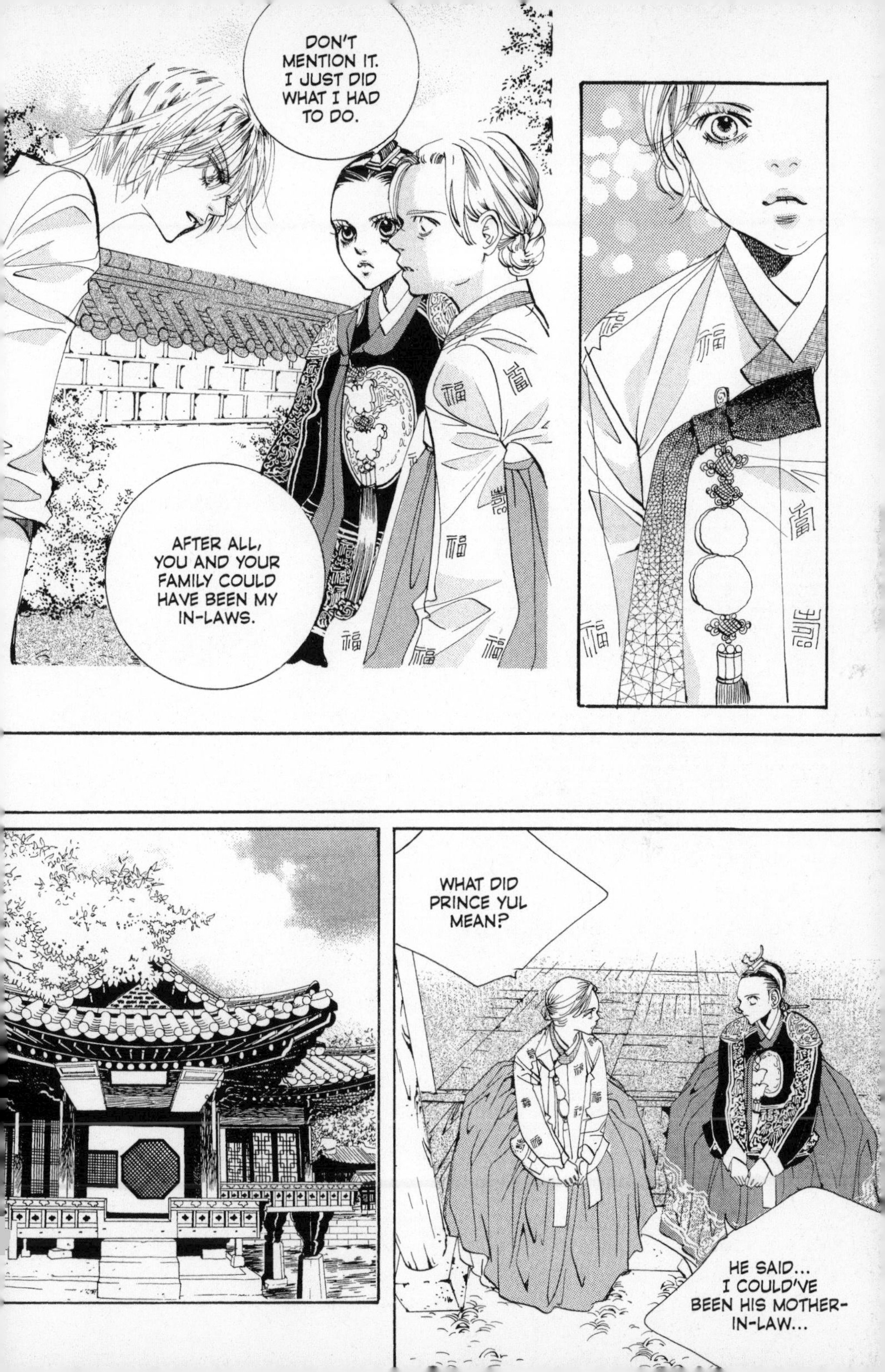
DON'T MENTION IT. I JUST DID WHAT I HAD TO DO.
AFTER ALL, YOU AND YOUR FAMILY COULD HAVE BEEN MY IN-LAWS.
WHAT DID PRINCE YUL MEAN?
HE SAID... I COULD'VE BEEN HIS MOTHER-IN-LAW...

WHAT YUL SAID IS TRUE. INITIALLY, I WAS ENGAGED TO YUL, NOT SHIN.

THE LATE KING PROMISED GRANDFATHER, "I WILL MAKE YOUR GRANDDAUGHTER THE QUEEN."

BACK THEN, YUL WAS THE ROYAL GRAND-SON, FIRST IN LINE FOR THE THRONE.

BUT WHEN YUL'S FATHER PASSED AWAY, SHIN BECAME THE ROYAL GRANDSON... AND MY FIANCÉ.

SO IF YUL'S FATHER HADN'T DIED...

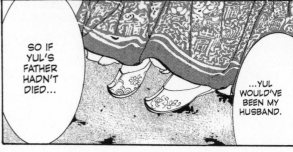

...YUL WOULD'VE BEEN MY HUSBAND.

I THINK...

...THAT WOULD'VE BEEN BETTER FOR YOU...

MOM ~!

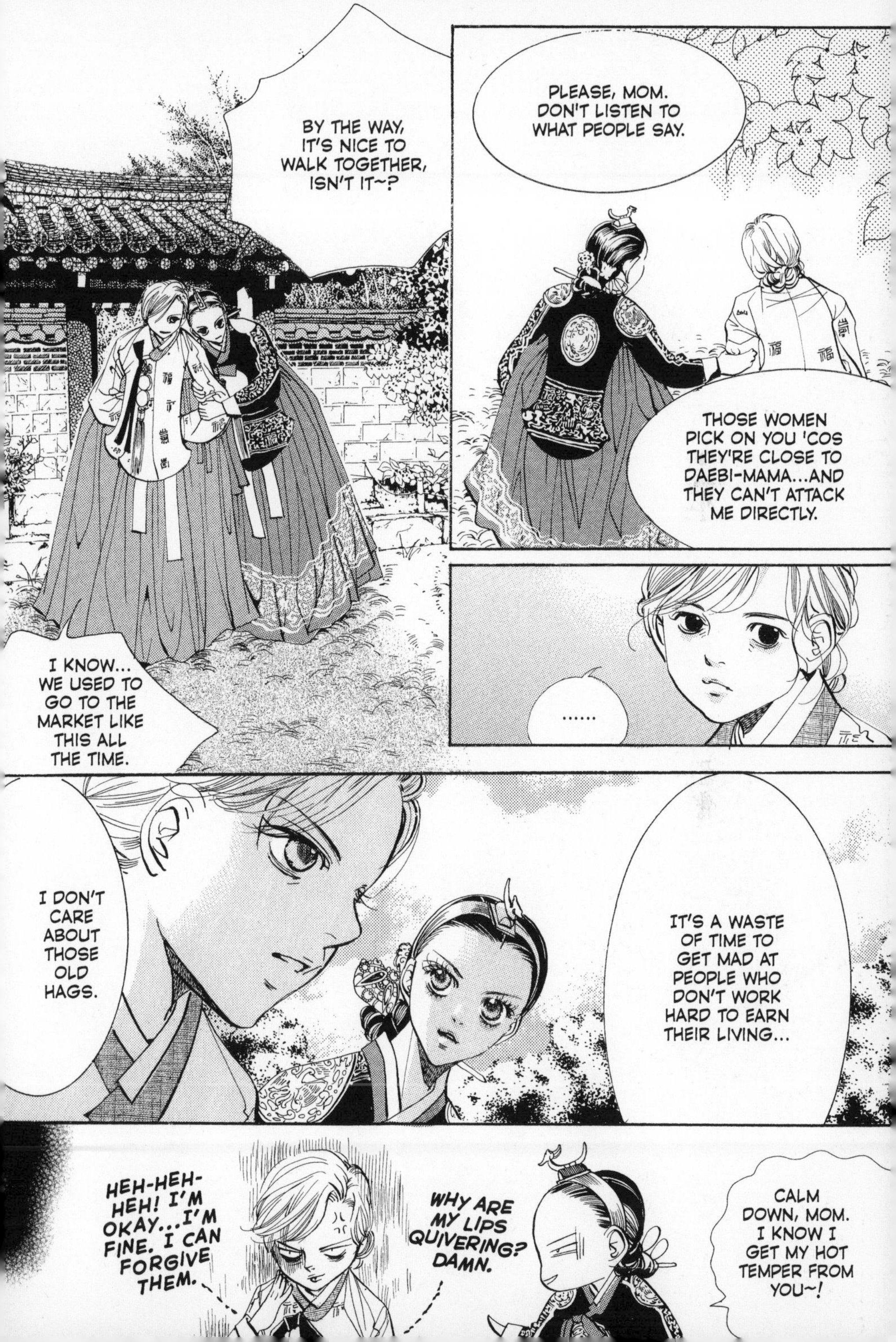
BY THE WAY, IT'S NICE TO WALK TOGETHER, ISN'T IT~?
I KNOW... WE USED TO GO TO THE MARKET LIKE THIS ALL THE TIME.
PLEASE, MOM. DON'T LISTEN TO WHAT PEOPLE SAY.
THOSE WOMEN PICK ON YOU 'COS THEY'RE CLOSE TO DAEBI-MAMA...AND THEY CAN'T ATTACK ME DIRECTLY.
......
I DON'T CARE ABOUT THOSE OLD HAGS.
IT'S A WASTE OF TIME TO GET MAD AT PEOPLE WHO DON'T WORK HARD TO EARN THEIR LIVING...
HEH-HEH-HEH! I'M OKAY...I'M FINE. I CAN FORGIVE THEM.
WHY ARE MY LIPS QUIVERING? DAMN.
CALM DOWN, MOM. I KNOW I GET MY HOT TEMPER FROM YOU~!

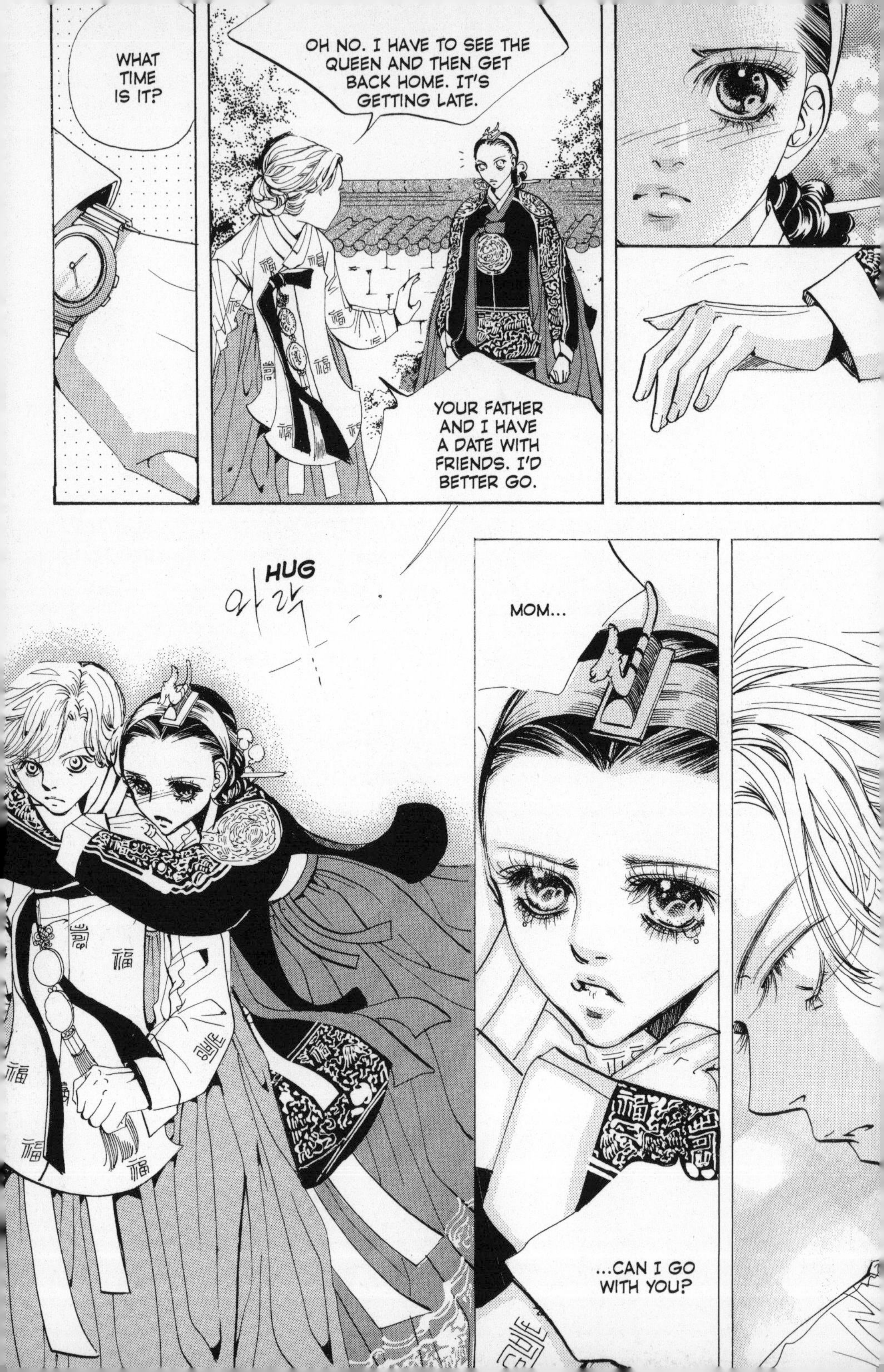
WHAT TIME IS IT?
OH NO. I HAVE TO SEE THE QUEEN AND THEN GET BACK HOME. IT'S GETTING LATE.
YOUR FATHER AND I HAVE A DATE WITH FRIENDS. I'D BETTER GO.
HUG
와락
MOM...
...CAN I GO WITH YOU?

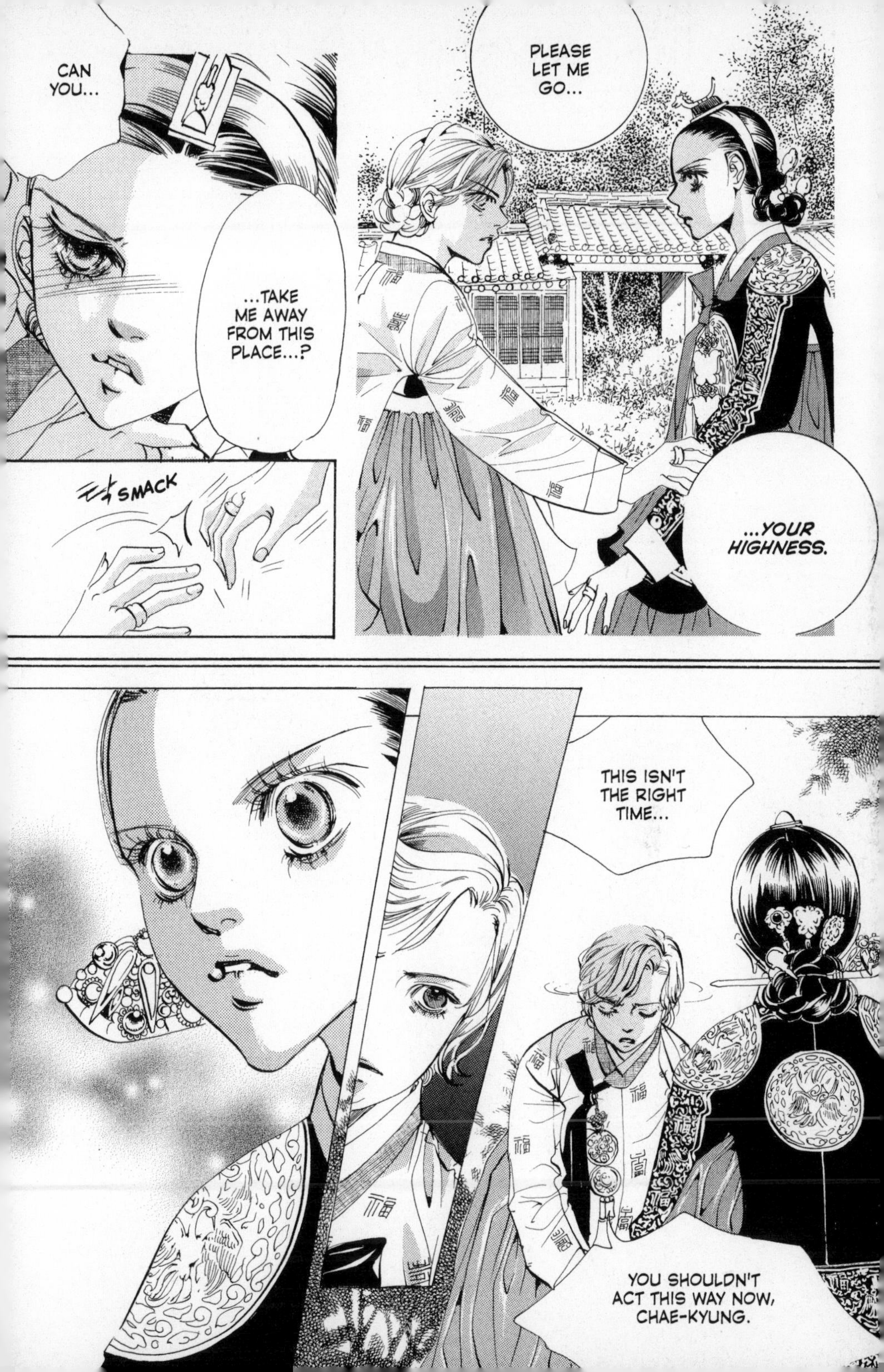
CAN YOU...
...TAKE ME AWAY FROM THIS PLACE...?
SMACK
PLEASE LET ME GO...
...YOUR HIGHNESS.
THIS ISN'T THE RIGHT TIME...
YOU SHOULDN'T ACT THIS WAY NOW, CHAE-KYUNG.

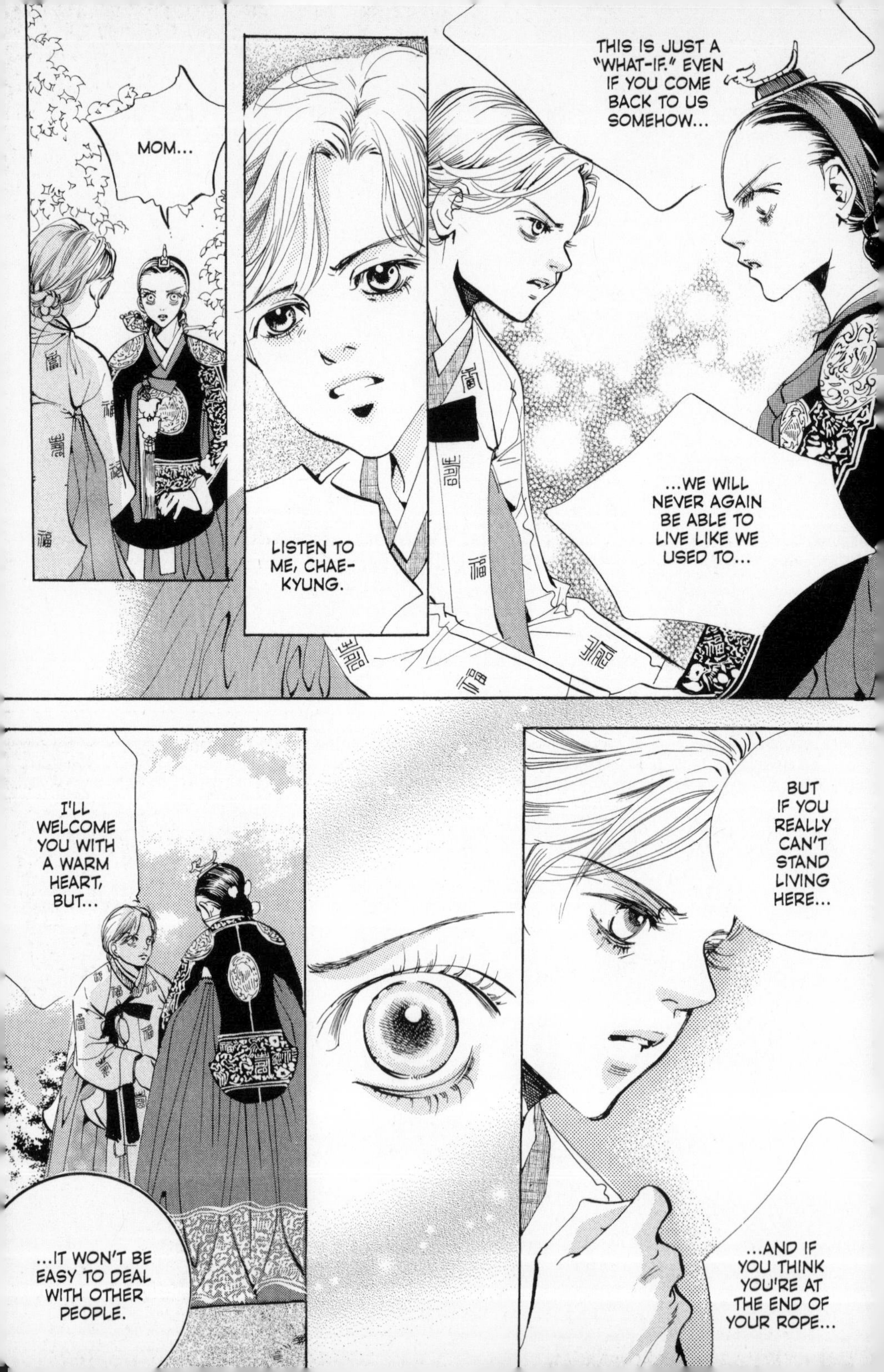
MOM...
LISTEN TO ME, CHAE-KYUNG.
THIS IS JUST A "WHAT-IF." EVEN IF YOU COME BACK TO US SOMEHOW...
...WE WILL NEVER AGAIN BE ABLE TO LIVE LIKE WE USED TO...
I'LL WELCOME YOU WITH A WARM HEART, BUT...
...IT WON'T BE EASY TO DEAL WITH OTHER PEOPLE.
BUT IF YOU REALLY CAN'T STAND LIVING HERE...
...AND IF YOU THINK YOU'RE AT THE END OF YOUR ROPE...

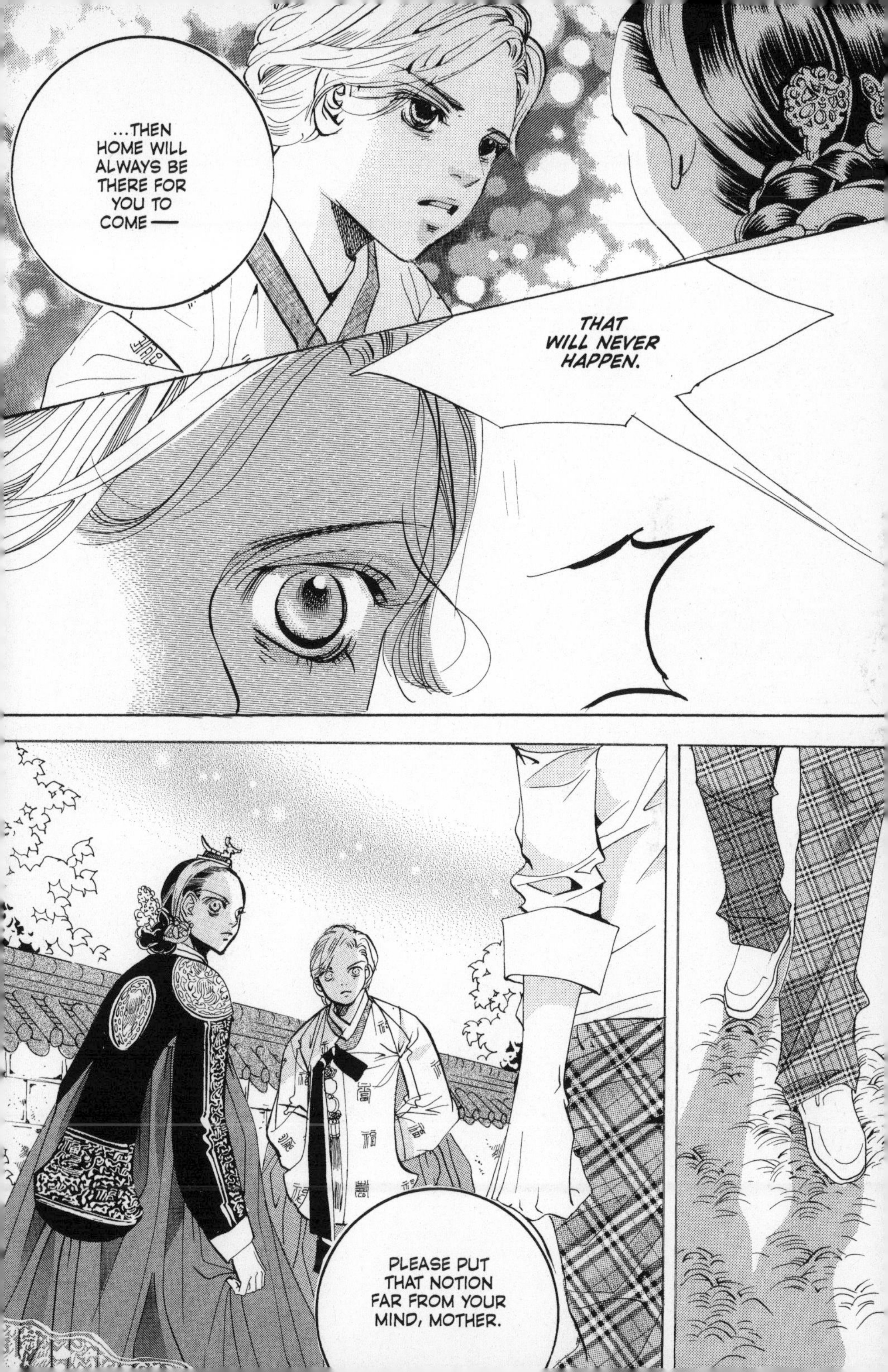
...THEN HOME WILL ALWAYS BE THERE FOR YOU TO COME—
THAT WILL NEVER HAPPEN.
PLEASE PUT THAT NOTION FAR FROM YOUR MIND, MOTHER.

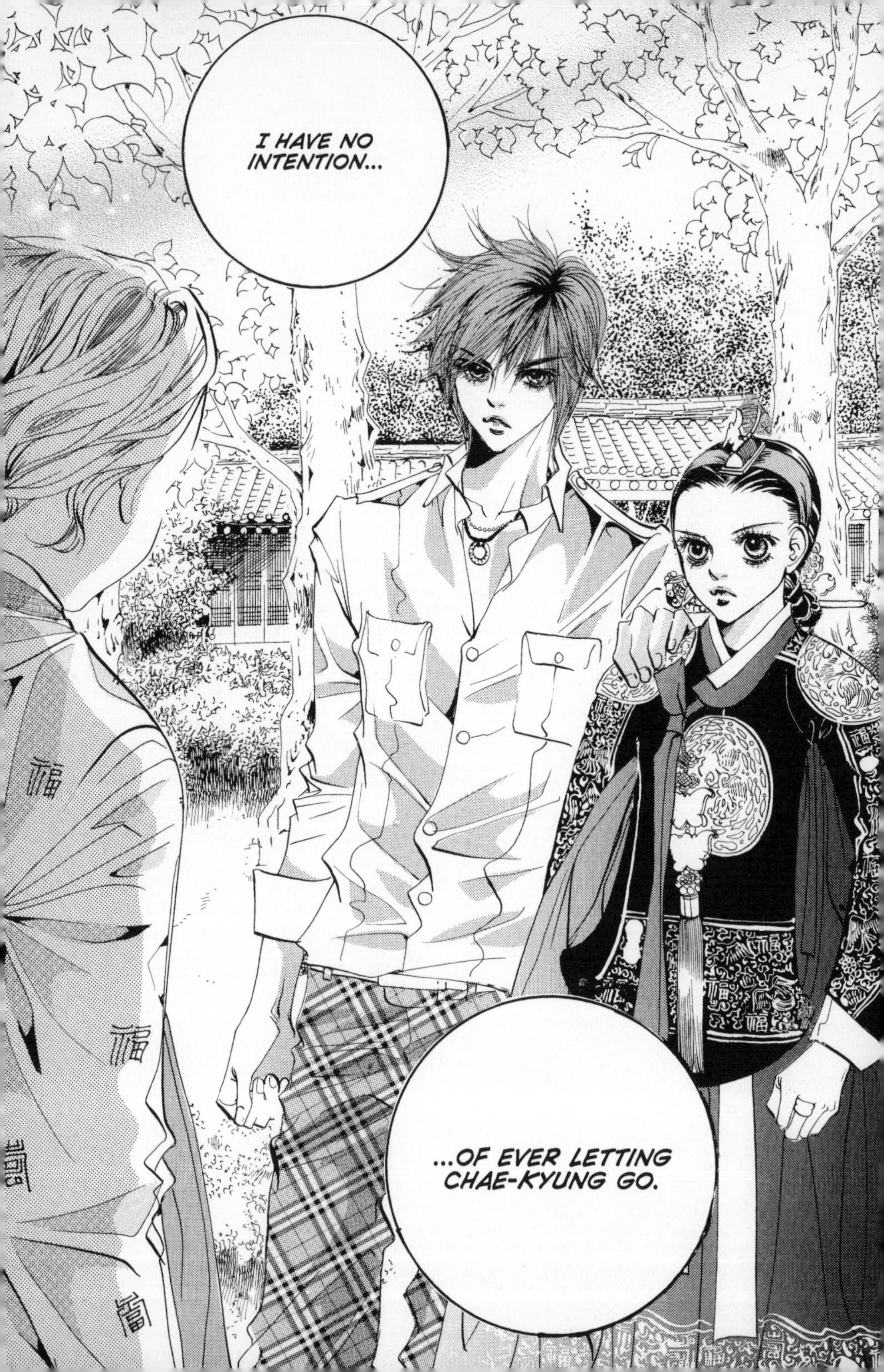
I HAVE NO INTENTION...
...OF EVER LETTING CHAE-KYUNG GO.

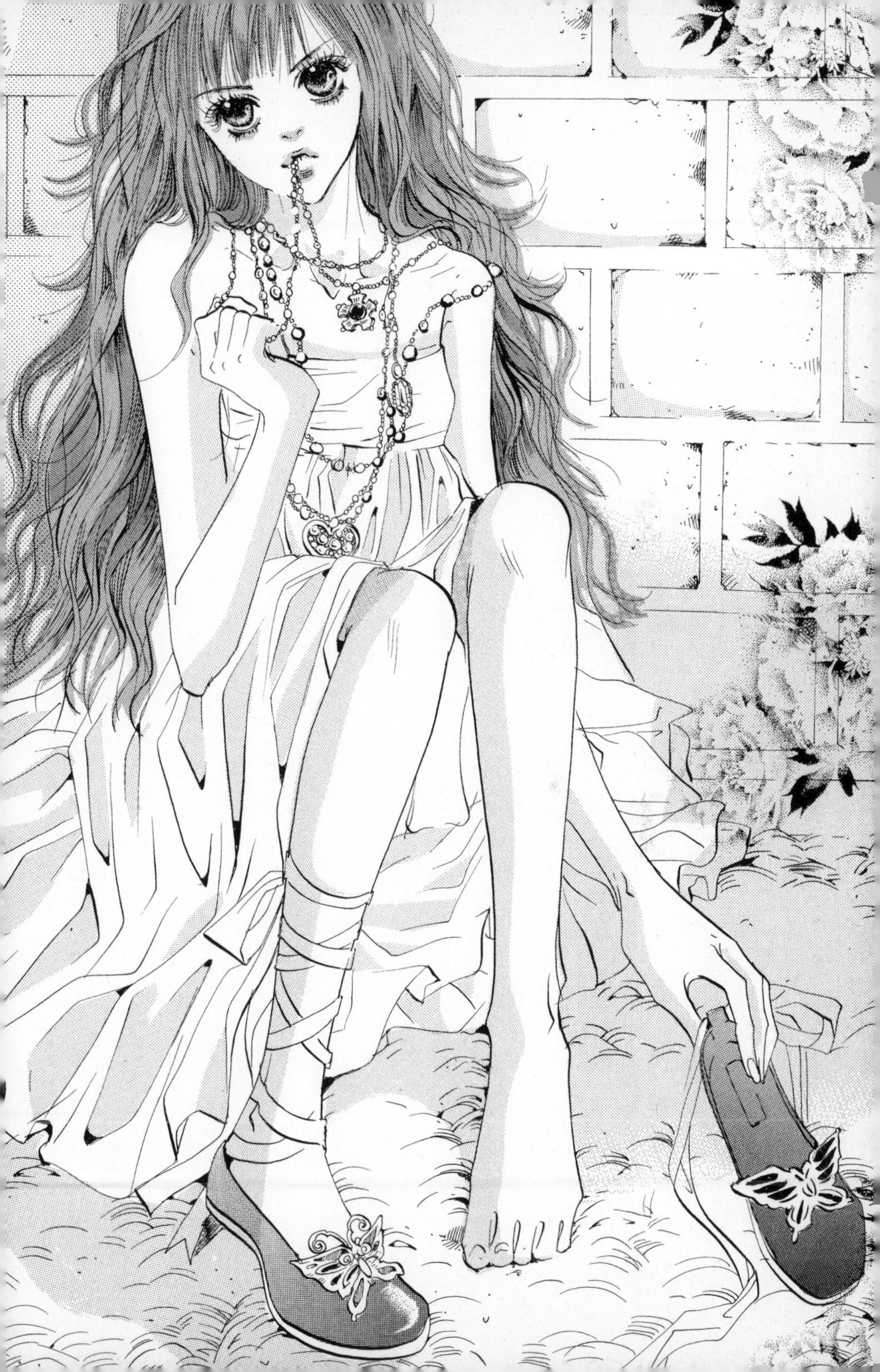

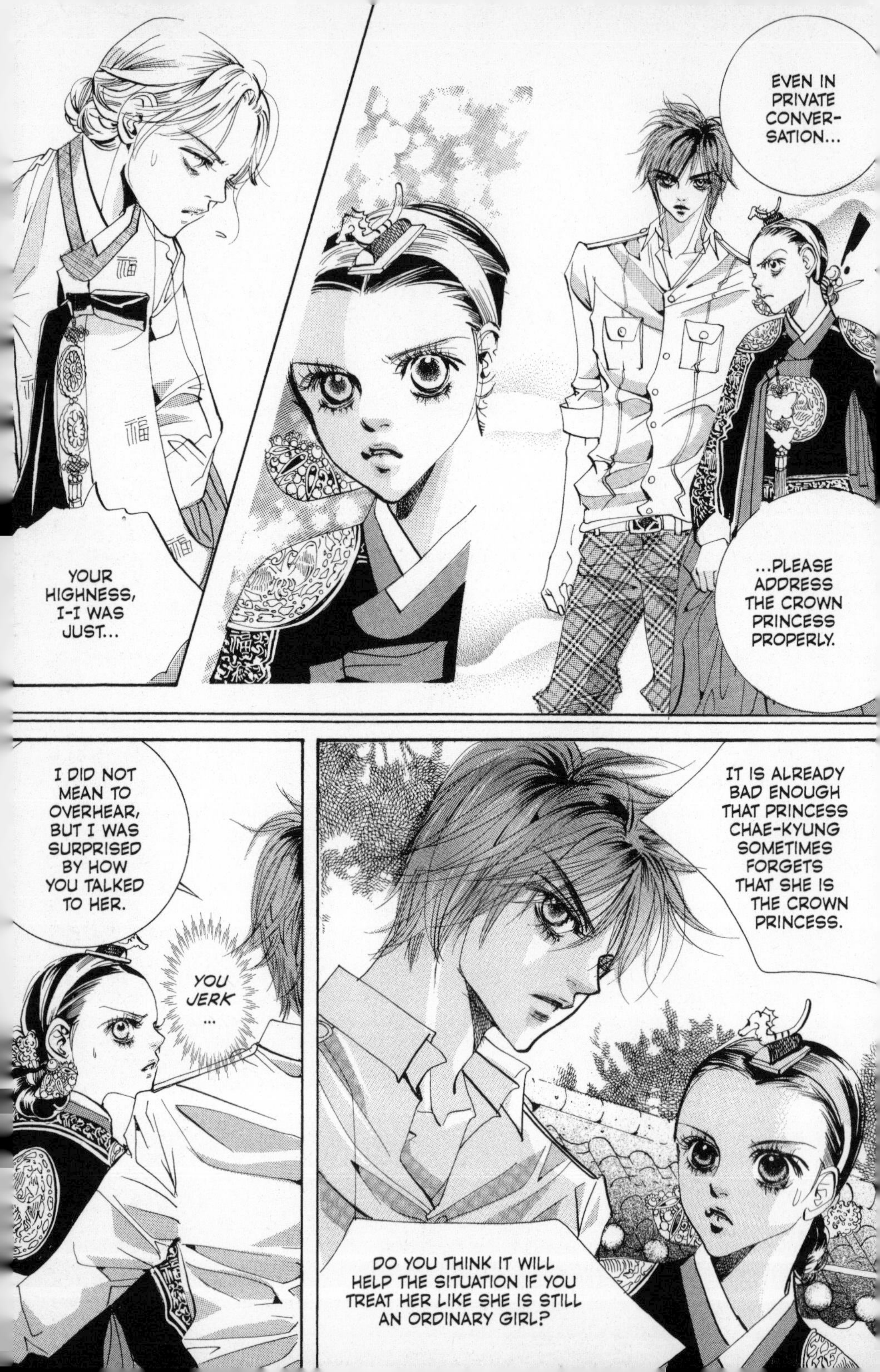
YOUR HIGHNESS, I-I WAS JUST...
EVEN IN PRIVATE CONVER-SATION...
...PLEASE ADDRESS THE CROWN PRINCESS PROPERLY.
I DID NOT MEAN TO OVERHEAR, BUT I WAS SURPRISED BY HOW YOU TALKED TO HER.
YOU JERK ...
IT IS ALREADY BAD ENOUGH THAT PRINCESS CHAE-KYUNG SOMETIMES FORGETS THAT SHE IS THE CROWN PRINCESS.
DO YOU THINK IT WILL HELP THE SITUATION IF YOU TREAT HER LIKE SHE IS STILL AN ORDINARY GIRL?

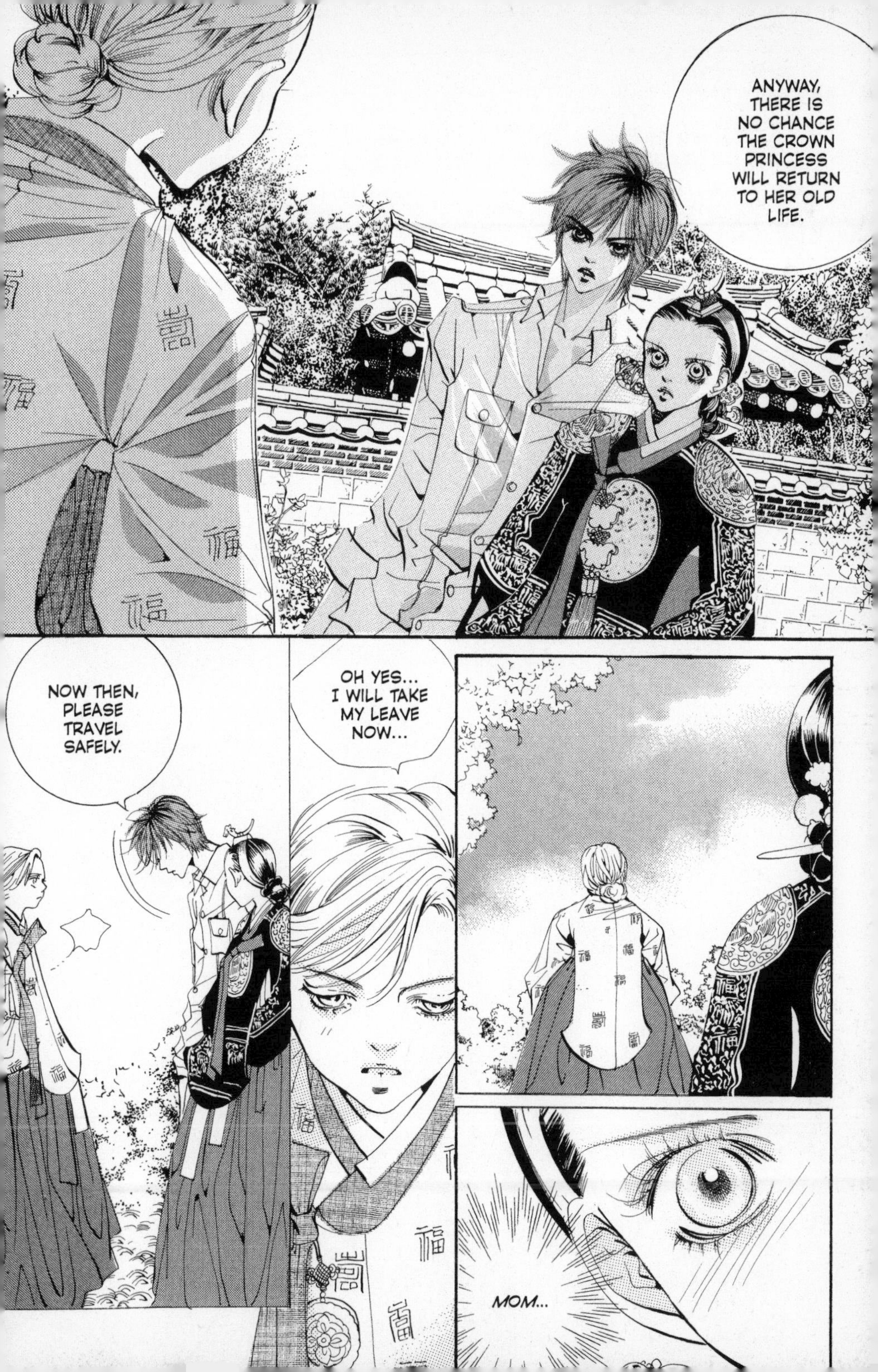
ANYWAY, THERE IS NO CHANCE THE CROWN PRINCESS WILL RETURN TO HER OLD LIFE.
NOW THEN, PLEASE TRAVEL SAFELY.
OH YES... I WILL TAKE MY LEAVE NOW...
MOM...

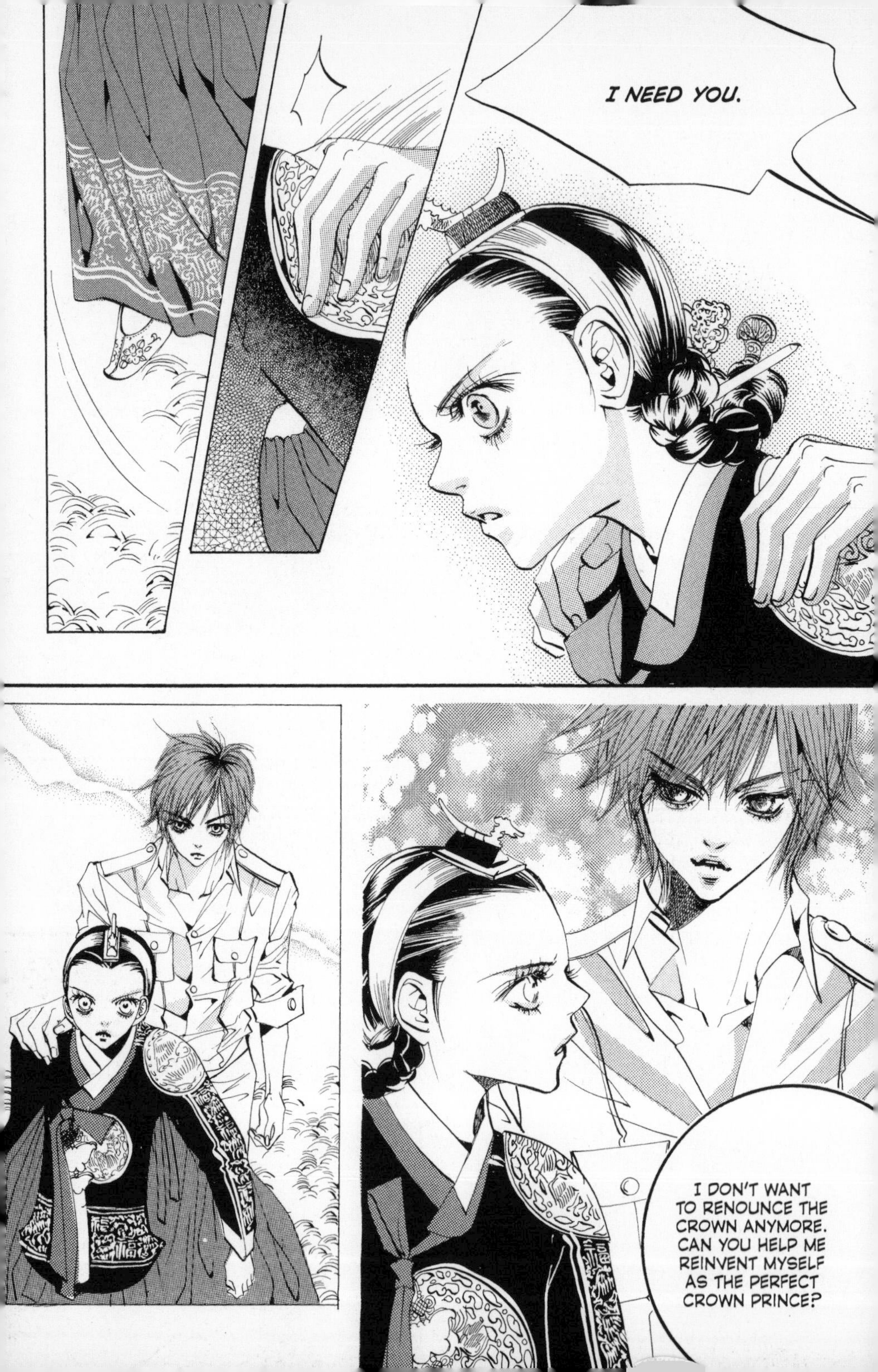
I NEED YOU.
I DON'T WANT TO RENOUNCE THE CROWN ANYMORE. CAN YOU HELP ME REINVENT MYSELF AS THE PERFECT CROWN PRINCE?

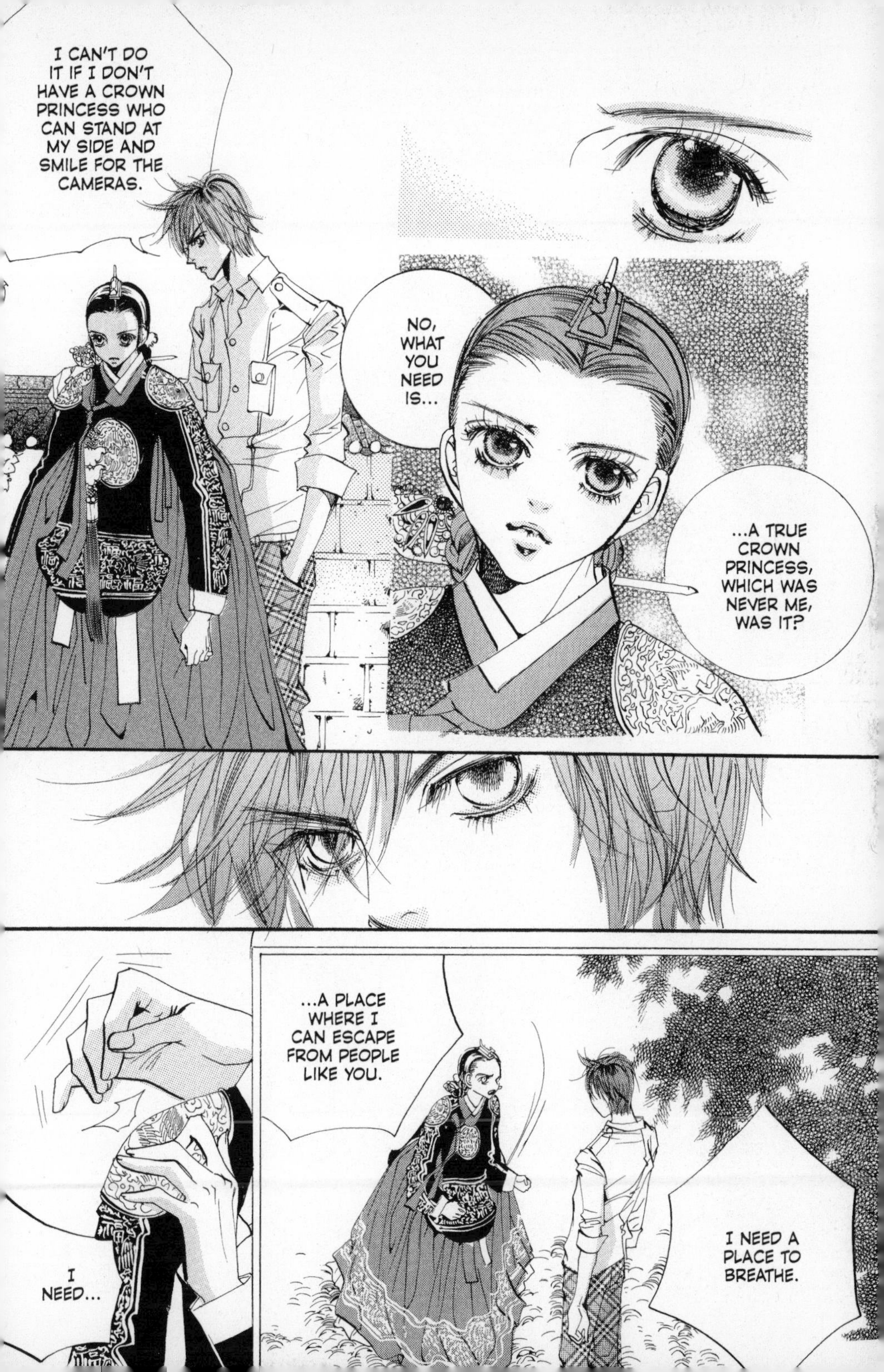
I CAN'T DO IT IF I DON'T HAVE A CROWN PRINCESS WHO CAN STAND AT MY SIDE AND SMILE FOR THE CAMERAS.
NO, WHAT YOU NEED IS...
...A TRUE CROWN PRINCESS, WHICH WAS NEVER ME, WAS IT?
I NEED...
...A PLACE WHERE I CAN ESCAPE FROM PEOPLE LIKE YOU.
I NEED A PLACE TO BREATHE.

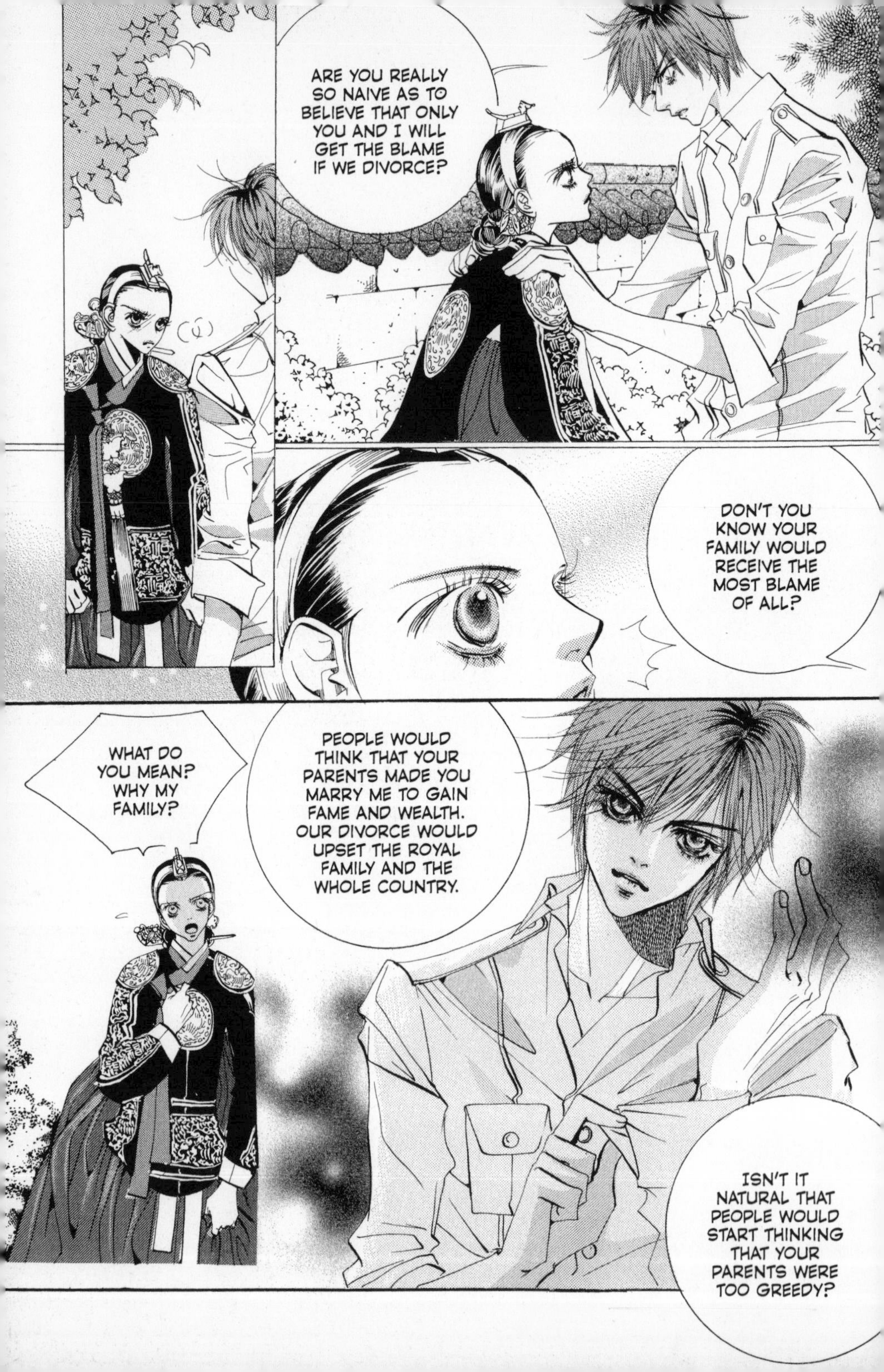
ARE YOU REALLY SO NAIVE AS TO BELIEVE THAT ONLY YOU AND I WILL GET THE BLAME IF WE DIVORCE?
DON'T YOU KNOW YOUR FAMILY WOULD RECEIVE THE MOST BLAME OF ALL?
WHAT DO YOU MEAN? WHY MY FAMILY?
PEOPLE WOULD THINK THAT YOUR PARENTS MADE YOU MARRY ME TO GAIN FAME AND WEALTH. OUR DIVORCE WOULD UPSET THE ROYAL FAMILY AND THE WHOLE COUNTRY.
ISN'T IT NATURAL THAT PEOPLE WOULD START THINKING THAT YOUR PARENTS WERE TOO GREEDY?

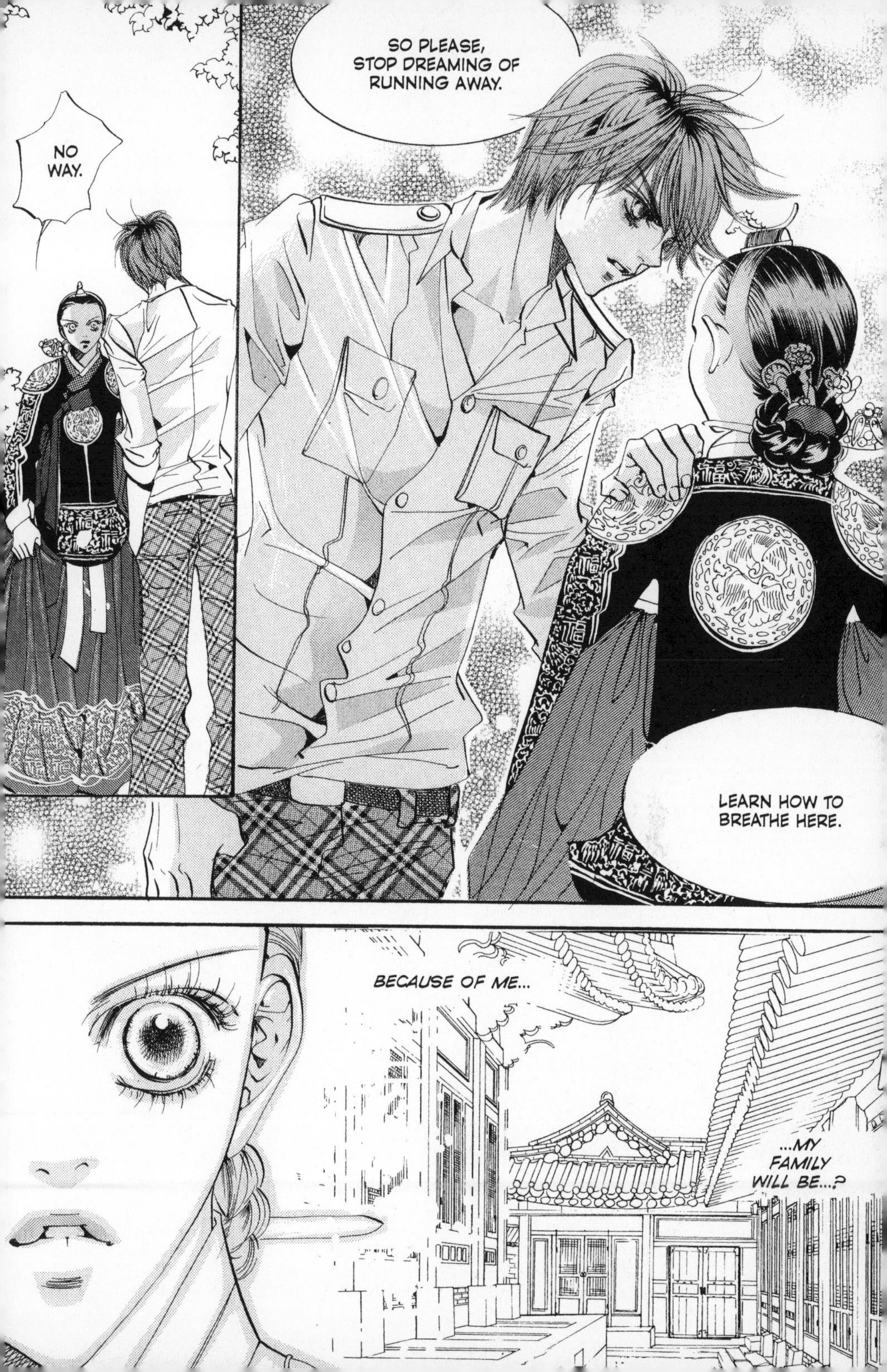
NO WAY.
SO PLEASE, STOP DREAMING OF RUNNING AWAY.
LEARN HOW TO BREATHE HERE.
BECAUSE OF ME...
...MY FAMILY WILL BE...?

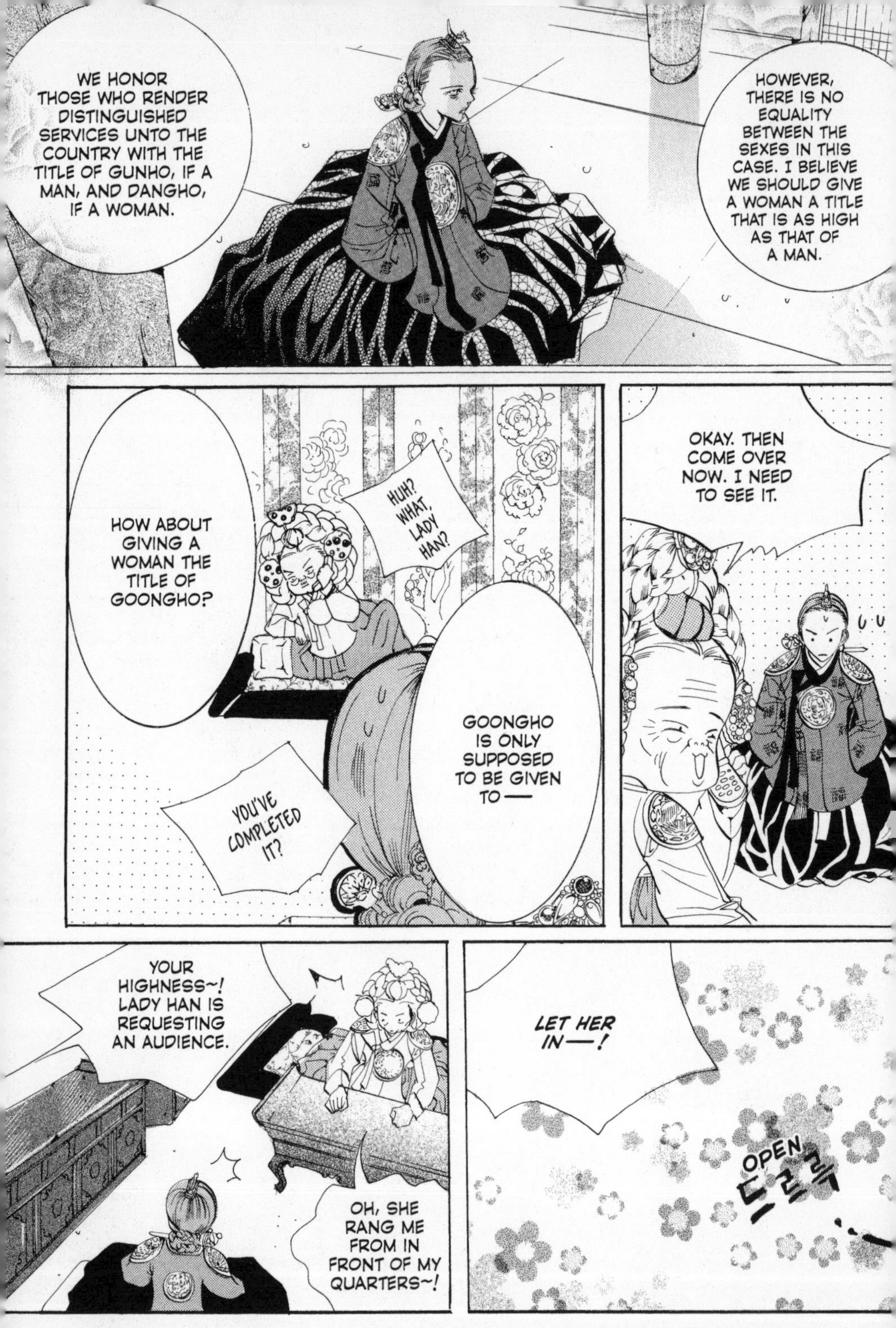
WE HONOR THOSE WHO RENDER DISTINGUISHED SERVICES UNTO THE COUNTRY WITH THE TITLE OF GUNHO, IF A MAN, AND DANGHO, IF A WOMAN.
HOWEVER, THERE IS NO EQUALITY BETWEEN THE SEXES IN THIS CASE. I BELIEVE WE SHOULD GIVE A WOMAN A TITLE THAT IS AS HIGH AS THAT OF A MAN.
HOW ABOUT GIVING A WOMAN THE TITLE OF GOONGHO?
HUH? WHAT, LADY HAN?
GOONGHO IS ONLY SUPPOSED TO BE GIVEN TO—
YOU'VE COMPLETED IT?
OKAY. THEN COME OVER NOW. I NEED TO SEE IT.
YOUR HIGHNESS~! LADY HAN IS REQUESTING AN AUDIENCE.
OH, SHE RANG ME FROM IN FRONT OF MY QUARTERS~!
LET HER IN—!
OPEN
드르륵

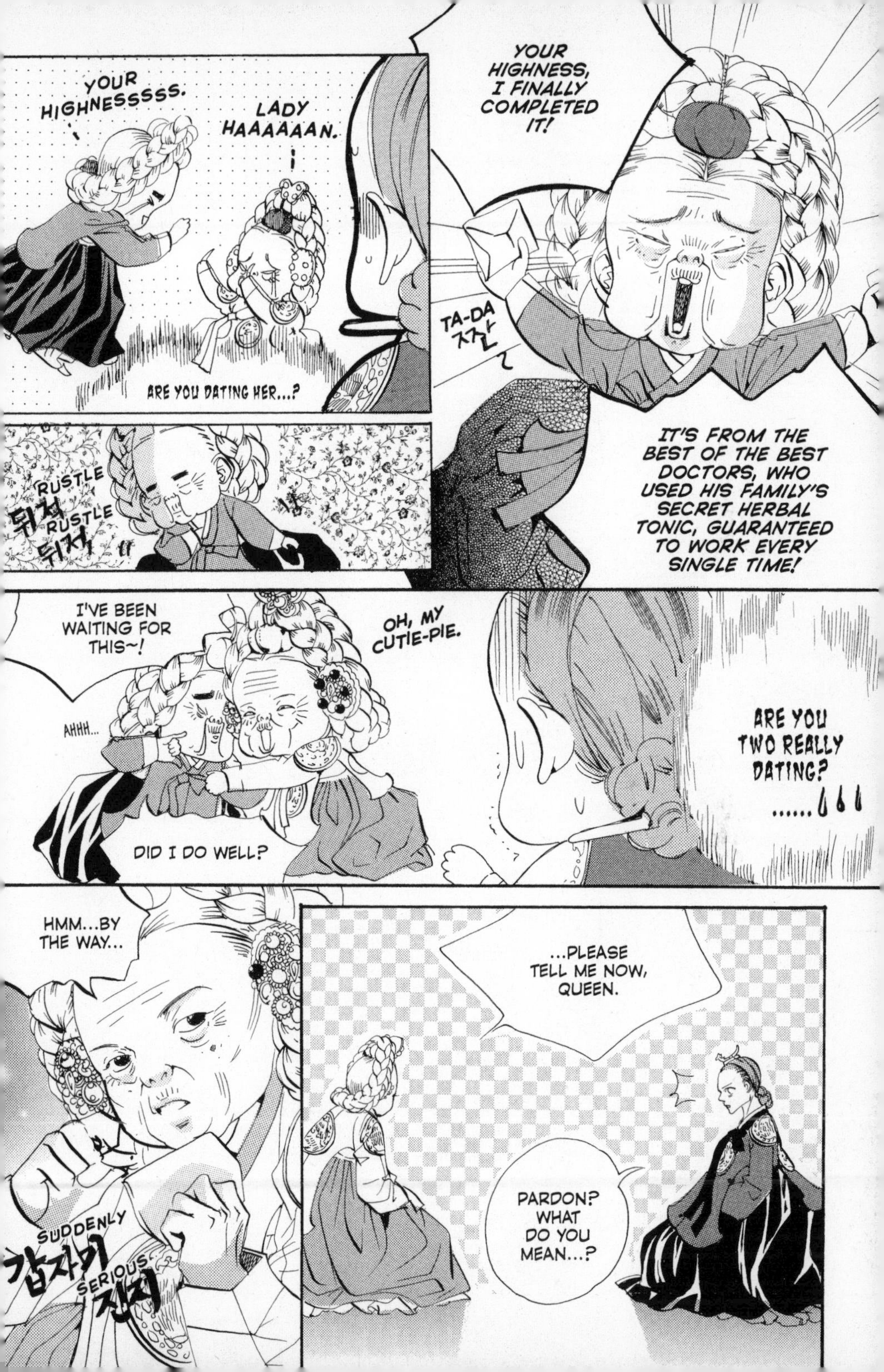
YOUR HIGHNESSSSS.
LADY HAAAAAAN.
ARE YOU DATING HER...?
RUSTLE 뒤적 RUSTLE 뒤적
YOUR HIGHNESS, I FINALLY COMPLETED IT!
TA-DA 짜잔
IT'S FROM THE BEST OF THE BEST DOCTORS, WHO USED HIS FAMILY'S SECRET HERBAL TONIC, GUARANTEED TO WORK EVERY SINGLE TIME!
I'VE BEEN WAITING FOR THIS~!
OH, MY CUTIE-PIE.
AHHH...
DID I DO WELL?
ARE YOU TWO REALLY DATING?
......
HMM...BY THE WAY...
SUDDENLY 갑자기 SERIOUS 진지
...PLEASE TELL ME NOW, QUEEN.
PARDON? WHAT DO YOU MEAN...?

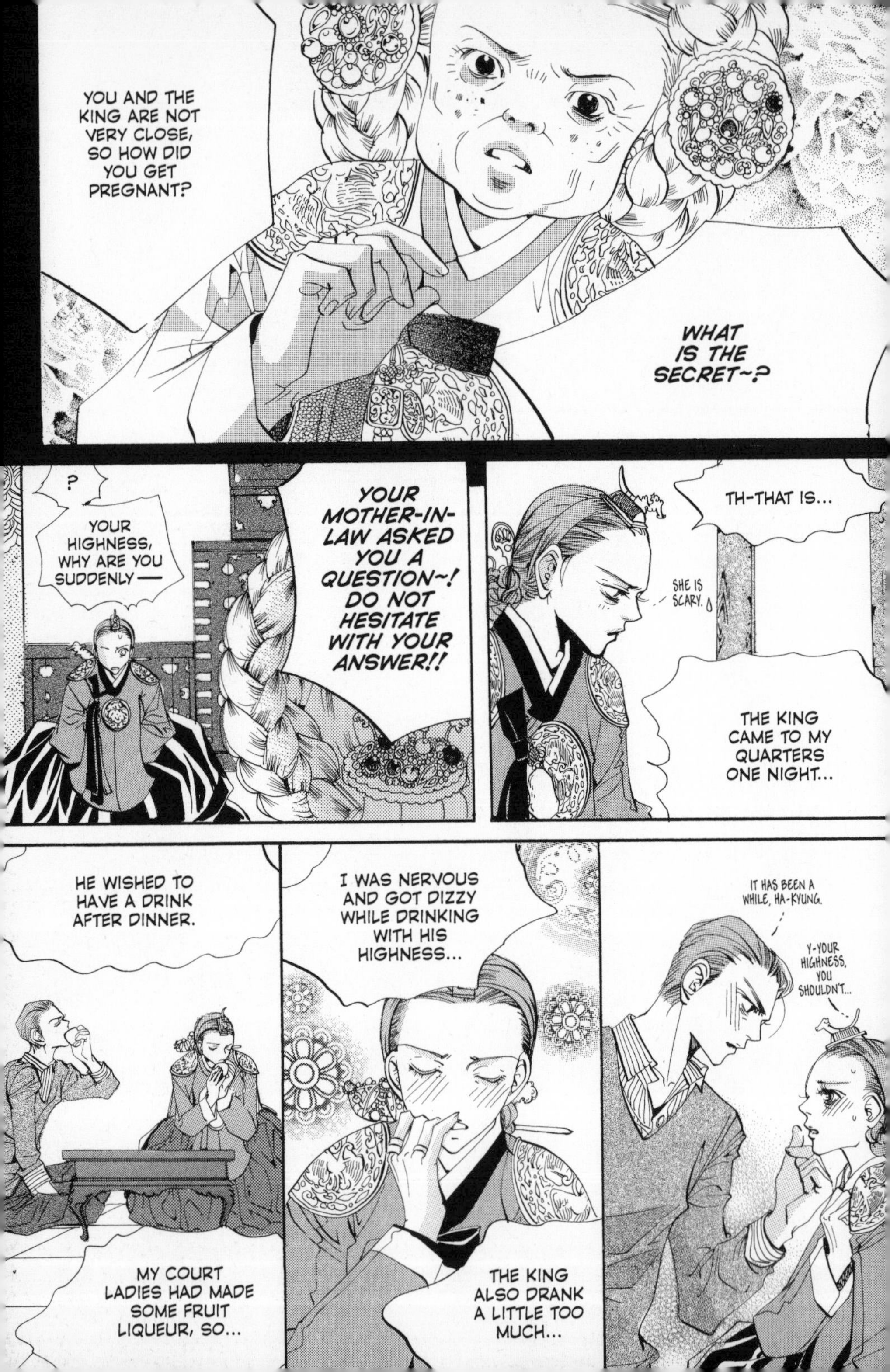
YOU AND THE KING ARE NOT VERY CLOSE, SO HOW DID YOU GET PREGNANT?
WHAT IS THE SECRET~?
?
YOUR HIGHNESS, WHY ARE YOU SUDDENLY—
YOUR MOTHER-IN-LAW ASKED YOU A QUESTION~! DO NOT HESITATE WITH YOUR ANSWER!!
TH-THAT IS...
SHE IS SCARY.
THE KING CAME TO MY QUARTERS ONE NIGHT...
HE WISHED TO HAVE A DRINK AFTER DINNER.
MY COURT LADIES HAD MADE SOME FRUIT LIQUEUR, SO...
I WAS NERVOUS AND GOT DIZZY WHILE DRINKING WITH HIS HIGHNESS...
THE KING ALSO DRANK A LITTLE TOO MUCH...
IT HAS BEEN A WHILE, HA-KYUNG.
Y-YOUR HIGHNESS, YOU SHOULDN'T...

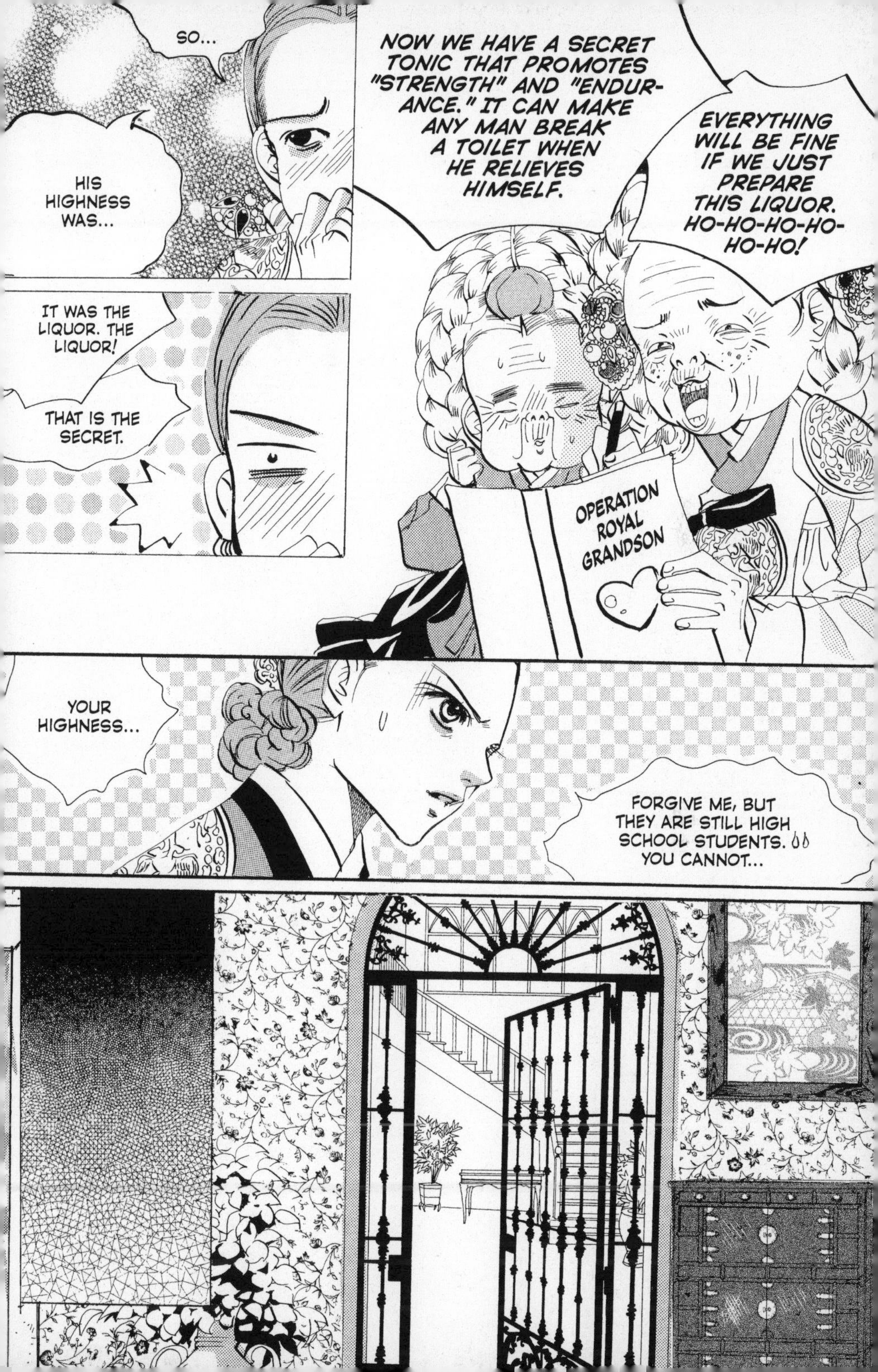
SO...
HIS HIGHNESS WAS...
NOW WE HAVE A SECRET TONIC THAT PROMOTES "STRENGTH" AND "ENDURANCE." IT CAN MAKE ANY MAN BREAK A TOILET WHEN HE RELIEVES HIMSELF.
EVERYTHING WILL BE FINE IF WE JUST PREPARE THIS LIQUOR. HO-HO-HO-HO-HO-HO!
IT WAS THE LIQUOR. THE LIQUOR!
THAT IS THE SECRET.
OPERATION ROYAL GRANDSON
YOUR HIGHNESS...
FORGIVE ME, BUT THEY ARE STILL HIGH SCHOOL STUDENTS.
YOU CANNOT...

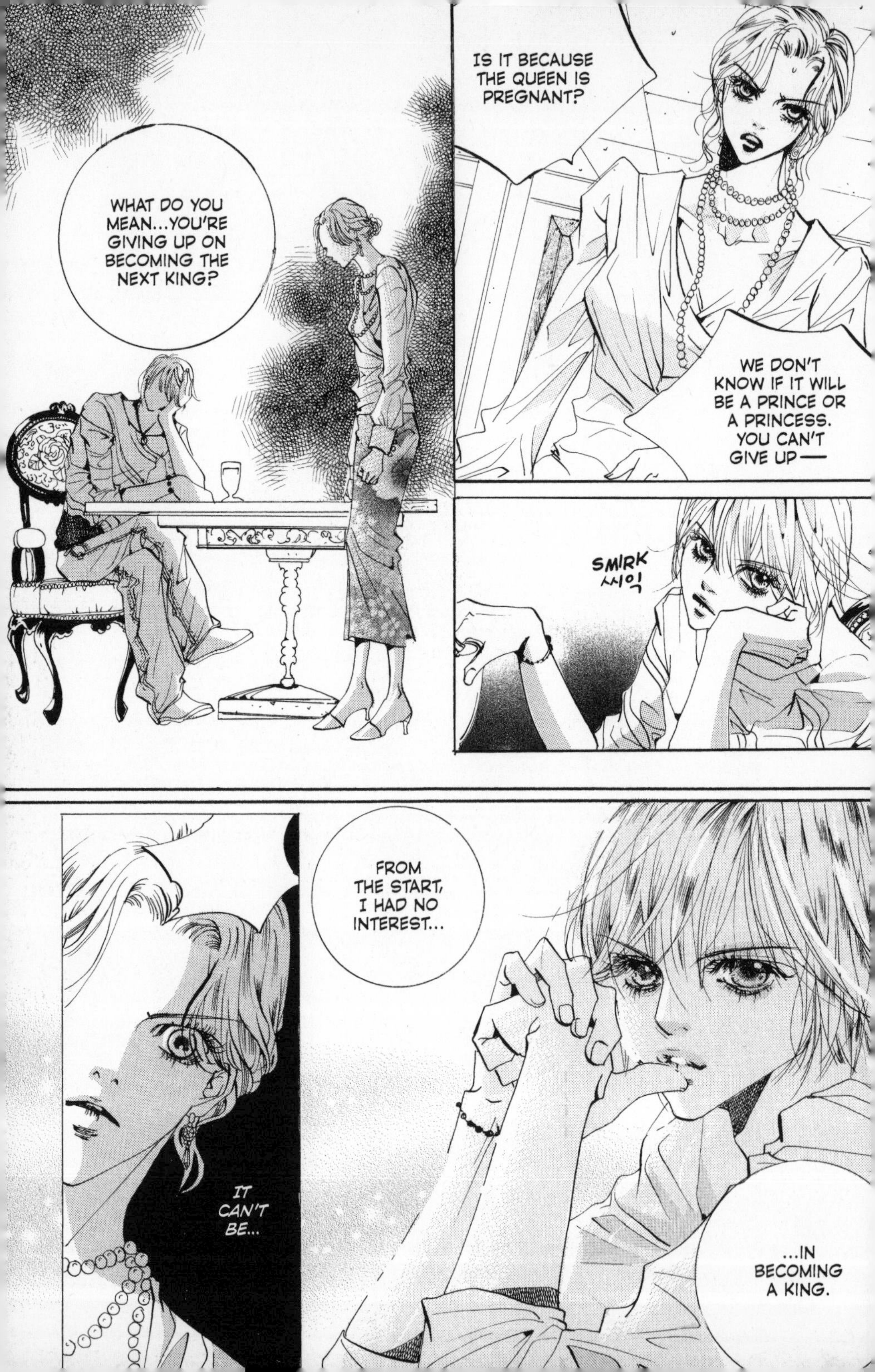
WHAT DO YOU MEAN...YOU'RE GIVING UP ON BECOMING THE NEXT KING?
IS IT BECAUSE THE QUEEN IS PREGNANT?
WE DON'T KNOW IF IT WILL BE A PRINCE OR A PRINCESS. YOU CAN'T GIVE UP—
SMIRK
씨익
IT CAN'T BE...
FROM THE START, I HAD NO INTEREST...
...IN BECOMING A KING.

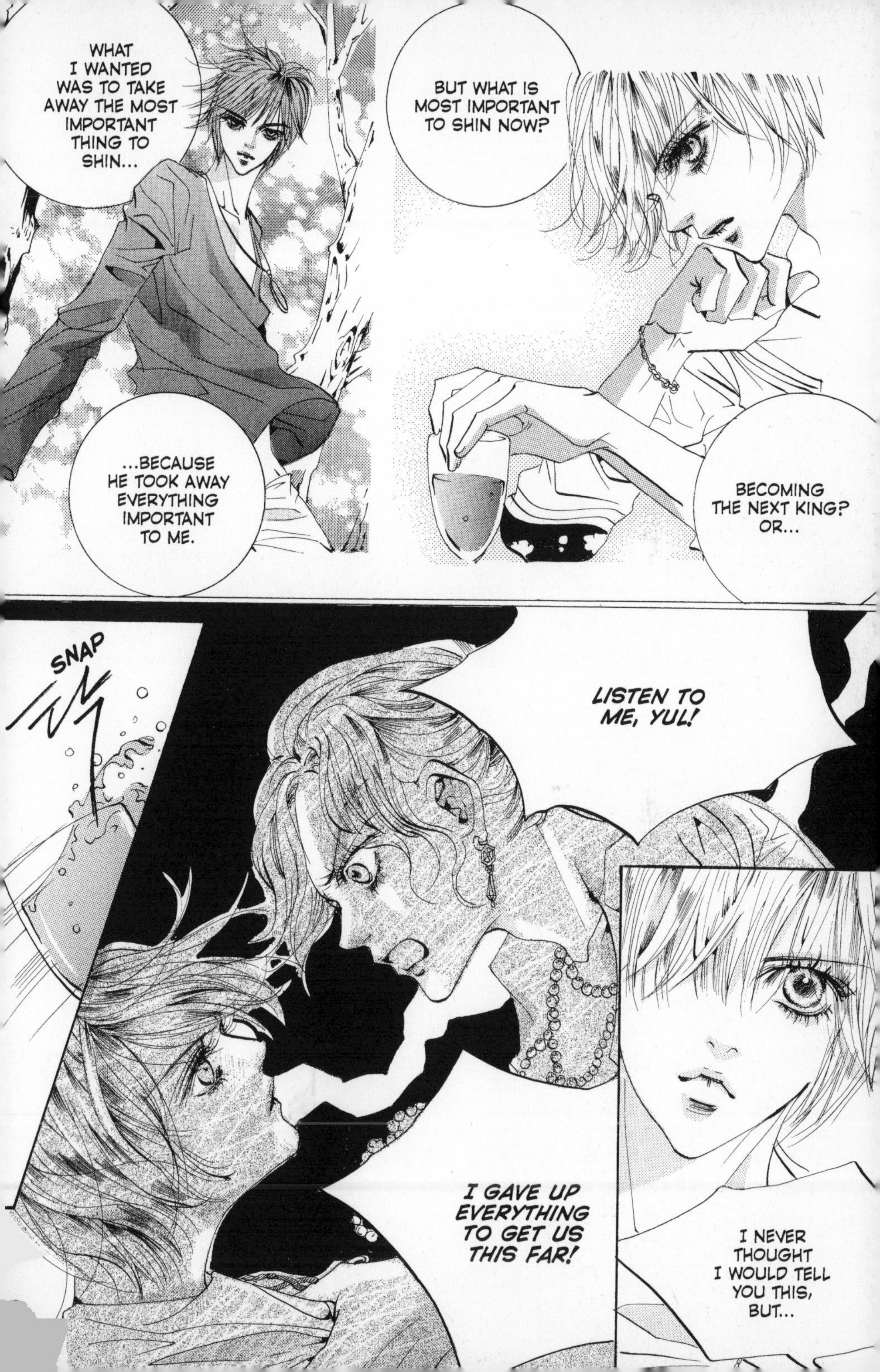
WHAT I WANTED WAS TO TAKE AWAY THE MOST IMPORTANT THING TO SHIN...
...BECAUSE HE TOOK AWAY EVERYTHING IMPORTANT TO ME.
BUT WHAT IS MOST IMPORTANT TO SHIN NOW?
BECOMING THE NEXT KING? OR...
SNAP
LISTEN TO ME, YUL!
I GAVE UP EVERYTHING TO GET US THIS FAR!
I NEVER THOUGHT I WOULD TELL YOU THIS, BUT...

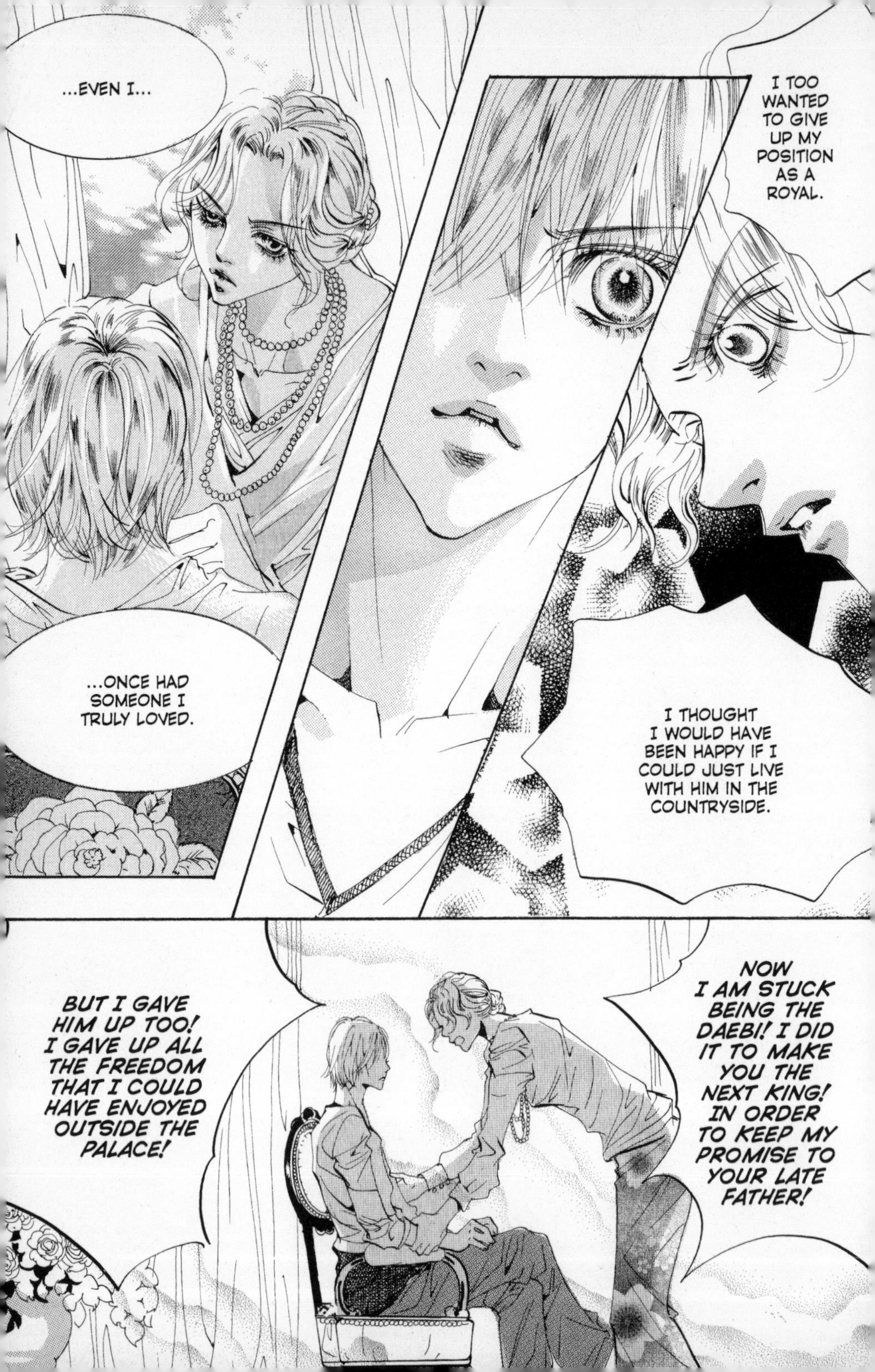
...EVEN I...
...ONCE HAD SOMEONE I TRULY LOVED.
I TOO WANTED TO GIVE UP MY POSITION AS A ROYAL.
I THOUGHT I WOULD HAVE BEEN HAPPY IF I COULD JUST LIVE WITH HIM IN THE COUNTRYSIDE.
BUT I GAVE HIM UP TOO! I GAVE UP ALL THE FREEDOM THAT I COULD HAVE ENJOYED OUTSIDE THE PALACE!
NOW I AM STUCK BEING THE DAEBI! I DID IT TO MAKE YOU THE NEXT KING! IN ORDER TO KEEP MY PROMISE TO YOUR LATE FATHER!

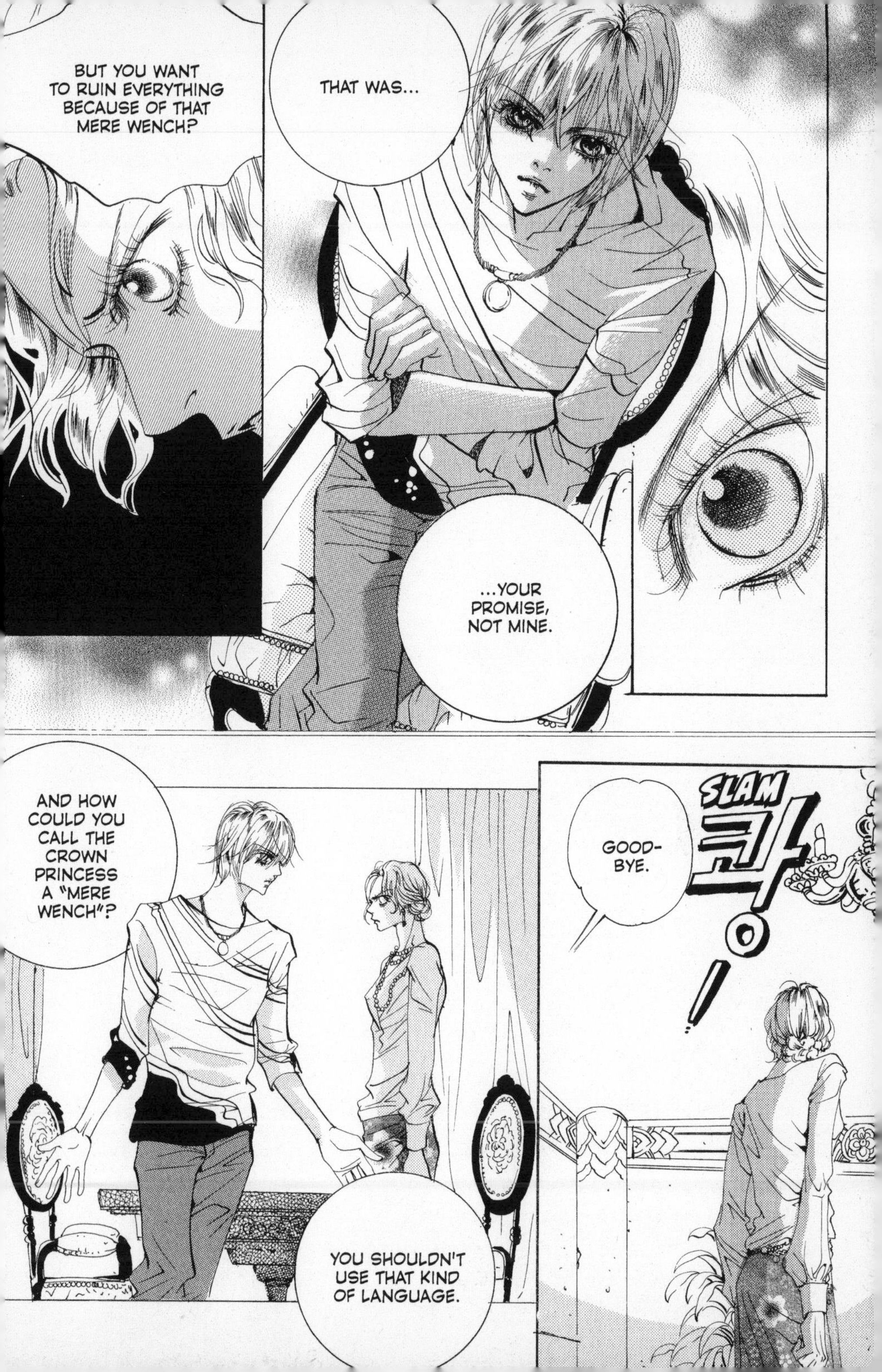
BUT YOU WANT TO RUIN EVERYTHING BECAUSE OF THAT MERE WENCH?
THAT WAS...
...YOUR PROMISE, NOT MINE.
AND HOW COULD YOU CALL THE CROWN PRINCESS A "MERE WENCH"?
YOU SHOULDN'T USE THAT KIND OF LANGUAGE.
GOOD-BYE.
SLAM
쾅!

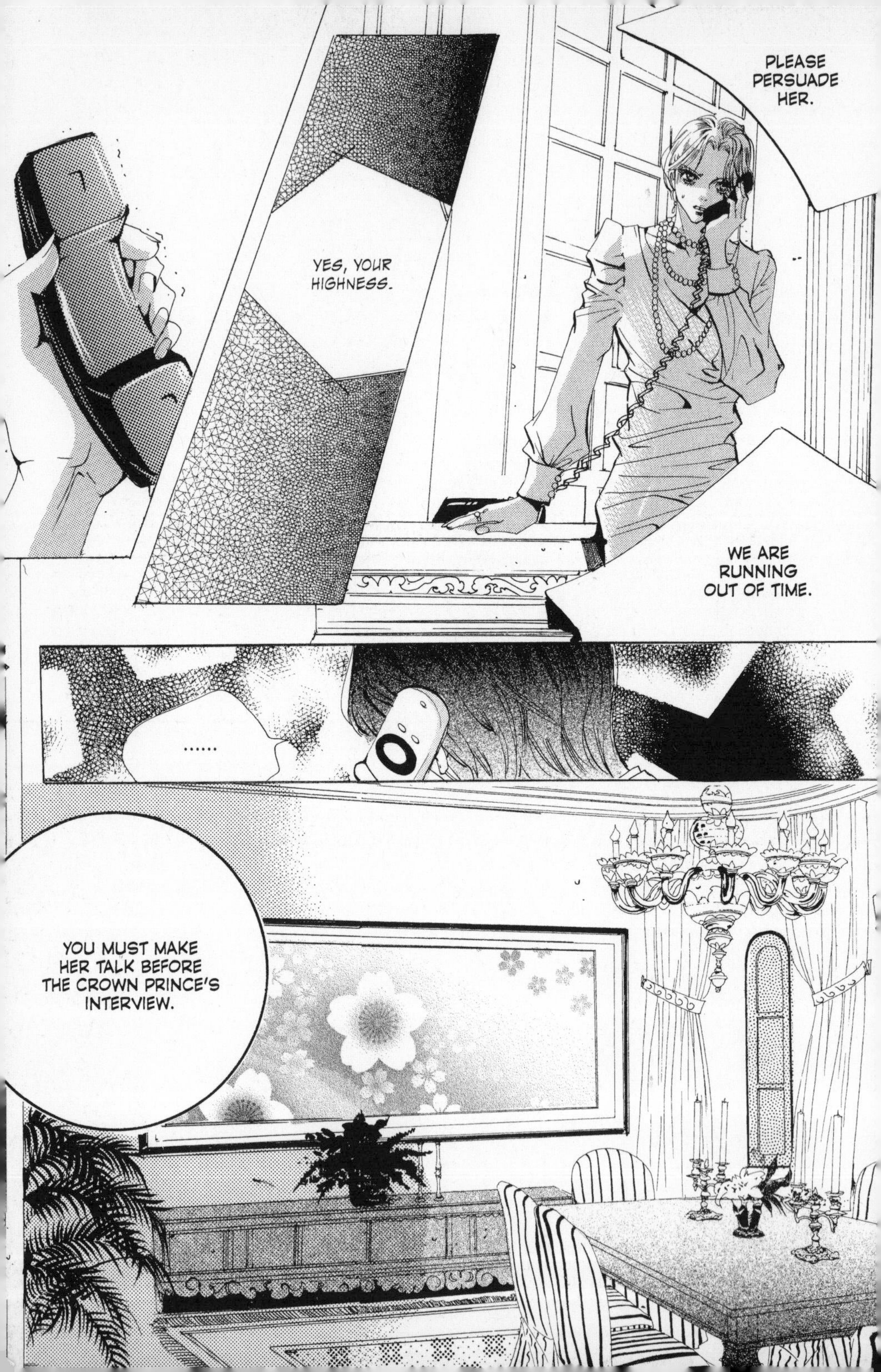
YES, YOUR HIGHNESS.
PLEASE PERSUADE HER.
WE ARE RUNNING OUT OF TIME.
......
YOU MUST MAKE HER TALK BEFORE THE CROWN PRINCE'S INTERVIEW.

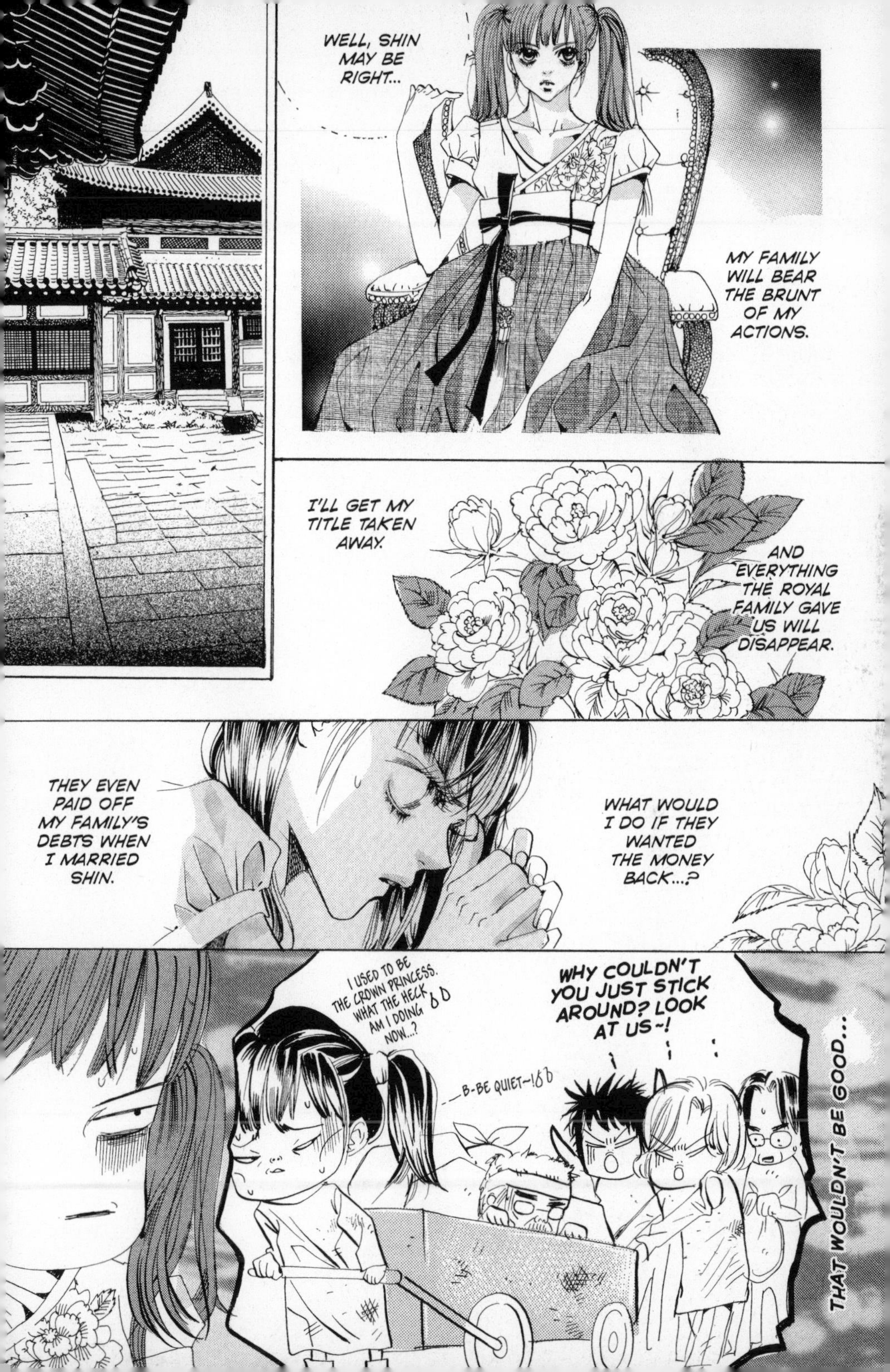
WELL, SHIN MAY BE RIGHT...
MY FAMILY WILL BEAR THE BRUNT OF MY ACTIONS.
I'LL GET MY TITLE TAKEN AWAY.
AND EVERYTHING THE ROYAL FAMILY GAVE US WILL DISAPPEAR.
THEY EVEN PAID OFF MY FAMILY'S DEBTS WHEN I MARRIED SHIN.
WHAT WOULD I DO IF THEY WANTED THE MONEY BACK...?
I USED TO BE THE CROWN PRINCESS. WHAT THE HECK AM I DOING NOW...?
WHY COULDN'T YOU JUST STICK AROUND? LOOK AT US~!
B-BE QUIET~!
THAT WOULDN'T BE GOOD...

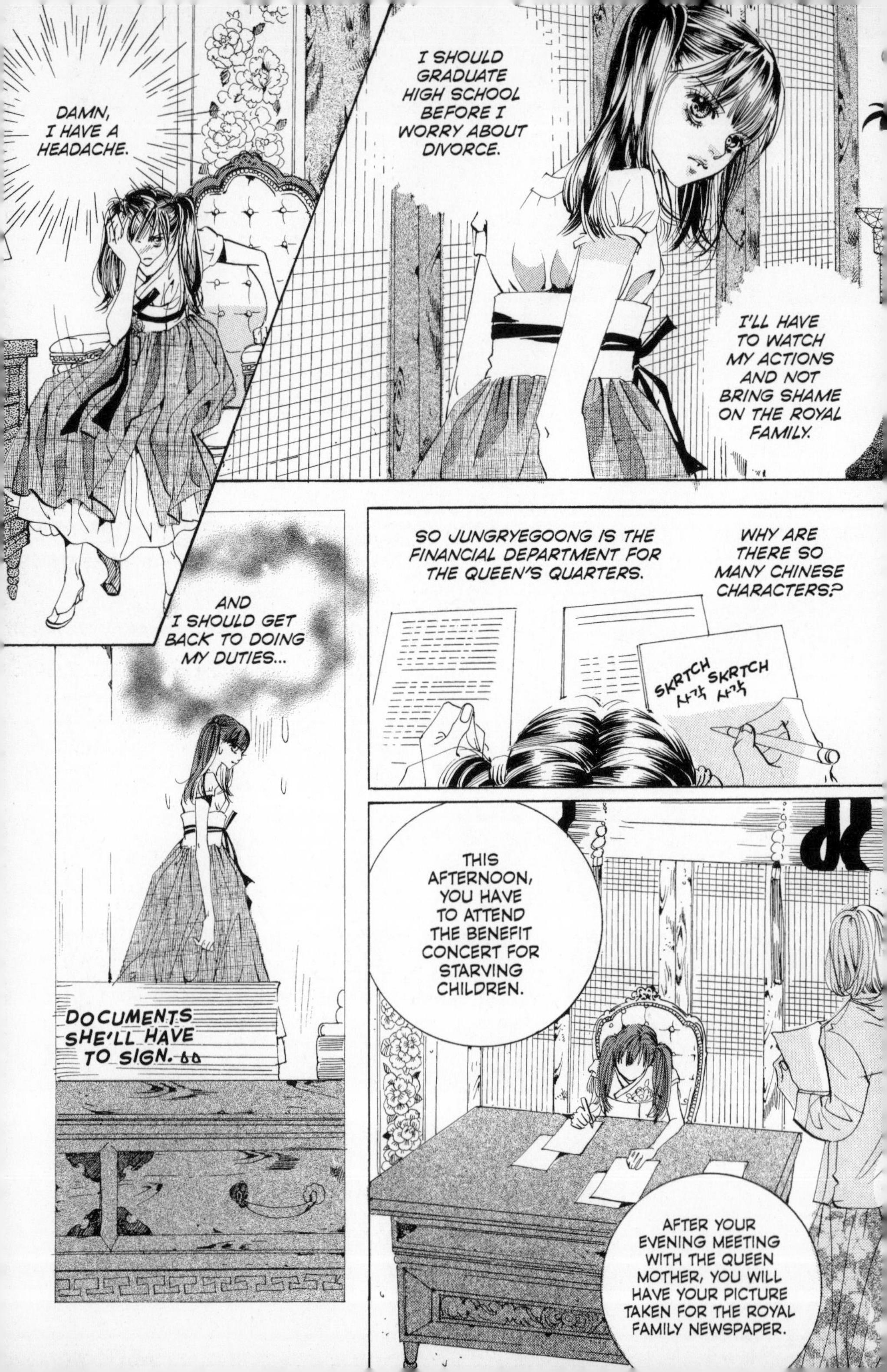
DAMN, I HAVE A HEADACHE.
I SHOULD GRADUATE HIGH SCHOOL BEFORE I WORRY ABOUT DIVORCE.
I'LL HAVE TO WATCH MY ACTIONS AND NOT BRING SHAME ON THE ROYAL FAMILY.
AND I SHOULD GET BACK TO DOING MY DUTIES...
DOCUMENTS SHE'LL HAVE TO SIGN.
SO JUNGRYEGOONG IS THE FINANCIAL DEPARTMENT FOR THE QUEEN'S QUARTERS.
WHY ARE THERE SO MANY CHINESE CHARACTERS?
SKRTCH 사각 SKRTCH 사각
THIS AFTERNOON, YOU HAVE TO ATTEND THE BENEFIT CONCERT FOR STARVING CHILDREN.
AFTER YOUR EVENING MEETING WITH THE QUEEN MOTHER, YOU WILL HAVE YOUR PICTURE TAKEN FOR THE ROYAL FAMILY NEWSPAPER.

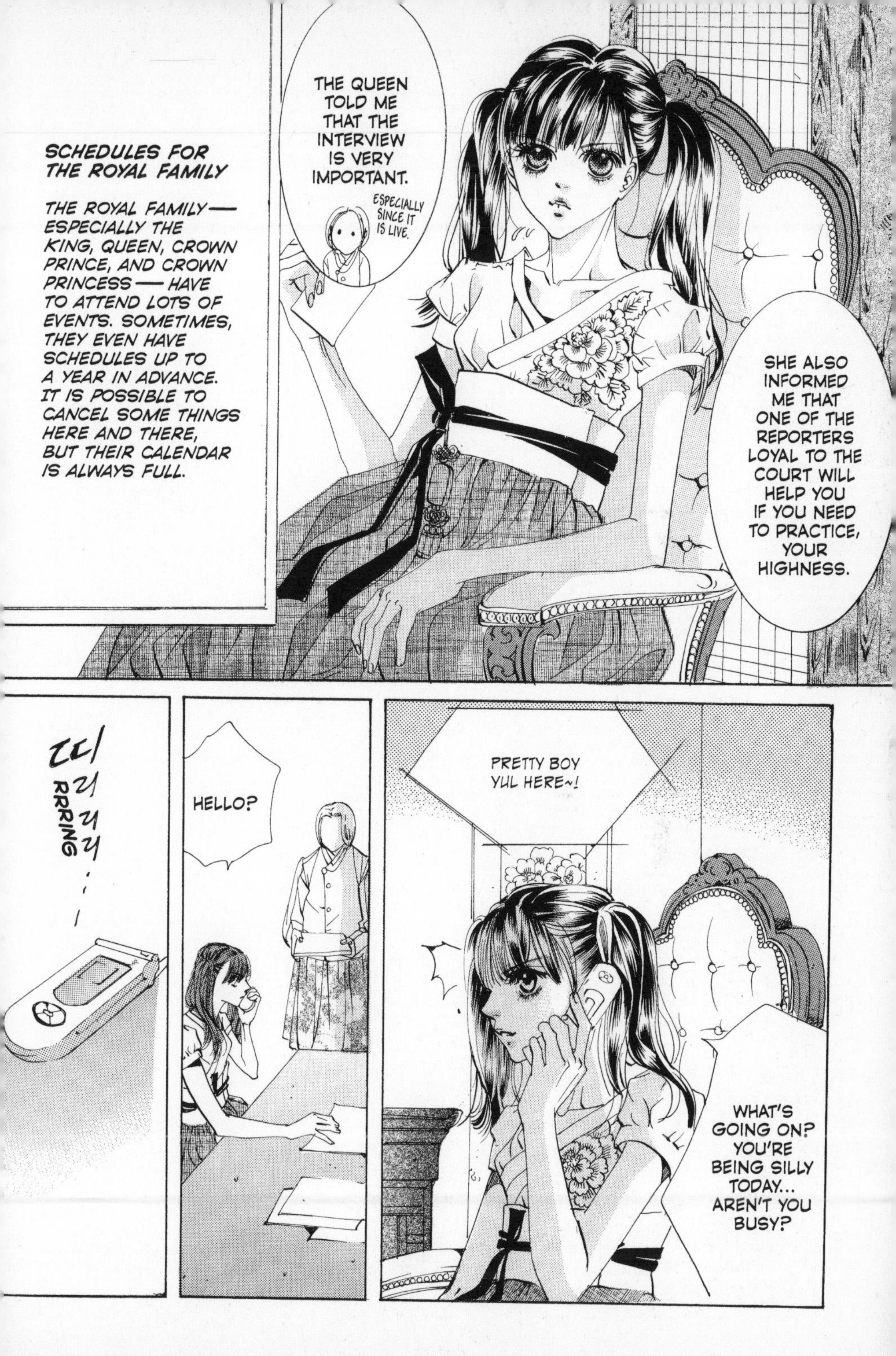
SCHEDULES FOR THE ROYAL FAMILY
THE ROYAL FAMILY—ESPECIALLY THE KING, QUEEN, CROWN PRINCE, AND CROWN PRINCESS—HAVE TO ATTEND LOTS OF EVENTS. SOMETIMES, THEY EVEN HAVE SCHEDULES UP TO A YEAR IN ADVANCE. IT IS POSSIBLE TO CANCEL SOME THINGS HERE AND THERE, BUT THEIR CALENDAR IS ALWAYS FULL.
THE QUEEN TOLD ME THAT THE INTERVIEW IS VERY IMPORTANT.
ESPECIALLY SINCE IT IS LIVE.
SHE ALSO INFORMED ME THAT ONE OF THE REPORTERS LOYAL TO THE COURT WILL HELP YOU IF YOU NEED TO PRACTICE, YOUR HIGHNESS.
RRRING
HELLO?
PRETTY BOY YUL HERE~!
WHAT'S GOING ON? YOU'RE BEING SILLY TODAY... AREN'T YOU BUSY?

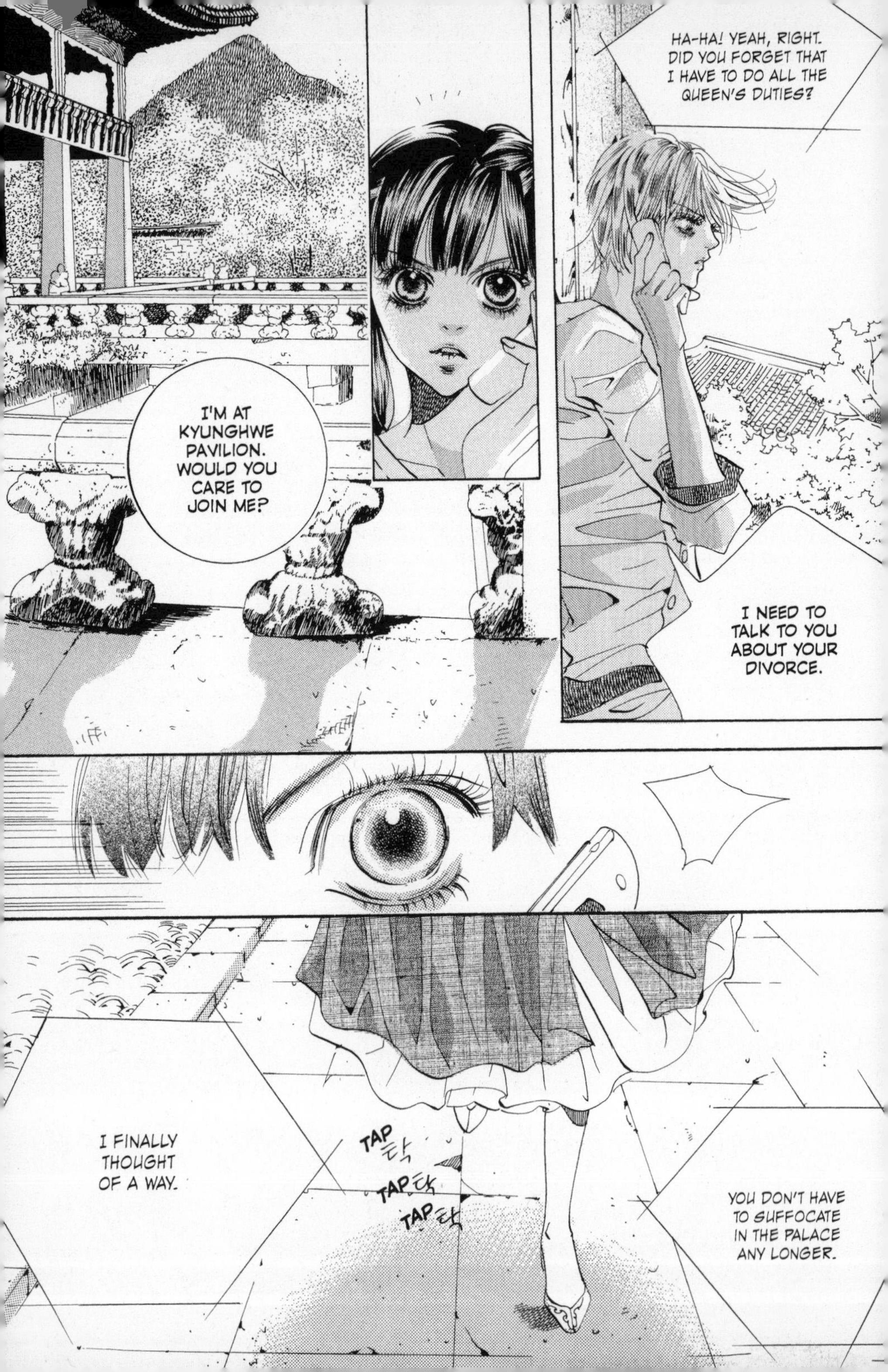
I'M AT KYUNGHWE PAVILION. WOULD YOU CARE TO JOIN ME?
HA-HA! YEAH, RIGHT. DID YOU FORGET THAT I HAVE TO DO ALL THE QUEEN'S DUTIES?
I NEED TO TALK TO YOU ABOUT YOUR DIVORCE.
I FINALLY THOUGHT OF A WAY.
TAP
탁
TAP
탁
TAP
탁
YOU DON'T HAVE TO SUFFOCATE IN THE PALACE ANY LONGER.

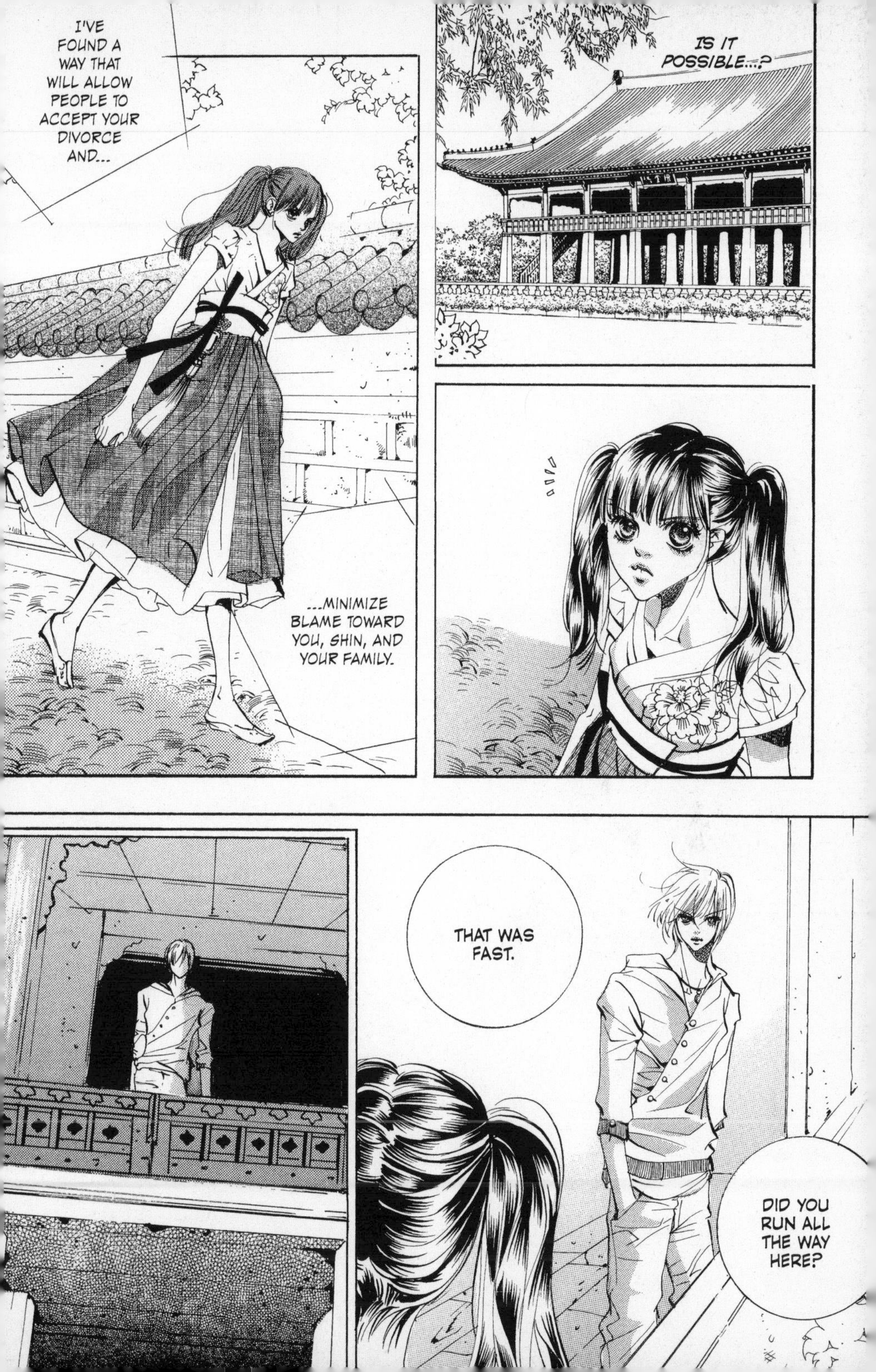
I'VE FOUND A WAY THAT WILL ALLOW PEOPLE TO ACCEPT YOUR DIVORCE AND...
...MINIMIZE BLAME TOWARD YOU, SHIN, AND YOUR FAMILY.
IS IT POSSIBLE...?
THAT WAS FAST.
DID YOU RUN ALL THE WAY HERE?

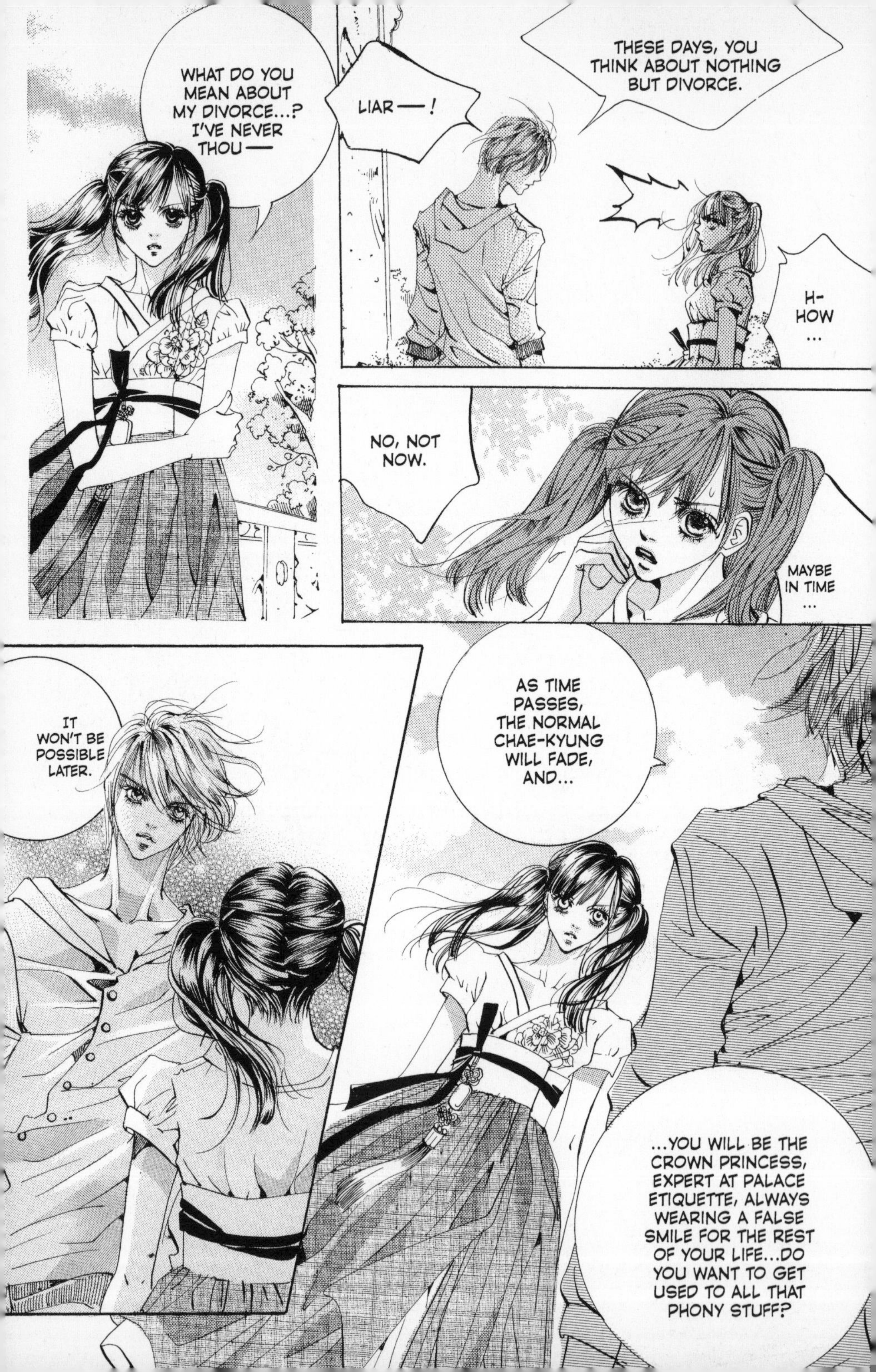
WHAT DO YOU MEAN ABOUT MY DIVORCE...? I'VE NEVER THOU—
LIAR—!
THESE DAYS, YOU THINK ABOUT NOTHING BUT DIVORCE.
H-HOW ...
NO, NOT NOW.
MAYBE IN TIME ...
IT WON'T BE POSSIBLE LATER.
..
AS TIME PASSES, THE NORMAL CHAE-KYUNG WILL FADE, AND...
...YOU WILL BE THE CROWN PRINCESS, EXPERT AT PALACE ETIQUETTE, ALWAYS WEARING A FALSE SMILE FOR THE REST OF YOUR LIFE...DO YOU WANT TO GET USED TO ALL THAT PHONY STUFF?

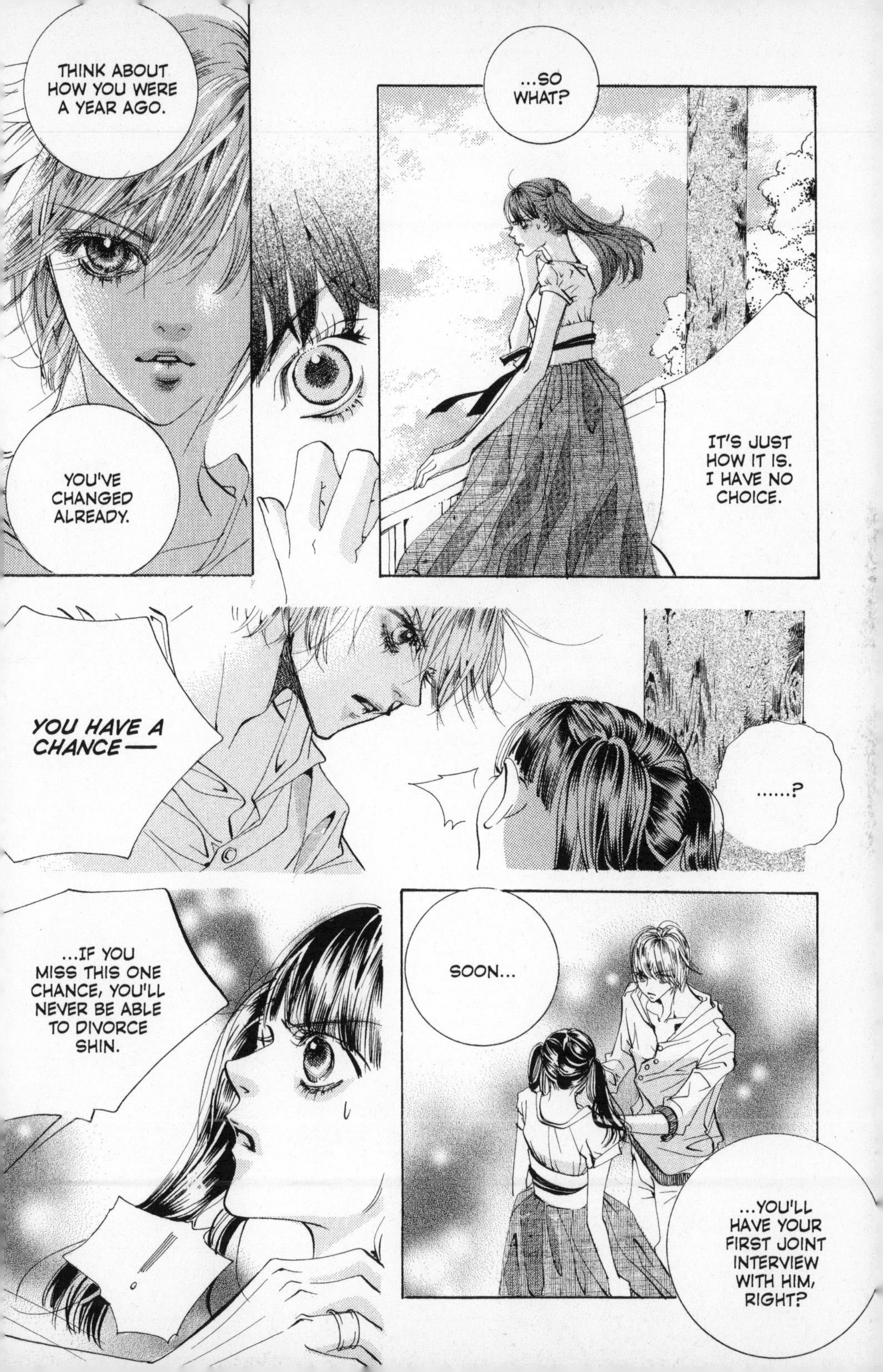
THINK ABOUT HOW YOU WERE A YEAR AGO.
YOU'VE CHANGED ALREADY.
...SO WHAT?
IT'S JUST HOW IT IS. I HAVE NO CHOICE.
YOU HAVE A CHANCE—
......?
...IF YOU MISS THIS ONE CHANCE, YOU'LL NEVER BE ABLE TO DIVORCE SHIN.
SOON...
...YOU'LL HAVE YOUR FIRST JOINT INTERVIEW WITH HIM, RIGHT?

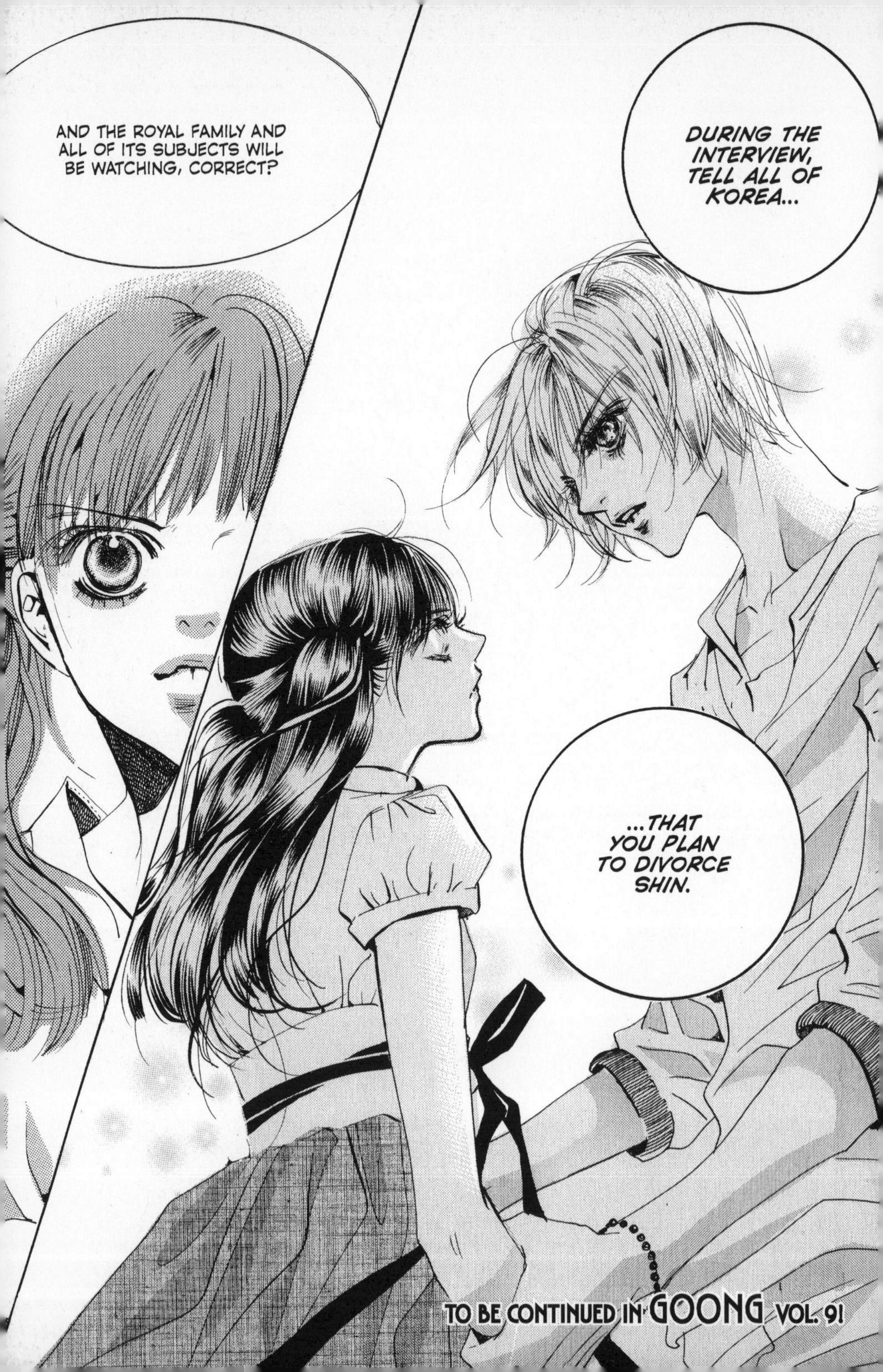
AND THE ROYAL FAMILY AND ALL OF ITS SUBJECTS WILL BE WATCHING, CORRECT?
DURING THE INTERVIEW, TELL ALL OF KOREA...
...THAT YOU PLAN TO DIVORCE SHIN.
TO BE CONTINUED IN GOONG VOL. 9!

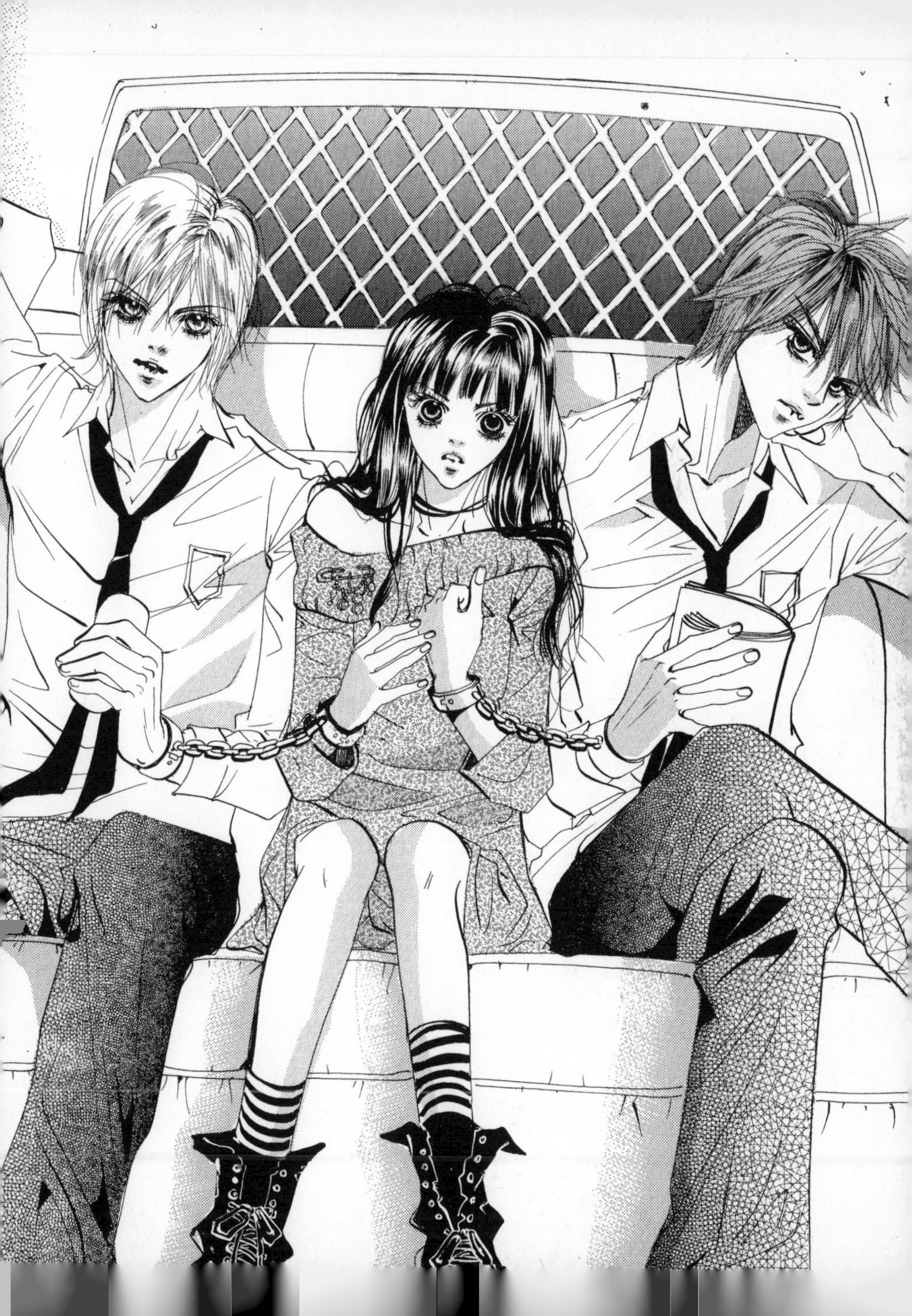

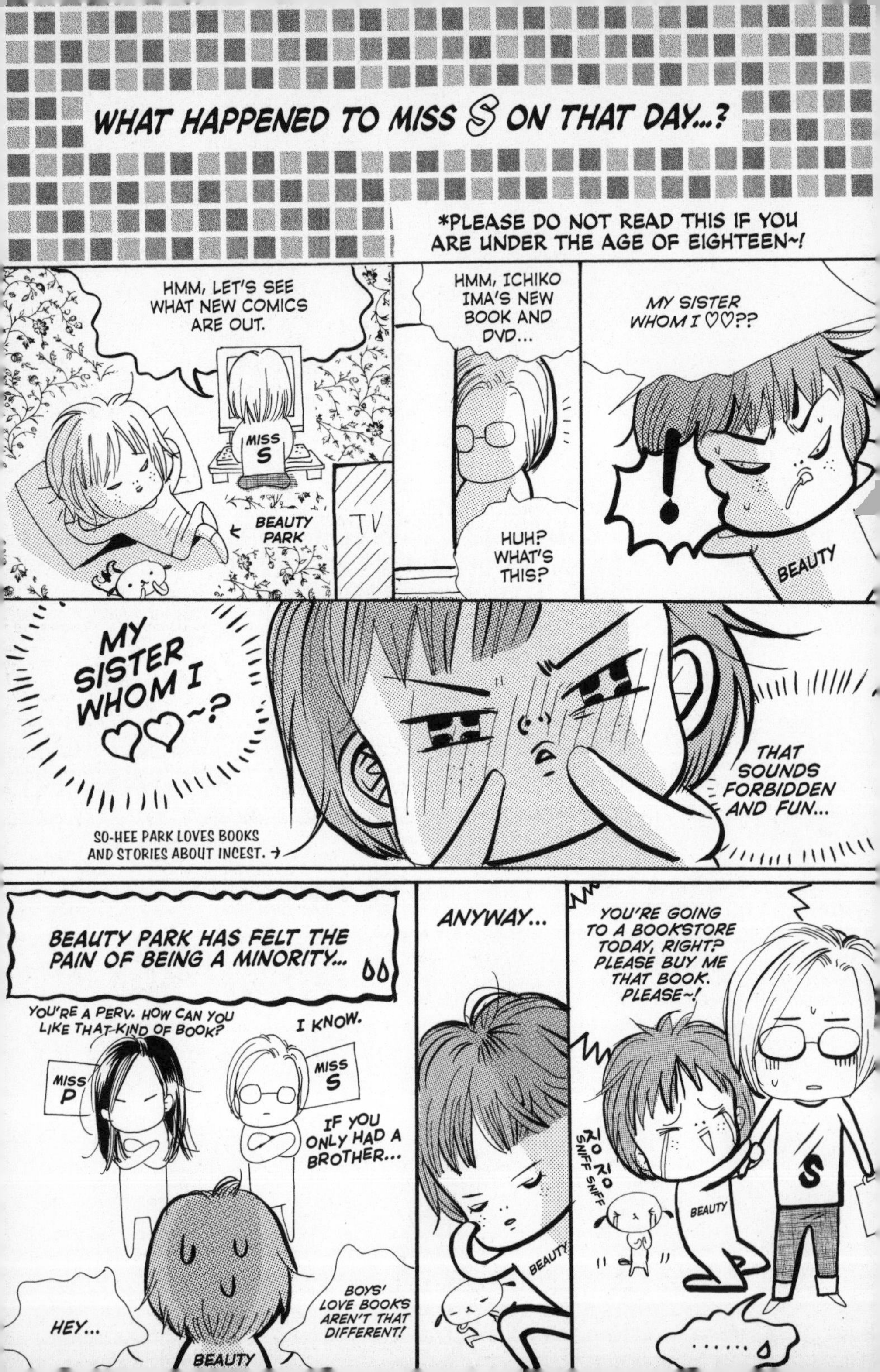
WHAT HAPPENED TO MISS S ON THAT DAY...?
*PLEASE DO NOT READ THIS IF YOU ARE UNDER THE AGE OF EIGHTEEN~!
HMM, LET'S SEE WHAT NEW COMICS ARE OUT.
MISS S
BEAUTY PARK
HMM, ICHIKO IMA'S NEW BOOK AND DVD...
TV
HUH? WHAT'S THIS?
MY SISTER WHOM I ♡♡??
BEAUTY
MY SISTER WHOM I ♡♡~?
SO-HEE PARK LOVES BOOKS AND STORIES ABOUT INCEST.
THAT SOUNDS FORBIDDEN AND FUN...
BEAUTY PARK HAS FELT THE PAIN OF BEING A MINORITY...
YOU'RE A PERV. HOW CAN YOU LIKE THAT KIND OF BOOK?
MISS P
I KNOW.
MISS S
IF YOU ONLY HAD A BROTHER...
HEY...
BEAUTY
BOYS' LOVE BOOKS AREN'T THAT DIFFERENT!
ANYWAY...
BEAUTY
YOU'RE GOING TO A BOOKSTORE TODAY, RIGHT? PLEASE BUY ME THAT BOOK. PLEASE~!
징 징
SNIFF SNIFF
BEAUTY
S
......

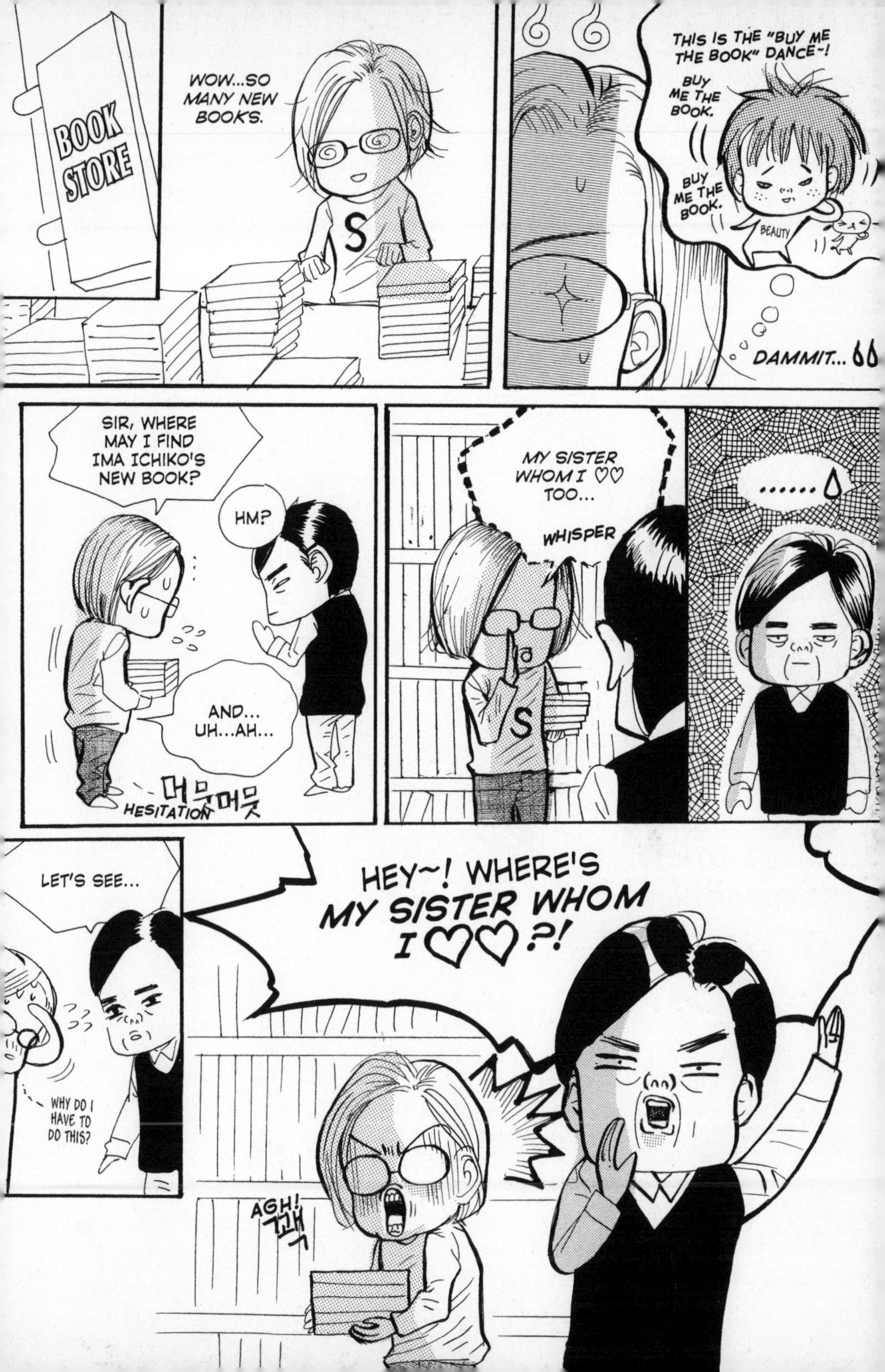
BOOK STORE
WOW...SO MANY NEW BOOKS.
THIS IS THE "BUY ME THE BOOK" DANCE~!
BUY ME THE BOOK.
BUY ME THE BOOK.
BEAUTY
DAMMIT...
SIR, WHERE MAY I FIND IMA ICHIKO'S NEW BOOK?
HM?
AND... UH...AH...
HESITATION
머뭇머뭇
MY SISTER WHOM I ♡♡ TOO...
WHISPER
......
LET'S SEE...
WHY DO I HAVE TO DO THIS?
HEY~! WHERE'S MY SISTER WHOM I ♡♡?!
AGH!
꽥

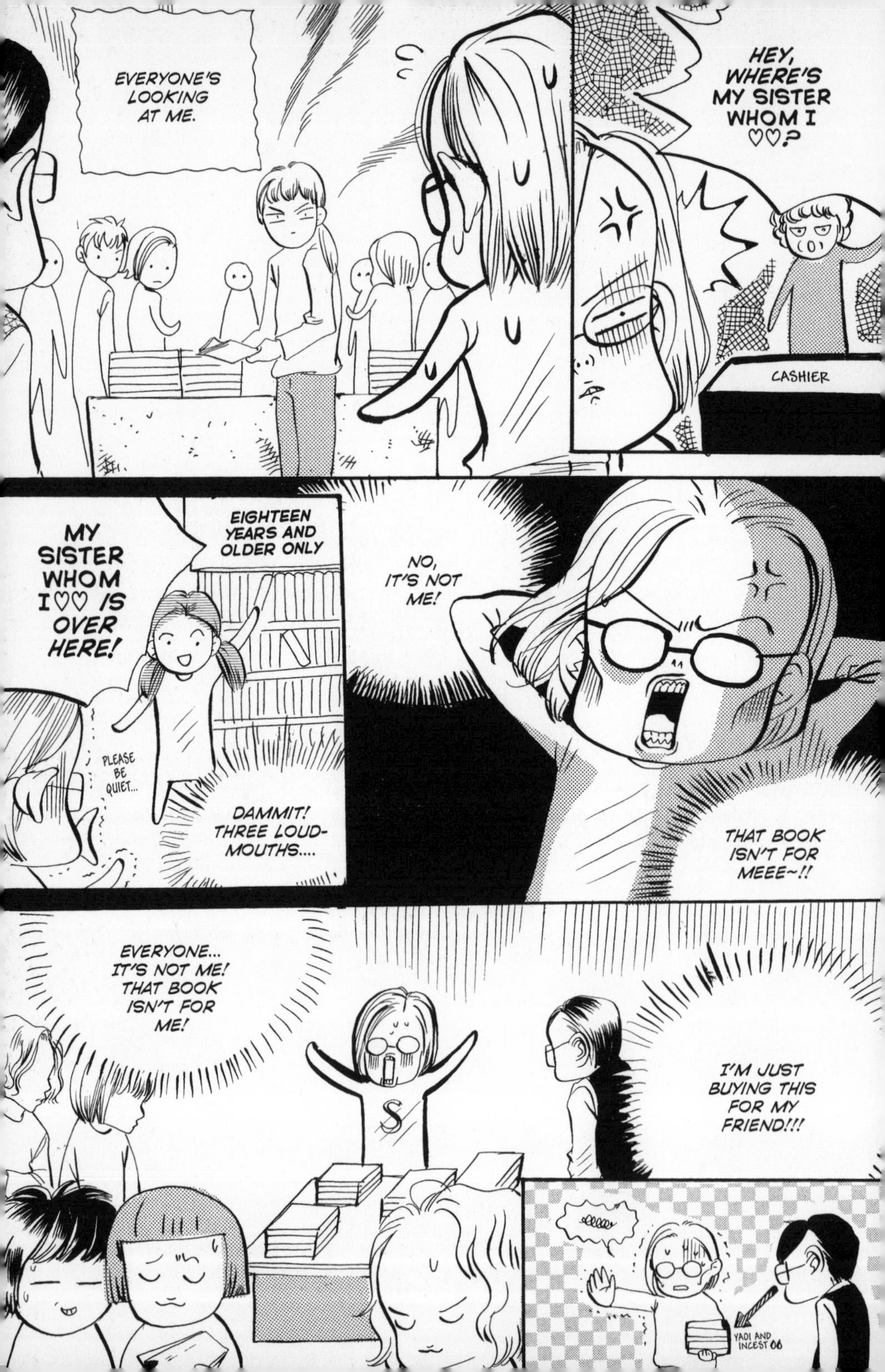
EVERYONE'S LOOKING AT ME.
HEY, WHERE'S MY SISTER WHOM I ♡♡?
CASHIER
EIGHTEEN YEARS AND OLDER ONLY
MY SISTER WHOM I♡♡ IS OVER HERE!
PLEASE BE QUIET...
DAMMIT! THREE LOUD-MOUTHS....
NO, IT'S NOT ME!
THAT BOOK ISN'T FOR MEEE~!!
EVERYONE... IT'S NOT ME! THAT BOOK ISN'T FOR ME!
I'M JUST BUYING THIS FOR MY FRIEND!!!
YAOI AND INCEST ♡♡

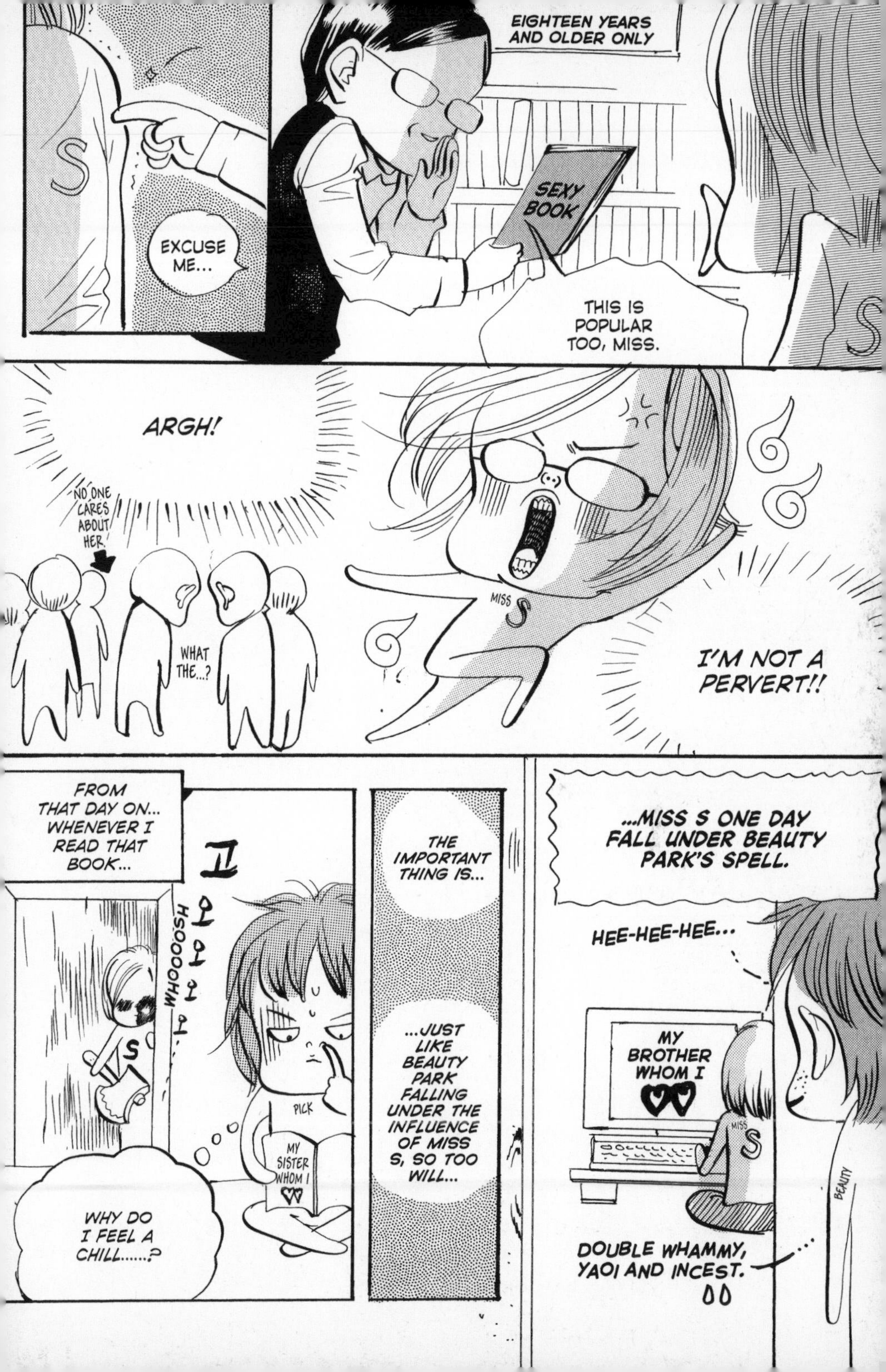
EXCUSE ME...
EIGHTEEN YEARS AND OLDER ONLY
SEXY BOOK
THIS IS POPULAR TOO, MISS.
ARGH!
NO ONE CARES ABOUT HER
WHAT THE...?
MISS S
I'M NOT A PERVERT!!
FROM THAT DAY ON... WHENEVER I READ THAT BOOK...
WHOOOOSH
S
PICK
MY SISTER WHOM I
WHY DO I FEEL A CHILL......?
THE IMPORTANT THING IS...
...JUST LIKE BEAUTY PARK FALLING UNDER THE INFLUENCE OF MISS S, SO TOO WILL...
...MISS S ONE DAY FALL UNDER BEAUTY PARK'S SPELL.
HEE-HEE-HEE...
MY BROTHER WHOM I
MISS S
BEAUTY
DOUBLE WHAMMY, YAOI AND INCEST.

Seeking the love promised by destiny . . .
Can it be found in the thirteenth boy?

13th ★ BOY

After eleven
boyfriends,
Hee-So thought
she was through
with love . . .
until she met
Won-Jun, that is . . .

But when
number twelve
dumps her, she's
not ready to
move on to the
thirteenth boy just
yet! Determined to win
back her destined love,
Hee-So's on a mission
to reclaim Won-Jun,
no matter what!

VOLUMES 1 AND 2
IN STORES NOW!

A totally new Arabian nights, where Scheherazade is a guy!

Everyone knows the story of Scheherazade and her wonderful tales from the Arabian Nights. For one thousand and one nights, the stories that she created entertained the mad Sultan and eventually saved her life. In this version, Scheherazade is a guy who disguises himself as a woman to save his sister from the mad Sultan. When he puts his life on the line, what kind of strange and unique stories will he tell? This new twist on one of the greatest classical tales might just keep you awake for another ONE THOUSAND AND ONE NIGHTS!

Available at bookstores near you!

One thousand and one nights 1~9

Han SeungHee · Jeon JinSeok

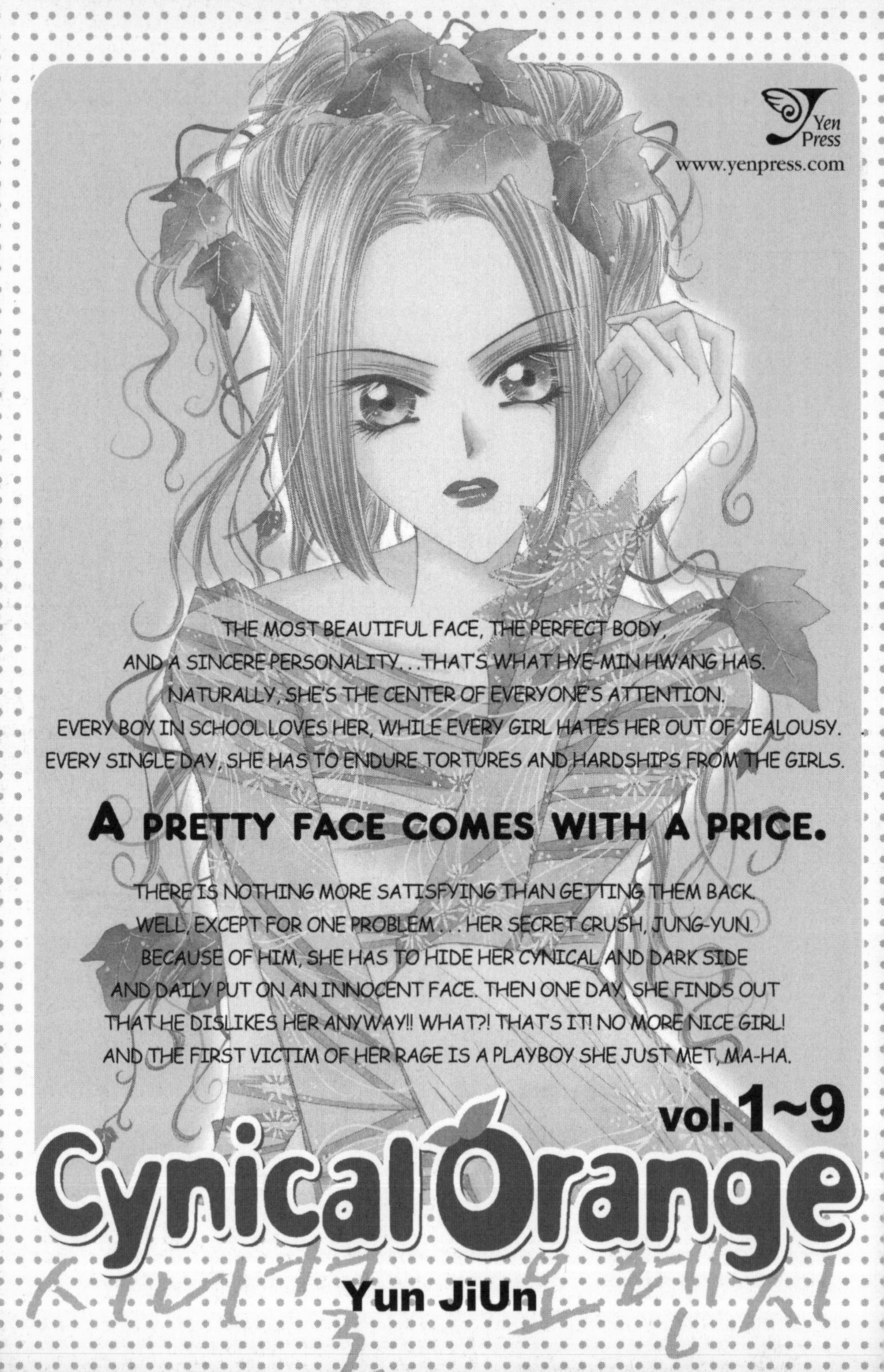
Yen Press
www.yenpress.com
THE MOST BEAUTIFUL FACE, THE PERFECT BODY,
AND A SINCERE PERSONALITY. . .THAT'S WHAT HYE-MIN HWANG HAS.
NATURALLY, SHE'S THE CENTER OF EVERYONE'S ATTENTION.
EVERY BOY IN SCHOOL LOVES HER, WHILE EVERY GIRL HATES HER OUT OF JEALOUSY.
EVERY SINGLE DAY, SHE HAS TO ENDURE TORTURES AND HARDSHIPS FROM THE GIRLS.
A PRETTY FACE COMES WITH A PRICE.
THERE IS NOTHING MORE SATISFYING THAN GETTING THEM BACK.
WELL, EXCEPT FOR ONE PROBLEM . . . HER SECRET CRUSH, JUNG-YUN.
BECAUSE OF HIM, SHE HAS TO HIDE HER CYNICAL AND DARK SIDE
AND DAILY PUT ON AN INNOCENT FACE. THEN ONE DAY, SHE FINDS OUT
THAT HE DISLIKES HER ANYWAY!! WHAT?! THAT'S IT! NO MORE NICE GIRL!
AND THE FIRST VICTIM OF HER RAGE IS A PLAYBOY SHE JUST MET, MA-HA.
vol.1~9
Cynical Orange
시니컬 오렌지
Yun JiUn

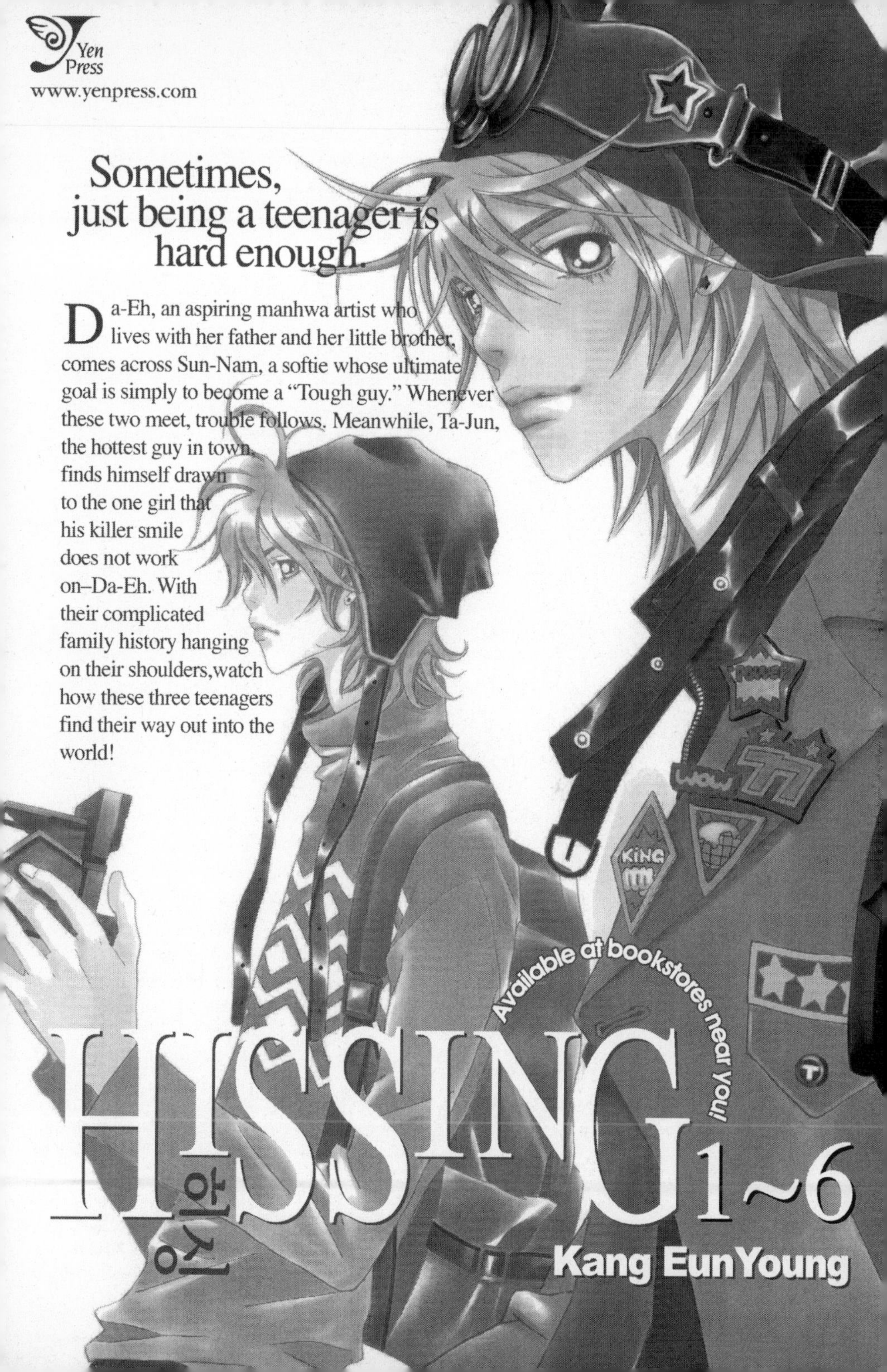
Yen Press
www.yenpress.com
Sometimes, just being a teenager is hard enough.
Da-Eh, an aspiring manhwa artist who lives with her father and her little brother, comes across Sun-Nam, a softie whose ultimate goal is simply to become a "Tough guy." Whenever these two meet, trouble follows. Meanwhile, Ta-Jun, the hottest guy in town, finds himself drawn to the one girl that his killer smile does not work on–Da-Eh. With their complicated family history hanging on their shoulders,watch how these three teenagers find their way out into the world!
Available at bookstores near you!
HISSING 1~6
히싱
Kang EunYoung

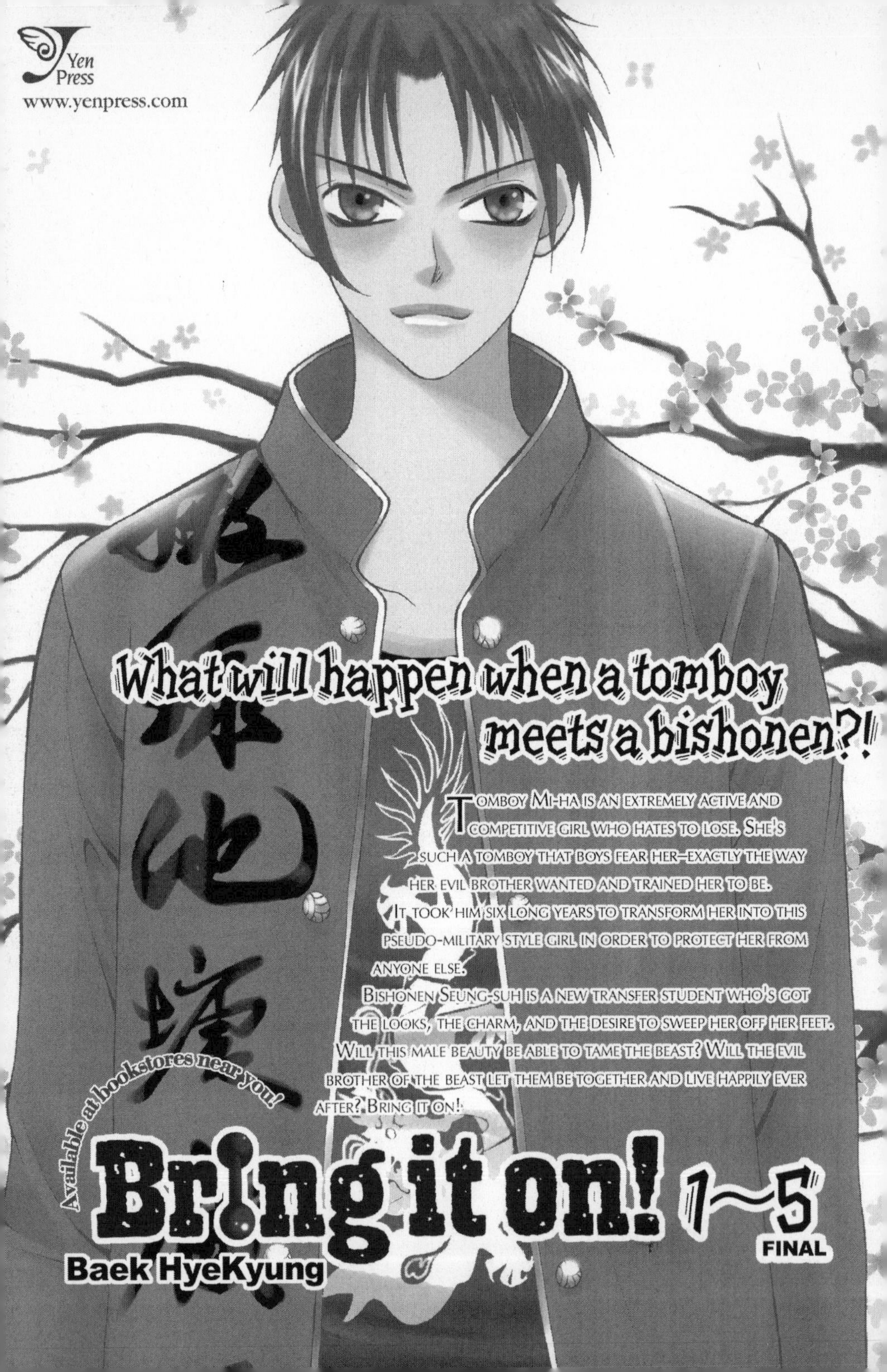
Yen Press
www.yenpress.com
What will happen when a tomboy meets a bishonen?!
Tomboy Mi-ha is an extremely active and competitive girl who hates to lose. She's such a tomboy that boys fear her–exactly the way her evil brother wanted and trained her to be.
It took him six long years to transform her into this pseudo-military style girl in order to protect her from anyone else.
Bishonen Seung-suh is a new transfer student who's got the looks, the charm, and the desire to sweep her off her feet. Will this male beauty be able to tame the beast? Will the evil brother of the beast let them be together and live happily ever after?! Bring it on!
Available at bookstores near you!
Bring it on! 1~5
FINAL
Baek HyeKyung

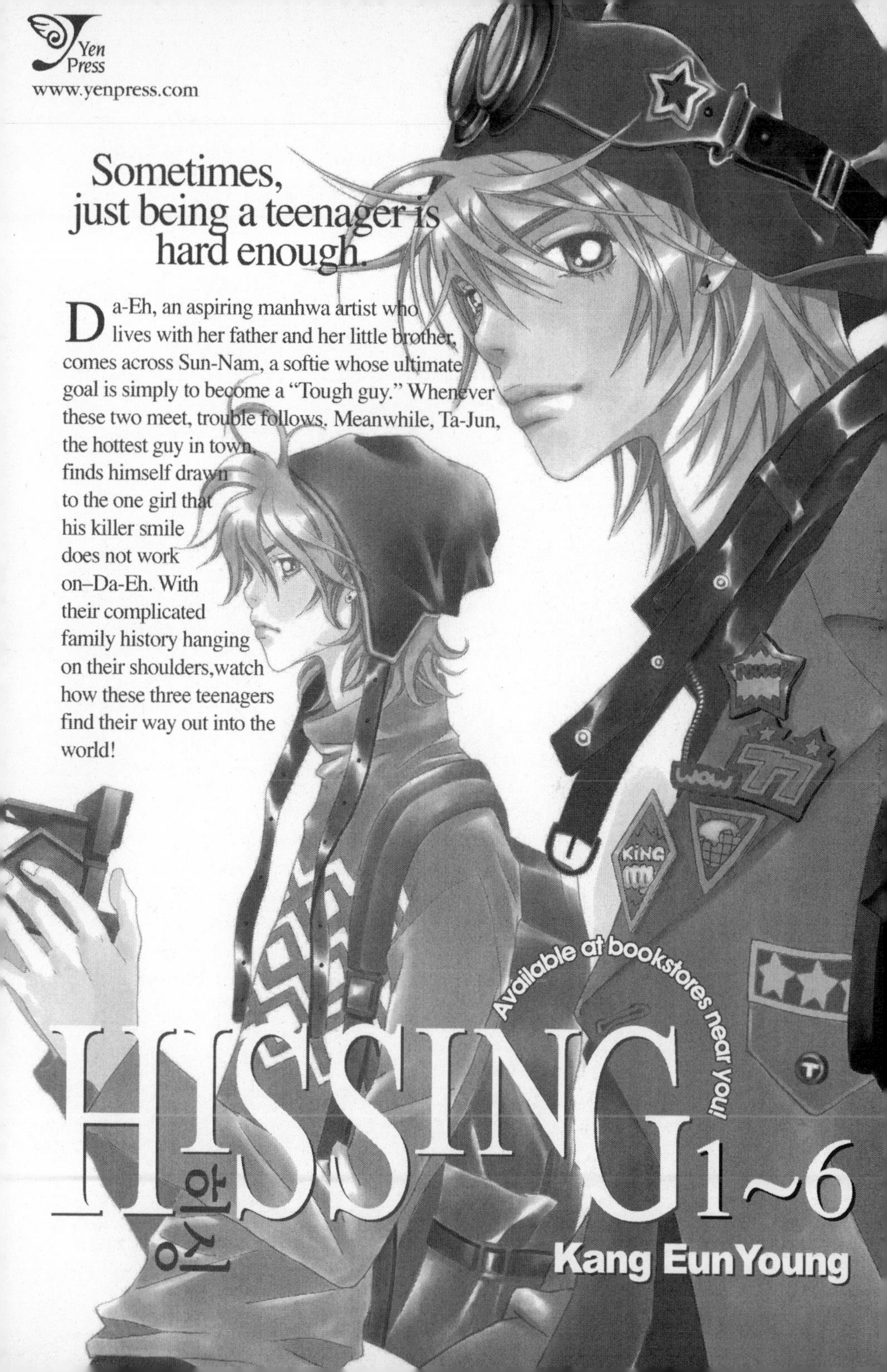

Sometimes, just being a teenager is hard enough.

Da-Eh, an aspiring manhwa artist who lives with her father and her little brother, comes across Sun-Nam, a softie whose ultimate goal is simply to become a "Tough guy." Whenever these two meet, trouble follows. Meanwhile, Ta-Jun, the hottest guy in town, finds himself drawn to the one girl that his killer smile does not work on–Da-Eh. With their complicated family history hanging on their shoulders,watch how these three teenagers find their way out into the world!

Available at bookstores near you!

HISSING 1~6

Kang Eun Young

What will happen when a tomboy meets a bishonen?!

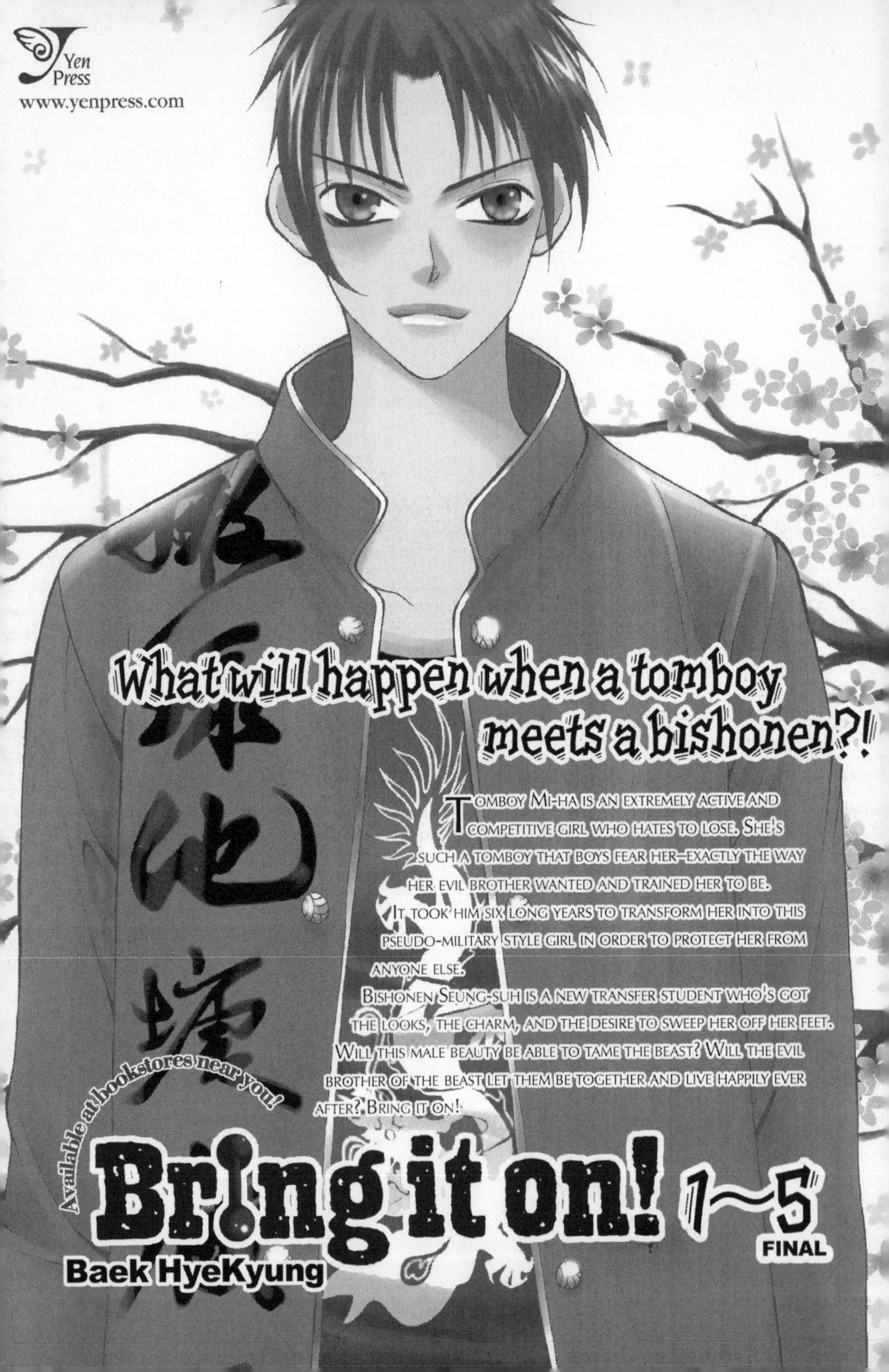

Tomboy Mi-ha is an extremely active and competitive girl who hates to lose. She's such a tomboy that boys fear her—exactly the way her evil brother wanted and trained her to be. It took him six long years to transform her into this pseudo-military style girl in order to protect her from anyone else.

Bishonen Seung-suh is a new transfer student who's got the looks, the charm, and the desire to sweep her off her feet. Will this male beauty be able to tame the beast? Will the evil brother of the beast let them be together and live happily ever after? Bring it on!

Available at bookstores near you!

Bring it on! 1~5 FINAL

Baek HyeKyung

Available at bookstores near you!

CHOCOLAT
1~7

Shin JiSang · Geo

Kum-ji was a little late getting under the spell of the chart-topping band, DDL. Unable to join the DDL fan club, she almost gives up on meeting her idols, until she develops a cunning plan–to become a member of a rival fan club for the brand-new boy band Yo-I. This way she can act as Yo-I's fan club member and also be near Yo-I,

How far would you go to meet your favorite boy band?

who always seem to be in the same shows as DDL. Perfect plan...except being a fanatic is a lot more complicated than she expects. Especially when you're actually a fan of someone else. This full-blown love comedy about a fan club will make you laugh, cry, and laugh some more.

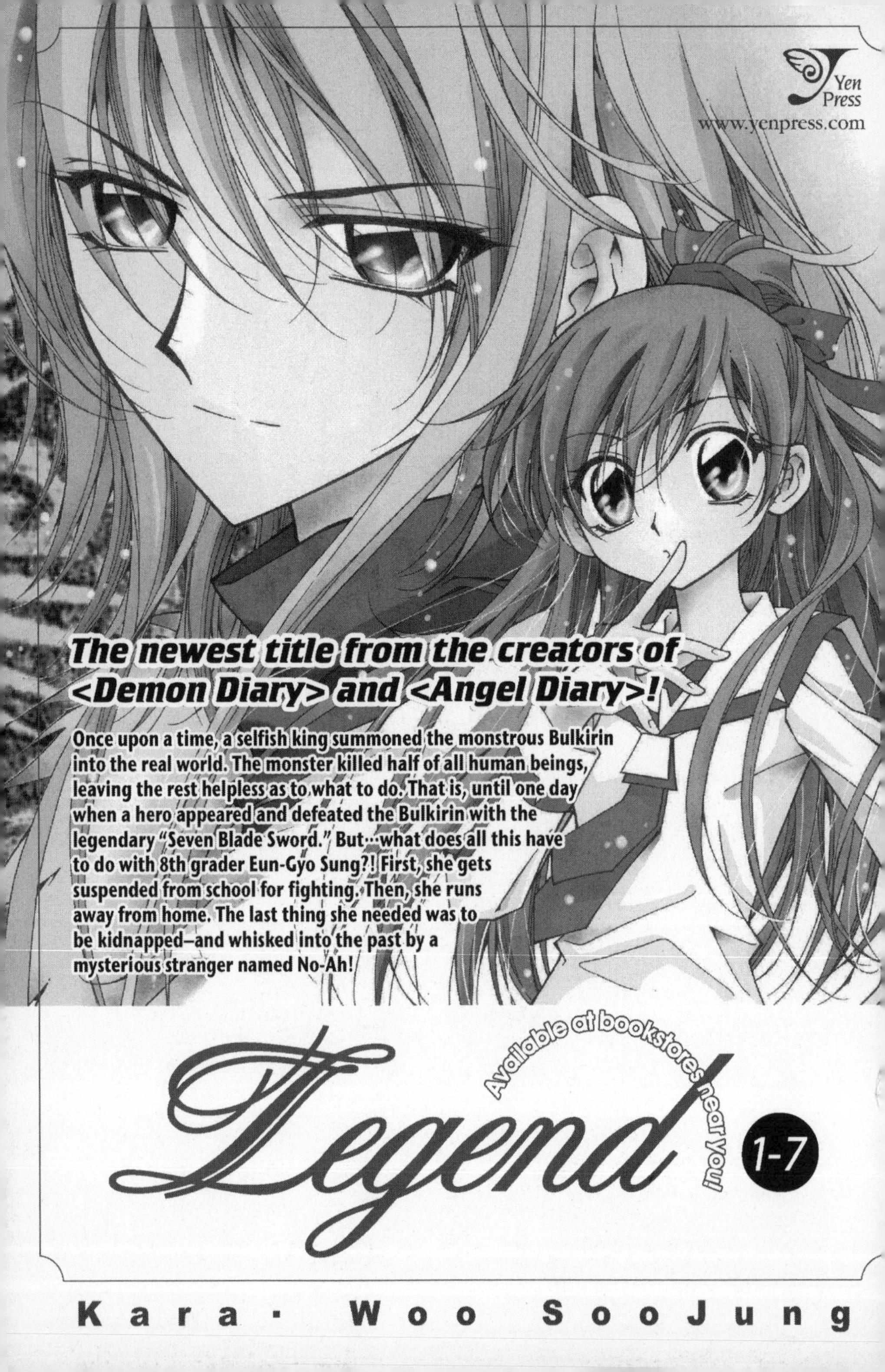
Yen Press
www.yenpress.com
The newest title from the creators of <Demon Diary> and <Angel Diary>!
Once upon a time, a selfish king summoned the monstrous Bulkirin into the real world. The monster killed half of all human beings, leaving the rest helpless as to what to do. That is, until one day when a hero appeared and defeated the Bulkirin with the legendary "Seven Blade Sword." But…what does all this have to do with 8th grader Eun-Gyo Sung?! First, she gets suspended from school for fighting. Then, she runs away from home. The last thing she needed was to be kidnapped–and whisked into the past by a mysterious stranger named No-Ah!
Legend
Available at bookstores near you!
1-7
Kara · Woo SooJung

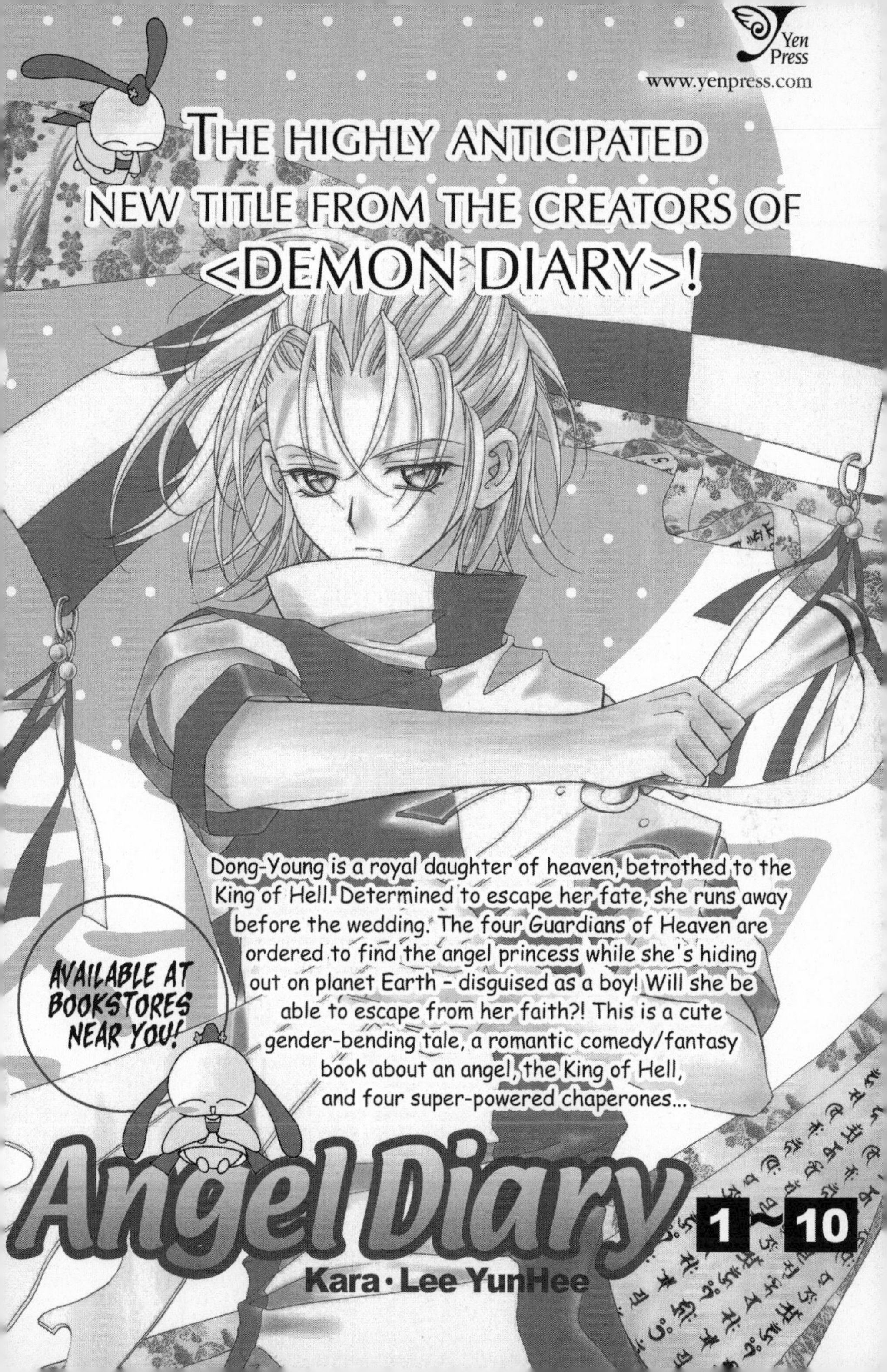
Yen Press
www.yenpress.com
THE HIGHLY ANTICIPATED
NEW TITLE FROM THE CREATORS OF
<DEMON DIARY>!
Dong-Young is a royal daughter of heaven, betrothed to the King of Hell. Determined to escape her fate, she runs away before the wedding. The four Guardians of Heaven are ordered to find the angel princess while she's hiding out on planet Earth - disguised as a boy! Will she be able to escape from her faith?! This is a cute gender-bending tale, a romantic comedy/fantasy book about an angel, the King of Hell, and four super-powered chaperones...
AVAILABLE AT BOOKSTORES NEAR YOU!
Angel Diary
1~10
Kara · Lee YunHee